Y0-BRU-825

E
210
.R33
1988

A Rage for liberty

EARLY
AMERICAN
HISTORY

An eighteen volume series reproducing
over three hundred of the most
important articles on all aspects of the
colonial experience

EDITED WITH INTRODUCTIONS BY
PETER CHARLES HOFFER
UNIVERSITY OF GEORGIA

A Garland Series

A RAGE
FOR LIBERTY

Selected Articles
on the Immediate Causes
of the American Revolution

EDITED WITH AN INTRODUCTION BY
PETER CHARLES HOFFER

Garland Publishing, Inc.
New York & London
1988

Library of Congress Cataloging-in-Publication Data

A Rage for liberty : selected articles on the immediate causes of
the American Revolution / edited with an introduction by
Peter Charles Hoffer.
p. cm.—(Early American history)
ISBN 0-8240-6246-9 (alk. paper)
1. United States—History—Revolution, 1775–1783—Causes.   I. Hoffer,
Peter C.   II. Series.
E210.R33   1988
973.3′11—dc19
87-17209
CIP

The volumes in this series are printed on
acid-free, 250-year-life paper.

Printed in the United States of America

CONTENTS

PREFACE

A motto (repeating John Robert Seeley) was prominently displayed on the front wall of the first library for history graduate students in America, at the Johns Hopkins University. The motto read: history is past politics and politics present history. While the most recent trends in early American history lead away from politics into the realms of family, domestic economy, labor relations, race relations, and culture, politics have always played a leading role in explanations of the onset of the American Revolution.

The conventional focus of political essays has been, and will remain, the colony. Traditional accounts of the coming of resistance focus upon Virginia and Massachusetts, a rivalry going back to the controversy between John Adams and William Wirt. Adams claimed primacy for the Bay colony, based upon the activities of James Otis, Jr., while Wirt, a Virginia lawyer, founded his state's claim to preem inence upon the contributions of Patrick Henry. As the reader of these essays will discover, the movement for independence was not limited to Otis's and Henry's homes, but had roots in all the colonies. What is more, the revolution was not an elite affair, the masses manipulated by secret committees of gentlemen. Instead, the crisis opened an avenue for the brightest and most ambitious commoners to climb to leadership roles.

In addition to the revelations about early revolutionary class structure and political power in this collection, the reader will find abundant evidence that the political struggle was no simple two-way tug of war. To be sure, from a distance, revolutionaries battled the agents of the crown and their loyalist allies. Closer to the action, scholars have traced rivalries within the revolutionary camp which disrupted the movement, and gave comfort to the loyalists. The loyalists, for their part, divided into militants, compromisers, and men and women passively obedient to whomever controlled the territory in which they resided.

The articles also reveal the importance of political symbols, a visual and verbal shorthand for emotion-charged ideologies of resistance. The elites' efforts to mobilize the masses was successful when it incorporated religious and social frames of reference, as well as explicit political grievances.

If the subjects of the articles in this volume are not the hottest topics for contemporary scholars, they have staying power nonetheless. As Gordon Wood has written in his section of *The Great Republic*, an American History textbook for college students, the Revolution is the most important event in our history because it established the values of the new nation.[1] Scholars and students will always be interested in the immediate causes of the Revolution.

Peter Charles Hoffer
University of Georgia

Notes

1. Gordon Wood, et al., *The Great Republic* (Boston, 1974), 229.

GROWTH OF REVOLUTIONARY PARTIES AND METHODS IN NEW YORK PROVINCE
1765–1774

IT has been seen that the new methods in nomination in New York province found their origin in the growth of the democratic spirit during the middle and last half of the eighteenth century.[1] The tendency of the coming consciousness of equality was to cut into the old factions based on personal influence, and to reorganize parties on a basis of principle. The Revolution gave this movement a great impetus by hastening—to some extent by completing—this change, and by teaching a minority the necessity of organization and the uses of political machinery ; the Revolution was the culmination in theory, and in fact to a considerable extent, at least in New York, of the effort of the masses to pull down authority from the top and place it upon the ground. In theory and in practice the masses, for the time being, got vital control of the business of governing. The lessons of the Revolution in this respect were incalculable, and no consideration of the nominating convention can be complete or intelligible without taking them into account. It will be necessary therefore to indicate the development of the Revolutionary parties in New York, to follow the changes from the old personal factions through the early inchoate divisions of the Stamp Act and Tea Act period, to the later well defined separation into radicals and conservatives. It is the design of this paper : (1) to trace the origin of these two factions up to the time when they began the contest for directing and shaping the Revolutionary movement in New York ; (2) to indicate incidentally the development of the popular extra-legal organization through which this directing and shaping influence was later exercised, largely through the nomination of candidates to the most important Revolutionary offices within the gift of the people.

In reality the anti-British struggle of the early Revolutionary period was a continuation of the anti-British struggle which had been going on since the administration of Governor Cosby in 1732. Until that time the administration of colonial New York, from the

[1] See article entitled, " Nominations in Colonial New York," AMERICAN HISTORICAL REVIEW, January, 1901.

point of view of British control, had been comparatively mild and indifferent. Party conflicts within the province had been largely personal. In so far as they were religious or political, they were an imitation, to a very considerable extent, of similar conflicts in the mother country. The bitter Leisler factions which disturbed New York for more than a quarter of a century were the outgrowth in the province of the English Revolution of 1688; and in this struggle political, religious and personal motives were inextricably mixed. Occasionally a governor like Bellomont made himself disliked, or one like Cornbury made himself despised. It is true also that even from the first there were two questions which served to divide the governor and council as the representatives of the British government, from the assembly as the representative of the colony; these were the question of enforcing the laws of trade and the question of controlling the colonial revenue. Bellomont indeed aroused disfavor by trying to enforce the former, while Cornbury and Hunter met a stubborn resistance in their efforts to reduce the power of the assembly over the appropriation of money and the control of the governor's salary. But the laws of trade were not an irritating question after Bellomont's time, and the matter of the revenue was compromised in 1715, during the administration of Governor Hunter. It was not, therefore, until the time of Cosby and Clarke and Clinton, that the anti-British party began to crystallize around the assembly, and the pro-British party around the governor. It was at this time that the growing democratic spirit, the coming consciousness of equality, a certain feeling of political self-sufficiency, resulted in a more jealous watchfulness of every claim put forth by the governor, and in an increasing tendency to look upon the governor as the agent of a power more or less foreign, if not actually hostile, to the colony's interests.

During the years from 1732 to 1760, the principal questions which were dividing parties into British and anti-British were the freedom of the press, the freedom of the judiciary from British control, the binding force of royal instructions and executive decrees, the frequency of elections, the appointment of colonial agents to England, and the control by the assembly of the revenue and, through the revenue, of the administration of the laws.

The question of the control of the revenue by the assembly had, as we have seen, come up before. All through the administration of Fletcher and during that of Cornbury and of Hunter, the assembly had carefully guarded what it considered its rights in this respect; it refused to grant revenue at the request or the demand of the governor; it refused to grant a life salary to the governor; it refused to allow the council to amend money bills; it insisted upon an elective treasurer. In this early struggle the assembly showed even the tendency, so manifest later, to interfere in the administration of the laws by specifying more or less minutely the purposes for which, and the methods and agents by which, the money was to be expended. But in the later period the quarrel was renewed and intensified; its full bitterness was not experienced until the period of the Indian wars of Governor Clinton's administration. During these years the policy of the assembly was clearly defined; it would not only control the levying of taxes, but it would also control appropriations and expenditures. By specifying minutely the methods and agents by which the money that it appropriated was to be expended, independent or discretionary power in the administration and execution of the laws was materially weakened if not destroyed. The persistent policy of limiting appropriations to one year made frequent sessions of the assembly a practical necessity,[1] while the struggle for frequent elections, which lasted some years, finally culminated in the Septennial Act of 1743.[2] The virtual helplessness of the governor led to a bill in Parliament proposing to give the force of law to royal instructions. It was to resist the passage of this bill that the assembly appointed two agents to England, and raised five hundred pounds for their expenses;[3] at a later time the assembly took the matter of the agency into its own hands through the appointment of an agent by resolution without consulting the governor, providing for his salary by a rider to the salary of the governor himself.[4] The freedom of the press was vindicated in the famous and somewhat dramatic trial of Zenger, the effect of which, in fostering the spirit of resistance to what was considered oppression, can hardly be overestimated.[5] Finally, the question of the freedom of the judiciary from British control, or more directly from the governor's control, was at issue in the Cosby-Van Dam controversy;[6] it was a matter which the people watched with jealous care, and every attempt of the governors to interfere in any way with the judicial arrangements was resisted stubbornly.

3

[1] See the address of the assembly, September, 1737, wherein the assembly frankly assured the governor that no appropriations would be made for a longer period than one year. *Assembly Journal*, p. 706.

[2] *New York Colonial Documents*, VI. 136; Schoonmacher, *History of Kingston*, 118. The first act, passed December 16, 1737, provided for triennial assemblies with yearly sessions. *Laws of New York*, Chapter 650. Disallowed by the King November 30, 1738. *New York Colonial Documents*, VI. 136.

[3] *Laws of New York*, Chapter 788.

[4] See Tanner, "Colonial Agencies in England," *Political Science Quarterly*, XVI. 43.

[5] Pasco, *Old New York*, II. 52; *Memorial History of New York*, II. 237; Lamb, *History of New York*, I. 557; Thomas, *History of Printing*, II. 100.

[6] *Memorial History of New York*, II. 583.

Such were the questions which were forming the British and anti-British parties. At first these questions were viewed very largely from the old standpoint of personality. With the governor stood De Lancey and the powerful following which he controlled ; with the assembly went the party of Livingston, supported by the able lawyers William Smith and John Morin Scott, and by very nearly if not quite all the rising young men of the day.[1] Increasingly this latter party shaped and guided the growing interest of the people in political questions. To counteract the mild influence of the court paper, Bradford's Gazette, Zenger's Journal was established ; it became the mouthpiece of the anti-court party, and gave utterance to those views, wise or unwise, which it was thought would serve to win for that party the popular support. And not indeed without avail ; the popular party gained steadily as it backed up the assembly in its resistance to the governor.[2] More or less steadily the purely personal element died out. Before 1750 De Lancey himself was at odds with the governor.[3] The old court party became demoralized. In 1750 the so-called 'Whig club was formed, and for many years the popular party was distinctly in the lead. When the Stamp Act

[1] Van Dam was supported in the trial with Cosby by William Smith and James Alexander. Of the three judges, De Lancey and Philipse were for Cosby, but the chief justice, Lewis Morris, was for Van Dam. Morris very soon after lost his judgeship which went to De Lancey, but he then stood for Westchester county for the assembly, and won in a contest which excited more popular interest than perhaps any election ever held in New York province. From this time, and more especially after the Zenger trial, the De Lancey faction became more avowedly the court party, while its enemies espoused upon every occasion the popular side. *Memorial History of New York*, II. 217, 233, 583 ; Bolton, *History of Westchester County*, I. 136 ; Valentine, *History of New York*, p. 264 ; *New York Journal*, November 5, 1733.

[2] *Memorial History of New York*, II. 248, 249, 262 ; Broadside dated August 25, 1750, in the New York Historical Society Library, Vol. I. of the collection ; *New York Colonial Documents*, VI. 247, 417, 578 ; Onderdonk, *Queens County in Olden Times*, pp. 21, 31, 33 ; Smith, *History of New York*, II. 37 ; Stone, *Life of William Johnson*, I. 39, 157 ; Valentine, *Manual of the Corporation*, 1865, p. 779 ; 1866, p. 703 ; *New York Weekly Post Boy*, June 24, 1745.

[3] *Memorial History of New York*, II. 261, 296. " Nothing could have been so unhappy," writes Clinton to the Duke of New Castle, Feb. 13, 1748, " for this province and myself, as the unexpected promotion [of De Lancey to the Lt.-Governorship] which became known when the elections were coming on for a new Assembly. Wherein I had carried the choice of several members for the counties that were well attached to his Majesty's interest . . . and should have succeeded with several others, but that messengers were immediately dispatched throughout the province with the news of Mr. De Lancey's being made Lt.-Governor, which damped the inclinations of all my friends, as dreading the exhorbitant power and resentment of this man." *New York Colonial Documents*, VI. 417. Again in 1750, Clinton laments that nothing has been done that he desired, for the encouragement of those that remained faithful. Otherwise, " I make no doubt but that every man of the Faction would have been left out of this election . . . and this notwithstanding that I am informed that Chief Justice De Lancey is gone into the country, since the writs issued, personally to influence the people in their election." *Ibid.*, 578.

was passed the popular party controlled the assembly and the province; the letters of Lt. Governor Colden reveal his helplessness.[1]

The Stamp Act raised the first of a series of questions which were to complete the formation of the Revolutionary parties in New York province and state. The popular party of Livingston was then in control of the assembly. Of the four well marked classes into which New York society was divided, three of them—the land owners, the professional classes and the merchants—were closely united in interests through business and family relationships.[2] Opposition to the governor and council as the agent of the British government had come to, be recognized as the cue in all political questions. When the Stamp Act came, the opposition which had been directed against the agents of the home government, was transferred to the home government itself. The conflict was felt to be more or less a continuation of the old one which had engaged the colony for so many years; it was merely a new act of oppression against which was directed the whole force of the popular party, which meant at first nearly the whole force of the colony.

The lead in the opposition was at first taken by the assembly. As early as October 18, 1764, the assembly had ordered that the committee which had been appointed to correspond with the assembly's agent in England, should also be a committee to correspond with other assemblies with reference to the late acts of Parliament on the "trade of the northern colonies."[3] The next year when the

---

[1] See *Colden's Letter Book*, I. 187, 231, 362, 422, 468; II. 68, 86. (New York Historical Society Collections, Vols. IX. and X.)

[2] The following division into classes is taken from Lieutenant-Governor Colden s report on the state of the province in 1765. "The people of New York are properly distinguished into different ranks. (1) The proprietors of the large tracts of land who include within their claims from 100,000 acres to above one million of acres under one grant. Some of these remain in one single family. Others are by devises and purchases claimed in common by considerable numbers of persons. (2) The gentlemen of the law make the second class in which are properly included both bench and bar. Both of them act on the same principles, and are of the most distinguished rank in the policy of the province. (3) The merchants make the third class. Many of them have rose suddenly from the lowest rank . . . to considerable fortunes, and chiefly in illicit trade in the last war. They abhor every limitation of trade . . . and therefore gladly go into every measure whereby they hope to have trade free. (4) In the last rank may be placed the farmers and mechanics. Though the farmers hold their land in fee simple, they are, as to condition of life, in no way superior to the common farmers in England. This last rank includes the bulk of the people and in them consists the strength of the province . . . The gentlemen of the law are either owners, heirs, or strongly connected in interest with the proprietors." *Letter Book*, II. 68–70. Likewise the merchants were for the most part, "strongly connected with the owners of these great tracts by family interest." Colden to the Lords of Trade, September 20, 1764. *Ibid.*, I. 363.

[3] *Assembly Journal*, II. 780. In his *History of Westchester County During the American Revolution*, Mr. Dawson points to this committee, with a certain note of triumph illustrative of a curious provincialism, as the first of the Revolutionary committee.

Stamp Act raised an opposition which carried away nearly all classes alike, the movement in New York was still directed by the assembly. It approved the plan of a congress of delegates to consider the matter and decide upon measures of resistance, which had been suggested by the assembly of Massachusetts, and it provided for the appointment of delegates to represent New York by referring the whole matter to the committee of correspondence that had already been named.[1] Thus until October 28, the day on which the congress adjourned, the opposition to the Stamp Act was distinctly in the hands of the leading men of the colony outside of the small remnant of the governor's party. As a movement it represented the property, professional and commercial interests of the province. But from this date the resistance takes on a more radical character; especially in the city of New York where the Revolutionary movement centered from first to last, it was more and more dominated by the lowest of the four classes—the unfranchised mechanics and artisans, the " inhabitants." As a result we find the propertied and commercial classes began soon to draw back and assume a more conservative attitude. The organization which represented the unfranchised class, and assumed the leadership in this more radical phase of the movement, was the so-called " Sons of Liberty."

The origin of the Sons of Liberty is somewhat in doubt. According to Governor Colden, whose statement has been followed by Dawson, the society was the outgrowth of an organization of the lawyers in 1750, whose object from the very first was political and revolutionary.[2] This is, however, probably far fetched. The papers

of correspondence. " Six years before Massachusetts appointed her faint hearted committee, whose fear of Great Britain prevented the preparation of even a single letter, and nearly nine years before that celebrated meeting at the Raleigh Tavern, Richmond, where Virginia gave birth to her first born, the Assembly of New York originated the movement and appointed a committee of correspondence with Robert R. Livingston at its head." p. 63. See also, p. 61 n. If it is a question of origin in mere form, one may equally well go back to the committee of safety of the Leisler régime, or to the committees of safety of the English civil war. See Leisler Narrative, *New York Colonial Documents*, III. 670.

[1] *Colden's Letter Book*, II. 35.

[2] " After Mr. Delancey had, by cajoling Mr. Clinton, received the commission of Chief Justice during good behavior, the profession of the law entered into an association, the effect of which your lordship had formerly opportunity of observing in some striking instances. They purposed nothing less to themselves than to obtain the direction of all the measures of the government, by making themselves absolutely necessary to every governor, in assisting him when he complied with their measures and by distressing him when he did otherwise." Colden to the Earl of Halifax, February 22, 1765. *Colden's Letter Book*, I. 469. Quoted in Dawson, *The Sons of Liberty in New York*, p. 40 n. "As early as the year 1754 there were men in America, I may say in the towns of Boston, New York, Philadelphia, and Williamsburg, who held independence in prospect." Examination of James Galloway, *New York Journal*, October 25, 1779. " The gentlemen of the law some years since entered into an association with intention, among other

of John Lamb, one of the moving spirits of the society of the Sons
of Liberty, indicate little if any connection between the two organizations; from these papers it appears that the Sons of Liberty were
formally organized shortly after the passage of the Stamp Act, as a
secret society which did not assume an open and public character
until some years later.[1]   Neither is it strictly true, as Dawson main-
tains, that they directed the whole struggle.   Livingston, Smith,
and John Morin Scott, who were prominent in the early part of the
Stamp Act trouble, do not appear to have been connected with the
Sons of Liberty, in any active capacity even at the first, and certainly
at a later time the leaders in the society were the more radical
spirits, like Lamb, Sears, Wiley, Robinson, and the notorious Alexander McDougall.   What is true is that the Sons of Liberty represented the lowest of the four classes, the artisan and laboring
classes of the city, and that they directed the conflict in so far as
popular agitation and mob violence formed a part of it.[2]

7

   This mob violence and popular agitation, during the Stamp Act
episode, reached a climax from the 1st to the 3d of November, as a
result of the arrival of the stamps at Fort George.   The mob went
through the city crying " liberty," destroying property, and burning
in effigy certain persons high in authority, including the governor

things, to assume the direction of the government upon them, by the influence they had
in the Assembly, gained by their family connections and by the profession of the law,
whereby they are invariably in the secrets of many families.   Many court their friendship,
all dread their hatred.   By these means, though few of them be members, they rule the
Assembly in all matters of importance."   Colden's Report on the state of the province,
December 6, 1765.   *New York Colonial Documents*, VII. 796.

   [1] " The association of the Sons of Liberty was organized soon after the passage of
the stamp act, and extended throughout the colonies."   Leake, *Life and Times of General Lamb*, p. 2.   See also, *Memorial History of New York*, II. 347, 374.

   [2] The members of the committees, fairly expressive of leadership in the society it
may be supposed, are given by Leake as follows: — *New York City:* John Lamb, Isaac
Sears, William Wiley, Edward Laight, Thomas Robinson, Flores Bancker, Charles Nicoll,
Joseph Allicoke, and Gershom Mott.   *Albany:* Jeremiah Van Rensselaer, Myndertse
Raseboom, Robert Henry, Thomas Young.   *Huntington:* J. S. Hobart, Gilbert Palter,
Thomas Brush, Cornelius Conklur, Nathaniel Williams.   *Life and Times of General
Lamb*, p. 4.   See also, *House Journal*, January 7, 1848; and, Sears, *Pictorial History
of the United States*.

   The first popular meeting of importance was called by the merchants.   On the 17th
of October, 1765, the following notice appeared in the *New York Gazette:*—"A meeting
of the friends of liberty and the English Constitution, in this city and parts adjacent, is
earnestly desired by great numbers of the inhabitants, in order to form an association of
all who are not already slaves, in opposition to all attempts to make them so."   Soon
after, October 31, a meeting was held, probably as a result of this notice, at George
Burns's inn.   Resolutions agreeing not to ship English goods until the Stamp Act was
repealed were signed by some 200 merchants.   *New York Gazette*, November 7, 1765.
Leake states that the meeting also appointed a committee of correspondence, of five
members, all Sons of Liberty.   *Life and Times of General Lamb*, pp. 14, 15.   The
Gazette does not mention it.   See also, *Memorial History of New York*, II. 367 n.

himself.[1] But opposition of this sort was not to the liking of the propertied classes, however much they may have disapproved of the levy and collection of the stamp tax. A little rioting was admirable it is true, so long as it remained entirely under their own control and was directed to the one end of bringing the English government to terms. But when the destruction of property began to be relished for its own sake by the classes which were propertyless, and when the cry of liberty came loudest from those who were most conspicuous for their lack of all political privileges, it seemed well to draw back ; these men might not cease their shouting when purely British restrictions were at an end. The ruling class in New York saw clearly that "liberty" and "no taxation" were arguments which might be used with as great potency against themselves as against the home government—arguments which indeed the unfranchised classes were already making use of. Consequently on Monday, the 4th of November, the mayor and several leading citizens, among them Livingston, attended a council called by the governor. The governor promised not to deliver or suffer to be delivered any of the stamps in Fort George. This promise was affixed to a statement purporting to express the satisfaction of the "Freemen and Freeholders," and their further determination to keep the peace until other causes of conflict arose; the document was signed by Livingston, Cruger, Beverley, Robinson, and J. Stevens, printed on a broadside, and circulated throughout the city. But in spite of the fact that the proposition bore the names of Beverley and Robinson, the "people" were not satisfied. It was demanded that the stamps be delivered to the corporation, and a popular meeting was called for the 5th of November. The common council then took the initiative ; a committee was sent to the governor, and the stamps, in return for a receipt, were taken and lodged in the city hall. The mob dispersed.[2]

This reaction of the propertied classes[3] against the more rad-

---

[1] "31st October, 1765. Several people in mourning for the near issue of the stamps, and the interment of their liberty. Descended even to the Bag-Gammon boxes at the Merchants Coffee House being covered with black and the dice in crape. This night a mob in three squads went through the streets crying 'liberty,' at the same time breaking the lamps and threatening particulars that they would the next night pull down their houses." *The Montresor Journals* (New York Historical Society Collections for 1881), p. 336. For a further account of the doings of the mob, especially the burning of the governor in effigy, see *Colden's Letter Book*, II. 54; *Memorial History of New York*, II. 360; *Montresor*, p. 337.

[2] *Memorial History of New York*, II. 363. For the receipt which was given, see *Colden's Letter Book*, II. 57.

[3] While the propertied class was seconded to some extent, in this reactionary movement, by the merchants and the lawyers, it is still true that the land owners were at this date the prime movers in the reaction. The main body of the merchants certainly assumed

ical methods of the Sons of Liberty, which was also a feeling of
jealousy at the interference of the lower classes in politics, was attended with more success in the matter of instructing the city's
representatives in the assembly. The leaders now made use of
their experience in political methods to secure success by a little
diplomacy, where, in point of mere numbers, they were very likely
at a disadvantage. On the 25th of November, certain of the leaders of the radicals, after consultation, posted a notice about the
city, according to their custom, calling a meeting of the freemen
and freeholders for the purpose of considering the matter of issuing instructions to their representatives.[1] On the day appointed
the conservative leaders, it appears, attended the meeting in considerable numbers, and by an ingenious device appointed their own
committee, laid aside the originally prepared instructions, and
adopted less radical ones in their stead.[2] The following day their
committee in person presented the instructions to the assembly.[3]

9

a conservative attitude only at a later date; as for the lawyers, some ultimately became
Tories others remained with the radical party. "The lawyers leveled at . . . to be at
the bottom of this disgraceful insurrection." "The lawyers deemed by the people here
to be hornets and firebrands . . . the planners and incendiaries of the present rupture."
The Montresor Journals, p. 339.

[1] "LIBERTY PROPERTY AND NO STAMPS! A general meeting of the
freeholders, freemen, and inhabitants of the city and county of New York is desired on
Tuesday afternoon, at the house of Mr. Burns . . . in order to agree upon some instructions to be given to their representatives in the general Assembly." *New York Mercury*,
December 2, 1765. See also, *The Montresor Journals*, p. 340.

[2] When the meeting had assembled, "one or more of the company, supposed to be
previously instructed, proposed some particular gentlemen present to be appointed a committee for the county. These gentlemen, without the general assent of the people, agreed
to the proposal on condition they might be joined by several other gentlemen present who
were named." The unexceptional character of the men named prevented any exception
being taken to them. Thus the men first appointed, who seemed the prime movers but
were not at all, took the lead and diverted the meeting from its original design. *New
York Mercury*, December 2, 1765. The instructions which the meeting drew up expressed the belief that it could not be unreasonable, in these troublous times, for constituents, "in this constitutional way," to urge upon their representatives the need of watchfulness in the public interest, and proceeded to point out the dangerous tendency of the
duties recently levied, etc. *New York Gazette*, November 28, 1765.

[3] The committee included William Livingston, William Smith, James DeLancey,
and John Morin Scott. For the whole list, see *New York Gazette*, November 28, 1765.
They were received kindly by the assembly, and were assured that the matter had already
been taken into consideration. *Ibid.* About a month later the assembly passed resolutions embodying the instructions of the committee, but adding a profession of allegiance
to the King. *Ibid.*, December 26. On the very day that the above instructions were
presented to the assembly, November 26, a curious anonymous document was received
by that body, which was also in the nature of instructions. It was not the resolutions
which were originally prepared for the meeting of the 26th of November (for these, see
New York Mercury, December 2, 1765), but was the work of some of the Sons of Liberty, or of individuals calling themselves such. The document was delivered to the clerk
of the assembly in a sealed envelope, and when opened read as follows:—"Gentlemen
of the House of Representatives you are to consider what is to be done first drawing of

After this rebuff the Sons of Liberty threw off the mask of secrecy, declared themselves the true representatives of the city and county, complained that they were not being supported by the best element of the people, and discussed the question as to whether the stamps in the state house should be burnt or sent back to England.[1] The first factional divisions of the Revolution were becoming clearly marked.

The result of the Stamp Act episode in detaching the propertied classes and especially the landed classes from the more radical followers of the Sons of Liberty, was thrown into strong relief by the elections of 1768 and 1769. In both of these elections the popular party of Livingston was defeated, and the royal or court party of De Lancey for the last time gained control of the assembly. It is true the moderate measures of resistance to the Stamp Act, which were also the most effective ones, had been carried through by the Livingston party in control of the assembly; but that party was at first hardly distinguishable from the mob element, and never perhaps became completely differentiated from it. It followed as a natural

---

as much money from the Lieutenant Governor's sellery as will Repare the fort and on spike the guns on the Battery & the nex a Repeal of the gunning act & then there will be a good Militia but not before and also as you are a setting you may consider of the Building act as it is to take place next yeare wich it Cannot for there is no supply of some sort of the materials Required this law is not ground on Reasons but there is a great many Reasons to the contrary so gentlemen we Desire you will do what Lays in your power for the good of the public but if you take this ill be not so conceited as to say or think that other people know nothing about government you have made these laws & say they are Right but they are Rong & take away Liberty, Oppressions of your make gentlemen make us SONS OF LIBERTY think you are not for the public Liberty, this is the general opinion of the people for this part of your conduct By order signed one and all, FREEDOM." *Documentary History of New York*, III. 495 (ed. 1850–1851). The assembly voted the letter scandalous and offered a reward of £50 for the detection of the author. Dawson, *The Park and its Vicinity*, p. 15 note.

[1] "23rd. (Dec., 1765) Assembled a mob for householder's votes—yea or nay to burn the Stamps or send them to England back. Undetermined." *The Montresor Journals*, p. 343. "4th Feb., 1766. Meeting of the Libertines, who seem to decline, being much concerned that the gentlemen of property in the town dont publicly join them. They formed a Committee of Correspondence with the Liberty Boys of the neighboring Provinces." *Ibid.*, 348. For the further activity of the Sons of Liberty during this period, see *Memorial History of New York*, II. 374; *New York Gazette*, January, 2, 9, 17, 23, 30, and February 6, 1766; *New York Mercury*, February 17, 1766; Onderdonk, *Documents and Letters Intended to Illustrate the Revolutionary Incidents of Queens County*, pp. 13, 14. "Our political affairs are in great confusion. Today will be decided if the moble will command the town or will be subjected to the better sort of citizens. The latter are called by the Mayor and corporation to meet at 11 o'clock at the city hall to resolve upon the point. The Sons of Liberty, so as they stile themselves, pretend to take by arbitrary force the stamps out of the town house and send them to England. . . . The last resolves of the Assembly concerning the present circumstances are very well. Why have they not been so moderate long ago? The effect would have been favorable and their conduct honorable. We set the house afire and then endeavour to put it out." Peter Hasenclerer to William Johnson, New York, December 23, 1765. Johnson MSS., II. 279.

consequence that the party had to bear the discredit of the whole movement, the most clearly remembered features of which were mob violence and lawlessness. The assembly, thus placed in the hands of the reactionists, became more and more conservative and royalist in character. Its influence decreased steadily until it was replaced by the popularly established government known as the Provincial Congress.

The Townsend Act, which followed close upon the repeal of the Stamp Act, aroused much the same sort of opposition from the Sons of Liberty as the Stamp Act had done. Even the merchant class had not yet been entirely detached from the radical party. But they were nevertheless somewhat more cautious in their resistance, and acted to some extent by themselves. An agreement was drawn up and signed by nearly all of the merchants of New York, in which they pledged themselves not to import anything more from England until the duties were repealed. For those who broke the agreement boycott was to be the punishment. The enforcement of the agreement was placed in the hands of a general committee of one hundred.[1] Having determined upon this policy the merchants settled down to await the repeal. Meanwhile popular agitation and resistance, which were continued largely under the direction of the Sons of Liberty, were directed against the assembly in the proportion to which that body became reactionary and royalist. The Sons of Liberty exercised themselves dramatically in erecting liberty poles, quarrelling with the soldiers,[2] arousing opposition to the acts of the assembly, urging their views upon the city's representatives by means of instructions,[3] and illustrating in many ways the

11

[1] *New York Mercury*, September 12, 1768.
[2] See *New York Colonial Documents*, VIII. 208; *Colden's Letter Book*, II. 211. Broadsides entitled "To the Public," and, "To the Inhabitants of the City," in the New York Historical Society Library, volume one of the collection of broadsides. *New York Mercury*, February 5, 1770; Leake, *Life of Lamb*, p. 54, *et seq.*
[3] The practice of drawing up instructions to representatives was a natural accompaniment of the coming political self-consciousness of the unfranchised classes. Almost inevitably the electors in a republican government look upon their representatives as mere agents of their own will; inevitably they will try to shape and control legislation by forcing this will upon their representatives. Instructions furnished the first method used by the popular element in America for controlling their representatives in this respect. The perfected nominating convention, with its platform, represents a later and perhaps a more efficient method. The practice of giving instructions was very common during the period under consideration. The "great majority of the freeholders of Queens and Suffolk counties" were pleased with the action of their representatives relative to the British acts of oppression, but directed them further to counteract the ruinous effect of the high fees of the supreme court, to continue the £5 act, and if possible raise the limit to £10. *New York Mercury*, April 17, 1769. Instructions to the same effect were sent in from many counties, and the object they had in view was ultimately attained. *Ibid.*, June 5, 1769. Another question that was agitated at this time was the proposed bill for substi-

influence of popular activity in political matters. The most prominent issue between the assembly and the Sons of Liberty at this period was raised by a bill proposing to appropriate money for the support of the British troops in the province. The episode presents perhaps as good an illustration as can be found of the popular political activity of the time, and shows therefore how the Revolutionary questions were teaching a minority the uses of popular organization. Mass meetings, committees, resolutions, instructions, were the crude ore out of which the nominating convention finally came a perfectly tempered instrument.

Soon after the bill proposing to aid the soldiers was brought forward, in December, 1769, a hand bill appeared, entitled " To the Public," and signed " Legion."[1] The sheet referred to the " late

tuting the ballot for viva voce voting. The Sons of Liberty had long desired such a change. They held a meeting at which they instructed the representatives of the city to support the measure. *New York Mercury*, Jan. 8, 1770. On the following day notice was given to " all such who are disposed to sign the petition to the Honorable House of Representatives praying it to pass a law to elect our representatives by ballot, that there will be petitions lodged at the houses of Messrs James M'Cartney in Bayard street, Henry Becker in the Broadway, David Philips in Horse and Cart street, and at Jasper Drakes between Beekman's and Burling's slip." (Broadside, Jan. 5, 1770, in the New York Historical Society Library, Vol. I. of the collection of broadsides.) But there was also strong opposition to the proposed change On the 4th of January, the following notice was circulated on a broadside, entitled " TO THE INDEPENDENT FREEHOLDERS AND FREEMEN OF THIS CITY AND COUNTY. It having been industriously propagated that numbers of the voters of this city and county have been long intimidated at elections, and are therefore desirous of voting for the future in a secret manner by way of the ballot : which report being by many surmised to be void of a proper foundation, and only intended to answer the particular private purposes of certain persons : it is therefore requested that the independent Freeholders and Freemen . . . will meet at the Merchants Coffee House, tomorrow at eleven o'clock in the forenoon, to convey their sentiments respecting this matter to their representatives." (Broadside, Jan. 4, 1770. As above, Vol. I.) On January 5th a number of people assembled at the Coffee House, " when a gentleman at request of a number of his friends delivered himself in the following words : Gentlemen, I am desired to address you on the present very important occasion, and I beg your attention to what I am about to propose, in order to secure to us the exercise of one of our most invaluable privileges . . . And then the question was put in the following words : Gentlemen, do you approve of the old free constitutional mode of voting publicly and openly for the representatives you like? When a great number of the inhabitants signified by loud acclamation their entire approbation of the old mode." *New York Mercury*, Jan. 8, 1770. Instructions were prepared which dilated at length upon the danger of radical innovations, and closed with the following words : " Therefore we desire you . . . would endeavor to protect us in our . . . constitutional right of election, for we will not that the old custom of the land should be changed." *Ibid.* These instructions were signed by some 1700 names it is said, and were presented to the assemby by a committee which the meeting had appointed. The bill had already been defeated, but the representatives assured the committee that they would always give careful attention to " constitutional instructions from a majority of their constituents." *Ibid.*, Jan. 22, 1770. For instructions from the " inhabitants of Westchester county," see *New York Mercury*, Jan. 15, 1770.

[1] Broadside, no date, in the New York Historical Society Library, volume one of the collection. *Documentary History of New York*, III. 534, ed. 1850–1851.

base inglorious " action of the assembly in " opposition to the loud and general voice of their constituents," and called upon all inhabitants to convene at eleven o'clock on the morning of the 17th of December in the Fields, to pronounce upon this violation of the well known will of the people. On the 16th a still more radical tirade appeared, entitled " To the Betrayed Inhabitants of New York," and signed " A Son of Liberty." It also urged a meeting for drawing up instructions and appointing a committee.[1] On the appointed day some fourteen hundred people assembled in the Fields near Mr. Montagnie's coffee house. After waiting till twelve o'clock, " they appointed a gentleman (John Lamb) to propound the necessary questions. . . . He stated and explained the vote passed by the Assembly for granting the money to support the troops. After a small pause the question was put : Whether they approved of the vote of the . . . Assembly . . . which was carried in the negative, there being but very few in the affirmative, not more in our opinion than five or six. And then the question was put : Whether they were for giving any money to the troops under any consideration whatever ? which was carried in the negative, there being not more in the affirmative than there were on the other question." A committee of ten was then appointed, which the assembly received " with decency, and in general returned for answer: That they were of the opinion that a majority of the inhab-

13

[1] Broadside, as above. *Documentary History of New York*, III. 528 ; Dawson, *The Park and its Vicinity*, p. 25 For the author of these articles rewards were offered of £50 and £100 respectively. *Documentary History of New York*, III. 532, 534 ; Dawson, *The Park and its Vicinity*, p. 25. From Parker, the editor of the *Gazette*, it was learned that the probable author was Alexander M'Dougall, who was consequently imprisoned for nearly three months. *Documentary History of New York*, III. 536. This arrest made McDougall the hero of the hour. He posed as the Wilkes of America, and was oppressed with visits of condolence ; so much so that the following manifesto was put forth from the New Gaol on the 10th of February, 1770 : " Many of my friends, who, having honored me with their visits since my oppressive confinement in this place, have advised me, as I intend to devote a good deal of my time to do justice to the public, in the cause for which I am imprisoned, to appoint an hour from which it will be most convenient for me to see my friends : I do therefore hereby notify them that I shall be glad of the honor of their company from three o'clock in the afternoon till six." Dawson, *The Park and its Vicinity*, p 32. From time to time he issued addresses to the freeholders from the New Gaol. See Broadsides, December 22, 1770, and January 26, 1771, in the New York Historical Society Library, Vol. I. of the collection. For further information on this affair see Thomas, *History of Printing*, II. 260–262 ; *New York Colonial Documents*, VIII. 208 ; *Colden's Letter Book*, II. 211. Leake, *Life and Times of General Lamb*, p. 60. The letter entitled " To the Betrayed Inhabitants of New York " was answered by "A Citizen," in another broadside dated December 18, 1769. Five days later this was in turn answered by " Plebeian," who pointed out that the assembly could not plead ignorance of the will of the people. Even before the meeting in the Fields they might have had full instructions, for " they must know *how ready the people are to come together to consult on matters that respect their liberties and property*." Broadsides as cited.

itants were disposed to give money to support the troops, and that it was now too late to pay any regard to the above report of the committee."[1]

This may serve to illustrate the attitude and the methods of the Sons of Liberty, during the period from the levying of the new duties until 1770, when all but the duties on tea were repealed. The Stamp Act episode had detached the landed classes generally, if one may make a rough generalization, but there was yet no sharp separation of the merchants from the mechanics and artisans—the "Inhabitants"—who filled up the ranks of the Sons of Liberty. Two forces were now operating however to separate the merchants from the mechanics and artisans. In the first place, the merchants, who were mostly men of property, were becoming conscious, as the landed classes had already become, of the consequences of the "mobish violence" which was constantly disturbing the peace of the city; and like the landed classes they resented the growing interference of an unfranchised class in political matters. More important however was the fact that, as the years passed and the duties were unrepealed, the commercial interests of the city began to suffer on account of the sweeping character of the non-importation agreement. The merchants began to consider therefore whether it were not possible to dispense with the liberty in return for a little trade—whether it were not quite as well to be a "Son of Liberty and Trade," as to be a mere "Son of Liberty." Early in 1770 this feeling became strong enough to reform the non-importation agreement on a more conservative basis; the same movement split the old organization into two—the Sons of Liberty and the Sons of Liberty and Trade.

The division came when the Rhode Island merchants first broke away from the old non-importation agreement. Upon learning of this violation, the committee of vigilance called a meeting of the inhabitants, by public notice, to meet on the 5th of June.[2] A "considerable number of inhabitants" assembled on that day; and to them was twice read a series of resolutions, previously prepared by the committee, condemning the Rhode Island merchants, declaring them enemies of the country, proposing to boycott them, and renewing the adherence of the New York merchants to the non-importation agreement. The assembled inhabitants assented to these resolutions, it is said, by a great majority.[3] Meanwhile the con-

---

[1] *New York Mercury*, December 25, 1769.

[2] General direction of the affairs of the non-importation league in New York was in the hands of a committee of one hundred. A subcommittee of vigilance acted for it in an administrative or executive capacity. The call for the meeting was posted May 30th. *New York Mercury*, June 11, 1770; Leake, *Life and Times of General Lamb*, p. 67.

[3] For these resolutions see *ibid.*

servative had been carrying through a plan of their own. A number of merchants had already asked the general committee of one hundred to "take the sense" of the city, "by subscription," whether "an alteration should not be made in our non-importation agreement." A meeting was held and persons were appointed to go through the wards proposing to each of the inhabitants the following question : " Do you approve of a general importation of goods from Great Britain except teas and other articles which are or may be subject to an importation duty? Or do you approve of our non-importation agreement continuing in the manner it now is ?" [1] A majority was found to be in favor of importation according to the proposed change.[2] Somewhat to the surprise, and much to the chagrin, of the committee of vigilance, which seems to have been composed of the radical element, both the meeting and the resolutions of the 5th of June were therefore disavowed by the general committee of one hundred, a majority of which were in sympathy with the views of the conservatives. From this time the division was complete.[3]

15

[1] *New York Mercury*, June 18, 1770; Leake, *Life and Times of General Lamb*, p. 67.

[2] *Ibid.* According to Colden 1,180 persons, among them the principal inhabitants, declared for importation, "about 300 were neutral or unwilling to declare their sentiments and few of any distinction declared in oppostion to it." *Letter Book*, II. 223.

[3] The separation had of course been long in coming. The actual struggle over non-importation was introduced by a curious and amusing prologue earlier in the year. It had been customary for the Sons of Liberty and others to celebrate, annually on the 18th of March, the repeal of the Stamp Act. At first this celebration was held at Bardin's Tavern. *New York Mercury*, March 9, 1767. As early as 1769 the friends of the repeal had divided into two factions, one holding its celebration at Bardin's as usual, the other at Van DeWater's. The former party Holt, editor of the *Journal*, characterized as " the genuine Sons of Liberty," composed mostly of merchants; the latter were "probably mechanics." *Memorial History of New York*, II. 397. At the next celebration the division was complete. The radical faction posted a notice calling a meeting of the Sons of Liberty at Montagnie's (Bardin's establishment had meanwhile been taken by Montagnie) as usual. Whereupon Mr. Montagnie published the following notice in the *Journal:* " To The Public : An advertisement having appeared in last Monday's papers inviting the Sons of Liberty to dine at my house on Monday, the 19th of March next . . . not having proceeded from any of the gentlemen who engaged my house for that day, I think myself obliged to give this notice that several gentlemen, as a committee from a great number of other gentlemen, having engaged my house some time ago for the 19th of March next, I shall not be able to entertain any other company." *New York Journal*, Feb. 8, 1770 ; Dawson, *The Park, etc.*, p. 42. A few days later the following appeared from the committee mentioned by Montagnie : " The friends of Liberty and Trade, who formerly associated together at Bardin's . . . to celebrate the . . . repeal of the stamp act, are requested to meet for that purpose on Monday, the 19th of March next, at the house of Mr. Abraham De La Montagnie." Dawson, *The Park, etc.*, p. 43. Finally, on the 15th, the other faction announced : " To all the Sons of Liberty," that whereas the house of Mr. Montagnie could not be secured, " a number of Sons of Liberty " had secured "the corner house in the Broadway, near Liberty Pole, lately kept by Mr. Edward Smith." *Ibid.* This house was purchased for the permanent use of the Sons of Liberty. It stood at the corner of Broadway and " the Bourie Road," and was christened Hampden Hall. Leake,

The general merchant body was now detached from the Sons of Liberty proper; henceforth it favored non-importation only as respects articles actually taxed; and its influence was exerted in support of conservative measures and in opposition to mob violence and all hasty and ill-considered action. For a time therefore the Sons of Liberty remained under a cloud, especially during the years of 1771 and 1772, which, partly because of the repeal of all duties except those on tea, were a period of quiet and unsuited to the turbulent activity which had brought them into prominence in previous years.[1] But their opportunity came again within the next two years when the East India Company attempted to force the importation of tea into the colonies. The Sons of Liberty renewed not only their spirit but also their organization; and from this time dates the struggle between the radicals and the conservatives to direct the Revolutionary policy of New York by controlling this organization. It is necessary to notice therefore: (1) What was the new attitude of the British government which presented the question directly at issue; (2) the renewed organization of the Sons of Liberty which claimed to represent the city; (3) the result of the tea episode upon the attitude of the conservatives.

The Stamp Act had been repealed in the spring of 1766. On the 20th of November, 1767, an import tax had been laid upon tea, glass, painter's colors, and paper. All of these duties were in turn repealed in 1770, with the exception of those on tea, which were retained as a test " of the parliamentary right to tax." But it was difficult to make any test so long as the American merchants refused to import any of the tea. Meanwhile the affairs of the East India Company were in a deplorable state, the result, it was thought, of the loss of the American market which had been regularly supplied by illegal traffic with Holland. Partly to test the right of taxation, partly to relieve the East India Company, a scheme was proposed by which the Americans could get their tea from England with the duty, cheaper than from Holland without it. This was effected by giving the company a drawback, on the tea exported to America, of all duties paid on such tea when entering England from the east. With this advantage the company was enabled to offer tea to America at a price which, even with the slight duty, was less

Life and Times of General Lamb, p. 62. From this time on the parties celebrated separately. See *New York Mercury*, March 4, 1771; *Memorial History of New York*, II. 419.

[1] " It gives me particular satisfaction to find this party [non-importation] entirely defeated last week in a violent struggle to turn out such of the elective magistrates of the city as had distinguished themselves in any way in favor of government." Colden to Hillsborough, October 15, 1770. *Letter Book*, II. 229. See *Ibid*. 222, 223.

than the price which must be paid for it in Holland. But the company was given to understand that the Americans would not be influenced by any mere appeal to their pecuniary interests, and that an attempt to land any dutied tea in America would be attended with disastrous results. The directors were nevertheless assured by Lord North that the King would have it so; he was determined to "try the question with America." Four ships were consequently sent to the four ports of Boston, New York, Philadelphia, and Charleston, in the fall of 1773, and agents appointed by letter to receive the cargos in each port.[1] The expected arrival of Captain Lockyear at the port of New York furnished the occasion for a reorganization of the Sons of Liberty.

17

On Thursday, the 16th of December, 1773, some of the Sons of Liberty, who still acted as a committee of the society, though the organization had fallen away somewhat during the quiet years since 1770, issued a broadside calling a meeting for the following day at the city hall. Besides the members, "every other friend to the liberties and trade of America," was invited to be present.[2] In spite of bad weather, "a very numerous and respectable number of citizens met at the City Hall" on the following day. Mr. John Lamb, of the committee, addressed the meeting on the questions at issue, and read several letters which had been received from the Boston and Philadelphia committees of correspondence relative to the "importation of the East India's tea." A committee of fifteen was then chosen to answer these letters and "to correspond with the sister colonies on the subject of the dutied tea." A series of resolutions, bearing the date November 29th,[3] entitled "The Association of the Sons of Liberty of New York," was then read. The preamble of these resolutions related briefly the history of the import duty on tea, the failure to secure American importers, and the

---

[1] Broadsides dated November 29, and December 17, 1773, in the New York Historical Society Library, Vol. I. of the collection. *Rivington's Gazetteer*, November 18, and December 2, 1773; Fiske, *American Revolution*, I. 82, 83.

[2] "The members of the association of the Sons of Liberty are requested to meet at the City Hall at one o'clock tomorrow (being Friday) on business of the utmost importance, and every other friend to the liberties and trade of America are hereby most cordially invited to meet at the same time and place.
    The Committee of the Association.
Thursday, 16th December, 1773."
Broadside, December 16, 1773, in the New York Historical Society Library, Vol. I. of the collection.

[3] These resolutions bearing date of November 29th were drawn up and adopted at a meeting of that date. Broadside, November 29, 1773, as above cited. The later meeting of the 17th of December was probably held for the purpose of securing a more general support of the resolutions. At any rate the latter meeting may be said to mark the complete reorganization of the Sons of Liberty.

recent acts of Parliament favorable to the East India Company,
finally closing with the assurance that the tea ships might be daily
expected. "Therefore," the document continues, "to prevent
slavery . . . we the subscribers, being influenced from a regard
to liberty and disposed to . . . transmit to our posterity those
blessings of freedom which our ancestors have handed down to us,
and to contribute to the support of the common liberties of America
which are in danger to be subverted: Do, for those important purposes, agree to associate together under the name and stile of
the SONS OF LIBERTY OF NEW YORK, and engage our honor to
and with each other faithfully to observe and perform the following resolutions." The five resolutions which follow the preamble
recite that the subscribers bind themselves to consider as an enemy
of the liberties of America any and every person who aids or abets
the introduction or the landing of the dutied tea, or buys or sells
it, or aids or abets the purchase or sale of it; whether the duty was
paid in England or America was immaterial; as for him who trans-
gressed these rules " we will not deal with or employ or have any
connection with him." The resolutions having been read, " Mr.
Lamb then putting the question whether they agreed to these resolutions? it passed in the affirmative nem. con." At this point the
mayor and recorder came in with a message from the governor.
Permission having been received to deliver it, the mayor stated that
the governor wished to make the following proposal to the people,
viz: that the tea should upon arrival be put into the fort at noon
day, that it should remain there until the council or the King or the
proprietors should order it delivered, that it should then be delivered at noonday. "Gentlemen," said the mayor, "is this satisfactory to you?" For all answer he got only "no" repeated three
times. Mr. Lamb in his turn, having made some pertinent remarks,
put the following question: " Is it then your opinion gentlemen that
the tea should be landed under these circumstances?" So general
was the negative reply that there was no call for a division. The
meeting then adjourned till the arrival of the tea ships. The association, together with an account of the meeting, was ordered printed
and transmitted to the committees of the other colonies.[1]

Such were the Sons of Liberty newly organized. They claimed
to represent the city, and through their committee to express its
will. When the tea ships arrived on the 18th of April, 1774, the

---

[1] An account of the proceedings of the meeting, including the advertisement by which
it was called and the resolutions of association in full, was published by John Holt. This
document is in the New York Historical Society Library. Vol. I. of the collection of
broadsides. See also, Leake, *Life and Times of General Lamb*, pp. 79, 80.

city was informed by the committee's hand bills, and from day to day other announcements of a similar character furnished information as to what had been and what would be done.[1] It is likely that the claim of representing the city was not altogether unjustified in this particular case, for the attempt to force importation upon the colony was certainly not popular with any class. The merchants themselves, as we have seen, had never given up the principle that duted goods should not be imported, and they were quite willing to resist any effort to force such articles into the province. Even the extreme conservatives were willing to record their protest, and the assembly took action for the last time by appointing a committee of its own, "to obtain the most early and authentic intelligence of all such acts and resolutions of the British Parliament . . . as do or may relate or affect the liberties and privileges of his Majesty's subjects in America, and to keep up . . . a correspondence . . . with our sister colonies."[2] Thus all parties were practically at one in respect to the importation of the duted tea; the conservatives, in so far as they refused to act with the Sons of Liberty, were actuated rather by jealousy of the growing political influence of the unfranchised classes, and by fear of their undisciplined methods of resistance, than by difference of opinion as to the nature of the British policy itself.[3] And this fear was not altogether unfounded as the sequel proved. The radical methods which the Sons of

19

---

[1] "TO THE PUBLIC:—The long expected tea ships arrived last night at Sandy Hook, but the pilot would not bring up the Captain until the sense of the city was known. The committee were immediately informed that the Captain solicits for liberty to come up to provide necessaries for his return, the ship to remain at Sandy Hook. The committee conceiving that he should have such liberty signified it to the gentleman who is to supply him and others with necessaries. Advise of this was immediately dispatched to the Captain, and whenever he comes up care will be taken that he does not enter the customs house and that no time be lost in dispatching him. New York, April 19, 1774." Broadside, as above cited. "TO THE PUBLIC: The sense of the city relative to the landing of the East India Company's tea being signified to Captain Lockyear by the committee, nevertheless it is the desire of a number of the citizens that, at his departure from hense, he should see, with his own eyes, their detestation of the measures persued by the ministry to enslave the country. This will be declared by the convention of the people at his departure . . . which will be on next Saturday morning about 9 o'clock, where no doubt every friend of this country will attend. The bills will give the notice about an hour before he embarks from Murry's wharf. By Order of the Committee." (Dated April 21, 1774.) Broadside, as above cited.

[2] *Assembly Journal*, January 20, 1774; *Rivington's Gazetteer*, January 27, 1774. The committee consisted of John Cruger, James DeLancey, Jacob Walton, Benjamin Seaman, Isaac Wilkins, Frederick Philipse, Daniel Kissam, Zebulon Seaman, John Rapalja, Simon Boerum, John DeNoyelles, and George Clinton, "or any seven of them." See also Dawson, *History of Westchester County During the American Revolution*, p. 23.

[3] A few voices were raised favoring the importation of the company's tea, on the ground of commercial necessity. See a series of articles by Popliocola in the Broadsides, as above cited. See also *Rivington's Gazetteer*, November 18, and December 2, 1773.

Liberty were likely to favor, had already been foreshadowed in the attitude of the meeting of the seventeenth of December, with reference to the proposals of the governor. The action of the citizens of Boston in throwing the tea into the harbor had meanwhile fired the zeal of the New York radicals, and the "Mohawks," a kind of rough riding detachment of the regular army of the Sons of Liberty, were prepared for similar measures if occasion offered. Eventually, in spite of the somewhat conservative attitude of the new committee, a part of Captain Lockyear's cargo was dumped into the harbor, while the band, a little incongruously perhaps, played "God Save the King."[1]

Once more therefore the Sons of Liberty, the representatives of the unfranchised classes, had scored a victory over the propertied enfranchised classes. The event served to separate the factions the more sharply and to introduce the coming struggle for control, because the difference was seen to be largely a question of methods of resistance rather than a question of resistance itself. As this fact became more and more' obvious, the extreme conservatives were dropping out of the contest entirely, eventually to swell the numbers of the Tory party. Within a few months the passage of the coercion acts precipitated the permanent Revolutionary contest, and the question became, at least within the city, less and less one of resistance or non-resistance and almost entirely one of the methods and character of the resistance. Was the policy of New York in this struggle to be dominated and guided by the radical unfranchised classes, whose methods were characterized by rashness and mob violence, or was it to be under the direction of moderate men of property, who were accustomed to exercise political privileges, whose methods were those of reason and good sense, and who would firmly assert the rights of the colony without over-stepping the bounds which separated law from lawlessness? The conservatives now saw clearly that a policy of mere negation, a policy of holding aloof, would not in any sense suffice; action of a positive character was necessary. Yet they shrewdly refrained from opposing the organization, now in the hands of the Sons of Liberty, which claimed to represent the city. They were conscious that this organization, whether legal or extra-legal, was grounded in a wide popular support, that it was the essential political institution of the hour, and that through it or not at all they must give practical effect to their ideas. Their energies were now directed therefore to obtaining control of this organization, through which they hoped to

[1] Leake, *Life and Times of General Lamb*, pp. 76, 77, 82, 83.

guide and direct the popular will. They captured the organization at the election of the new committee of fifty-one. A protracted struggle then followed over the election of delegates to the first Continental Congress ; incidentally the first attempt was made by the city committee to organize the rural districts for the Revolutionary contest.

CARL BECKER.

21

Notes and Documents

The Ward-Hopkins Controversy and the American Revolution in Rhode Island: An Interpretation

Mack E. Thompson*

FROM 1755 to 1770 the colony of Rhode Island was torn by an internal political struggle that historians usually refer to as the Ward-Hopkins controversy, since the two factions contending for political supremacy were led by Samuel Ward from Westerly and Newport and Stephen Hopkins from Providence. Those who consider the American Revolution as an internal social and political conflict as well as a revolt from political obedience to England seem to see their thesis substantiated by the Ward-Hopkins controversy. Their assumption is that in pre-Revolutionary Rhode Island the people were sharply divided politically along economic class lines. One author states that Rhode Island was "a battleground for conservative merchants and radical farmers," and that "radicalism won victories earlier than in the other colonies." "When the break with England came," this author concludes, "Newport and the Narragansett country remained loyal, whereas the agrarian north, which was in control of the government, declared Rhode Island's independence of Britain two months before the radical party was able to achieve that end in the Continental Congress. Throughout the revolutionary period the Rhode Islanders were staunch defenders of democracy and state sovereignty."[1] In other words, the colony was taken into the Revolution by

* Mr. Thompson is a member of the faculty of the Division of Humanities, University of California at Riverside.

[1] Merrill Jensen, *The Articles of Confederation: An Interpretation of the Social-Constitutional History of the American Revolution, 1774-1781* (Madison, 1940), p. 40. Marguerite Appleton, in her biographical sketch of Samuel Ward in the *Dictionary of American Biography*, XIX, 437, writes that Rhode Island "was divided into two

northern agrarian radicals who had earlier won a victory for democratic rights against southern conservative merchants. The purpose of this paper is to offer an alternative interpretation of the Ward-Hopkins controversy and the Revolution in Rhode Island.

It is true that Rhode Island was split politically along geographic lines. Hopkins's supporters were located in the northern towns and Ward's in the southern. But to view the north's rise to political power as a victory for agrarian radicalism is to miss entirely the significance of Stephen Hopkins's political success. Fundamental to an understanding of domestic politics in Rhode Island is a clear picture of the colony's economic growth during the middle half of the eighteenth century.

To speak of the north as "agrarian" and the south as "mercantile" is a fairly accurate description of Rhode Island in 1720, if we mean that commercial activity was confined largely to Newport and the Narragansett country in the south.[2] Before that date, and for some years after, only in Newport, on Aquidneck Island in Narragansett Bay, did there exist in Rhode Island an urban community with a fairly sizable population employed in commerce and manufacturing. And only in the southern part of the colony, in the Narragansett country, were there substantial numbers of capitalistic farmers. In the rest of the colony an overwhelming majority of the people were engaged in subsistence agriculture, and commercial activity was relatively unimportant.

Until the 1750's the agrarian interests managed to have a decisive voice in the formation of public policy because the architects of the colony's gov-

23

hostile camps: the conservative group, the merchants, found a champion in Ward, while the radicals looked to Hopkins." Bernhard Knollenberg has a somewhat different view. He writes, "I have found no evidence of such a line of cleavage; personal and sectional rivalry seem to have been the chief factors." *Correspondence of Governor Samuel Ward, May 1775-March 1776, with a Biographical Introduction Based Chiefly on the Ward Papers Covering the Period 1775-1776,* ed. Bernhard Knollenberg (Providence, 1952), p. 6. Carl Becker, in his *History of Political Parties in the Province of New York, 1760-1776* (Madison, 1909), was one of the earliest writers to interpret the American Revolution as the "result of two general movements; the contest for home rule and independence, and the democratization of American politics and society." Recently the Becker-Jensen thesis as applied to Massachusetts has been sharply challenged by Robert E. Brown, *Middle-Class Democracy and the Revolution in Massachusetts, 1691-1780* (Ithaca, 1955).

[2] Carl Bridenbaugh, *Cities in the Wilderness: The First Century of Urban Life in America, 1625-1742* (New York, 1938), pp. 175-205, passim, but see particularly pages 175, 176-177, 182, 184, 190; Richard Pares, *Yankees and Creoles: The Trade between North America and the West Indies before the American Revolution* (London, 1956), p. 33.

ernment in the seventeenth century had fashioned a system to serve the needs of an agricultural population, and their charter had placed control of the central government in the hands of men residing in small farming communities.[3] As long as Rhode Island's economic base remained predominantly that of subsistence agriculture the most important unit of government was town, not colony, government. With few exceptions the problems of these people could be solved by the town council. For decades the powers of the General Assembly were neither numerous nor vigorously exercised except in the area of monetary policy. From 1710 to 1751 Rhode Island farmers passed nine paper money bills or "banks" in an attempt to solve their monetary problems.[4] They were forcefully but unsuccessfully opposed by the commercial interests in Newport.[5]

But the Rhode Island economy was not static. During the half century preceding the Revolution, external as well as internal events caused a remarkable economic growth that profoundly altered long existing political conditions. Newport, already one of the five leading ports in America by 1720, continued to grow.[6] As the West India market expanded and the number of trading ships to Newport increased, Narragansett planters geared their production to meet the demands of agricultural exporters. Increasingly these planters turned from subsistence to capitalistic farming, sending their surpluses to Newport for distribution. Opportunities in manufacturing, particularly distilling, shipbuilding, and ropemaking, caused many farmers to diversify their activities and in some cases to leave the land altogether. Long existing cultural, religious, and family affinities between the Newport and Narragansett residents were strengthened by intimate economic association, and the planters of Narragansett drifted

[3] The unit of representation in the General Assembly was the town: six deputies from Newport, four each from Providence, Portsmouth, and Warwick, and two from each of the remaining towns. As long as the smaller towns remained united they could always defeat the larger towns.

[4] *Records of the Colony of Rhode Island and Providence Plantations in New England,* ed. John Russell Bartlett (Providence, 1856-65), IV, 96, 202, 295, 350, 405, 454, 487, 440, 579, 592, V, 40, 75, 99, 130, 318-319. Hereafter cited as *Rhode Island Records.*

[5] For example, see the protest of Newport deputies against the 1744 "bank," and the "Petition to the King, relative to bills of credit," Newport, Sept. 4, 1750, *ibid.,* V, 75-76, 311-313. Among the 72 signers were Newport's leading merchants. In 1731 Governor Joseph Jenckes vetoed a bill issuing £60,000, but he was overruled by the General Assembly and the home government. *Ibid.,* IV, 456-461.

[6] Bridenbaugh, *Cities in the Wilderness,* pp. 330-363, passim, and particularly pp. 331, 334, 337, 347.

slowly into political alliance with merchant, mechanic, and professional classes of Newport. Newporters or men closely identified with the interests of that town began to monopolize the governorship and other important offices in the colonial government. They also tried to run the General Assembly in their own interests but were never quite able to wrest control from the grip of the small farmers.

While Newport was expanding its commercial activities and extending its economic and political influence into the southern agricultural communities, in the north, on the banks of the Seekonk and Providence Rivers, another commercial center was rising. For almost a century Providence, the oldest town in the colony, had remained an agricultural community, but in the second quarter of the eighteenth century it responded to the same influences that were making Newport one of the leading ports in British North America. By the mid 1750's Providence was a thriving port with a young and enterprising group of merchants.[7]

Providence's economic growth is not surprising. In some respects that city was more advantageously located than Newport. Providence not only had a protected outlet to the sea, but her merchants could draw on a larger hinterland for their cargoes than could Newport's. In response to increased demand for exports, several Providence merchants began to manufacture candles, chocolate, barrel hoops, rum, and rope and to serve as middlemen, supplying Newport merchants with cargo they could not find on the island or in the Narragansett country across the bay. By the early 1750's Providence was prepared to challenge Newport for economic leadership of the colony.[8]

It is against this background of economic change that Rhode Island politics must be projected. Newport's continued expansion and Providence's rise as an important commercial center were both cause and effect of the violent political controversy that erupted in 1755 and continued for over a decade. In that year the freemen elected Stephen Hopkins, one of Providence's leading merchants, to the governorship, an office he held for nine of the next thirteen years. His election shows that a realignment of political forces had taken place—the hitherto fairly unified agrarian interest had disintegrated, and two composite factions, one in the north and another in the south, had appeared. The new factions were made up of

25

    [7] William E. Foster, *Stephen Hopkins: A Rhode Island Statesman, A Study in the Political History of the Eighteenth Century* (Providence, 1884), pp. 91-102.
    [8] James B. Hedges, *The Browns of Providence Plantations: Colonial Years* (Cambridge, Mass., 1952), pp. 1-69.

cross sections of society—large and small farmers, merchants and trades-men, professional men and other freemen. The previous division of political forces along agrarian-commercial lines was no more. Hopkins's election also shows that political leadership had finally passed from the agrarian-small town interests to commercial and manufacturing groups and that the chief instrument for the promotion of economic growth was likely to be the General Assembly rather than the town council. Although rural towns continued to exert considerable influence in the political life of the colony, thirty years passed before they again consolidated to seize control of the government.[9]

26

With the disintegration of agrarian solidarity and the growth of two factions composed of men from both the urban and rural areas, political success went to the man who could reconcile conflicting interests within his own section and attract a majority of the few uncommitted freemen. As the contest between the north and south developed, leaders of both sides realized that the voters holding the balance of power were concen-trated most heavily in the farming communities in the central part of the colony, equidistant from the two commercial centers of Newport and Providence.[10] Stephen Hopkins, one of the most accomplished politicians

[9] There is no recent study of the Ward-Hopkins controversy, but see Hedges, *The Browns of Providence Plantations,* pp. 189-192, and my unpublished Ph.D. dissertation, "Moses Brown, A Man of Public Responsibility," Brown University, 1955, chaps. IV-VI. Carl Bridenbaugh has some interesting remarks concerning the Ward-Hopkins controversy in his *Cities in Revolt: Urban Life in America, 1743-1776* (New York, 1955), pp. 11, 53, 222-223, 264, 378. An older but still valuable treatment is contained in *State of Rhode Island and Providence Plantations at the End of the Century: A History,* ed. Edward Field (Boston, 1902), I, 199-219. A re-cently published work on the subject by David S. Lovejoy, *Rhode Island Politics and the American Revolution, 1760-1776* (Providence, 1958), arrived too late to be of as-sistance in the preparation of this paper.

[10] For a breakdown by towns of votes in the elections of 1761-64, see Ward Manuscripts, Box I, 1725-70, nos. 43, 49, Rhode Island Historical Society, Providence, R. I.; Brown Papers, L63-71M, John Carter Brown Library, Providence, R. I. In the election of 1765, Ward carried every town in King's and Kent counties by sub-stantial majorities. In the election of 1766, while he still won all the towns, his mar-gin of victory had decreased appreciably, and in the next election the drift toward Hopkins had gone so far as to give him the election by 414 votes, the largest majority in years. *The Providence* [Rhode Island] *Gazette and Country Journal,* Apr. 18, 1767, announced that not one vote was cast for Ward in Providence, and that in Cumberland he got only 4 votes. An analysis of the vote by towns shows that in 1767 Ward lost what little support he had in the north, while Hopkins made large dents in Ward's majorities in South Kingston, North Kingston, Westerly, (Ward's home town), Charleston, and East Greenwich. "Public Notice to the Printer," sub-mitted by one of the Browns, Apr. 17, 1767, Brown Papers, P-P6; Field, *State of Rhode Island,* I, 211.

in colonial America, was more successful in appealing to these freemen and better able to prevent any serious defections in his party than was his opponent, Samuel Ward.

The climax to the prolonged struggle came in the election of 1767, when Hopkins decisively defeated Ward for the governorship and dealt the southern party a shattering blow from which it never recovered. Hop-kins's success was the result of a combination of factors. By 1767, after controlling the government for two consecutive years, Ward and his followers in Newport had alienated the Narragansett planters and farmers by refusing to support a measure to regulate interest rates, and some of the latter began to look elsewhere for political leadership. Ward's party was further discredited by the gerrymandering activities of Elisha Brown, the deputy governor.[11]

Hopkins helped his cause by collecting a large election fund and conducting an energetic campaign. Personal influence, money, and liberal amounts of rum were brought to bear, and where possible, the old, the sick, and the infirm were carried to the polls to cast their ballots for Hopkins-party men. Freemen were not only paid to vote for Hopkins and his supporters but "many persons that is stranious for Mr. Ward who may be agreed with for a Small Sum to Lay Still," were also approached.[12] One Hopkins-party campaign worker, "Clostly Engaged in the Grand Cause" in Cumberland, reported that he would "be short with Regard to the Necessary argument (haveing Last Evening fell into Company with Two men who was against us Last year, who was hard to Convince of their Error, but I over come them) shall want five Dollars more which I must have; for I must meat the above two men To morror morning almost up to Woonsoketfalls where I expect to Settle Some things very favourable To the Campaign . . . . " He ended his urgent letter with the candid remark: "am Engaged Clostly in makeing freemen and hope I shall merrit the Beaver Hat."[13]

Hopkins's success in 1767 was materially aided by the growing identification of outlying towns with Providence as a result of the economic opportunities that flourishing port offered. Providence's economic growth may be compared to an expanding whirlpool; when it began slowly to

27

[11] *Acts and Resolves . . . of Rhode Island . . .* (Providence and Newport, 1747-1815), 1765-69, pp. 24, 30-32; *Rhode Island Records*, VI, 436-437; Moses Brown Papers, misc. papers, I, 15, XVIII, 77, R. I. Hist. Soc.

[12] Nicholas Brown and Company, Apr. 9, 1767, Brown Papers, P-P6.

[13] John Dexter to Nicholas Brown and Company, Apr. 14, 1767, *ibid.*, L67M.

spin in the second quarter of the century, it drew nearby agricultural communities into its vortex. In the next decades, as its force increased, it slowly but inexorably sucked more distant towns into its center. Political sympathies apparently were swept along with economic interests, for these towns eventually supported Stephen Hopkins and the northern party. Southern response to this economic and political alignment was what triggered the Ward-Hopkins controversy and kept it alive for over a decade.

Stephen Hopkins's elections to the governorship in 1755 and in subsequent years was not a victory for social and political radicalism. On issues commonly associated with radicalism there was little discussion and almost no discussion at all directly relating to internal political controversies. During Hopkins's numerous administrations no new laws were passed or even introduced in the General Assembly abolishing or lowering the property qualifications for the vote. The people were apparently not concerned with such issues. And ironically, on the most important problem of the period, currency, the men who assumed the leadership in solving it were not the southern "conservative merchants" but the northern "radical farmers." Stephen Hopkins, one of Providence's leading merchants, and the Browns of Providence, Obadiah and his four nephews, Nicholas, Joseph, John, and Moses, who operated one of the largest shipping firms in the colony, led the fight for currency reform.[14] By the early 1760's Stephen Hopkins's northern followers were committed to a program of sound money and in 1763 they were able to push through the assembly the first bill to regulate currency in the history of the colony.[15]

[14] The material on this subject is extensive, but see Governor Stephen Hopkins to the General Assembly, Providence, Oct. 28, 1756, *The Correspondence of the Colonial Governors of Rhode Island, 1723-1775*, ed. Gertrude Selwyn Kimball (Boston, 1902-03), II, 234-236; and Petition to General Assembly, Providence, Feb. 1763, Rhode Island Archives, II, 58, State Archives, State House, Providence, R. I. Over a hundred men signed this petition, including the leading merchants and landowners of Providence, but the names of small businessmen, tradesmen, and farmers also appeared on the list. See also Brown Papers, P-P6, and the *Providence Gazette and Country Journal*, Apr. 2, 1763.

[15] *Rhode Island Records*, VI, 358-362. While Hopkins, the Browns, and other northerners desired currency reform, they did not oppose paper money issues on principle. And in response to the Currency Act of 1764, which prohibited the colonies from making paper money legal tender, proponents of currency reform indicated that paper money was essential to the economic prosperity of the colony. *Rhode Island Records*, VI, 407-410. E. James Ferguson, "Currency Finance: An Interpretation of Colonial Monetary Practices," *William and Mary Quarterly*, 3d Ser., X (1953), 155.

While some southerners supported currency reform, the Browns would never have been able to pass the bill without the support of representatives from the nearby agricultural towns, a fact which points up the composite nature of the northern faction. Subsequent legislation provided Rhode Island with a stable currency until the Revolution.

To see in Rhode Island political controversy a class struggle—agrarian radicals fighting conservative merchants—is to see something that did not exist. That came only in the post-Revolutionary years and had its roots in the changes brought about by the war and the success of the Revolution. This is not to say that before 1776 there were no class distinctions or that members of the lower classes did not resent advantages enjoyed by the upper classes; but there is little evidence that such distinctions or sentiments resulted in social tensions serious enough to label revolutionary.

Briefly stated, then, the chief cause for the intense political struggle in Rhode Island before the Revolution was the desire of men in the north and the south to gain control of the government to promote private and public interests. When the southern and northern economies expanded, and merchants, tradesmen, and capitalistic farmers emerged whose needs could no longer be satisfied by the town meeting, they began to compete with one another for control of the colonial government. The General Assembly could bestow many profitable favors on deserving citizens; it could issue flags of truce to merchants authorizing them to exchange French prisoners and provisions in the West Indies;[16] it could determine which merchants could outfit privateers;[17] it could grant monopolies to enterprising businessmen;[18] it could vote funds to build or repair light-

[16] Governor Hopkins to William Pitt, Rhode Island, Dec. 20, 1760, *Correspondence of William Pitt when Secretary of State with Colonial Governors and Military and Naval Commissioners in America*, ed. Gertrude Selwyn Kimball (London, 1906), II, 373-378; *Rhode Island Records*, V, 241-242, VI, 173-174, 220, 252.

[17] As governor during the French and Indian War, Stephen Hopkins frequently issued letters of marque to Providence ship captains, among them members of his own family. Rhode Island Historical Society Manuscripts, XII, 17.

[18] In 1765 when the Browns of Providence went into the iron manufacturing business, they had to petition the assembly to get legislation permitting them to build a dam for the furnace on the Pawtuxet River. The petition was considered no less than twelve times by the lower and upper houses within a period of less than two months. Governor Ward and the assistants resorted to numerous devices to block the granting of the petition, and, although they were unsuccessful, they were able to place several restrictions on the construction and use of the dam. The furnace owners had to return to the assembly to get them removed, but they waited until Ward was no longer governor. Journal of the House of Deputies, 1765-66, Sept. sess., 1765, R. I. Archives.

29

houses, bridges, schools, and to make other local public improvements;[19] it could alter the apportionment of taxes to the benefit of towns in particular sections.[20] These and other powers only the General Assembly had. The section that controlled the government could use the assembly as an instrument to promote its economic and cultural growth.

A good illustration of this interpretation of domestic politics in Rhode Island occurs in the struggle that took place in 1769 and 1770 over the permanent location of the College of Rhode Island. After considerable discussion, the choice of sites for the college narrowed to Providence and Newport. The contestants considered the controversy one more episode, and perhaps the last, in the long drawn-out competition for economic and political leadership between the north and the south. In a letter to the town councils of Scituate and Glocester, Stephen Hopkins and Moses Brown of Providence wrote:

When we consider that the building the College here will be a means of bringing great quantities of money into the place, and thereby of greatly increasing the markets for all kinds of the countries produce; and, consequently, of increasing the value of all estates to which this town is a market; and also that it will much promote the weight and influence of this northern part of the Colony in the scale of government in all times to come, we think every man that hath an estate in this County who duly weighs these advantages, with many others that will naturally occur to his mind, must, for the bettering of his own private interest, as well as for the public good, become a contributor to the College here, rather than it should be removed from hence. . . .

[19] For example, in 1764, Moses Brown, one of the deputies from Providence, tried unsuccessfully to get the assembly to appropriate money to restore the washed out Weybosset Bridge in Providence and to repair the lighthouse on Beavertail Island in Narragansett Bay. Later he was more successful. Brown Papers, P-U5, I. Towns also had to get assembly approval for lotteries, one of the common methods for raising money for local improvements, and their representatives were expected to see that such legislation passed the assembly. *Rhode Island Acts and Resolves,* Sept. sess., 1761, pp. 39-40.

[20] In 1761 Hopkins and his party passed legislation shifting the burden of taxation from commercial interests in the northern towns to agricultural property owners in Narragansett country, a Ward-party stronghold. When Ward gained control of the government in 1765, the assembly lightened the tax burden for some of the southern agricultural towns and increased it for Providence, Scituate, and Cumberland, solid Hopkins-party towns. In 1767, when Hopkins decisively defeated Ward, the assembly not only rescinded the Ward-party legislation but passed a bill acquitting the three northern towns of court judgments for nonpayment of taxes. *Ibid.,* 1765-69, May and June sess., 1767.

We are more zealous in this matter as we have certain intelligence that the people in Newport, who are become sinsible of the importance of this matter, are very deligently using every method in their power to carry the prize from us, and as the few remaining days of this month is the whole time in which we can work to any purpose, we hope none will slumber or sleep. We think ourselves in this matter wholly engaged for the public good; and therefore hope to be borne with when we beg of you and all our neighbors, to seriously consult their own interest and pursue it with unremitted zeal.[21]

The governing body of the College of Rhode Island eventually voted to make Providence the permanent home of the institution. In the 1770 election, Samuel Ward, his brother Henry, who was the colony secretary, and a few other southern politicians made a determined effort to capture control of the government in order to get a charter for a college in Newport. They failed and their bill to charter a second college was defeated by deputies committed to northern leadership.[22]

To say that the central theme of the Ward-Hopkins controversy was the political struggle between similar interests in two different sections does not necessarily assume a uniformity of motives on the part of the participants. Undoubtedly some men on both sides were propelled above all else by the financial rewards public office afforded, by personal animosities, and by desire for social prestige, while others devoted their time and money to politics because of a sense of public responsibility or simply because they enjoyed the game of politics. But what bound the men of each party together was their recognition that the promotion of their own section, and thus their own interests, could best be done through control of the government.[23] Social and economic classes could co-operate for this purpose in the two sections. In fact, co-operation, not dissension, between classes is the distinctive characteristic of pre-Revolutionary political life in Rhode Island.

If we turn now to consider the claim that Rhode Island split into radical and conservative camps over British attempts to extend Parliamen-

---

[21] Stephen Hopkins and Nicholas Brown and Company [Moses Brown] to Town Councils of Scituate and Glocester, Providence, Dec. 8, 1769, Rhode Island College Miscellaneous Papers, 1763-82, I, 71, John Hay Library, Providence, R. I.

[22] *The Literary Diary of Ezra Stiles, D. D., LL.D., President of Yale College,* ed. Franklin Bowditch Dexter (New York, 1901), I, 46, 108, 109.

[23] A detailed discussion of these influences is contained in my unpublished Ph.D. dissertation, "Moses Brown, A Man of Public Responsibility," chap. III.

tary authority to America, we find that the facts do not bear out this claim. Rhode Island was one of the first colonies to react to the Sugar Act of 1764 and to the Stamp Act of the following year.[24] In the General Assembly, members of the two factions united to petition the Lords Commissioners for Trade and Plantations for their repeal. This early response set the tone for resistance to subsequent Parliamentary legislation and ministerial attempts to enforce customs regulations.[25]

The political leaders of both factions opposed British policy with equal vigor. Stephen Hopkins made a strong defense of American rights in *The Rights of the Colonies Examined,* and the General Assembly sent this pamphlet to the colony's agent in England for use in the move for repeal of the Stamp Act.[26] Hopkins's subsequent service for the cause of American independence is too well known to necessitate further comment. His political opponent, Samuel Ward, was no less a patriot. In fact, Ward held the governorship during the Stamp Act crisis when the colony successfully prevented the use of stamps. He made every effort to frustrate attempts of the king's officers to enforce the Acts of Trade and was an outspoken critic of British trade regulations. When the First Continental Congress met in Philadelphia in September 1774, Ward and Hopkins attended as delegates from Rhode Island.[27]

Stout resistance by these key figures to Parliament's attempts to extend its authority to the American colonies was emulated by the second rank

[24] "Remonstrance of the Colony of Rhode Island to the Lords Commissioners of Trade and Plantations," South Kingston, Jan. 24, 1764, and Resolves against the Stamp Act, Sept. 1765, in *Rhode Island Records,* VI, 378-383, 451-452. Rhode Island's response to the Sugar Act and the Stamp Act is described in detail in Edmund S. and Helen M. Morgan, *The Stamp Act Crisis: Prologue to Revolution* (Chapel Hill, 1953), pp. 27-28, 36, 98-99. In connection with Rhode Island's reaction to the Sugar Act, the Morgans note that "In Rhode Island where the whole government was popularly elected, no conservative politicians hampered the preparation of a spirited protest." This statement (p. 36) describes the nature of Rhode Island resistance for the entire period.

[25] *Rhode Island Records,* V, 559-561, 561-566, 563. Arthur M. Schlesinger, *The Colonial Merchants and the American Revolution, 1763-1776,* Library Edition (New York, 1939), p. 112.

[26] *Rhode Island Records,* VI, 412. For Hopkins's pamphlet, see *ibid.,* 416-427.

[27] *Correspondence of Governor Samuel Ward,* pp. 3-36; *Rhode Island Records,* VI, 472-513, passim. As late as December 12, 1774, Governor Joseph Wanton was firm in his opposition to the British efforts to suppress revolt. *American Archives,* ed. Peter Force, 4th ser. (Washington, 1837-46), I, 1039. Rhode Island resolutions against Parliamentary taxation and the Boston Port Act, Newport, June 15, 1774, *ibid.,* 416-417.

of leaders of both factions and strongly supported by the freemen. The only person of importance in the north who attempted to abide by the Stamp Act was John Foster, a justice of the peace and clerk of the Inferior Court of Common Pleas for Providence County, who refused to open his court and transact business without stamps.[28] A crowd of angry people gathered before his house and threatened to ride him out of town on a rail unless he changed his mind. This was enough to convince Foster of his error. In 1769 after the Townshend Acts were passed and again in 1772, royal officials trying to perform their duties were roughly treated by the northerners; and in 1773, when British naval vessels were patrolling Narragansett Bay in an effort to stop contraband trade, John Brown, the leading merchant in Providence, and a number of citizens, burned the revenue vessel, the *Gaspee*, to the water's edge. Royal investigators could get no assistance from Rhode Islanders in their search for the culprits. In the south, in Newport, throughout the period 1765-75, the people frequently demonstrated their hostile attitude toward British policy and supporters of the Crown.[29]

33

One of the striking things about anti-British leadership in Rhode Island is its continuity. The same people who successfully organized the opposition to the Stamp Act and the Townshend Acts led the resistance to the Tea Act and the Intolerable Acts and declared Rhode Island's independence. For the most part these leaders were not radical agrarians but members of the commercial and professional classes of both Providence and Newport. This does not mean that the farmers were pro-British. There was stronger loyalist sentiment among the merchants in Newport than among the farmers in the agricultural communities.[30] What it does mean is that the farmers were content to follow the lead of men like Hopkins

[28] Affidavit, Dec. 12, 1765, Moses Brown Papers, misc. MSS, B-815, Box 1, R. I. Hist. Soc.

[29] Oliver M. Dickerson, *The Navigation Acts and the American Revolution* (Philadelphia, 1951), p. 258; Morgan and Morgan, *The Stamp Act Crisis*, pp. 144-151; Bridenbaugh, *Cities in Revolt*, pp. 309-311. *Rhode Island Records*, VI, 593-596; Schlesinger, *Colonial Merchants*, pp. 485-486; *American Archives*, 4th ser., I, 1098-1099. For response of Newport to Boston Port Act, see Resolves of Newport town meeting, May 20, 1774, *ibid.*, 343-344. That there were a few royalists in Newport and Providence during this period is suggested by an "Extract of a Letter to a Gentleman in New-York, dated Newport, Rhode Island, Dec. 14, 1774," and in a Resolution of the Providence town meeting, Aug. 31, 1774, *ibid.*, 1041, 747.

[30] Carl Bridenbaugh, *Peter Harrison, First American Architect* (Chapel Hill, 1949), p. 125. Most Quakers, of course, opposed the Revolution or tried to remain neutral, and some of the Episcopalians joined the British.

and Ward. The merchants, shipowners, and lawyers who were the leaders in domestic politics were also the leaders in the Revolutionary movement.

Articulate supporters of Parliamentary supremacy in Rhode Island during the 1760's were almost without exception royal government employees.[31] They constituted an infinitesimal percentage of the population and exerted no influence within the colonial government and very little outside it. And when they did speak out, they made every effort to hide their identity and to cloak their real intentions. If discovered, they were either forced into silence or hounded out of the colony. During the five years before the outbreak of violence, supporters of British policy were even less noticeable than during the earlier period. Even Joseph Wanton, Rhode Island's Episcopalian governor who eventually went over to the British, was a strong defender of American liberties throughout these years. When Rhode Island declared its independence, the few citizens who could not accept the decision either withdrew from active participation in public affairs or left the colony.

The colony's vigorous, continuous opposition to British policy proves that Rhode Islanders were trying to preserve a system with which they were well satisfied, rather than to change it. The struggle for home rule in Rhode Island was not paralleled by any fight between agrarian and commercial classes to determine who should rule at home. The transition from colony to commonwealth was made with practically no changes in the existing institutions, leadership, or social structure. And there were few demands for any changes. The struggle for democratic rights came in the postwar decade and its origins must be sought in the changes produced by the war and independence and not in the Ward-Hopkins controversy.

[31] Governor Joseph Wanton refused to sanction General Assembly military preparations and was removed from office. *Rhode Island Records*, VII, 392-393. Deputy Governor Darius Sessions and Assistants William Potter and Thomas Wicks also expressed doubts about military resistance to royal authority, but they soon recovered and became good patriots. *Ibid.*, 311, 398-399, 347-349. There was no great turnover in the personnel sitting in the assembly during 1775-76. Those who left did so to serve in the army or to assume some other government post; their successors were in some instances former members who had retired because of age or to devote full time to business; in other cases they were local leaders who would probably have moved up to the assembly eventually.

Rights Imply Equality:
The Case Against Admiralty Jurisdiction
in America, 1764-1776

David S. Lovejoy*

EQUALITY has become a fundamental principle of American democracy. Although we are frequently reminded that Americans fail to practice altogether what they preach, still, the concept of equality is as much a part of the democratic ideal as manhood suffrage and public education. But the Spirit of '76, although not aristocratic, was not egalitarian either. Despite Thomas Jefferson's eloquent declaration that all men are created equal, most Americans of the Revolutionary generation showed little interest in the broad aspects of human equality which since that time have helped to direct the course of American history.

One very good reason why eighteenth-century Americans did not worry much about equality among themselves was that in America there were not the glaring inequalities between individuals and between groups which obtained in Europe. Colonial society was less stratified than that across the Atlantic. Since land was much easier to acquire here than there, economic opportunity was greater, and wider distribution of land meant wider distribution of suffrage. In this sense the American colonies were generally more democratic by nature both politically and socially than either England or France or any European nation.

What inequality did exist among people in the colonies, whether it was political or social, economic or religious, was secondary to another kind of inequality which took the colonists' attention in the 1760's and which became a compelling force driving them toward revolution in the years following. This was inequality not among Americans but between Americans and Englishmen as subjects of the same empire, and when Americans became aware of it, they were grateful to the English for pointing it out to them. At the close of the French and Indian War, when

* Mr. Lovejoy is visiting lecturer in history, Northwestern Universcity.

Englishmen discovered that their national debt was about as large in pounds sterling as the new empire was in acres of American wilderness, they initiated a new colonial policy which would require Americans to contribute through taxation to the financial responsibilities of this empire. Englishmen were surprised to learn that several generations of salutary neglect of the colonists were accompanied by a striking process of economic and political maturity, changing obedient children into precocious and fractious adolescents. Ambitious Americans regarded Parliamentary taxation as conduct becoming a stepmother's severity rather than parental kindness, and they stubbornly refused to accept it. In justification they argued a theory of empire which denied Parliament's right to tax them without their consent, and, more important, they maintained that Americans were as good as Englishmen and had claim to the same kind of treatment from government.

No one saw more clearly than John Adams the distinction Parliament made between American and British subjects. A few years before his death he wrote to a friend: "However tedious and painful it may be for you to read, or me to transcribe any part of these dull [Parliamentary] statutes, we must endure the task, or we shall never understand the American Revolution."[1] At the age of eighty-three, forty-two years after independence, Adams still bristled and fumed when he thought of the insulting, the degrading attitude of superiority which Parliamentary statutes expressed. What he meant was that the inferior status forced upon the American colonists was an important cause—maybe to Adams, an ambitious man, the most important cause—of the Revolution which, in his mind, was a struggle for equality between American and Englishman.

I

Although Parliamentary taxation was the most celebrated threat to colonial rights in the early years of the Revolutionary movement, it was not the only threat, despite the fact that it has received more attention than any other issue by historians since that time. What historians have failed to emphasize is that the means of enforcing the new taxes were as much an innovation in colonial policy and as much a threat to equality of treatment in the empire as the taxes themselves, and, according to the

[1] John Adams to William Tudor, Quincy, Aug. 6, 1818, *The Works of John Adams*, ed. Charles Francis Adams (Boston, 1850-56), X, 339.

colonists, just as unconstitutional. For Parliament directed that the new tax laws could be enforced in either the regular colony courts where common-law procedures operated or in the courts of admiralty which proceeded without juries according to the civil law.

Admiralty court justice was not new to Americans in 1764, or to the English for that matter. Since medieval times these courts in England had functioned according to the law of nations, and their jurisdiction was limited to disputes occurring on the high seas and traditionally below the first bridge over navigable rivers. The common-law courts and common lawyers constantly kept admiralty jurisdiction in check, and Sir Edward Coke owed some of his reputation as a defender of the common law to frequent trimming of admiralty jurisdiction when it exceeded the limits allowed. Certainly admiralty courts were necessary, and if not popular, they were tolerated since they disposed of disputes, particularly prize cases, which could be settled in no other way. However, Englishmen were jealous of the common law and successfully protected it from unwarranted encroachment by civil courts.[2]

37

During most of the seventeenth century the colonial governments allowed governors and councils and common-law courts to hear and determine disputes which in England would have been tried before admiralty judges. When it became ' apparent that Americans were not disposed to enforce the Navigation Acts, Parliament took strong measures. In shoring up the whole imperial structure in 1696, the legislature directed that certain laws of trade could be enforced either in the common-law courts at Westminster or in Ireland or in American courts of admiralty within the colonies where the offenses occurred. Since admiralty courts did not actually exist in the colonies, they were established the next year and judges were appointed. The act of 1696, however, was ambiguously phrased, and it left some doubt whether Parliament meant all forfeitures and penalties under the acts of trade, or just those mentioned in the new act itself, were recoverable in admiralty courts in America. (Probably Parliament intended the new courts to enforce all the acts of trade since 1660; otherwise there would have been little sense in extending the jurisdiction to America. In any event, Crown officials came later to regard

[2] Helen J. Crump, *Colonial Admiralty Jurisdiction in the Seventeenth Century* (London, 1931), chap. I; Winfred T. Root, *The Relations of Pennsylvania with the British Government, 1696-1765* (New York, 1912), pp. 95-97.

these courts as suitable for enforcement of all Parliamentary acts which regulated trade in the colonies.)

Regardless of which interpretation was correct, the act of 1696 gave a larger jurisdiction to admiralty courts in America than had ever been given to the same courts in England, thus distinguishing between Americans and Englishmen in matters of justice. His Majesty's courts at Westminster, that is, common-law courts with juries, enforced the acts of trade in England, while admiralty courts, which proceeded under the civil law without juries, could enforce some, if not all, of the same acts in America.[3]

A few people recognized the alarming extension of admiralty jurisdiction in the colonies and protested against it. Among these was William Penn who understood the necessity of trade and commerce for nurturing an infant colony. In 1701 he condemned the comprehensive powers of the new court in Pennsylvania which, he said, "swallowed up a great part of the Government here. . . ." Penn understood, too, that his colonists had not come to America to be deprived of their rights by an arbitrary court: the determining of these causes, he wrote, "without a jury, gives our people the greatest discontent, looking upon themselves as less free here than at home, instead of greater privileges, which were promised."[4]

Despite the ominous powers given to the new courts by the act of 1696, American merchants and traders were not as badly off as they imagined. It was not long before the common-law courts found ways to circumvent the admiralty courts or at least to limit their effectiveness. The act itself

[3] 7 & 8 Gul. III, c. 22, sect. VII, *The Statutes at Large* . . . , ed. Danby Pickering (Cambridge, Eng., 1762-1866), IX, 432; Crump, *Colonial Admiralty Jurisdiction*, pp. 1, 128-132, 148-149, 163-164, and *passim;* Lawrence A. Harper, *The English Navigation Laws* (New York, 1939), chap. XV; Charles M. Andrews, *The Colonial Period of American History* (New Haven, 1934-38), IV, 225-229; see also Andrews's Introduction to *Records of the Vice-Admiralty Court of Rhode Island, 1716-1752,* ed. Dorothy S. Towle (Washington, D. C., 1936), pp. 5-13; Edward Channing, *History of the United States* (New York, 1905-25), II, 275-277; Root, *The Relations of Pennsylvania*, pp. 95-97.

Crump implies that all acts of trade could come under admiralty jurisdiction in America, while Andrews, although recognizing the momentous change brought about by the act of 1696, seems to think the jurisdiction of the courts was somewhat limited. For confusing judicial opinions on this matter, see *Calendar of State Papers, Colonial Series, America and West Indies, Jan.-Dec. 1, 1702,* ed. Cecil Headlam (London, 1912), 389, 451, 554-555.

[4] William Penn to Robert Harley [c. 1701], *The Manuscripts of His Grace the Duke of Portland,* IV, Historical Manuscripts Commission, Fifteenth Report, Appendix, Part IV (London, 1897), 31.

was not as clearly worded as it might have been—"weakly penned," as William Penn put it—[5]and was open to several less rigorous interpretations which the colonists were quick to exploit. The struggle in England between common law and admiralty law, which had helped to push Sir Edward Coke into the limelight in the seventeenth century, was transferred to the colonies in the eighteenth with some of the same results. Courts of common law grew bold, often usurping jurisdiction from admiralty courts by issuing writs of prohibition against their decrees and even discharging prisoners detained by them.[6] The people of Massachusetts generally assumed that their Superior Court exercised locally all the powers of the Court of King's Bench in England and on this basis justified the court's halting admiralty proceedings when the latter got out of line.[7] Jeremiah Dummer defended this conduct as early as 1721 in his *Defence of the New-England Charters* . . . , in which he equated the Massachusetts court not only with the King's Bench, but also with the Courts of Common Pleas and Exchequer in England. If these English courts had a right to restrain admiralty jurisdiction, so then did the court in Boston; for, he wrote, if "some bounds are not set to the Jurisdiction of the Admiralty, beyond which it shall not pass, it may in Time, like the Element to which it ought to be confin'd, grow outrageous and overflow the Banks of all the other Courts of Justice." The fact that admiralty judges received only fees and no salaries worried Dummer since they were "strongly tempted to receive all Business that comes before them, however improper for their Cognizance."[8]

Rhode Islanders made life miserable for an admiralty judge appointed there: in 1743, just after his arrival, the legislature enacted a law regulating his fees and reducing them so low, it was said, "that the Judge has not a competent Allowance to support the Dignity of the Office." When the ministry in London accused the colony of interfering with the execution

39

---

[5] *Ibid.*

[6] Root, *The Relations of Pennsylvania,* pp. 95-97; Edward Channing, *History,* II, 277-279; Harper, *The English Navigation Laws,* p. 188.

[7] Thomas Hutchinson, *The History of the Colony and Province of Massachusetts-Bay,* ed. Lawrence Shaw Mayo (Cambridge, Mass., 1936), III, 65, 116.

[8] (London, 1721), pp. 50-52, 58, 60. Dummer also argued that an Englishman ought not to be deprived of his property by civil law since it is "what he has not consented to himself, or his Representative for him." Therefore, admiralty court justice should cover only transactions which occur on the high seas and not triable at common law (p. 51).

of the court's duties, Governor William Greene reassured the Duke of Newcastle that the court enjoyed complete independence in Rhode Island. Surprisingly, in the same letter to His Grace, he admitted that the former deputy judge was then in jail for not paying his debts.[9]

Just about the time Dummer published his *Defence,* Parliament again extended the jurisdiction of the admiralty courts in America, this time, not just beyond the shore line, to which he believed it ought to be confined, but beyond even the banks of the rivers which penetrated the interior. The colonists, it seems, were as careless at times about Parliament's laws reserving particular pine trees for the use of His Majesty as they were about the Navigation Acts. As a consequence, in 1721 Parliament placed enforcement of the white-pine laws in the courts of admiralty where suspected colonists could be tried by a single judge according to the civil law.[10] The extension of admiralty court jurisdiction to include cutting the King's masts does not seem to have caused much complaint. As with the enforcement of the laws of trade, probably the common-law courts frequently interfered and thwarted the efforts of Crown officers and admiralty judges.[11]

Had the Molasses Act of 1733 been enforced, doubtless the American colonists would have added to their complaints about its prohibitive duties the objection that offenses against the act in America were triable in either their own courts of record (common-law courts) or the courts of admiralty. Moreover, the act made clear to those colonists who read it closely just how discriminatory Parliament could be. Besides levying duties on imported goods from the foreign islands, the act prohibited the importation of these same goods into Ireland except when they had been "loaden and shipped in *Great Britain"* in proper vessels. But Parliament specifically directed that offenses committed against this section of the act were triable *only* in courts of record at Westminster or Dublin.[12]

[9] See letters in *Correspondence of the Colonial Governors of Rhode Island, 1723-1775,* ed. Gertrude S. Kimball (Cambridge, Mass., 1903), II, 242-245, 251.

[10] 8 Geo. I, c. 12, sect. V, Pickering, *The Statutes at Large,* XIV, 387.

[11] This was not always the case. In 1770 William Dean and his sons, who lived in the vicinity of what is now Brattleboro, Vermont, went to jail rather than pay the £800 sterling the admiralty court at New York demanded for cutting sixteen trees on land near their home. *Reports of Cases in the Vice Admiralty of the Province of New York and in the Court of Admiralty of the State of New York, 1715-1788,* ed. Charles M. Hough (New Haven, 1925), pp. 227-233.

[12] 6 Geo. II, c. 13, Pickering, *The Statutes at Large,* XVI, 375-376.

Since customs officials in America generally avoided enforcement of the Molasses Act[13] and common-law courts were already adept at preventing cases from coming to the admiralty courts, the constitutional issue did not arise.

As long as admiralty courts confined themselves to the condemnation of prizes and problems of salvage, wrecks, and seamen's wages, Americans willingly admitted their jurisdiction. But courts of admiralty were charged with enforcing the acts of trade in America, and when they did so, they were thoroughly disliked.[14] Despite the fact that the seriousness of the colonists' complaints varied in direct proportion to the degree the courts interfered with illegal trade, a constitutional issue was involved. When courts of admiralty exercised all the powers in America that the act of 1696 intended, then Americans were distinguished from their cousins in England and were subject to a different judicial system—one that deprived them, they said, of trial by jury. But Americans escaped any serious difficulty over admiralty jurisdiction until after the French and Indian War when Parliament levied taxes on the colonists and used admiralty courts to see that they were paid.

41

II

The Sugar and Stamp Acts of 1764 and 1765 inaugurated a major change in British colonial policy. Never before had Parliament directly taxed the American colonists, and their violent reaction to these taxes set in motion a resistance movement which in twelve years culminated in independence. Besides levying a threepence tax on each gallon of molasses imported into the colonies from the foreign West Indies and imposing duties on several other imports, the Sugar Act explicitly directed that forfeitures and penalties imposed by the act and by any of the earlier laws of trade were recoverable at the election of the informer or prosecutor in a court of record or a colonial admiralty court. Any doubt entertained heretofore, owing to the "obscurity, if not inconsistency,"[15] of the 1696 act, that admiralty courts could try violations of the Navigation Acts was now laid to rest. What is more, in order to put admiralty justice clear of the

---

[13] For exceptions, see Andrews, *Colonial Period, IV*, 242-244; also Andrews's Introduction to Towle, *Records of the Vice-Admiralty Court of Rhode Island*, pp. 53-54.

[14] Crump, *Colonial Admiralty Jurisdiction*, pp. 128, 164.

[15] Penn to Harley, *The Manuscripts of the Duke of Portland*, IV, 31.

pressure of colonial common-law courts, the Sugar Act authorized, and an Order in Council established, a vice-admiralty court for all America to be located at Halifax, Nova Scotia, with both appellate and original jurisdiction.[16]

A few months after the Sugar Act became effective, Parliament passed the American Stamp Act which would tax the colonists' use of paper and exact sterling money from most legal and business transactions. Penalties and forfeitures under the Stamp Act were also recoverable in courts of record *or* courts of admiralty in America.[17] At the election of informers or prosecutors the whole British colonial system—Navigation Acts, Sugar Act, and Stamp Act—now came under admiralty court jurisdiction where judges, linked to the prerogative, decided issues according to civil law without benefit of juries.

The documents and pamphlets drafted during the Stamp Act crisis clearly demonstrate that the extension of admiralty court jurisdiction was a major grievance. The Stamp Act Congress listed it prominently in the four documents the members produced.[18] Most colonial legislatures coupled it with Parliamentary taxation in their resolves and complained about the subversion of the rights of Americans.[19] Daniel Dulany in his famous pamphlet declared that the Stamp Act, its power to tax and its substitution of an "arbitrary Civil Law Court, in the Place of . . . the Common-Law-Trial by Jury . . ." left Americans without "even the Shadow of a Privilege."[20] The sacred right of trial by jury, said John Dickinson, was violated "by the erection of arbitrary and unconstitutional jurisdictions."[21] *The Constitutional Courant,* probably the most inflammatory piece of political literature at the time, likened admiralty courts to the "high commission and star chamber courts" and warned Americans that, since the Stamp Act gave these courts "jurisdiction over matters that

[16] 4 Geo. III, c. 15, sects. LX, LXI, Pickering, *The Statutes at Large,* XXVI, 49; *Acts of the Privy Council of England, Colonial Series,* ed. James Munro (London, 1908-12), IV, 663-664.

[17] 5 Geo. III, c. 12, sects. LVII, LVIII, Pickering, *The Statutes at Large,* XXVI, 202, 203.

[18] *Proceedings of the Congress at New-York* (Annapolis, 1766).

[19] *Prologue to Revolution: Sources . . . on the Stamp Act Crisis,* ed. Edmund S. Morgan (Chapel Hill, 1959), pp. 46-62, *passim.*

[20] *Considerations on the Propriety of Imposing Taxes in the British Colonies* (North America, 1765), p. 25.

[21] *The Late Regulations respecting the British Colonies on the Continent of America, Considered . . .* (Philadelphia, 1765), p. 35.

have no relation to navigation or sea affairs, they may, with equal propriety, have jurisdiction in cases of life and death. This is a real representation of the slavish state we are reduced to by the Stamp Act, if we ever suffer it to take place among us."[22] Admiralty courts, said James Otis, "savour more of modern Rome and the Inquisition, than of the common law of England and the constitution of Great-Britain."[23]

In 1765 John Adams, who still lived in Braintree, and whose reputation as a lawyer and patriot was modest, to say the least, compared with that of James Otis, began a series of attacks upon admiralty justice which contributed to his growing stature as a major Revolutionary figure. Adams as much as any colonist hated the Stamp Act and all Parliamentary statutes which discriminated against Americans. But, in the instructions he drafted for Braintree's representatives, he saved his severest condemnation for the "alarming extension" of admiralty court powers, which, he claimed, was the "most grievous innovation of all," for it violated the Great Charter itself and shamelessly distinguished between Americans and English in matters of justice.[24] This was only the opening gun of Adams's attack; he later demonstrated even more forcefully the disgraceful inequalities which Parliament cavalierly established under courts of admiralty in America.

Granted the colonists objected to Parliamentary taxation for very human and self-interested reasons. Granted they objected to admiralty court trials for the same human and selfish reasons—after all, the chances of losing one's shirt would be about a hundred times greater at Halifax or before any admiralty judge than in a local court before a jury of one's peers. Granted, then, the colonists had self-interested motives; their dislike for parting with their property does not vitiate the constitutional arguments they brought to bear against the process used to take it away from them. In the colonists' eyes, the new use of admiralty justice in America compounded Parliament's original error, for these courts would enforce unconstitutional taxes by unconstitutional means.

[22] Reprinted in a paper by Albert Matthews on the snake devices, 1754-76, and the *Constitutional Courant*, 1765, in Colonial Society of Massachusetts, *Publications*, XI (Boston, 1910), 429-430.
[23] *The Rights of the British Colonies Asserted and Proved* (Boston, 1764), p. 28.
[24] Adams, *Works*, III, 466-467.

III

To understand the Tory and English defense of admiralty court jurisdiction in America is to understand in part the growing difference between American and English interpretations of the empire and the rights of colonists as British subjects. Justification for admiralty jurisdiction over American trade, said its defenders, was simply its necessity. Juries "in these causes were not to be trusted," said Governor Francis Bernard of Massachusetts. No candid man "will take upon him to declare, that at this time an *American* jury is impartial and indifferent enough, to determine equally upon frauds of trade."[25] Martin Howard, a Newport Tory, came to the same conclusion, and although he admitted that the court at Halifax was a "severity in the method of prosecution," it was a severity Americans had brought upon themselves. Smuggling was so prevalent, he argued, that the "government is justifiable in making laws against it, even like those of *Draco,* which were written in blood."[26]

In 1776 Thomas Hutchinson achieved the dubious honor of answering for Englishmen, article by article, the Declaration of Independence. When he came to the grievance that Americans in many cases were deprived of trial by jury, he demonstrated the same blindness to American argument that had afflicted the ministry for some time. Omitting completely any reference to the fact that admiralty courts in America could enforce Parliamentary taxation, he cited only admiralty court jurisdiction over breaches of the laws of trade and over trespass upon the King's woods as cases in which trial by jury was denied. In both of these, he argued, the "necessity of the case justified the departure from the general rule."[27]

A few years later, George Chalmers, a Tory historian in England, referred to the year 1697 as the era of "memorable change in colonial jurisprudence," which "superseded in some measure the trial by jury, that had been found to be inconvenient in proportion as it was favorable to popu-

[25] *Select Letters on the Trade and Government of America* (London, 1774), pp. 16-17. Governor Bernard's words were echoed in London by defenders of the Stamp Act. See anon., *The Conduct of the Late Administration Examined,* 2nd ed. (London, 1767), p. 36.

[26] *A Letter from a Gentleman at Halifax, to his Friend in Rhode-Island* (Newport, 1765), pp. 17-20.

[27] *Strictures upon the Declaration of the Congress at Philadelphia; In a Letter to a Noble Lord &c.* (London, 1776), p. 24, recently reprinted by the Old South Association, *Old South Leaflets,* no. 227, ed. Malcolm Freiberg (Boston, 1958).

lar rights." Chalmers cushioned this "memorable change," or so he believed, by informing his readers that John Locke himself had "expressly advised his sovereign 'to settle courts of admiralty under proper officers of his own appointment, in order to prevent illegal trade in those parts.'"[28] Tory argument implied very clearly that Parliament was justified in violating the rights of its subjects so that the Navigation Acts might be enforced.

Justification for admiralty court enforcement of Parliamentary taxation grew in part out of the defense of these courts for the regulation of trade. Enforcement of the Stamp Act in the admiralty courts, said its advocates, was really not a "novel measure" at all, because "a jurisdiction had been assigned to the judges of the court of admiralty, upon the laws of revenue and trade, without juries, for near a century past."[29] This argument goes to the very bottom of the chasm which divided the colonists and the Parliament in these years. Unlike Englishmen, Americans did not speak of trade and revenue in the same breath. They had always accepted regulation of their trade, and although they smuggled on occasion, they seldom doubted Parliament's right to control their commerce. But the colonists distinguished absolutely between statutes which regulated their trade and statutes which taxed their trade and themselves. Members of the Stamp Act Congress and Daniel Dulány, in 1765, and John Dickinson, a few years later, made this distinction clear, and most Americans were disposed to agree with them.[30]

Englishmen, on the other hand, thought this distinction absurd, be-

45

---

[28] Although written during and just after the Revolution, only a part of this work was published in London in 1780 and entitled *Political Annals of the Present United Colonies.* The complete work was published in two volumes in Boston in 1845 and called *An Introduction to the History of the Revolt of the American Colonies.* See I, Introduction and p. 275.

[29] Thomas Pownall, *The Administration of the Colonies, to which is added, an Appendix, No. III, containing, Considerations on the Points lately brought into Question as to the Parliament's Right of taxing the Colonies, and of the Measures necessary to be taken at this Crisis* (London, 1766), pp. 43-44 (of *Considerations*); anon., *Conduct of the Late Administration,* pp. 22-25, 34-37; anon., *Correct Copies of the Two Protests against the Bill to Repeal the American Stamp Act* (Paris, 1766), pp. 16-19.

[30] *Proceedings of the Congress at New-York,* p. 23; Dulany, *Considerations on the Propriety of Imposing Taxes,* p. 34; John Dickinson, *Letters from a Farmer in Pennsylvania, to the Inhabitants of the British Colonies* (Philadelphia, 1768), pp. 29-30.

cause to them there was little difference between regulation of trade and taxation, since both brought in revenue to the Crown. Navigation Acts since 1660 had regulated the commerce of the empire, but they had also, when enforced, produced some revenue. For Americans to argue that regulation was right and taxation was wrong made no sense to most members of Parliament and the ministry. According to their argument, Parliament had always taxed American trade; and violations of these laws were cognizable in courts of admiralty in America. Most Englishmen saw no reason, then, why admiralty courts were not competent to try cases involving further taxation of Americans under the Sugar and Stamp Acts, particularly since these courts were made necessary by the reluctance of colonial juries to convict Americans.

46

One can imagine that this argument made no impression whatsoever upon colonists who for some time had questioned admiralty jurisdiction over the trade laws. To extend the jurisdiction of these courts to enforce direct taxation of Americans was intolerable, not merely because the taxes were believed unconstitutional but because the court procedure offended their sense of justice as British subjects.

Englishmen further argued that an admiralty trial for a violation of the Stamp Act in America did not really distinguish Americans from English subjects with respect to trial by jury.[31] And if the issue were trial by jury alone, the Englishmen had the better of the argument. Americans, apparently, were unmindful that Englishmen had paid stamp taxes since 1694. In addition, forfeitures and penalties for several violations of the English acts, specifically for printing or selling pamphlets and newspapers on unstamped paper, had been cognizable since 1711 before two or more justices of the peace only, with appeal to a quarter sessions court, consisting of more justices of the peace, in the county, riding, or shire where the offenses occurred.[32] Actually neither subject enjoyed trial by jury when

[31] Anon., *Correct Copies of the Two Protests against the Bill*, p. 17; anon., *Conduct of the Late Administration*, p. 36.

[32] For the English stamp acts, see in particular 5 & 6 Gul. III, c. 21; 9 & 10 Gul. III, c. 25; 10 Anne, c. 19, sects. CXIX, CXX, CLXXII; 16 Geo. II, c. 26, sect. V; Pickering, *The Statutes at Large*, IX, 306-321, X, 153-167, XII, 377-378, 388-389, XVIII, 134-135. See also Edward Hughes, "The English Stamp Duties, 1664-1764," *English Historical Review*, LVI (1941), 244-246, 249, 252, 253; Stephen Dowell, *A History of Taxation and Taxes in England* (London, 1884), III, 323-377. Dowell says nothing about enforcement of the stamp acts.

he disobeyed a stamp act. But the English argument in defense of the American act on these grounds did not go far enough. It failed to point out that the Englishman was brought before a court in his own neighborhood or county where he could count on traditional common-law procedure, while the American might find his trial set in some other colony besides his own or even at Halifax, Nova Scotia, and presided over by a single judge trained in the civil law.

Had Parliament authorized the enforcement of the Stamp Act in the colonies by the same means that similar acts were enforced in England, the colonists might not have complained as loudly as they did, for justices of the peace were certainly more amenable to the will of the people than were admiralty judges appointed by the Crown. Doubtless members of Parliament were well aware of this when they made enforcement of the American act possible in the courts of admiralty. Experience in England had demonstrated that the stamp acts were not well obeyed there.[33] But Parliament had never dared to enlarge admiralty jurisdiction to assure obedience in England. Parliament did dare to enlarge this jurisdiction in America. This was the distinction: British subjects were under the common law in England but would be under civil law in America for violations of stamp taxes. Although the principle involved, as far as equal treatment was concerned, was not trial by jury, it was equally fundamental. Had the colonists answered the argument regarding equal loss of jury trial, they probably would have exclaimed, and not very respectfully: "If an Englishman was deprived of trial by jury for disobeying a stamp act, he ought not to be!"

The repeal of the Stamp Act in 1766 gave the act's proponents an opportunity to portray their enemies as unsympathetic to American complaints against distant courts and interested judges. Just as the Sugar Act had authorized an over-all vice-admiralty court in America, so the Stamp Act under Grenville had empowered the creation of several more of these courts, with both appellate and original jurisdiction, to be distributed among the thirteen colonies. Once Parliament had passed the act, the Treasury recommended to the Privy Council that the court at Halifax be switched to Boston and two others be established, one at Philadelphia and one at Charlestown, South Carolina—also that dignified salaries be settled on the judges to relieve them of the criticism that poundage and fees

[33] Hughes, "The English Stamp Duties," *Eng. Hist. Rev.*, LVI, 249, 252, 253.

tempted them to action.[34] But shortly after they had passed the Stamp Act, George Grenville and his friends went out of government, giving way to the Marquis of Rockingham and his people. Secretary Henry S. Conway, whose duty it would have been under Rockingham to act upon the proposals for new vice-admiralty courts, failed to do so before Parliament, led by his faction, repealed the Stamp Act, thus revoking the authorization for additional courts. The question of constitutionality, as we have seen, the Stamp Act defenders brushed off with the argument that admiralty courts had always enforced acts of trade and revenue in America and that stamp duties even in England were not enforced by jury trials. Now, they said, the blame for injustice and inconvenience, in dragging a colonist to a court far distant from his home where he was unknown and where the judge was paid in fees, must be laid at the feet of the administration which repealed the Stamp Act.[35]

This was cold comfort for the American colonists. The only complaint against admiralty jurisdiction which seemed to get a hearing in England was that the vice-admiralty court at Halifax was grievous because it was too far removed from the centers of trade. And, as it turned out, relief from this particular grievance was frustrated by the repeal of the very act they protested—an act which taxed Americans without their consent and authorized enforcement of the tax in courts of civil law.

Parliament repealed the Stamp Act, not because it was unconstitutional, as the colonists claimed, but for the sake of expediency, since it was economically unwise and, probably more important, since the colonists generally refused to obey it. Although the courts of admiralty never got the chance to enforce the Stamp Act, the possibility had unsettled a good many people. Moreover, the constitutional issue, according to the colonists, remained unresolved; if Parliament could levy one tax and place its enforcement within the jurisdiction of the admiralty courts, it could levy another and enforce it in the same way. Furthermore, the Sugar Act remained on the statute books—although the tax on molasses was reduced

---

[34] 5 Geo. III, c. 12, sect. LVIII, Pickering, *The Statutes at Large*, XXVI, 203; Munro, *Acts of the Privy Council, Colonial Series*, IV, 664; anon., *Correct Copies of the Two Protests against the Bill*, pp. 17-18; anon., *Conduct of the Late Administration*, pp. 36-37.

[35] Anon., *Correct Copies of the Two Protests against the Bill*, pp. 16-19; anon., *Conduct of the Late Administration*, pp. 22-25, 37.

to one penny a gallon—[36] and the court at Halifax was still open for business.

The Stamp Act crisis forced Americans to examine more closely their status within the empire. Probably very few agreed with Benjamin Gale of Connecticut that the Stamp Act had "laid the foundation for Americas being an Independant State."[37] Nevertheless, the people, said John Adams, "even to the lowest ranks, have become more attentive to their liberties, more inquisitive about them, and more determined to defend them, than they were ever before known or had occasion to be."[38]

In defending these liberties, several Americans concluded that British subjects were equal in other matters besides the rights to consent to taxes and to demand the protection of the common law. The Boston town meeting declared that "Britons have been as free on one side of the Atlantic as on the other"; when a people become colonists they are still naturally a part of the state and "intitled to all the essential rights of the mother country."[39] Rhode Islanders petitioned the King and reminded him of their "equal freedom" with their fellow subjects in Great Britain.[40] Their governor, Stephen Hopkins, besides declaring that colonists anywhere throughout history had always enjoyed the same rights as subjects who remained at home, boldly argued that the separate American colonies and England constituted a commonwealth of nations, each with its own government—the colonies were subject to the superintendence of Parliament only for such general matters as the regulation of trade.[41] A pamphleteer in North Carolina admitted that "the more closely united the Mother Country and the Colonies are, the happier it will be for both"; but, he cautioned, "such an union will never take effect, but upon a foundation of equality."[42] Richard Bland of Virginia complained bitterly of Parliamentary acts which put heavier restrictions on American than on

49

---

[36] 6 Geo. III, c. 52, Pickering, *The Statutes at Large*, XXVII, 275-276.

[37] *Extracts from the Itineraries . . . of Ezra Stiles*, ed. Franklin B. Dexter (New Haven, 1916), p. 494.

[38] Adams, *Works*, II, 154.

[39] "Substance of a Memorial presented the House," May 1764, bound in Otis, *Rights of the British Colonies*, p. 70, John Carter Brown Library, Brown University.

[40] *Records of the Colony of Rhode Island*, ed. John R. Bartlett (Providence, 1856-65), VI, 415.

[41] *The Rights of Colonies Examined* (Providence, 1764), reprinted *ibid.*, VI, 424-425.

[42] Maurice Moore, *The Justice and Policy of Taxing the American Colonies, in Great-Britain, Considered* (Wilmington, N. C., 1765), p. 15.

English commerce. Such acts, he declared, "constituted an unnatural Difference between Men under the same Allegiance, born equally free, and entitled to the same civil Rights." I am speaking of the "*Rights* of a People," and "*Rights* imply *Equality* in the Instances to which they belong . . . ." Colonists, he concluded, "were not sent out to be the Slaves but to be the Equals of those that remain behind."[43]

The crisis over taxation provoked among a number of Americans the doctrine that British subjects, regardless of where they lived, ought to be treated as equals. Americans, it seems, were content to be colonials as long as their status as colonists was in no way inferior to that of subjects within the realm—an interpretation of the British Empire which was a slap in the face to most eighteenth-century Englishmen. If Americans believed this in the 1760's, and there is certainly evidence that a number of them did, then Benjamin Gale's conclusion, although extreme for the time, was not very far from the truth. An empire in which all subjects were "born equally free" and live upon a "foundation of equality" was no empire at all, as both Englishmen and Americans came to see in the next few years.

IV

Just how hollow a victory the Americans won in the repeal of the Stamp Act became clear the next year when Charles Townshend persuaded Parliament to levy more taxes on the colonists, this time on certain goods imported from England: glass, lead, paper, paint, and tea. Again, suits for recovery of forfeitures and penalties inflicted by the new taxes were cognizable in the courts of admiralty. The Townshend Acts set up elaborate machinery for rigorous enforcement not merely of import taxes but of all the laws of trade as well. An American Board of Customs was created with headquarters in Boston where it could keep an eye on colonial ships and merchants and where its members soon earned unenviable reputations as racketeers and pirates.[44]

Americans learned, too, that what Parliament had intended to do under the Stamp Act, but did not do because of the act's sudden repeal, it accomplished under the Townshend Acts. The new legislation authorized several vice-admiralty courts distributed in America, and the Privy Coun-

[43] *An Inquiry into the Rights of the British Colonies* (Williamsburg, 1766), pp. 23, 27.
[44] 7 Geo. III, c. 46; 7 Geo. III, c. 41; 8 Geo. III, c. 22; Pickering, *The Statutes at Large*, XXVII, 505-512, 447-449, XXVIII, 70-71.

cil eventually established four—one at Halifax (recommissioning the court already there) and one each at Boston, Philadelphia, and Charlestown, South Carolina—giving them original and appellate jurisdiction over the areas under their control. To meet the complaint that the judges' profits increased in proportion to the number of condemnations they made, salaries of £600 per annum were fixed upon them, and they were forbidden to accept fees or gratuities of any kind.[45] The establishment of more courts in America with better opportunities for their use by customs collectors only antagonized the colonists and provoked louder complaints. The constitutional issues were the same; and as far as convenience was concerned, a Connecticut merchant, instead of following his vessel to Halifax to see it condemned, might now have to go only as far as Boston, or a Virginian to Philadelphia, for the same privilege.

51

The choice of judges for these new courts did not make the pill any easier for the colonists to swallow. Jonathan Sewall accepted a commission for the court at Halifax without relinquishing his post as King's attorney in Massachusetts, while the Boston judgeship went to Robert Auchmuty, already well established as judge of the Bay Colony's admiralty court.[46] The two remaining positions at Philadelphia and Charlestown were given to former Stamp Masters Jared Ingersoll of Connecticut and Augustus Johnston of Rhode Island, obviously in compensation for their trying experiences during the Stamp Act riots when both were hanged in effigy, threatened in person, and forced to resign.[47]

V

Before the government had quite established the new vice-admiralty courts, the commissioners of customs and the local admiralty courts combined in the late 1760's to give American merchants and traders the roughest handling they had ever received from the customs people. By a calculated system alternating between deliberate negligence and utmost severity, the Crown officials inaugurated what Oliver M. Dickerson has

[45] 8 Geo. III, c. 22, *ibid.*, XXVIII, 70-71; Munro, *Acts of the Privy Council, Colonial Series*, V, 151-153.

[46] Josiah Quincy, Jr., *Reports of Cases Argued and Adjudged in the Superior Court of Judicature of the Province of Massachusetts Bay, 1761-1772* (Boston, 1865), pp. 300, 311-312n.

[47] Lawrence H. Gipson, *Jared Ingersoll* (New Haven, 1920), pp. 294-297, 299n; *Newport* [Rhode Island] *Mercury*, Dec. 5, 1768, May 15, 1769.

called an "era of customs racketeering" which pushed many a neutral merchant into the patriot camp.

Customs collectors could seize vessels and libel cargoes, but it took admiralty courts to condemn them and legalize the division of spoils. The two most notorious instances occurred in Charlestown and Boston in 1767 and 1768; both demonstrated the obvious intent of customs officials to destroy influential merchants, and both provoked violent attacks upon the admiralty courts, increasing the hatred already felt for them. The first involved Henry Laurens, wealthy merchant and planter and popular figure in South Carolina. Within twelve months the customs collector and his deputy at Charlestown seized on frivolous charges three of Laurens's vessels and a fourth in which he had part interest, immediately taking the cases to the colony's admiralty court for trial and condemnation. The cases were heard before Egerton Leigh who was not only judge of the admiralty court, but also attorney general of the colony, surveyor-general of His Majesty's customs, a member of the colony's council appointed by the King, and a prominent practicing lawyer. Each case, whether he won it or not, cost Laurens a good deal of money in costs of court and fees for the judge. The last case, involving the packet *Ann* caused so much adverse publicity for Judge Leigh and his court that he was obliged to dismiss the charge—not, however, before Laurens had exposed and declared to the world by newspaper articles, letters, and pamphlets the infamous conduct of both customs people and the court.[48]

Laurens disclosed what he called the "amazing Accession of Jurisdiction given to Courts of Admiralty" in America. British subjects, he declared, quoting William Blackstone, had always asserted, " 'That it is the most transcendent Privilege which any Subject can enjoy or wish for, that he cannot be affected either in his Property, his Liberty, or his Person, but by the unanimous Consent of twelve of his Neighbours and Equals.' " Like other ambitious Americans who had accumulated property and reputation and who intended to go right on accumulating both, Laurens was struck by the discriminatory treatment admiralty courts gave the colonists. How were causes relating to the revenue decided in England, or even in Ireland, he asked. Are they tried before the Admiral? Laurens

---

[48] Oliver M. Dickerson, *The Navigation Acts and the American Revolution* (Philadelphia, 1951), pp. 224-231; Laurens, *Extracts from the Proceedings of the High Court of Vice-Admiralty, in Charlestown, South-Carolina . . .* (Charlestown, 1769).

answered with a thumping NO! America was the "only Place where Cognizance of such Causes is given to the Admiralty." Why are Americans so "particularised, to be disfranchised and stript of so invaluable a Privilege as the Trial by Jury?" Are the liberties of an American less dear or of smaller consequence "than those of any other Subject of the *British* Empire?" Laurens presumed they were not.[49]

Judge Leigh fought back with a dreary discourse of over 150 pages, scrupulously avoiding any discussion of the constitutional issues at stake. He focused his attack on Laurens, who, he said, thirsted "after the phantom Popularity," and whose libelous writings demonstrated the "evil workings of a *cruel* and *malignant* heart." Besides defending himself at the other's expense, Leigh held up to ridicule Laurens's "unlettered judgment" in the law and declared him clearly out of his depth in an inquiry completely foreign to the "whole study and labour of his life."[50]

Henry Laurens answered shortly, defending his character, his conduct, and his recent publication of the admiralty court proceedings which had followed the seizure of his vessels. He reproduced a good deal of the correspondence involved in the controversy which, along with the court proceedings, was particularly damaging to the reputation of Judge Leigh. Again he drove home for all the world to see the major grievance he and other Americans suffered: "the Disadvantages to which a *British* Subject, whose Property, perhaps his ALL, and his Reputation into the Bargain, is exposed by a Trial in an *American* Court of Vice-Admiralty before a *Volunteer* sole Judge." Any doubt in Laurens's mind up to this time as to where his allegiance belonged was soundly resolved.[51]

Laurens and his friends received some satisfaction from their long drawn-out struggle: both the collector and his deputy were replaced, and the government in England gave Egerton Leigh his choice of keeping the judgeship or his post as the King's attorney. He chose to remain as attorney general probably because of the larger fees, although Laurens

53

[49] "A Few General Observations on American Custom-House Officers, and Courts of Vice-Admiralty," appended to *Extracts from the Proceedings of the High Court of Vice-Admiralty*, p. 3.

[50] *The Man Unmasked: or, the World Undeceived, in the Author of a Late Pamphlet, Intitled, "Extracts from the Proceedings . . ."* (Charles-Town, 1769), pp. 13, 22, 26, 40, and *passim.*

[51] *An Appendix to the Extracts from the Proceedings of the High Court of Vice-Admiralty . . . , containing Strictures upon, and proper Answers to . . . The Man Unmask'd* (Charlestown, 1769), p. 24 and *passim.*

doubtless would have testified that the fees as judge were nothing to sneeze at since for the past year or so Laurens himself had paid most of them out of his own pocket. Laurens received a measure of satisfaction he may not have counted on, for he managed, during the course of one of the trials, after a *"by your leave,* in the phrase and manner of a London porter,"* to pull the collector by the nose.[52]

Henry Laurens's counterpart in Massachusetts was the wealthy merchant and recognized patriot, John Hancock, who had never got along well with customs people and disliked in particular the commissioners who descended on Boston in 1768. Hancock's dislike was bountifully returned, and at the same time the customs officials in Charlestown were ganging up on Laurens, the commissioners, the collectors, and Governor Bernard himself launched an attack on Hancock unprecedented for its illegality and greed.

In June of 1768 the customs officials seized Hancock's sloop *Liberty* for loading whale oil and tar without first giving bond that the cargo's destination was within the limits of the laws of trade. Despite the fact that Hancock and all other Boston traders, with full knowledge of the customs people, had always loaded first and given bond later before clearance, the letter of the law in this instance was enforced, and Hancock stood by helpless while the King's men sailed the sloop out into the harbor and anchored it under the covering guns of a man-of-war. He was not entirely alone, however; a number of sympathizers met and rioted throughout Boston in reaction to what they believed to be outright plunder. During the summer months the admiralty court met, condemned, and confiscated both vessel and cargo and divided the proceeds according to law: one-third to the colony, one-third to Governor Bernard, and one-third to the informers, in this case, the customs officials.

Although Hancock lost both vessel and cargo, the action did not impair his fortune, his prestige, or his influence in Massachusetts. The customs officials tried again and in the fall of 1768 brought suit in the admiralty court, this time against Hancock himself, for smuggling wine in the *Liberty* several months earlier. His vessel, it seems, had arrived at Boston in May ot that year with a cargo from the islands; the tax was paid on the declared amount of wine and the cargo unloaded. But in the

---

[52] Dickerson, *The Navigation Acts,* p. 231; Leigh, *The Man Unmasked,* pp. 35-36, 100-101, 102-103; Laurens, *An Appendix to the Extracts,* p. 11.

54

fall the customs commissioners, partly on the evidence of a perjured witness, claimed that Hancock had actually unloaded in May large quantities of undeclared wine valued at £3,000 and therefore, according to the Sugar Act, was liable to a penalty of treble the costs of the cargo. Moreover, the law said, anyone who aided in unloading contraband was also guilty of the offense, and the customs people claimed that five of Hancock's friends had assisted him. The government filed suit against six Boston merchants for £9,000 each or a total of over £50,000 sterling for allegedly smuggling one hundred pipes of wine into the port. The admiralty court accepted the case against Hancock *in personam,* issued a warrant for his arrest, and demanded and got bail of £3,000, an exorbitant amount for a case of this kind. Obviously the commissioners of customs and Governor Bernard, each of whom would benefit handsomely from a conviction, had plotted and planned at some length for Hancock's demise.[53]

When Hancock appeared in court before Judge Auchmuty in November 1768, he happily brought John Adams with him as counsel. The Braintree lawyer, now moved to Boston, was by this time of wider reputation as both lawyer and patriot than when he began his siege against admiralty jurisdiction at the time of the Stamp Act. Not content merely to defend Hancock against a smuggling charge, Adams, like James Otis seven years earlier in the famous writs of assistance case, transcended the immediate issue and defined fundamental principles which were to become stock in trade in the Revolutionary movement. But while Otis attacked the writs and general warrants in 1761 as contrary to natural law and the natural rights of Americans, Adams stuck to the rights of subjects under the British constitution. In what was doubtless for Adams his best opportunity to date, he attacked with considerable eloquence the legislative authority of Parliament and in particular, admiralty court jurisdiction in America.

Adams, who has left his defense laboriously transcribed in his "Admiralty Notebook," was much more interested in the validity of the Sugar Act itself than in the specific charge of its violation (although he defied the court to prove that Hancock was aware that any undeclared wine had

[53] For information about the events leading to Hancock's trial, I have relied upon Dickerson, *The Navigation Acts,* pp. 231-250; Quincy, *Reports of Cases,* pp. 456-457, 459; George G. Wolkins, "The Seizure of John Hancock's Sloop *Liberty,*" Massachusetts Historical Society, *Proceedings,* LV (1921-22), 260-261.

been removed from the *Liberty*). Three years earlier the colonists, almost to a man, had denied Parliament's right to tax them without their consent. Since that time Parliament had done nothing to convince them they were wrong. In fact, between 1765 and 1774 Americans enlarged their attack from taxes without consent to laws without consent, and by the latter date they denied Parliament any authority in America. John Adams contributed generously to this shift in American opinion, and in Hancock's trial before the court of admiralty, he harangued at length about subjection to laws which the colonists had not approved. In words which must have maddened and at the same time amused the ministry and Parliament when they read them, he boldly remarked of the statute in question : "My Clyant Mr Hancock never consented to it."[54]

Not only, argued Adams, was the Sugar Act passed without the colonists' approval; not only were the penalties inflicted by it—that is, treble the value of the smuggled cargo—out of all proportion to the severity of the crime; but, added Adams, violations of this act, these penalties and forfeitures are "to be heard and try'd.—how? Not by a Jury, not by the Law of the Land," but by the civil law before a single judge, contrary to the will of the ancient barons who, in similar circumstances, had answered in one voice: "We will not that the laws of England be changed, which of old have been used and approved." The barons of modern times, Adams went on, were quite willing that the laws of England should be changed, at least as far as America was concerned, and, more important, "in the most tender Point, the most fundamental Principle." But the crowning insult to Americans was that this statute, on the same page that it deprived Americans of trial by jury and the law of the land, directed that the penalties and forfeitures incurred under the act in Great Britain be prosecuted, sued for, and recovered in His Majesty's courts of record which proceeded under the common law.

John Adams's next remarks demand a full hearing, because they go to the core of a fundamental cause of the American Revolution, a cause which has been only partly appreciated and not specifically demonstrated. Here, said Adams, "is the Contrast that stares us in the Face!"

The Parliament in one Clause guarding the People of the Realm, and

<hr />

[54] For information about Hancock's trial, I have relied upon John Adams, "Admiralty Notebook," in Adams Family Papers, Miscellany, Legal Papers (microfilm, reel 184, Brown University Library); Quincy, *Reports of Cases*, pp. 457, 459.

securing to them the Benefit of a Tryal by the Law of the Land, and by the next Clause, depriving all Americans of that Priviledge.—What shall we say to this Distinction? Is there not in this Clause, a Brand of Infamy, of Degradation, and Disgrace, fixed upon every American? Is he not degraded below the Rank of an Englishman: Is it not directly, a Repeal of Magna Charta, as far as America is concerned . . . [and here Adams quoted in Latin: No freeman shall be taken or imprisoned or disseised of his freehold or liberties or free customs or outlawed or exiled or any otherwise destroyed, nor will we pass upon him nor condemn him, but by lawful judgment of his peers or the law of the land.] This 29. Chap. of Magna Charta has for many Centuries been esteemed by Englishmen, as one of the noblest Monuments one of the firmest Bulwarks of their Liberties. . . . The Stat 4 G. 3 [Sugar Act] takes from Mr Hancock this precious Tryal Per Legem Terra, and gives it to a single Judge. However respectable the Judge may be, it is however an Hardship and Severity, which distinguishes my Clyent from the rest of Englishmen. . . .[55]

57

After challenging the authority of Parliament and the constitutionality of the court, Adams proceeded to tear to shreds the court's use of evidence and examination of witnesses, claiming that the court had so mixed up the rules of civil and common law, using favorable parts of each for the benefit of the government alone, that no one could tell under which system of law his client was being unfairly tried. This last impressed the judge, or so it seemed, and after an interlocutory decree in March 1769, pronouncing that the Crown's method of examination was improper, the attorney general stopped proceedings and withdrew the case.[56]

It would be easy to conclude that Hancock owed the happy outcome of the trial to Adams alone, but there was more involved here than Adams's eloquent persuasiveness. Several things occurred in the spring of 1769 which convinced the customs people that they would be better off out of the business. Governor Bernard, it was learned, was soon to be recalled; the government in England became suspicious of the motives of the commissioners and curious as to just what the customs people had done with all the revenue. Meanwhile, Auchmuty and the attorney general were promoted to vice-admiralty judgeships in Boston and Halifax with fixed

[55] John Adams, "Admiralty Notebook."
[56] Ibid.

salaries of £600 apiece, a fact which may have reduced the necessity of plundering Hancock. In any event the case was dropped.[57]

Unlike James Otis's attack against writs of assistance in 1761, which received little publicity then or later,[58] Adams's speech before the admiralty court did not long lie hidden from public view. During and after the extended trial, from November 1768 well into the spring of the next year, the colonial presses, adept at the use of propaganda, were fed a running account of what occurred behind the closed doors of the court.[59] Not two months after his final appearance before the court, Adams lifted from the "Admiralty Notebook" whole sections of his argument against admiralty courts and incorporated them into Boston's instructions to its representatives in the General Court where they would receive wide currency and again prompt printing in the newspapers.[60] The next year the Massachusetts House of Representatives digested Adams's argument including the quotation from Magna Charta—this time in English—and sent it to Benjamin Franklin, its agent in London.[61] The fate which befell the speech of James Otis was not repeated in the case of John Adams. The vigorous attack on admiralty justice and on the authority of Parliament and the clear denunciation of Parliamentary statutes, which, he said, fixed upon every American a "Brand of Infamy, of Degredation, and Disgrace," received wide publicity at home and abroad through his own efforts.

58

[57] Dickerson, The Navigation Acts, pp. 245-246; Boston under Military Rule, 1768-1769, as revealed in A Journal of the Times, ed. Oliver M. Dickerson (Boston, 1936), pp. 83-84.

[58] For a discussion of Otis's speech, see Oliver M. Dickerson, "Writs of Assistance as a Cause of the Revolution," in The Era of the American Revolution, ed. Richard B. Morris (New York, 1939), pp. 40, 42-43.

[59] During the winter and spring, 1768-69, The New-York Journal printed, and several other colonial newspapers reprinted in whole or part, what was called a "Journal of the Times," describing contemporary events in Boston including Hancock's trial. These articles, some of which appeared later in English journals, have been collected and published in Dickerson, Boston under Military Rule. For an account of Hancock's trial, see pp. 18-84, passim. For further discussion of the "Journal," see Arthur M. Schlesinger, Prelude to Independence, the Newspaper War on Britain, 1764-1776 (New York, 1958), pp. 100-103, 312-313.

[60] May 15, 1769, Adams, Works, III, 507-510. Half of the content of these instructions is devoted to admiralty court justice as a major grievance. On June 29, 1769, The New-York Journal, Supplement, printed an attack on admiralty court jurisdiction using many of Adams's own words and phrases. See Dickerson, Boston under Military Rule, pp. 97, n. 2, and 98-99.

[61] Nov. 6, 1770, Papers Relating to Public Events in Massachusetts Preceding the American Revolution, III, Massachusetts Papers, Seventy Six Society (Philadelphia, 1856), p. 174.

VI

Adams, Hancock, Laurens, and other Americans were not to be degraded below the rank of Englishmen. A government in London which by Parliamentary statute relegated Americans to an inferior position within the empire was not long to be tolerated. Inferiority was galling to an ambitious people, and inferiority was never more explicitly demonstrated than in the extension of admiralty court jurisdiction in America. Enactments, which deprived colonists of trial by jury and the law of the land, denied them that equality of treatment they insisted was their birthright as British subjects. John Adams sooner than most Americans recognized that mere denial of Parliament's power to tax Americans was a feeble defense of American rights; for it was the legislative authority of Parliament over America which was doing the damage, and one had to go no further than the extension of admiralty court jurisdiction to see just how much damage this authority had done. The concerted attack on Hancock, Laurens, and their property was sufficient warning of what might follow. And despite the slight easing of tension owing to the repeal of most of the Townshend taxes, the colonists did not let up in their complaints against the extending to "so enormous a degree" the powers of these courts. Sam Adams included the grievance in his "List of Infringements and Violations of Rights" which he persuaded the Boston town meeting—John Hancock, moderator—to adopt in the fall of 1772.[62] And wily old Benjamin Franklin the next year vexed the English in London with the biting explanation that depriving Americans of trial by jury and subjecting them to arbitrary judges—the "lowest characters in the country"—was one of the *Rules by which a Great Empire may be Reduced to a Small One*.[63]

In five short years after Hancock's trial, a majority of Americans had caught up with John Adams; a series of events, beginning with the Boston Massacre and ending with the Coercive Acts of 1774, convinced Americans that the sooner they got out from under Parliament the better. They sent to the Continental Congress in September of that year delegates who fashioned a theory of empire which admitted allegiance to the King but

[62] *Sources and Documents Illustrating the American Revolution, 1764-1788*, ed. Samuel Eliot Morison (Oxford, 1929), p. 94.
[63] *The Writings of Benjamin Franklin*, ed. Albert H. Smyth (New York, 1905-07), VI, 132.

59

denied Parliament any authority whatever in America except when the colonists consented. The Resolves of the Congress were a declaration of equality, announcing that Americans and Englishmen were equally subject to the same King and to their local legislatures, Parliament in England and the colonial assemblies in America. The Congress also declared, as had most protests since 1764, that the American colonies were "entitled to the common law of England, and more especially to the great and inestimable privilege of being tried by their peers. . . ." Any statutes denying these rights—and the Congress suggested several—Parliament must immediately repeal.[64]

The only trouble with the concept of empire which Americans formulated in the fall of 1774 was that its acceptance was limited to one side of the Atlantic. King, Parliament, and ministry scoffed at such ideas and stirred their troops in America to see to it that the colonists remained subject to the authority of Parliament. Within a year hostilities commenced.

Unable to establish themselves equal to the English within the empire, Americans in July 1776 cast off and declared themselves equal to the English as members of the human race; for, said Jefferson, *all* men are created equal. The appeal to the law of nature above the constitution was not so much a stroke of genius in 1776 as it was a stark necessity. The home government's refusal to accept the colonists' terms and the outbreak of fighting dissolved the hope of Americans' being equal on any other grounds. Despite the fact that Jefferson's magnificent declaration of human equality has come to mean many things to many men since 1776, it had only a particular meaning at the time it was written. Americans were not yet interested in the rights of all men. They had been interested in the rights of British subjects and particularly American subjects, and these rights, they said, implied equality. When the government in London repeatedly offended their sense of equality, as it did when meddling with the common law and trial by jury, the Americans called a halt and set up for themselves. John Adams knew what he was talking about when he advised his friend to read the statutes if he wanted to understand the American Revolution.

[64] *Journals of the Continental Congress, 1774-1789*, ed. Worthington C. Ford (Washington, D. C., 1904-37), I, 69.

60

Prelude to Revolution in New York:
Jury Trials and Judicial Tenure

Milton M. Klein *

A GENERATION of historical reinterpretation of the causes and character of the American Revolution has brought us full circle back to the view that the conflict between England and her American colonies was primarily political and constitutional. At issue, wrote the Earl of Dartmouth to General Thomas Gage, the British commander in chief in North America, was the "Constitutional Authority of this Kingdom over its Colonies" and the assertion of its laws "throughout the whole Empire."[1] Americans accepted the challenge and argued the case on Britain's terms. The central question, responded Sam Adams, was whether the constitution of Great Britain permitted the Parliament to "rightly leap the bounds of it" in exercising unwarranted "power over the subjects in America."[2] American Tories, like Governor Francis Bernard of Massachusetts, agreed that patchwork solutions would not settle the basic question. What was needed was a definition of the constitutional relationship between Britain and the colonies and the establishment of an American government upon "fixed Constitutional Principles."[3]

The constitutional and legal grounds on which the great debate was conducted from 1763 to 1776 could scarcely have been better designed to serve the American cause: the colonists had both the ammunition and the generalship to fight a constitutional contest. They were well fortified with political theory borrowed from England and expounded, reformulated, reiterated, and perfected in the course of over a century of local conflict

61

* Mr. Klein is a member of the Department of History, Long Island University, Brooklyn, New York.

[1] June 3, 1774, *The Correspondence of General Thomas Gage with the Secretaries of State . . . 1763-1775*, ed. C. E. Carter (New Haven, 1931-33), II, 165.
[2] To the Earl of Shelburne, Jan. 15, 1768, *The Debate on the American Revolution, 1761-1783*, ed. Max Beloff (London, 1949), p. 127.
[3] Bernard to Lord Barrington, Nov. 23, 1765, *Barrington-Bernard Correspondence*, ed. Edward Channing and A. C. Coolidge (Cambridge, Mass., 1912), pp. 96-97.

between assemblies and royal governors; and in each colony they possessed a first-rate corps of veterans to lead the constitutional defense, the lawyers.

The leadership of the American Revolution was drawn from many sources—the clergy, the merchants, the planters, and the newspaper editors—but no single group was better able to articulate the colonial position within the political, legal, and constitutional framework of the Anglo-American debate than the men of the legal profession. Curiously, modern historians have done them less credit than did their contemporaries. While there are excellent monographs on the roles of the merchants, the clergy, and the press in the Revolution, there is none on the lawyers.[4] Perhaps the fullness of the subject has discouraged systematic investigation. The roster of even the better-known lawyers who were active in the years before the Revolution is impressive: Jefferson, the Adamses, James Wilson, Patrick Henry, John Dickinson, Daniel Dulany, James Otis, John Jay, Alexander Hamilton, Josiah Quincy, William Livingston, Jared Ingersoll, William Smith, Jr., Richard Bland, George Mason, William Samuel Johnson, and James Iredell.

The colonial lawyer may not have been "deeply learned by the English standards," as Daniel J. Boorstin claims,[5] but this is somewhat irrelevant. Americans studied law widely if not deeply; their political theory was rooted in and fused with their knowledge of law; lawyers as a class, by the eve of the Revolution, possessed both social prestige and political power;[6] and they played a decisive role in many of the colonies in precipitating the Revolution. Friends of the Crown at least were in no doubt of the legal profession's pernicious influence. "The Lawyers are the Source from whence the Clamors have flowed in every Province," General Gage assured the home government during the Stamp Act disorders.[7] American

[4] On the role of these other groups, see, for example, Arthur M. Schlesinger, *The Colonial Merchants and the American Revolution* (New York, 1918), Alice M. Baldwin, *The New England Clergy and the American Revolution* (Durham, 1928), Schlesinger, *Prelude to Independence: The Newspaper War on Britain, 1764-1776* (New York, 1958), and Philip Davidson, *Propaganda and the American Revolution, 1763-1783* (Chapel Hill, 1941). An excellent introduction to the role of the lawyers is Richard B. Morris, "Legalism versus Revolutionary Doctrine in New England," *New England Quarterly*, IV (1931), 195-215.

[5] Boorstin, *The Americans: The Colonial Experience* (New York, 1958), p. 202.

[6] Milton M. Klein, "The Rise of the New York Bar: The Legal Career of William Livingston," *William and Mary Quarterly*, XV (1958), 334-336; Carl Bridenbaugh, *Cities in Revolt* (New York, 1955), pp. 95, 289.

[7] To Henry S. Conway, Dec. 21, 1765, Carter, *Gage Correspondence*, I, 79.

Tories echoed the charge in their assertion that the lawyers were "culti-
vating, with unwearied Pains, the Seeds of Infatuation and Tumult."[8]

New York's lawyers were no exception. Their influence and power were
recognized and feared by Tories and Churchmen. The Reverend Samuel
Johnson, a staunch Episcopalian and the first president of King's College,
vouchsafed the literary talents of three of New York's legal fraternity—
William Livingston, William Smith, Jr., and John Morin Scott—when he
expostulated that it was "indeed fencing against a flail to hold any dispute with them as there is nothing that they will stick at, however so false
and injurious, in opposing and discrediting the Church, and which they
will not cease to repeat and inculcate over and over again, however so
thoroughly it was answered."[9]

The irritated clergyman's compliment to the legal profession was only
oblique. That of Cadwallader Colden, New York's ageless lieutenant governor, was more direct. In a long lament to the Board of Trade, diagnosing
the source of New York's violent disorders in connection with the Stamp
Act, Colden pictured himself as the helpless victim of the lawyers' near-
diabolical power:

The Gentlemen of the Law, both the Judges and principal Practitioners
at the Bar, are either Owners Heirs or strongly connected in family Interest
with the Proprietors. . . . the power of the Lawyers is such that every Man
is affraid of offending them and is deterr'd from makeing any public opposition to their power and the daily increase of it. . . . many Court their
Friendship, and all dread their hatred. . . . they rule the House of Assembly in all Matters of Importance. . . .

By this association, united in interest and family Connections with
the proprietors of the great Tracts of Land, a Domination of Lawyers was
formed in this Province . . . . A Domination founded on the same Principles and carried on by the same wicked artifices that the Domination of
Priests formerly was . . . . Every Man's character who dares to discover
his Sentiments in opposition to theirs is loaded with infamy by every
falsehood which malice can invent, and thereby exposed to the brutal Rage
of the Mob. Nothing is too wicked for them to attempt which serves

[8] Quoted in Clinton Rossiter, *Seedtime of the Republic* (New York, 1953), p. 345.
[9] To Thomas Secker, Mar. 1, 1759, *Samuel Johnson, President of King's College:
His Career and Writings,* ed. Herbert and Carol Schneider (New York, 1929), I,
283.

their purposes—the Press is to them what the Pulpit was in times of Popery. . . .[10]

Colden had personal reasons for his antipathy toward the legal profession, but other observers, without his hypersensitivity or his political myopia, conceded the accuracy of his judgment. General Gage ascribed New York City's Stamp Act troubles to the pervasive influence of the lawyers. "In this Province Nothing Publick is transacted without them." Without the instigation of the lawyers and their merchant-allies, "the inferior People would have been quiet."[11] A young British engineering officer, stationed in the city during the disturbances, corroborated the impression. While many people of property participated in the "disloyal Insur[r]ection," he noted in his diary, the lawyers were "at the bottom" of it. They were the "Hornets and Firebrands . . . . The Planners and Incendiaries of the present Rupture."[12]

Neither New York's turbulent reaction to the Stamp Act nor the leadership assumed by the gentlemen of the law was entirely unexpected. The "seditious spirit" of which Colden complained so bitterly was the fruit of local political discontent as much as of resentment against imperial reorganization, and the political maturity exhibited by New York's lawyers in 1765 did not emerge full-blown in that year. It was rather the climax of a succession of local contests during the previous fifteen years, in each of which the lawyers managed to pose successfully as spokesmen of the "popular" cause against the extensions of royal prerogative. Two of these contests took place on the very eve of the Stamp Act's passage, between 1760 and 1765. Both were judicial in nature, involving, respectively, the tenure of judges and the traditional right of trial by jury. As matters of technical and professional interest, these disputes naturally engaged the attention of the legal fraternity; but by clothing their arguments in the twin dress of popular rights and constitutional privilege, the lawyers succeeded in making them issues of transcendent public interest. With the "grand Engine" of the press as their instrument and the doctrine that "all authority is derived from the People" as their theme, the lawyers created

[10] To the Secretary of State and Board of Trade, Dec. 6, 1765, *The Colden Letter Books, 1760-1775* (New-York Historical Society, *Collections,* IX-X [New York, 1877-78]), II, 70-71; hereafter cited as *Colden Letter Books.*

[11] To Conway, Dec. 21, 1765, Carter, *Gage Correspondence,* I, 79.

[12] Entries of Nov. 6, 7, 1765, *The Montresor Journals* (N-Y Hist. Soc., *Colls.,* XIV [New York, 1882]), p. 339; hereafter cited as *Montresor Journals.*

a climate of opinion that the Sons of Liberty turned to ready advantage in 1765. If the violence accompanying the Stamp Act marked the first act of the Revolution in New York, then the local contests over judges and jury trials constituted a fitting prelude.

The first of the judicial clashes came in 1760. It originated in the vacancy on the Supreme Court bench created by the death of James De Lancey, who had held that post since the days of the John Peter Zenger trial. During his long tenure as chief justice and, after 1753, lieutenant governor as well, De Lancey had built a powerful political machine which controlled the provincial government for more than a decade. De Lancey's prestige was due in no small measure to his success in championing the rights of the Assembly against the "encroachments" of Governor George Clinton, particularly over control of the purse. Clinton's strife-ridden ten-year administration (1743-53), during which the Governor failed first to secure from the De Lancey Assembly a permanent revenue for the support of the government and then to secure wholehearted legislative support for the prosecution of King George's War, left its mark on Cadwallader Colden. As Clinton's principal adviser, Colden shared his chief's frustrations in the losing struggle with De Lancey. Colden became convinced by this experience that a chief justice had "more influence on the public affairs in this Country" than a governor, and that the source of De Lancey's power was the number of lawyers whose "bread and fortune" depended on his "Countenance" and who served as "his emissaries and spies in every part of the Country."[13]

In 1760 Colden assumed command of New York's government, a responsibility that devolved upon him as the senior member of the Council. Seventy-three years old and a veteran of over forty years in the colony's politics, Colden had not mellowed one bit in his inordinate fear of the bench and bar or, indeed, of any disruptive element that threatened the stability of church and state. Colden had held royal office almost from the day of his arrival in New York in 1718. As "one of the most permanent of all permanent officials" in British North America,[14] he was the arche-

[13] Colden to William Shirley, July 25, 1749, *The Letters and Papers of Cadwallader Colden* (N-Y Hist. Soc., Colls., LIII-LVI [New York, 1921-24]), IV, 124-125; hereafter cited as *Colden Papers*.

[14] Wilbur C. Abbott, *New York in the American Revolution* (New York, 1929), p. 15.

type of the loyal servant of the Crown and the staunch defender of royal prerogative. Temperamentally, the role suited him well. Vain, ambitious, petulant, inflexible, and unimaginative, this dour Scotsman saw government as a kind of irrepressible conflict between the insidious forces of republicanism and independency and the stabilizing influence of the British monarchy and the Anglican Church. During his active career in politics, Colden managed to secure a widespread reputation as a physician, botanist, philosopher, physicist, historian, and colonial savant, but the breadth of his intellectual interests never liberalized his political outlook.

As the new chief executive of New York, Colden was still firmly persuaded that the lawyers were the most dangerous enemies to good government in the colony. The courts were their private domain, and there no honest citizen could expect redress unless he were initiated into the legal mysteries that the bar so jealously guarded. The great landed proprietors were their henchmen, the two in combination perpetrating huge land frauds which legal legerdemain protected from royal investigation. The Assembly, filled with simple citizens too ignorant to exercise independent judgment in weighty matters of government, was easily swayed by the smooth-talking lawyers; and for good measure, the gentlemen of the law insinuated themselves into popular good grace by propagating the doctrine that more power ought to be lodged in the "Popular side of Government" while they depreciated the "Powers of the Crown."[15] With monotonous persistency, Colden reiterated the theme that "All associations are dangerous to good Government . . . and associations of Lawyers the most dangerous of any next to Military."[16]

The demise of the formidable James De Lancey and the impairment of the De Lancey party's strength did not leave Colden without political foes. Two years earlier the Livingstons, who had long vied with the De Lanceys for political power in the province,[17] had gained control of the Assembly; and the Livingstons bore no love for "the Scotch gentleman." Under Governor Clinton's administration, Philip Livingston, the second manor lord, had been accused of trading with the French and defrauding the Indians, and the Livingstons saw Colden as the real instigator of the

[15] Colden to the Earl of Halifax, Feb. 22, 1765, *Colden Letter Books*, I, 470.
[16] *Ibid.*
[17] Milton M. Klein, "Democracy and Politics in Colonial New York," *New York History*, XL (1959), 223-228.

odious charges.[18] Angrily, Philip Livingston dubbed Colden, New York's "Haman" and suggested tartly that he "ought to be turn[e]d off or sent back to his own place."[19]

Colden, for his part, shared Clinton's mordant observation that the Livingstons were "a vile family."[20] In one way or another, they had been disturbers of peace and good government for two decades: the second generation had been unconscionable land-grabbers, and now the third generation was taking over De Lancey's old role as champion of the Assembly against the Crown. Worse, the mouthpiece of the Livingstons outside the Assembly's halls was a brash young triumvirate of lawyers with whom Colden had already locked horns. The trio, William Livingston, William Smith, Jr., and John Morin Scott, were all Presbyterians and graduates of Yale College, and it was at this nursery of sedition, in Colden's view, that they had imbibed their republican principles in politics and religion. Colden's suspicions of the triumvirate had been fanned by their vigorous assault against the Anglican Church at the time of the founding of King's College. Their proposal for a "free college" under legislative sponsorship smacked to him of the "narrow principles" of religious free-thinking and political "independency" that had already polluted Harvard and Yale.[21] But Colden's distaste for the triumvirate was personal as well as political.

In 1751 Colden had approached Livingston and Smith while they were preparing a digest of the colony's laws and requested them to omit from their compilation a reference that might cast doubt on the legality of a land grant in which he held property. Despite a "soothing" entreaty to Livingston and a stormy threat to Smith, the editors held fast to their original resolution, telling Colden to "go to the Devil." For maintaining

[18] Alice M. Keys, *Cadwallader Colden: A Representative Eighteenth Century Official* (New York, 1906), pp. 138-141.

[19] To Jacob Wendell, Oct. 19, Nov. 9, 1747, Livingston Papers, Museum of the City of New York, New York City.

[20] Clinton to the Duke of Newcastle, Nov. 18, 1745, *Documents Relative to the Colonial History of the State of New York*, ed. E. B. O'Callaghan (Albany, 1853-87), VI, 286; hereafter cited as *N. Y. Colonial Documents*.

[21] Colden to Hezekiah Watkins, Dec. 12, 1748, G. H. Moore, *Origin and Early History of Columbia College* (New York, 1890), pp. 39-40. As a petty expression of his dislike of the triumvirate on this occasion, Colden is said to have refused membership in the newly founded New York Society Library simply because the three lawyers were among its organizers. A. B. Keep, *History of the New York Society Library* (New York, 1908), p. 180.

"our Opinions," Smith later recalled, Colden "never forgave us."[22] In 1757, when Smith's famous history of New York appeared, Colden objected violently to some of its veiled references to his conduct in connection with a land transaction.[23] When his demands for "proper redress" and withdrawal of the "Misrepresentation, Falsehood and Calumny" were refused, he denounced the whole publication as not fit to "pass for a chronicle of the Province of New York."[24]

As chief executive of the province, Colden was in a position to wreak sweet vengeance on the Livingstons, the triumvirate, and all the gentlemen of the law; and like David, he strode forth garbed in his robes of viceregal virtue to do battle with the legal Goliath. It did not seem at first that the Livingstons would bar his path. The enthusiasm aroused by the success of British arms in the French and Indian War seemed to suffuse local politics with a warm glow of cordiality. The Livingston Assembly congratulated Colden on his accession to the governorship, and the head of the triumvirate himself penned the salutation.[25] Colden was deluded into thinking that his administration would go "easy." The illusion was only slightly dispelled by a brief disagreement between Colden and the Livingstons over the selection of a sheriff for Albany County,[26] but it was completely shattered by the uproar that greeted Colden's announcement of his views regarding the opening on the Supreme Court bench created by De Lancey's death.

[22] William Smith Papers, V, "30 October 1776," New York Public Library, New York City. The incident arose when Livingston and Smith failed to find the original of a 1699 law vacating certain extravagant land grants. Since a number of persons including Colden had been regranted land in the vacated patents, the law was of "vast Importance." The editors decided to reproduce the law as it had appeared in an early printed edition and to make a marginal notation to the effect that the original could not be located. The act, with the marginal notation, may be found in the Livingston-Smith edition of the *Laws of New-York, from the Year 1691, to 1751, Inclusive* (New York, 1752), pp. 33-36.

[23] William Smith, Jr., *The History of the Late Province of New York* . . . (N-Y Hist. Soc., *Colls.*, IV [New York, 1829]), I, 247-248; hereafter cited as Smith, *History*.

[24] *Colden Papers*, V, 283-295, 310-319; "The Colden Letters on Smith's History, 1759-1760," N-Y Hist. Soc., *Colls.*, I (New York, 1868), 214, 226-230; William Smith Papers, V, "30 October 1776."

[25] Smith, *History*, II, 284-286; *Journal of the Votes and Proceedings of the General Assembly of the Colony of New York . . . 1691 . . . [1765]* (New York, 1764-66), II, 637-638; hereafter cited as *Assembly Journals*.

[26] Robert Livingston to Abraham Yates, Sept. 9, Oct. 13, 1760, Abraham Yates Papers, New York Public Library, New York City.

Colden had two fixed notions with respect to the vacant chief-justice-ship: that the office should be filled by a stranger to New York's politics and that the appointment should be at the Crown's pleasure rather than during good behavior. With De Lancey's long rule on the bench in mind, Colden insisted that only a chief justice unconnected with the great landed families of New York or with the legal fraternity could restrain the insolent local aristocracy and compel it to respect the royal will. A chief justice dependent on the governor's pleasure would prove a useful servant of the Crown; life tenure for the head of the bench, conversely, would make the governor the Supreme Court's "tool."[27]

Colden's position could not have been "more universally disgustful," to use the words of one of the triumvirate.[28] The Livingstons had their own candidates for the vacant judicial post, William Smith, Sr., or Robert Hunter Morris; so did the De Lanceys, in the persons of two of the inferior judges of the Supreme Court, John Chambers and Daniel Horsmanden. Colden's stand infuriated both the local factions, but his behavior was particularly offensive to the Livingstons. At least the De Lancey nominations were forwarded on to England; Morris's name was peremptorily rejected, and the elder Smith was offered the appointment on terms that he had clearly announced he would refuse.[29]

The contest now initiated between Colden and the Livingstons had its counterpart in almost every other colony before the Revolution. At stake was control of the courts, and the contestants were the assemblies and the governors. One issue was the right to erect new courts and to determine their jurisdiction, the assemblies insisting that this was a legislative power and the governors claiming the power as belonging to prerogative. In New York this issue had already produced the famous Zenger case. It was Governor William Cosby's attempt to erect a new court of equity that brought down upon him the anguished protests of the Zengerites.[30] By 1760, however, the issue had been fairly well resolved in the legislature's favor, the English authorities tolerating, if not approving, various acts of the As-

69

[27] Colden to the Lords of Trade, Jan. 11, 25, Apr. 7, 1762, Colden to the Earl of Egremont, Sept. 14, 1762, *Colden Letter Books*, I, 149-150, 157, 191, 231.

[28] Smith, *History*, II, 289.

[29] *Colden Letter Books*, I, 13, 15, 22-24; Smith, *History*, II, 285, 288-289; William Smith Papers, IV, "24 November 1761"; Thomas Jones, *History of New York during the Revolutionary War* (New York, 1879), I, 224.

[30] Livingston Rutherfurd, *John Peter Zenger* (New York, 1904, reprinted 1941), pp. 9-10; Vincent Buranelli, *The Trial of Peter Zenger* (New York, 1957), pp. 12-13.

sembly establishing New York's courts and defining their jurisdiction.[31]

The other issue, more vexing, was that of judicial tenure. Although the Glorious Revolution had settled the question in England by providing that judges should hold their offices for life, that is, "during good behavior," the privilege of life tenure had not been extended to the colonial judiciary. The Board of Trade's specious explanation was that English judges rarely had to be removed since they were both able and financially incorruptible —as a result of permanent salaries—while American judges were usually so incompetent that the Crown of necessity required the right to remove them at will in order to replace them with abler men. A more substantial ground for the Board's position was its explanation that an independent colonial judiciary would be "subversive of that Policy by which alone Colonies can be kept in a just dependance upon the Government of the Mother Country."[32] The Board preferred, therefore, that American judges receive their commissions "during the King's pleasure" only. The colonists, in turn, countered with the charge that impartial justice could scarcely be expected from judges whose terms of office could be arbitrarily terminated whenever their decisions irritated an unfriendly governor.[33]

Principles, politics, and personalities were all intertwined in the Livingstons' position. As the majority party in the Assembly they felt compelled to uphold the privilege of judicial tenure during good behavior that the De Lanceys had wrested from Governor Clinton a decade earlier.[34] De Lancey's own commission as chief justice had been for life; the commissions of the inferior judges had been similarly drawn. By 1760 New Yorkers regarded the principle to be as firmly fixed in their own constitution as it was in England's since the Act of Settlement of 1701. Colden's refusal to honor the precedent bespoke still another example of his "sycophantic" attachment to prerogative.

On practical grounds, the Livingstons feared that an appointee for New

[31] Leonard W. Labaree, *Royal Government in America* (New Haven, 1930), pp. 375-380; *History of the State of New York,* ed. Alexander C. Flick (New York, 1933-37), III, 18-26.

[32] Report of the Lords of Trade, Nov. 11, 1761, O'Callaghan, *N. Y. Colonial Documents,* VII, 473, 474-475; Labaree, *Royal Government,* pp. 390-391.

[33] Labaree, *Royal Government,* pp. 394-395.

[34] Although Clinton later regretted having been so generous as to grant De Lancey the chief justice's commission during good behavior, the legality of the commission was upheld by the Crown's law officers. O'Callaghan, *N. Y. Colonial Documents,* VI, 356, 792.

York named in London might be the type of incompetent fortune seeker as, on two recent occasions, had been sent over from England to fill the chief-justiceship of New Jersey.[35] But the Livingstons' desire for a friendly head of the bench was undoubtedly also underlined by the family's economic interests. During his first few months in office, Colden had begun vigorously to curb illicit trade with the West Indies and to vacate large land patents granted in violation of royal instructions.[36] The Livingstons were vulnerable on both counts.

The contestants warmed to the fight slowly. The Assembly prepared an address requesting Colden to honor tradition in filling the judicial post. Reluctant to brew up a storm until his commission as lieutenant governor arrived from England—he was as yet merely acting governor—Colden promised to consider the Assembly's advice.[37] Then George II's death late in October 1760 relieved him temporarily of the need for redeeming this pledge. The Assembly was dissolved and new elections called; and Colden hoped for better fortune in the next house. To his dismay, the Livingstons were returned to power. They quickly passed a bill providing for the organization of the Supreme Court on the basis of life tenure. The legal fraternity simultaneously prodded the incumbent judges to request new commissions on the plea that their old ones had been vacated by the King's demise. They made it clear that they would refuse reappointment unless they received tenure during good behavior, as before. At the same time, and quite apart from the controversy over the judges, the Assembly passed an innocuous bill—at the lawyers' suggestion—validating all legislation enacted between the death of George II and the date the news of his successor reached New York.[38]

Hypercritical and oversuspicious, Colden responded to these measures with almost psychopathic rage. He refused the judges' request for new

---

[35] The New Jersey justices, each of whom had short-lived terms of office, were William Aynsley, lately treasurer of a turnpike company in northern England, and Nathaniel Jones, a Newgate solicitor of allegedly questionable character and dubious morality. Smith, *History*, II, 284; Donald L. Kemmerer, *Path to Freedom: The Struggle for Self-Government in Colonial New Jersey, 1703-1776* (Princeton, 1940), pp. 268-270.

[36] Colden to Pitt, Oct. 27, 1760, to the Lords of Trade, Jan. 25, 1762, *Colden Letter Books*, I, 26-28, 155 :58; Keys, *Colden*, pp. 275-276.

[37] Smith, *History*, II, 285; Colden to Halifax, Nov. 11, 1760, *Colden Letter Books*, I, 35.

[38] *Colden Letter Book.*, I, 79, 88-89, 104; William Smith Papers, IV, "24 November 1761."

commissions, told them to "sit upon" their old ones, and snapped: "Yours are as good as mine, and you'll stand on the same foundation."[39] The validating act he denounced as a legal subtlety fabricated by the bar to create "a kind of Law Popery" and by "setting Law and Common sense in opposition ... [to] obtain a most extensive power over the Minds of the rest of Mankind."[40] Neither the validating act nor the court bill received his assent.

The opposition struck back rapidly. The judges announced their refusal to serve under their old commissions; the business of the Supreme Court slowed to a standstill. The Assembly declined a Colden compromise offer to trade new judicial commissions for permanent judicial salaries. The legislature, having gained both advantages, was unwilling to surrender either. Instead, it repassed the original bill organizing the Supreme Court, and again Colden withheld his assent.[41]

In this deadlock, the Ministry came to Colden's rescue by naming one of Boston's prominent lawyers, Benjamin Pratt, to the critical chief-justiceship. Colden's exultation was immediately dampened by Pratt's disinclination to accept the post as long as the wrangle with the Assembly continued. He was well aware that if he defied public sentiment by accepting his commission during pleasure, the Assembly would vote him no salary.[42] Only Colden's importunate letters and a vague promise to get the terms of his commission changed, in time, persuaded Pratt to give up his comfortable practice in Boston for the uneasy privilege of a judicial robe.[43] Delighted with his victory, Colden saw it completed by the arrival of the lieutenant governor's commission he coveted so dearly.[44]

The aged Scotsman did not enjoy his triumph for long. Pratt was received "with Contempt and Displeasure" by New York's legal community. His associates on the Supreme Court refused to sit with him, the Assembly withheld his salary, and after six months he gave up in disgust and returned to Boston. His analysis of his troubles in New York was per-

[39] Smith, *History*, II, 290; William Smith Papers, IV, "11 November 1761."
[40] Colden to the Lords of Trade, June 2, 1761, *Colden Letter Books*, I, 89.
[41] Colden to the Lords of Trade, Aug. 12, Sept. 25, 1761, Colden to Pitt, Sept. 24, 1761, *ibid.*, pp. 106, 117, 119-120.
[42] O'Callaghan, *N. Y. Colonial Documents*, VII, 460; Colden to Pratt, Oct. 12, 1761, *Colden Letter Books*, I, 123-124; Pratt to Colden, Aug. 22, Sept. 14, Oct. 3, 1761, *Colden Papers*, VI, 68-69, 76-78, 81-82.
[43] Colden to Pratt, Sept. 7, 1761, *Colden Letter Books*, I, 113-114.
[44] *Ibid.*, p. 103.

spicacious: "The granting Commissions as they were before, that is During good Behavior, is now the Popular Demand and made the inflaming Topic but at Bottom the Point in View is to compel the Crown to appoint one of themselves Ch: Justice."[45]

Colden did not surrender as easily. For a month he was forced to view the proceedings from the sidelines while General Robert Monckton, the newly appointed governor, ran the administration; but when Monckton departed to lead an expedition to Martinique in November 1761, Colden was able to resume the contest. He now had fresh personal grievances against the triumvirate. Monckton had demanded that Colden account to him for any executive fees that might be collected during his absence, and Colden had been compelled to sign a bond to that effect. The terms and the language of the bond seemed humiliating to Colden, and he blamed it all on the younger Smith, who had been Monckton's counsel in the affair. To Colden, Smith was no better than "a crafty malicious smooth tongued hypocrite" and "the greatest Scoundrel in the Province."[46]

Colden's vengeance was directed against the bar as a whole. He demanded that the Assembly investigate the "dilatory Proceedings in the Courts of Law" and the "heavy Expence in obtaining Justice."[47] The legal fraternity accepted the move as a declaration of war against all "the Professors of the Law"; and they were not without means to return the compliment. As Robert Livingston put it picturesquely: "I think his Hon[o]r has Ill tim[e]d it; the Gentlemen of the Law are very able . . . to lead him a dance Sufficient to mortify him and family and friends . . . and p[e]rhaps make his administration more uneasye to him than heretofore . . . ."[48] The Assembly, under the bar's influence, threatened to pass a bill fixing executive as well as legal fees, a move that would have hit Colden in his own purse. Pressing their advantage, the Livingstons pushed through a bill providing for life tenure for the judges to which they attached the annual appropriation for official salaries. Unwilling to cut his own throat, the en-

73

---

[45] Pratt to Thomas Pownall, Jan. 7, 1762, *Colden Papers*, VI, 113-116. See also, O'Callaghan, *N. Y. Colonial Documents*, VII, 500-502; Jones, *History of New York*, I, 226-231; Colden to the Secretary of State and Board of Trade, Dec. 6, 1765, *Colden Letter Books*, II, 73.

[46] Smith, *History*, II, 296-298; Colden to John Pownall, Nov. 26, 1761, *Colden Letter Books*, I, 137-141; William Smith Papers, IV, "17 March 1762."

[47] *Assembly Journals*, II, 669; William Smith Papers, IV, "24 November 1761."

[48] To Abraham Yates, Dec. 8, 1761, Abraham Yates Papers.

raged Lieutenant Governor approved, while immediately penning lengthy explanations of his conduct to the home government.[49]

Colden now sought some relief by proroguing the Assembly; the triumvirate, determined to give the old gentleman no peace during the legislative recess, sharpened their quills and began a press war against him. A new paper, the *American Chronicle*, was founded for the purpose, none of the regular newspaper publishers being very anxious to challenge the Lieutenant Governor. Its hurried first issue, on March 20, 1762, was timed to permit the rural members of the Assembly to take copies along with them to their constituencies.[50] For the next two months the *Chronicle* carried a veritable barrage of the triumvirate's sharpest literary barbs. Colden was successively lampooned for his ignorance of law, criticized for his "outrageous Abuse of Power," accused of upsetting the provincial constitution, and indicted for using his public office to accumulate private wealth. In a burlesque on Colden's frequent references to the artificial intricacies of the law, the triumvirate facetiously proposed that "all the Laws of this Province . . . be retrenched to the Size of *Poor Richard's* Almanack; and every Law-suit decided in six Hours."[51] In more serious vein, the paper asserted New York's *"undoubted Right,* of having the Judges of our Courts on a constitutional Basis," called attention to the independence of the judiciary in England, and insisted that Americans were entitled to "the same Liberties and Privileges" as their fellow subjects in Britain.[52]

The anti-Colden crusade did not last very long. Lengthy tirades against the Lieutenant Governor could fill a few issues, but they could not sustain a permanent newspaper. The publishers of New York's other papers placed obstacles in the *Chronicle*'s path; a fire of suspicious origin destroyed its press. In July the new journalistic enterprise expired, but the crusade against Colden had already lost its steam before then. Eight months earlier the King in Council, disturbed with the growing colonial movement for judicial independence, had ordered the issuance of new instructions absolutely forbidding governors to grant judicial offices during good behavior,

---

[49] *Assembly Journals,* II, 672-673; William Smith Papers, IV, "9 March 1762"; Colden to the Lords of Trade, Feb. 11, 1762, *Colden Letter Books,* II, 159-161.

[50] Clarence E. Brigham, *History and Bibliography of American Newspapers, 1690-1820* (Worcester, 1947), I, 607-608. The publisher of the *Chronicle* was Samuel Farley, an English printer recently arrived in New York.

[51] *American Chronicle* (N. Y. C.), Mar. 20, Apr. 12, 1762.

[52] *Ibid.,* Apr. 3, 12, 19, 1762.

on pain of removal.[53] Triumphantly, Colden waved the new instructions before the recalcitrant judges and threatened them with dismissal unless they accepted new commissions during pleasure. William Livingston and William Smith, Jr., urged them to stand fast. One justice, John Chambers, resigned, but the other two—Daniel Horsmanden and David Jones—submitted to Colden's ultimatum.[54] The controversy was finally resolved a year later by Governor Monckton, whose friendship with the Livingstons made a compromise possible. Horsmanden—no friend of Colden—was persuaded to accept the chief-justiceship, even though "during the King's pleasure," and as a measure of consolation two members of the Livingston party, William Smith, Sr., and Robert Livingston, were named to the other two vacancies on the bench.[55]

The "affair of the Judges is settled," Colden reported in high enthusiasm to the Board of Trade. "The minds of the people are as much at ease, and the Province in as great tranquility, as ever it was at any time."[56] With characteristic obtuseness, Colden failed to recognize that what he had won was merely an armistice. His jubilation over the immediate victory could not entirely conceal an apprehension that the "three popular Lawyers" might continue to "propagate their principles both in Religious and Civil matters and for that end make use of every artifice they can invent to calumniate the administration in every Exercise of the Prerogative." And while their literary crusade had not aroused the same "clamor" as their earlier attacks on episcopacy in connection with the King's College affair, their vitriolic pens could not be ignored. Colden was sure that no gentlemen had been taken in by the Livingston trio's campaign against authority, but "What effect it may have on the low rank of Mankind, for which it is cheifly calculated is not so easy for me to know . . . ."[57] The next round would tell, and it was only a year in coming.

The second test between Colden and the legal fraternity began innocently enough with an action for assault and battery filed by one Thomas

[53] Colden to Monckton, Mar. 30, 1762, *Colden Letter Books*, I, 183-184; "Order of the King in Council," Nov. 23, 1761, O'Callaghan, *N. Y. Colonial Documents*, VII, 472-476.
[54] New York Executive Council Minutes, XXV, 432, 433, New York State Library, Albany; William Smith Papers, IV, Mar. 27, 31, 1762.
[55] Colden to the Lords of Trade, July 18, 1763, *Colden Letter Books*, II, 218.
[56] Apr. 7, June 12, 1762, *ibid.*, I, 190, 213.
[57] To the Lords of Trade, Apr. 7, 1762, *ibid.*, pp. 187, 190.

Forsey against Waddel Cunningham during the summer of 1763. The case bore no particular significance apart from the widespread public sympathy that Cunningham's attack brought the victim. Cunningham had allegedly accosted Forsey in the street, drawn a concealed sword, and "did beat Thrust Stab wound and evilly treat" the victim so badly that he was incapacitated for eighty-two days. The triumvirate were involved in the litigation but as opposing counsel. Scott represented Forsey, the plaintiff; Livingston and Smith, Cunningham. A criminal action ended with Cunningham's paying a fine of thirty pounds in January 1764. A civil suit decided later in the year awarded Forsey damages of more than £1500.[58]

It was the civil suit that became the bone of contention. Up to this time appeals from the decisions of the common-law courts had been taken to the Governor in Council only by "writ of error." The review in such cases was confined to errors of law in the record or in the bill of exceptions filed by the attorney and to irregularities in the lower court's proceedings. Matters of fact were outside the appellate court's jurisdiction: it did not attempt to examine the evidence or to pass judgment on the jury's verdict. It could hardly do so without conducting another trial, since neither the evidence nor the testimony of witnesses in trial proceedings was recorded. Cunningham, regarding the damages awarded as excessive, determined to break tradition by requesting a review of the facts as well as the law. In the fall of 1764 he petitioned the Supreme Court to allow an appeal to the Governor in Council. His attorneys now refused to associate themselves with the case, convinced that the move was a dangerous threat to the inviolability of jury trials; and they persuaded virtually the entire New York bar to stand with them. Cunningham was compelled to turn over the case to his business partner—a notary public—and to several obscure lawyers, one of whom had only recently been deported from England under a conviction for fraud.[59]

The Supreme Court sided with the legal profession, firmly denying Cunningham's request for the minutes of the trial on the ground that

<hr/>

[58] Supreme Court Minutes, 1762-64, pp. 224-225, 308, 358-359; 1764-67, pp. 18, 32, parchment rolls 21-A-3, 28-K-9, 186-K-3, Hall of Records, New York City; William Livingston, "Supreme Court Cost Books," II, 207, New York Public Library, New York City.

[59] Colden Letter Books, I, 416-418; Supreme Court Minutes, 1764-67, pp. 35, 125-126; William Smith Papers, IV, "Autumn 1764."

"no proper writ" for sending up the record had been produced. Colden, under no such inhibitions and anxious to lock horns with the gentlemen of the law, examined his instructions; and finding no specific mention of appeals in cases of error only—an unintentional oversight, it later proved —accepted Cunningham's plea. He stayed execution of the Supreme Court's judgment and ordered the Chief Justice to deliver up to him the proceedings in the case. The Supreme Court judges resolutely declined; the Attorney General offered his opinion that the Lieutenant Governor's action was without precedent; the leading members of the bar endorsed the chief law officer's opinion; the Council agreed with the lawyers. Yet Colden insisted that his interpretation was as good as that of the legal fraternity. He would do what was right "without regard to any Man."[60]

Convening the Council in November, Colden ordered the judges before it and repeated his demand that they allow the appeal. Chief Justice Daniel Horsmanden again refused and with the assistance of the triumvirate presented a lengthy vindication of his position. He declared that Colden's attempt to review the facts as well as the law would alter "the ancient and wholesome Laws of the land," endanger the right of jury trial, and institute a novel procedure "repugnant to the Laws both of England and this Colony."[61] Infuriated, Colden publicly charged both judges and Councilors with "Indecency, Want of Respect to the King's Authority and . . . unwarrantable Freedoms." Hysterically, he advised the Secretary of State and the Board of Trade to remove the Supreme Court judges, hinted darkly at a plot on the Chief Justice's part to bring about his death—by induced apoplexy, no doubt—and warned that unless the home government supported him in this crisis, the whole structure of royal government in America would topple, with the lawyers rising "uncontroulable" on its ruins.[62]

New Yorkers were not amused at Colden's frenetic exaggerations. An irresponsible chief executive with delusions of grandeur who saw

[60] John Tabor Kempe to Colden, Oct. 31, Nov. 16, 1764, George Harrison to Colden, Nov. 24, 1764, *Colden Papers*, VI, 368-371, 378, 387-388; *Colden Letter Books*, I, 395-396, 415-416.

[61] *Calendar of Council Minutes, 1668-1783*, ed. Berthold Fernow, New York State Library Bulletin 58 (Albany, 1902), p. 509; *Colden Letter Books*, I, 407-416; *Colden Papers*, VI, 379-386.

[62] Colden to the Lords of Trade, Dec. 13, 1764, Jan. 22, 27, 1765, *Colden Letter Books*, I, 421-425, 455, 552; William Smith, Jr., to Monckton, Jan. 25, 1765, Chalmers Papers, New York, IV, 17, New York Public Library, New York City.

assassins in every dark corner could hardly be tolerated at any time, but in the midst of the uncertainty created by the new Parliamentary trade regulations, he would be positively dangerous. What was needed in the "uneasy temper of Mind" created by the measures of George Grenville was a governor who could ease public inquietude and inspire popular confidence. Colden's "unseasonable Effort" to introduce a judicial innovation served only to spread "a Jealousy, that the Crown is aiming to deprive the Subject of his most valuable Rights." The new commercial measures and the expected internal taxes were bad enough. The "good folks at Home" were "overshooting the Mark about Trade," one conservative New Yorker warned.[63] Colden's actions seemed to be even worse—"nothing less than the entire Subversion of the Constitution of the Province," by the destruction of its jury system and its courts as well.[64] Convinced that "the Ministry appears to have run mad" with its talk of stamp duties and land taxes, New Yorkers were all the more determined to maintain without reservation their ancient privilege of trial by jury.[65]

The opposition to Colden was not confined to the lawyers. Conservative merchants of the De Lancey party joined with landlord members of the Livingston family to denounce the Lieutenant Governor as an "evil Genius," an "old Mischief-maker," and a "Petty T[yran]t" and to condemn his "Fondness for showing himself in Law Matters, superior to the whole Body of the Law."[66] The judges and the bars of New Jersey and Pennsylvania lined up solidly on the side of the New York legal community.[67] Even Colden's own administration deserted him. In January 1765 he convened the Council and read it a long, turgid, and ill-informed defense of his position in the matter of appeals. With accustomed tactlessness, Colden went well beyond the limits of immediate necessity. To justify his acceptance of a solitary appeal, Colden was quite

[63] John Watts to Monckton, Dec. 29, 1763, Sept. 22, 1764, William Smith, Jr., to Monckton, Jan. 25, 1765, Chalmers Papers, New York, III, 65, 77, IV, 17.

[64] Horsmanden to Monckton, Dec. 8, 1764, Watts to Monckton, Nov. 10, 1764, ibid., III, 80, IV, 26.

[65] Robert R. Livingston to Robert Livingston, June 7, 15, 1764, Robert R. Livingston Papers, N-Y Hist. Soc., New York City.

[66] Watts to Monckton, Nov. 10, 1764, Chalmers Papers, New York, III, 80; Watts to Isaac Barré, Jan. 19, 1765, Letter Book of John Watts . . . (N-Y Hist. Soc., Colls., LXI [New York, 1928]), pp. 323-326, hereafter cited as Watts Letter Book; Robert R. Livingston to Monckton, Feb. 23, 1765, Livingston Family Papers, New York Public Library, New York City.

[67] Watts to Monckton, Jan. 25, 1765, Chalmers Papers, New York, III, 86.

willing to denounce the whole jury system for its iniquitous and false verdicts, to assert the Crown's power to set up courts at will and to define their jurisdiction and procedure, and to proclaim the virtue of appealing all jury verdicts to the reasonable judgment of governors, kings, and councils.[68] His astounded Council not only condemned Colden's position unanimously but prepared a formal reply—with an eye to publication—for the official minutes. Thereupon it denied Cunningham's appeal and refused him permission to carry his case directly to the Crown.[69]

Colden was as persistent as he was obtuse. Undaunted by the Council's action, he, forwarded Cunningham's petition for review to London, accompanied by a familiar barrage of letters describing the sinister legal conspiracy of which the Forsey case was but a part. The anti-Coldenites countered with a similar stream of letters, addressed chiefly to New York's absentee governor, General Monckton; but their most effective literary weapon was the public prints. The triumvirate, long experienced in this type of press warfare, directed the campaign. Chief Justice Horsmanden's defense of jury trials and his argument rejecting the original appeal petition was run serially in the newspapers.[70] John Morin Scott, one of the triumvirate, introduced them with a preface in which Colden's interpretation of his appellate powers was attacked as "entirely new, unconstitutional, and illegal," a "strange and unnatural" innovation, and "alarming to every British subject." When the series had completed its run in the papers, it was republished in book form, William Livingston, the chief of the triumvirate, himself underwriting the publication.[71] The grand jury was induced to extend congratulations to the judges for their defiance of Colden, and then copies of the address were sent to the newspapers.[72] A column titled the "Sentinel" was launched in the *New-York Gazette; or Weekly Post-Boy,* with all three of the triumvirate as contributors, and for the next six months it assailed Colden mercilessly in a

79

[68] "Cadwallader Colden's Opinion on Appeals [Jan. 1765]," *Colden Papers,* VII, 1-7.
[69] Fernow, *Calendar of Council Minutes,* p. 510; New York Executive Council Minutes, XXIX, 33-57; *Colden Papers,* ix, 205-206; *Colden Letter Books,* I, 444-445.
[70] *New-York Gazette; or Weekly Post-Boy* (N. Y. C.), Jan. 3—Feb. 21, 1765.
[71] *The Report of an Action of Assault . . . between Thomas Forsey . . . and Waddel Cunningham . . .* (New York, 1764 [1765]); William Livingston, Receipt Book, May 9, June 29, July 31, Oct. 31, 1765, Livingston Papers, Box 8, Massachusetts Historical Society, Boston.
[72] *New-York Gazette,* Jan. 24, 1765; *New-York Mercury* (N. Y. C.), Jan. 21, 1765.

mixture of essays ranging from serious discussions of the constitutional principles at stake to crude lampoons of Colden.[73] Many of the essays were anonymous, but neither Colden nor his critics were in doubt of the real authors. "All this publishing is the Lawyers doing," gleefully observed John Watts, a member of the Council but no friend of the Lieutenant Governor. "The old Gent. has abus'd 'em by the Lump and they are determined not to let him rest."[74]

In this literary venture the Livingston triumvirate had a decided advantage over their press warfare against Colden three years earlier. Try as they might on that former occasion they had not been able to fire public enthusiasm over a subject as technical and narrow as judicial tenure. Popular support had come only from the vague recognition that some vital liberty was being curbed by the crabbed old Lieutenant Governor. The Forsey case involved something of much broader character, and in the "Sentinel," Livingston and his associates made certain that the popular meaning and the constitutional significance of Colden's actions were forcefully emphasized and loudly proclaimed. Liberty itself was at stake, the "Sentinel" trumpeted. The question of appeals was "the most momentous affair that ever engaged our attention, since the existence of this province." Colden's behavior was "arbitrary" and "unheard of," and a "scandalous abuse of the king's name and authority."[75] The right to trial by jury was imbedded in the fabric of the English constitution, "matured by ages, founded as it were on a rock, repeatedly defended against lawless encroachments by oceans of blood . . . and guarded by the most awful sanctions." Was it now to be frivolously "altered or abolished, by—the dash of a pan?"[76]

To surrender an ancient and tried privilege like trial by jury to the caprice of any governor would be to substitute despotism for law, vassalage for freedom, tyranny for justice. "From such a System, the *Star Chamber* would be a redemption." The excellency of the English constitution and the freedom of its subjects depended on the "equal poise of the several branches," Crown, Lords, and Commons. Whoever would "swallow up or impair" any was a "traitor and felon to his country." Colden's demand for appellate powers could only be construed as "a most

[73] The series ran from Feb. 28 to Aug. 29, 1765.
[74] Watts to Monckton, Feb. 23, 1765, Chalmers Papers, New York, III, 88.
[75] "Sentinel, I," *New-York Gazette*, Feb. 28, 1765.
[76] "Sentinel, III," *ibid.*, Mar. 14, 1765.

premature and superlative ebullion of Zeal for the prerogative" at the expense of popular rights.[77]

From the defense of the right to jury trials, the triumvirate moved easily into a ringing affirmation of the theory of limited government and a vigorous defense of the right of popular resistance to arbitrary rulers. No monarch had a supernatural warrant to subvert the natural liberties of mankind, nor was there any divine prohibition against resisting tyrannical abuse of power. The virtue of the English constitution lay in its guarantees of personal liberty, firmly buttressed by the "impregnable bulwark of law" and "the most awful sanctions"; "and whoever asserts the contrary is *a lyar, and the truth is not in him.*"[78]

With only slightly veiled allusions to the new Parliamentary duties, the "Sentinel" challenged its readers to regard Colden's assault on American liberties as a call to arms:

. . . let us ever be jealous of lawless encroachments. . . . Let us prize our liberty, civil and sacred, as a jewel of inestimable value . . . . Let us oppose arbitrary rule in every shape by every lawful method in our power. Never let us sit supine and indolent while our precious privileges are abridged . . . . But let us, on every such alarming occasion, rouse ourselves; and act like men . . . who know the unspeakable advantages of freedom by happy experience . . . . Let no illegal attempt against us appear inconsiderable, or unworthy our notice. A smaller will ever pave the way for a greater . . . . Let us therefore . . . crush the cockatrice in the egg . . . [and] strive to transmit to our posterity, that inestimable blessing which our ancestors have handed down to us . . . .[79]

Despite Colden's assurances to the Board of Trade that the press campaign was of little consequence—a few "licentious" and "seditious" papers by "Men of no Esteem"—the Lieutenant Governor soon became more and more "odious" even to those closest to his administration, and public tempers became more and more "incens[e]d and alarmed." "The old Body was allways dislik'd enough," observed one critic, acidly, "but now they would prefer Belzebub himself to him."[80] News of the Stamp Act

[77] "Sentinel, III, XII," *ibid.*, Mar. 14, May 16, 1765.
[78] "Sentinel, XXI," *ibid.*, July 18, 1765.
[79] *Ibid.*
[80] Robert R. Livingston to Robert Livingston, Mar. 4, 1765, Robert R. Livingston Papers, N-Y Hist. Soc.; Watts to Monckton, Nov. 10, 1764, Chalmers Papers, New York, III, 80.

did not help Colden's cause, coming as it did right in the midst of the
"Sentinel's" impassioned pleas for opposition to "arbitrary rule in every
shape" and to "lawless encroachments" upon American liberties. Like
Colden's arbitrary stand on the matter of appeals, so the Grenville ministry's radical tax program appeared as still another attempt to upset the
delicate relationship between colonies and mother country—"by the dash
of a pen."

The parallel currents of popular unrest inspired by Colden's actions
at home and Parliament's abroad reached their stormy confluence in the
fall of 1765. In an atmosphere already made electric by Colden's preparations to receive the obnoxious stamps and by the warnings of the Sons of
Liberty to any who might purchase them, came the news—"like a Thun-
derbolt"—that the Privy Council had ordered Cunningham's appeal to be
heard. The decision was regarded by some observers as even "more de-
tested" than the Stamp Act itself.[81] The resolutions of the Stamp Act
Congress, even then meeting in New York, added fuel to the fire. The
Congress's bold assertion that "trial by jury is the inherent and invaluable
right of every British subject in these colonies" appeared as a direct response to Colden's casual dismissal of the importance of jury decisions.
With characteristic obstinacy, Colden chose to ignore the reminder. He
convened the Council in mid-October, laid before it the order from London, and forced it to agree to admit Cunningham's appeal.[82]

Colden's opponents had two weapons left: the Supreme Court and the
mob. The Supreme Court struck back a week later by again refusing to
send up the proceedings in the case without a writ of error.[83] The mob
made clear its sentiments on the night of November 1, the date the Stamp
Act was scheduled to go into operation. A "Wonderfull Large Mob"
collected in the fields, attempted unsuccessfully to storm Fort George
where Colden had taken refuge, hanged the old Scotsman in effigy, in-
vaded his coach house, seized his "chariot," two sleighs, and a chair, made
a bonfire of the lot, and threw his effigy into the flames for good measure.
The rest of the Lieutenant Governor's household goods were saved only
by his son's actions in moving them into the fort; and Colden's wife and

81 Watts to Monckton, Oct. 12, 1765, Massachusetts Historical Society, *Collections*,
4th Ser., X (Boston, 1871), 579.

82 Fernow, *Calendar of Council Minutes*, p. 514, Oct. 15, 1765.

83 Keys, *Colden*, p. 319; Robert R. Livingston to Robert Livingston, Oct. 19,
1765, American Art Association, *Robert R. Livingston Sale Catalogue*, No. 39 (New
York, 1918).

children were spared only because they were rushed aboard a warship in the harbor.[84]

The end of the Forsey case was anticlimactic. The New York Assembly came to the Supreme Court's defense in a series of vigorous resolutions denouncing Colden's "mischievous Innovation" as illegal and subversive of the ancient right of trial by jury and applauding the judges and the bar for leading the opposition.[85] Before Colden found time to compose a reply, word came from London that the Board of Trade, after consulting the highest law officers of the Crown, had decided in New York's favor. Only appeals "in error" could be heard by the Governor in Council, and lest Colden or any other chief executive remain in doubt of the procedure, the royal instructions were rewritten to make the point crystal-clear.[86]

Both Colden and his critics penned their epitaphs on the Forsey affair. Colden's took the form of a lengthy pamphlet, published in 1767, in which he reiterated the familiar complaint that the lawyers had used the issue of appeals in order to discredit him personally and to pull down the whole structure of royal authority in New York.[87] At least no one could accuse Colden of inconstancy. As for the November riots, Colden was equally certain that this was the lawyers' doing. Their aim had been to capitalize on the "Spirit of Sedition" created by the Forsey case and to turn "the Rage of the Mob" against him.[88]

Colden's critics were in close agreement with him on only one count: that the Forsey case had been the "true cause of the Malice" against him. His attempt to invade the traditional right of jury trial, William Smith, Jr., observed, was a "capital Article of the People's Jealousy" and "rivetted their Abhorrence" of his "obnoxious Character." His stand on appeals "more than any other Cause" had driven the mob to its "Pitch of Madness."[89]

[84] *Montresor Journals*, pp. 336-377; *Colden Letter Books*, II, 54-56, 74-77, 80-81; Division of Archives and History, University of the State of New York, *The American Revolution in New York* (Albany, 1926), pp. 16-17.

[85] *Assembly Journals*, II, 803-806; *New-York Gazette*, Dec. 26, 1765.

[86] O'Callaghan, *N. Y. Colonial Documents*, VII, 762-764, 814-816; *Colden Papers*, VII, 95-96; Fernow, *Calendar of Council Minutes*, p. 515.

[87] *The Conduct of Cadwallader Colden . . . Relating to the Judges Commissions, Appeals to the King, and the Stamp-Duty* (1767), in *Colden Letter Books*, II, 433-467.

[88] *Colden Letter Books*, II, 2, 5, 68-78, 84-86, 89-92.

[89] Smith to Monckton, Nov. 8, 1765, Chalmers Papers, New York, IV, 19.

Neither Smith nor Colden could view the affair with detachment. There were few who could, entirely. But even the most conservative New Yorkers believed that the lawyers were right and Colden wrong. The rights of internal taxation and of jury trials were both inviolate "privileges of Englishmen." To deny them would make "the Atlantick . . . the difference between a Freeman and a Slave which God forbid." The lawyers had voiced the same sentiments more eloquently in the press: "Without liberty no man can be a subject. He is a slave."[90]

[90] Watts to Monckton, Feb. 26, 1765, *Watts Letter Book*, p. 336; "Sentinel, III," *New-York Gazette*, Mar. 14, 1765.

The Coming of the Revolution in Virginia: Britain's Challenge to Virginia's Ruling Class, 1763-1776

Thad W. Tate*

CONTEMPLATING the approach of independence in May 1776, Landon Carter, Virginia planter and retired Burgess, recorded in his diary that the Revolution was an unfortunate contest which Great Britain "certainly began with America by attempting to tax her out of the constitutional road."[1] Carter took a view of the predominant issue leading to the American Revolution that every Patriot leader in Virginia shared. All the major public resolutions, addresses, and petitions of the colony spoke against a threat to "ancient, legal, and constitutional Rights."[2]

The final statement, a bill of indictment against George III in the preamble of the 1776 constitution, comprised twenty-two charges, which stand as an official summary of the issues as the colony saw them.[3] Five of the twenty-two related to punitive actions taken after the beginning of hostilities by Dunmore or by British military authorities elsewhere and did not, therefore, concern basic issues from which the conflict had arisen. Two other accusations were too general to relate to specific grievances. Of the remain-

* Mr. Tate is a member of the Department of History, the College of William and Mary. A version of this article was presented at the Ninth Conference on Early American History, Cleveland, Ohio, Mar. 25, 1960. The research for it was completed while the author was a member of the staff of Colonial Williamsburg, Inc.

[1] Entry of May 29, 1776, "Diary of Col. Landon Carter," *William and Mary College Quarterly*, 1st Ser., XVIII (1909-10), 43.

[2] The quotation is from the resolutions of the House of Burgesses creating the Committee of Correspondence, Mar. 12, 1773, in Henry R. McIlwaine and John P. Kennedy, eds., *Journals of the House of Burgesses of Virginia* (Richmond, 1905-15), *1773-1776*, p. 28. Other important statements derived from constitutional arguments are in *ibid.*, *1761-1765*, pp. 302-304; *1766-1769*, pp. 23-24, 165-171, 214; *1770-1772*, pp. 101-102; *1773-1776*, pp. 28, 124; Purdie and Dixon's *Virginia Gazette* (Williamsburg), July 21, 1768, Aug. 11, 1774.

[3] *Ordinance Passed at a General Convention . . . of Virginia . . . Monday the 6th of May Anno Dom: 1776* (Williamsburg [1776]), 5-7.

ing fifteen allegations, which were the heart of the case, fourteen attacked British political or military policies. Nine of the fourteen criticized restrictions on colonial legislatures, two objected to abridgment of legal rights of the individual, and three dealt with threats to liberty from the use of armed force. Only a single article from the entire list concerned economic conditions—a complaint against the restriction of colonial trade with non-British ports.[4] Apparently the Virginia protest explained the Revolution as a defense of constitutional rights against their subversion by the British government. Moreover, it made no distinction between measures that affected Virginia directly and those that seemed, by their threat to another colony, to raise the prospect of future tyranny over all. The Virginians seemed content to say they fought over a common issue.

Many historians have been dissatisfied with this answer. In part, they have been influenced by broad currents in historical writing, such as the imperialist view of the colonial period, the economic interpretation of history, and the belief that the American Revolution was primarily an internal conflict, all of which have questioned the traditional constitutional explanation. Doubt has come, too, from certain local characteristics of the Revolution in Virginia. It has not been easy to understand why a colony with Virginia's reputation for conservatism and loyalty reacted with such force and rapidity, when the actual burdens of the British acts fell more lightly upon Virginia than upon many other colonies. The Stamp Act and the Townshend duties, of course, affected all colonies equally; and Virginia was one of the colonies that the framers of the Currency Act of 1764 had particularly in mind. The Sugar Act, however, seemed likely to harm Virginia mostly through higher costs for a gentleman's favorite solace—good Madeira wine.[5] No military commander came to quarter his troops upon unwilling Virginians. The Crown had long enjoyed independent sources

[4] Thomas Jefferson, the author of the list of charges in the Virginia Constitution, made a more sweeping condemnation of imperial economic policies in *Summary View of the Rights of British America* . . . (London, 1774). The briefer statement with only a single mention of economic grievances was, however, the version that gained the approval of the Virginia Convention. See Julian P. Boyd, ed., *The Papers of Thomas Jefferson* (Princeton, 1950———), I, 123-124, 329-365, 377-378.

[5] "Proceedings of the Virginia Committee of Correspondence, 1759-'67," *Virginia Magazine of History and Biography*, XII (1904-5), 6, 9. For a suggestion that the Sugar Act might even benefit Virginia economically, see Charles Steuart to Messrs. [William] Aitchison and [James] Parker, May 4, 1764, Parker Family Papers, Liverpool Record Office, Liverpool, Eng. (available on microfilm at Colonial Williamsburg, Inc., Research Library).

of revenue from which to pay royal salaries within the colony.[6] "Customs racketeering" by the American Board of Customs Commissioners and its agents was possibly not so severe as elsewhere—the General Court, for one thing, never issued general writs of assistance.[7] Finally, the Coercive Acts neither affected Virginia directly nor, in the Massachusetts Government Act, imposed any conditions upon the Bay Colony that had not long prevailed in Virginia. Such considerations have caused speculation about the candor of Virginia Patriots and about the accuracy of interpreting the Revolution in that colony solely as a contest for political liberty.

Although no one has made a full-scale attack on the constitutional interpretation as it applied to Virginia, a number of scholars have emphasized other issues. Among the additional sources of conflict to which they have pointed are the existence of earlier disputes, antedating the taxation measures of George Grenville; the massive indebtedness of the planters to British merchants; the clash between imperial policy and speculative interests of Virginians in western lands; and the divisions between radical Patriots of the stripe of Patrick Henry and the entrenched leadership of the House of Burgesses. The over-all effect has been to reduce the importance of the issue of colonial rights, as it developed after 1763, by suggesting either that it was only one among a number of points in dispute or that it was largely an expression of deeper-seated and more material grievances.

Those who believe that there were important beginnings of the Revolution in Virginia before the peace of 1763 have placed their emphasis upon

87

[6] Note, for example, the reputation for loyalty on the part of Virginia implicit in Halifax's observation that it was "the only province in North America who had granted a permanent revenue to the crown for the support of government." Quoted in Keith B. Berwick, Loyalties in Crisis: A Study of the Attitudes of Virginians in the Revolution (unpubl. Ph.D. diss., University of Chicago, 1959), 51.

[7] Treasury, Ser. 1, 501, foll. 181-186, 261-265, 270-275, 308-311, Public Record Office, London (available on microfilm at Colonial Williamsburg, Inc., Research Library); John Randolph to Commissioners of Customs, May 15, 1769, Colonial Office Papers, Ser. 5, 1347, fol. 109, Public Record Office (available on microfilm at Colonial Williamsburg, Inc., Research Library). The fullest discussion of the Virginia General Court's refusal to issue writs of assistance is in Oliver M. Dickerson, "Writs of Assistance as a Cause of the Revolution," in Richard B. Morris, ed., The Era of the American Revolution (New York, 1939), 67-73. Dickerson's The Navigation Acts and the American Revolution (Philadelphia, 1951), 255, finds little evidence of customs racketeering in Virginia. There is a suggestion of the relative moderation of vice-admiralty court activity in Virginia in Carl Ubbelohde, The Vice-Admiralty Courts and the American Revolution (Chapel Hill, 1960), 93-94, 156-167.

the only serious political controversy at this time—the disputes over the Twopenny Acts, otherwise known as the Parsons' Cause. In the disallowance of these laws they have seen the making of an imperial dispute that commenced as early as 1759 and led directly to Virginia's involvement in the Revolution.[8]

The Twopenny Acts were passed by the Assembly in 1755 and again in 1758 to relieve taxpayers of the necessity of satisfying their public obligations in tobacco during two years of short crops and abnormally high prices. Both laws permitted the commutation of such payments at a rate of two pence per pound of tobacco—well below its market value.[9] The 1755 law was to remain in effect only ten months, and the 1758 law, twelve. Among the obligations affected were the salaries of the clergy of the Established Church, which had been fixed at sixteen thousand pounds of tobacco yearly by a 1748 law that had been confirmed by the Crown. Although the royal instructions stipulated that laws thus confirmed could not be altered

88

[8] There are a number of detailed accounts of the Parsons' Cause, many of which vary in their emphasis. Richard L. Morton, *Colonial Virginia* (Chapel Hill, 1960), II, 751-819, is especially good for its explanation of the background of ill feeling against the Anglican clergy in Virginia; Bernhard Knollenberg, *Origin of the American Revolution: 1759-1766*, rev. ed. (New York, 1961), 57-66, gives strong emphasis to the Parsons' Cause as a significant source of discontent in Virginia; George Maclaren Brydon, *Virginia's Mother Church and the Political Conditions under Which It Grew* (Philadelphia and Richmond, 1947-52), II, 288-320, stresses the effect on the clergy; Robert Douthat Meade, *Patrick Henry: Patriot in the Making* (Philadelphia and New York, 1957), 114-138, has a very full treatment of the suit by the Rev. James Maury in which Henry was involved; Lawrence Henry Gipson, *The Coming of the Revolution, 1763-1775* (New York, 1954), 46-54, treats the Parsons' Cause as an aspect of the question of planter debts; the same author's more recent *The Triumphant Empire: Thunder-Clouds Gather in the West, 1763-1766* (New York, 1961), Volume X of *The British Empire before the American Revolution*, 146-157, contains a suggestive treatment of the passage of the Twopenny Acts as part of a broad, determined effort by the Virginia House of Burgesses to modify the constitutional authority of the Crown in the colony; Glenn Curtis Smith, "The Parsons' Cause, 1755-65," *Tyler's Quarterly Historical and Genealogical Magazine*, XXI (1939-40), 140-171, 291-306, is the fullest discussion of the pamphlet controversy. Two studies of exceptional importance which do not stress the Parsons' Cause as a cause of the Revolution are Arthur P. Scott, "The Constitutional Aspects of the 'Parson's Cause,'" *Political Science Quarterly*, XXXI (1916), 558-577, which is particularly good in treating the rather questionable legal grounds of the lawsuits of the clergy, and Joseph Henry Smith, *Appeals to the Privy Council from the American Plantations* (New York, 1950), 607-626, which gives a very thorough analysis of all the legal aspects of the Parsons' Cause.

[9] William Waller Hening, ed., *The Statutes at Large: Being a Collection of All the Laws of Virginia . . .* (Richmond, 1809-23), VI, 568-569; VII, 240-241.

without the consent of the Crown and required the insertion of a suspending clause in any amending acts, the Virginia legislature included no such clause in either of the Twopenny Acts. To have done so, as defenders of the measure later pointed out, would have kept them from going into immediate effect and would have defeated the whole purpose of the legislation. Lieutenant Governor Francis Fauquier realized that he was violating his instructions in assenting to the 1758 measure, but he readily approved it because there had been no repercussions from the approval of the 1755 law by his predecessor Robert Dinwiddie.[10]

Passage of the 1758 act immediately evoked strong opposition from the clergy. Had the law not been enacted, the high-priced tobacco would have meant a substantial addition to their income. To avoid its loss a number of ministers determined to resist the Twopenny legislation. Their opposition took several forms: a convention of some, though not all, of the clergy;[11] a petition to the Privy Council requesting that the 1758 act be declared null and void from its inception;[12] a series of lawsuits for the recovery of the full market value of their assigned quota of tobacco;[13] and a pamphlet and newspaper controversy.[14] In all of these measures the chief clerical spokesman was the Reverend John Camm, Professor of Divinity at the College of William and Mary and rector of Yorkhampton Parish in nearby York County. It was he who largely instigated the complaints to England, carried the test suit to the Privy Council on appeal, and defended

[10] Morton, *Colonial Virginia*, II, 682, 784-785; Knollenberg, *Origin of the American Revolution*, 57-58; Gipson, *The Triumphant Empire*, 145-147; J. H. Smith, *Appeals to Privy Council*, 608-611.

[11] Richard Bland, *A Letter to the Clergy in Virginia* . . . (Williamsburg, 1760), 3; William Robinson to the Bishop of London, Aug. 12, 1765, in William Stevens Perry, ed., *Historical Collections Relating to the American Colonial Church* ([Hartford], 1870), I, 509-510.

[12] Memorial of the Clergy of Virginia to the Board of Trade, C.O. 5/1329, foll. 119-120.

[13] Morton, *Colonial Virginia*, II, 807-812, and J. H. Smith, *Appeals to Privy Council*, 615-621, are the best accounts of the initiation of all the suits and of their progress through the courts of the colony.

[14] The pamphlets in order of their appearance are: Landon Carter, *A Letter to the Right Reverend Father in God the Lord B——p of L——n* . . . (Williamsburg, 1759); Bland, *Letter to the Clergy in Virginia*; John Camm, *A Single and Distinct View of the Act, Vulgarly Entitled, the Twopenny Act* . . . (Annapolis, 1763); Landon Carter, *The Rector Detected* . . . (Williamsburg, 1764); John Camm, *A Review of the Rector Detected* . . . (Williamsburg, 1764); Richard Bland, *The Colonel Dismounted; or the Rector Vindicated* (Williamsburg, 1764); John Camm, *Critical Remarks on a Letter Ascribed to Common Sense* (Williamsburg, 1765).

the clerical position in writing against two outspoken burgesses, Landon Carter and Richard Bland.

The resultant controversy continued from 1759 until 1766, and in its course the clerics directly challenged the competence of the Virginia Assembly to pass the Twopenny Acts. Both the timing—its later stages coincided with the taxation dispute with the home government—and the underlying issue—the limits of the legislative power of a colonial assembly—have made it easy to see the Parsons' Cause as one of the first steps of approaching revolution. Patrick Henry's vehement argument in the best-known of the clerical suits that a king who would annul a beneficial law degenerated into a tyrant seems to support this view.[15] The same is true of the more sober arguments advanced by Carter and Bland. They justified the Twopenny Acts on several grounds that touched upon the nature of the imperial constitution: the necessity of the legislation to protect the welfare of the colony, the right of the people to be governed by laws made by their elected representatives, and the claim that a governor's instructions from the Crown were not obligatory and did not have the force of law.[16]

Yet it is possible to see the Parsons' Cause in a much different light by considering its full scope, including the progress of the dispute in England as well as in the colony. Patrick Henry's courtroom oration was, after all, only a single episode, occurring in a local case in which the court's initial finding in favor of the clergyman was at variance with the general outcome of the cases.[17] The pamphlet warfare was also a local controversy within the colony and did not directly involve any British officials or poltical leaders. Far more central to the nature and outcome of the Parsons' Cause were the two appeals to the Privy Council—one legislative and the other judicial—that John Camm instituted. These show the Parsons' Cause as primarily a dispute between the colony and its clergy, not between colony and mother country.[18]

After the failure of every appeal within the colony itself, Camm sailed

[15] James Maury to John Camm, Dec. 12, 1763, in Ann Maury, ed., *Memoirs of a Huguenot Family* (New York, 1853), 421.

[16] G. C. Smith, "The Parsons' Cause," 169-171, 291-306, summarizes the constitutional arguments of Bland and Carter.

[17] J. H. Smith, *Appeals to Privy Council*, 617-620.

[18] *Ibid.*, 611-624. In this discussion Smith treats the legal aspects of both cases with far greater precision than earlier accounts and thereby clears the way for a better understanding of whether the home government ruled largely in favor of the

90

for England in either late 1758 or early 1759 to represent the clergy in an effort to have the Twopenny Acts declared null and void from the moment of their passage.[19] The memorial of the clergy which Camm presented to the Privy Council did not ask for the customary disallowance, because the clergy knew that it would not take effect before the expiration of the laws. By customary usage the laws would thereby have the force of law until their expiration or disallowance. A decision that the acts had never possessed the force of law would, on the other hand, open the way for recovery of the full value of the clerical salaries. On August 10, 1759, however, after full hearings before the Board of Trade and before one of its own committees, the Privy Council refused to do more than disallow the laws.[20] Thereupon James Abercromby, who had represented the colony during the hearings, reported with evident satisfaction that "the point was determined in our Favour (to wit) to go no further than the Repeal."[21] Abercromby's attitude reflects something that is often forgotten about the Privy Council decision: that disallowance represented a defeat for the clergy far more than it did for the Virginia Assembly. Certainly Virginians would have preferred not to hear the criticism that the Privy Councilors made of their actions, but it was criticism that had no practical effect.

There were, however, aspects of the decision that created the possibility of more serious objections from Virginia. The action of the Privy Council had, after all, not gone so far as to approve the Twopenny Acts. The Privy Council, moreover, had coupled its disallowance with a tart instruction to Fauquier that he would incur the highest displeasure and face recall if he failed in the future to observe strictly article sixteen of his instructions directing him to assent to no act of less than two years duration and to no act without a suspending clause that repealed any other act, whether confirmed by the King or not.[22] This action by the Privy Council posed a definite future threat for the colony, to which the Assembly responded in the "Humble Representation of the Council and Burgesses of Virginia,"

---

clergy or the colony both in disallowing the laws and in upholding the decision of the General Court of Virginia in Camm's lawsuit.

[19] Francis Fauquier to Board of Trade, Jan. 9, 1759, C.O. 5/1329, foll. 119-120.

[20] William L. Grant and James B. Munro, eds., *Acts of the Privy Council of England, Colonial Series* (London, 1908-12), IV, 420-421 (Aug. 29, 1759).

[21] To John Blair, Aug. 3, 1759, James Abercomby Letter book, Virginia State Library, Richmond.

[22] Leonard W. Labaree, ed., *Royal Instructions to British Colonial Governors, 1670-1776* (New York and London, 1935), I, 128-131.

prepared in October 1760. The sixteenth article of the governor's instructions had not been observed for a long time, and its enforcement now, the Assembly observed, would "involve the Colony in the most insuperable Difficulties."[23]

Admittedly, the renewed emphasis on a long-dormant royal instruction was a source of concern—and perhaps a harbinger of the over-all shift in imperial policy just getting underway.[24] The tone of the Assembly's representation, however, does not suggest that Virginians yet saw either the disallowance of the Twopenny Acts or the additional instruction as part of a new and general restriction on colonial rights. The language of the document is mild, and its nature is explanatory. "It was not our Intention," the members of the Assembly declared, "by any Act of our's to lessen the Influence and Prerogative of the Crown upon which the Preservation of our privileges and the happy and rightful Administration of the Government depend."[25] The reaction of the colony was not dissimilar to that produced by comparable imperial actions earlier in the century.

The sharpest language of the Humble Representation was reserved for those who were accused of having misrepresented the position of the colony in England, thus constituting a scarcely veiled attack on John Camm and the Virginia clergy. The greater part of the reaction within the colony to the outcome of the Privy Council hearings was, in fact, directed against the ministers. First of all, Camm's return from Britain was the occasion for a well-known and explosive incident in which Fauquier committed the supreme insult of pointing the cleric out to his slaves and ordering them never again to admit him beyond the gates of the Governor's Palace.[26] Another irritant was the circulation within Virginia of the Bishop of London's letter of June 14, 1759, which he had originally written to the Board of Trade in support of the clerical request for nullification of the Twopenny Acts.[27] It was a copy of this letter which stung Carter and Bland

[23] C.O. 5/1330, foll. 51-53. The Assembly also sent a long letter to its agent with an order to work for countermanding of the additional instruction to Fauquier, but this letter is a paraphrase of the Humble Representation. Committee of Correspondence to Montagu, Nov. 5, 1760, "Proceedings of the Virginia Committee of Correspondence, 1759-'67," Va. Mag. of Hist. and Biog., XI (1903-4), 14-16.

[24] The Privy Council, moreover, in 1761 recommended against granting the request of the Humble Representation for modification of the new instruction. C.O. 5/1368, foll. 179-185.

[25] C.O. 5/1330, fol. 53.

[26] Morton, Colonial Virginia, II, 802.

[27] The letter is in C.O. 5/1329, foll. 131-133A.

into initiating the pamphlet war, although by this time it had failed in the immediate purpose of influencing the Privy Council decision. Still a third cause for anger was the institution of several suits by Virginia clergymen to recover their full salaries.[28] Vexing as all these actions of the clergy were, none of them had anything to do with specific governmental policies adopted by imperial officials.

This fact is even more clear from an examination of the clergy's attempt to recover their money through the courts. Thinking one of the Privy Councilors had suggested he might still recover his money at law, Camm—and ultimately at least four other clergymen—brought suits in various county courts of the colony. In effect, they sought either by deliberate misrepresentation or out of honest misunderstanding to contend that the Order in Council of 1759 had been what it was not: a declaration of nullity rather than a disallowance. Camm's suit, going on appeal from the General Court of Virginia to the Privy Council, became the test case. A committee of the Privy Council decided against him in 1766. The general impression has been that he lost on a question of procedure rather than of right—the implication is that the committee members thought his case valid but found a technical ground for denying his appeal in order to soothe the Virginians without creating a precedent. Nevertheless, the notes of Robert Walpole, clerk for the Privy Council, contain contradictory evidence. As Walpole recorded it, the committee ruled that the 1758 act "passed regularly in the regular course of Legislation" and was "a Law . . . till the disapprobation of the King in Council is signified in the Province." Whatever the basis of the decision, the Virginians had once and for all carried the day against the clergy in the Parsons' Cause.[29]

The view that the dispute over the Twopenny Acts was in its essence a dispute between Virginia and Great Britain depends upon two assumptions: that Patrick Henry's plea was a major event of the controversy in which he and the popular opinion that supported him defied the Privy Council decision of 1759 and that Virginians contended with British officials who generally—at least until a conciliatory gesture in 1766—sup-

[28] Long before returning from England Camm had written ahead to his attorney to bring suit, and the General Assembly moved before the end of 1759 to support the vestry of Camm's parish in their defense. Morton, *Colonial Virginia*, II, 797-798.

[29] Camm's case is treated through its final outcome in great detail by J. H. Smith, *Appeals to Privy Council*, 618-624. The statement of Robert Walpole is quoted by Smith from War Office Papers, Ser. 1, 404, fol. 66, Public Record Office.

ported the clerical arguments. Both are in large part erroneous, although it is possible that the clergy themselves helped obscure the issue in Virginia somewhat and although they did enjoy powerful support in England from bishops, merchants, and a few officials of the government.

There is an alternate set of propositions that serves much more accurately to delineate the nature of the Parsons' Cause. First, the dispute originated solely within the colony, between clergy and local political leaders, and was not the result of any deliberate act of imperial policy. The home government, moreover, became involved beyond the routine review of legislation only at the instigation of the Virginia clergy and their friends in England. Whether the action of Crown officials in the Parsons' Cause was, or was understood by Virginians to be, a part of the general tightening of colonial policy that began at much the same time is problematical. In the long run, the Virginians used the machinery of imperial administration, and they lost nothing by it. Two royal governors sided with them, and the Privy Council twice decided more in their favor than against them. If there was a genuine constitutional issue involved, it was that of the additional instruction to Fauquier in 1759, which, as it turned out, was a potential rather than an actual grievance. Unquestionably the pamphlets of Bland and Carter expressed many of the same ideas that soon appeared in more genuine Revolutionary disputes. They were, however, principally answering the extravagant claims of John Camm and the Bishop of London, whom no one mistook for official interpreters of the British constitution. Furthermore, they wrote in part after the crisis of the Sugar Act and the Stamp Act had begun to affect the controversy. In retrospect the Parsons' Cause may have seemed to some Virginians a grievance against Great Britain. Certainly, had British politicians been observant, it could have warned them of the extent of colonial constitutional claims.[30] This, however, was the extent of its relationship to the Revolution. It was not in the beginning a major issue between Virginia and the home government. At most, it was contributory rather than decisive to the advent of the Revolution in Virginia.

The Parsons' Cause is sometimes also seen as an economic issue, in which Virginians took a first step toward revolution by their reaction to alleged British interference with an effort at debtor relief.[31] But, since dis-

[30] In this connection see the conclusion in Scott, "Constitutional Aspects of 'Parson's Cause,'" 577.

[31] Gipson, *Coming of the Revolution*, 45-54.

94

allowance occurred after the expiration of the Twopenny Acts and did not affect their validity during the time they were in force, the British action did not have any practical economic effect. Still the question of whether planter debts influenced the coming of the Revolution, being far broader than a single incident, demands further consideration. Certainly the endless discussions of increasing debts, depressed tobacco prices, and shortages of currency that occupy so large a part of the surviving correspondence of Virginians suggests the possibility of a link between economic conditions in the colony and the Revolutionary movement. Indeed, by 1763 planter debts were already an issue of long standing, as the running controversy in the 1750's over the rate of exchange between Virginia currency and sterling money attested.[32]

In the 1760's and 1770's there are two aspects of the debt question. One centers around the Currency Act of 1764, which extended to the other continental colonies the 1751 restrictions on New England forbidding further emissions of paper money as legal tender.[33] Virginia, where the rate of exchange with sterling money had seldom kept pace with depreciation of the paper bills, had been a principal offender; and the demand for the statute was largely a result of pressure from British merchants who traded there and who were displeased with the persistent refusal of the House of Burgesses to comply with an instruction of 1759 requiring the removal of the legal tender provisions of previous currency issues. Men like Robert Beverley were consequently bitter at the "Machinations of those very Merchants who draw their Subsistence, as it were from our very Vitals."[34] After passage of the Currency Act Virginians were still incensed at the merchants but were surprisingly unconcerned about the act itself. In their communications with Virginia agent Edward Montagu, members of the

95

---

[32] It is this earlier period that is emphasized in Lawrence H. Gipson, "Virginia Planter Debts before the American Revolution," *Va. Mag. of Hist. and Biog.*, LXIX (1961), 259-277, and in his *The Triumphant Empire*, chap. 8. Jack P. Greene and Richard M. Jellison, "The Currency Act of 1764 in Imperial-Colonial Relations, 1764-1776," *Wm. and Mary Qtly.*, 3d Ser., XVIII (1961), 485-488, treat the same period as an immediate background to the Currency Act of 1764. See also Morton, *Colonial Virginia*, II, 745-749, and William Z. Ripley, *The Financial History of Virginia, 1609-1776* (New York, 1893), 153-159.

[33] The fullest treatment of the relationship between the Currency Act and the Revolutionary movement is Greene and Jellison, "Currency Act of 1764 in Imperial-Colonial Relations."

[34] Beverley to John Bland, Apr. 5, 1763, Robert Beverley Letter book, Library of Congress, Washington.

committee of correspondence expressed no hostility to the act. Rather, they were relieved that, by failing to do more than to demand retirement on schedule of the depreciated money in circulation, it had not gone as far as the merchants demanded.[85] As a result, a sufficient currency for at least a time remained in circulation, a circumstance to which the general lack of immediate protest in Virginia possibly owed a great deal. Beyond a few outbursts against the merchants, the immediate reaction to the Currency Act was mild.

If the prohibition of future paper money issues failed to stir initial hostility against the home government itself, it nevertheless soon created a shortage of circulating currency that brought occasional expressions of dissatisfaction and an unsuccessful attempt by the House of Burgesses in 1768 to obtain permission for a new issue of £200,000.[86] Ultimately, Virginia found ways to mitigate its currency problem through such expedients as non-legal tender issues in 1769 and 1771;[37] and, if there had been sufficient time before Independence for the Parliamentary Act of 1773, which modified the Currency Act of 1764, to run its course, the currency issue might well have disappeared completely. As it is, it is difficult to see the Currency Act as a major grievance in Virginia or as one which the colony believed it could not solve within the normal imperial framework.[88]

The second part of the debt question concerns the debts themselves— the ever increasing sums due British merchants as a consequence of the fortunes of the tobacco trade.[89] If a link does exist between them and the Revolutionary protest, it is not easy to establish, for the Virginians never included complaints about economic conditions in their petitions and resolutions. Between 1764 and 1766 Virginians occasionally grumbled about debts. Governor Fauquier found the people "uneasy, peevish, and

[85] "Proceedings of the Virginia Committee of Correspondence, 1759-'67," *Va. Mag. of Hist. and Biog.*, XII (1904-5), 6, 11.

[86] Francis Fauquier to Earl of Halifax, June 14, 1765, C.O. 5/1345, foll. 80-81; C.O. 5/1332, foll. 30-34; Board of Trade to Crown, June 10, 1768, C. O. 5/1346, foll. 9-12; Greene and Jellison, "Currency Act of 1764 in Imperial-Colonial Relations," 503.

[37] Hening, ed., *Statutes at Large*, VIII, 346-348, 501-503.

[88] Greene and Jellison, "Currency Act of 1764 in Imperial-Colonial Relations," 518.

[89] In addition to the emphasis upon the relevance of planter debts in the works of Professor Lawrence H. Gipson, cited in nn. 31 and 32 above, the study by Isaac S. Harrell of *Loyalism in Virginia . . .* (Durham, 1926), also stresses the debt question but concentrates upon its outcome in the period after 1776.

ready to murmur at every Occurrence" because of their debts, and he attributed some of the continued unrest after repeal of the Stamp Act to economic hardship.[40] Again, most of the hostility seemed directed against the merchants; the debts were not the occasion for any contests with the government.[41] Probably debtors welcomed the closing of the courts that had occurred while the Stamp Act was in force, because it prevented suits by creditors and put pressure on merchants to work for repeal of the stamp duties.[42] But the benefit to debtors was almost certainly a by-product and not a cause of the suspension of the courts, which had occurred very widely to avoid the use of stamped paper. A number of inferior courts, moreover, reopened in Virginia before the repeal of the Stamp Act.[43]

97

Certainly neither in the period of the Stamp Act nor in the crisis over the Townshend duties did Virginians make a full-scale attack upon the British navigation system and the closed trade by which it presumably held them irretrievably in debt.[44] In the very letter to George Washington in which he outlined his proposals for the nonimportation agreement of 1769, George Mason wrote that "our supplying our Mother Country with gross Materials, and taking her Manufactures in Return is the true Chain of Connection between Us; these are the Bands, which, if not broken by Oppression, must long hold Us together, by maintaining a constant Reciprocation of Interest."[45]

The attitude of Virginians concerning their debts grew harsher in the spring and summer of 1774. These months mark a distinct shift to a new phase of the debt question. The commercial system was still not an object of criticism, but there was frank discussion of withholding the payment

---

[40] Fauquier to Earl of Halifax, June 14, 1765, C.O. 5/1345, foll. 80-81; Fauquier to Commissioners for Trade, C.O. 5/1331, foll. 149-150.

[41] Fauquier to Secretary of State, Nov. 18, 1766, C.O. 5/1345, foll. 157-159; Purdie and Dixon's *Virginia Gazette,* Oct. 30, 1766.

[42] George Washington to Francis Dandridge, Sept. 20, 1765, in John C. Fitzpatrick, ed., *The Writings of George Washington* (Washington, 1931-44), II, 425-426; Richard Henry Lee to Landon Carter, Feb. 24, 1766, in James Curtis Ballagh, ed., *The Letters of Richard Henry Lee* (New York, 1911-14), I, 14-15.

[43] See the general discussion on the closing of the courts in twelve of the colonies in Edmund S. Morgan and Helen M. Morgan, *The Stamp Act Crisis: Prologue to Revolution* (Chapel Hill, 1953), 168-179. For the Virginia information see 172-173.

[44] One of the few exceptions is the letter by "A Virginian," Rind's *Virginia Gazette* (Williamsburg), Dec. 11, 1766.

[45] George Mason to George Washington, Apr. 5, 1769, George Washington Papers, Lib. Cong.

of debts.[46] Not all of it came as accusations from diehard Tories like James Parker, whose constant contention was that "the more a man is in debit, the greater patriot he is."[47] Even Parker must be believed, however, when he describes in some detail the advocacy of nonpayment by George Mason, Patrick Henry, Richard Henry Lee, and Robert Carter Nicholas.[48] Feeling reached the point where in November Patriots suspended a bag of feathers over a barrel of tar on the main street of Williamsburg and dragged offending merchants before it to recant their crimes against the people.[49] Moreover, the county courts and the General Court stopped hearing civil cases, giving as their reason the failure of the Assembly during its brief session in May to renew the law fixing court fees.[50] The next year British subjects, permitted to return home by the Virginia Convention, were forbidden to take with them papers or account books belonging to anyone in Great Britain.[51]

The closing of the courts—the most substantial of these actions since it blocked suits for debts—may have served as a weapon in the political struggle, as it had in part in 1765. Some merchants in Virginia conceded that its principal purpose was simply to force the merchants in Great Britain to use their influence against the repressive measures of the ministry instead of supporting them.[52] Any exact apportionment between its politi-

---

[46] Francis Lightfoot Lee to William Lee, July 3, 1774, Lee-Ludwell Papers, Virginia Historical Society, Richmond; James Parker to Charles Steuart, May 17, 1774, Charles Steuart Papers, National Library of Scotland, Edinburgh (available on microfilm at Colonial Williamsburg, Inc., Research Library).

[47] James Parker to Charles Steuart, June 7, 1774, Charles Steuart Papers.

[48] James Parker to Charles Steuart, postcript of June 17, 1774, to letter of June 7, 1774, ibid.

[49] James Parker to Charles Steuart, Nov. 14, 1774, Parker Family Papers; Parker to Steuart, Nov. 27, 1774, Steuart Papers.

[50] See, for example, Edmund Randolph, History of Virginia, Va. Hist. Soc.; William Reynolds to George F. Norton, June 3, 1774, William Reynolds Letter book, Lib. Cong.; Charles Yates to John Hardy, Dec. 1774, Charles Yates Letter book, Alderman Library, University of Virginia, Charlottesville.

[51] The Proceedings of the Convention and Delegates for the Counties and Corporations in the Colony of Virginia . . . on the 20th of March, 1775 . . . (Richmond, 1816), 77.

[52] Harry Piper to Dixon and Littledale, June 9, 1774, Harry Piper Letter book, Alderman Library. Piper wrote that "it is also proposed to stop all proceedings in the Courts of Justice with regard to the recovery of Debts, so that You see the Merchants are to be distressed at all events in order to make them Active in getting the Acts Repealed." See also Charles Yates to Samuel and William Vernon, Oct. 5, 1774, Charles Yates Letter book.

cal and economic purposes is impossible, but obviously political pressure on the merchants played some part.[53] On the other hand, the atmosphere in 1774 did differ from that of 1765. There was more open complaint about debts, and by 1773 the tobacco trade had entered a new period of depression, bringing a consequent restriction on credit. If there was, however, a genuine economic conflict, it appeared at a late stage in the advance toward revolution, when public sentiment had become sufficiently inflamed to aggravate latent grievances.

In sum, there seems little doubt that there was—and had been for a long time—feeling by the planters on the subject of their financial obligations. That it constituted a basic issue in bringing on the Revolution is questionable. Virginians directed hostility over the debts against the merchants rather than against the economic policies of the government, which in all its measures after 1763 actually exerted less pressure on the matter of debts than it had sometimes done earlier. For most of these years the colonists agitated the debt issue correspondingly less. And in the last five years of the 1760's the Assembly even enacted a few minor safeguards against efforts of debtors to escape their obligations.[54] Only with the interruption of the courts in 1774 did hostility grow notably sharper and did Virginia move to obstruct outright the collection of debts. The debt issue in short, does not loom particularly large in the years of political conflict with Great Britain. At best, the planter debts were an underlying source of difficulty brought to the surface only late in the Revolutionary crisis under the stimulus of a deepening political crisis.

Virginia had another economic interest—speculation in western lands—which the post-1763 measures of the imperial government affected more directly. The land claims of Virginia were sweeping, and many of the leaders of the colony had acquired a stake in their exploitation. The series of British directives, beginning with the Proclamation Line of 1763, that restricted the confirmation of new grants or the establishment of new settlements in the West ran counter to the plans of Virginians for further acquisitions and profitable sales. Even where lands were to be opened,

99

[53] The point is discussed in some detail in Emory G. Evans, "Planter Indebtedness and the Coming of the Revolution in Virginia," paper delivered at Southern Historical Association Annual Meeting, Chattanooga, Tenn., Nov. 9, 1961, and scheduled for publication. Mr. Evans gives an extended treatment of the debt question from a point of view basically sympathetic with that expressed in this paper.

[54] Hening, ed., *Statutes at Large*, VIII, 118-123, 240-241, 326-332.

Virginia investors faced a contest with British rivals. Yet, the West no more figured as an initial issue in the Revolutionary controversy in Virginia than did planter debts. On land questions the colony could usually count upon the royal governor to take its side.[55] Furthermore, the British allowed settlement in some areas west of the mountains by 1769 and never effectively interfered with it elsewhere. And Virginians, willing to trust their bargaining power with the home government, never questioned the Crown's rights to issue land grants.[56]

Only in the already explosive situation of 1774 did the problem of the West attract complaints.[57] In February of that year Dunmore, along with the other governors, received instructions to sell lands only at public auction, at a quintupled minimum price, and at twice the old rate for quitrents.[58] These requirements, unpopular to a degree that had not been true of earlier British actions on the West, were the first to which Patriot leaders in Virginia seriously protested.[59] As a potential grievance that failed to reach important proportions until the last stages of the con-

[55] Richard Orr Curry, "Lord Dunmore and the West: A Re-evalution," *West Virginia History*, XIX (1958), 231-243, treats Dunmore as a strong champion of colonial "rights" so far as western lands were concerned.

[56] From the extensive literature on the West and the American Revolution the following are most relevant to the specific question of the degree to which British policy in the West influenced the causes of the Revolutionary controversy in Virginia: Clarence W. Alvord, *The Mississippi Valley in British Politics* (Cleveland, 1917), which emphasizes the general importance of the West; the same author's "Virginia and the West, an Interpretation," *Mississippi Valley Historical Review*, III (1916), 19-38, which applies the same argument more specifically to Virginia; Harrell, *Loyalism in Virginia*, 7-22, which briefly but strongly supports the same view; St. George L. Sioussat, "The Breakdown of the Royal Management of Lands in the Southern Provinces, 1773-1775," *Agricultural History*, III (1929), 67-98, which covers in more detail than anyone else the reaction to British western policy after 1774; Thomas Perkins Abernethy, *Western Lands and the American Revolution* (New York, 1937), which minimizes the importance of the West as a cause of the Revolution in Virginia; and John R. Alden, *The South in the Revolution, 1763-1789* (Baton Rouge, 1957), 138-139, which is a useful and succinct statement of the Abernethy view.

[57] Through the early 1770's the Vandalia scheme loomed as a potential issue but never materialized as Crown authorities dragged their feet and eventually failed to approve it. Abernethy, *Western Lands and the American Revolution*, 40-58.

[58] Earl of Dartmouth to Governor of Virginia, etc., Feb. 5, 1774, C.O. 5/241, foll. 509-524; Alvord, *Miss. Valley in British Politics*, II, 209-216; Jack M. Sosin, *Whitehall and the Wilderness: The Middle West in British Colonial Policy, 1760-1775* (Lincoln, Nebr., 1961), 226-227.

[59] Jefferson, Draft of Instructions to the Virginia Delegates in the Continental Congress, in Boyd, ed., *Papers of Jefferson*, I, 123.

troversy, the issue of the West developed in a manner similar to that of the debt question.

Internal divisions appear to have been no more important in bringing on the Revolution. The image of a band of radicals ceaselessly contending against a powerful conservative bloc to move the Revolution at a faster pace and to achieve a stronger voice in the colonial government does not hold for Virginia. At no time during the 1760's and 1770's were there organized or rival groups that might be legitimately classified as factions or parties. In fact, once events moved beyond the apparent challenge by Patrick Henry to the old guard of the House of Burgesses over the Stamp Act Resolves of 1765, it is difficult to find evidence of serious internal disputes among Virginia Patriots.[60] In all the years from 1763 to Independence only one period of obvious controversy occurred, and that at a time when the agitation against Great Britain had quieted. A group of conflicts clustered in the months following repeal of the Stamp Act, but none of them were factional in nature. In one of them Richard Henry Lee attacked George Mercer for his acceptance of the Virginia stamp agency. When Mercer answered by disclosing that Lee had himself been an unsuccessful applicant for the post, the debate raged through a series of long newspaper articles.[61] Another dispute occurred when the death of John Robinson, Speaker of the House and Treasurer of the colony, disclosed shortages in his accounts because of secret loans from paper money that had been turned in for destruction. It resulted in the separation

[60] Writers who have emphasized a conservative-radical split are Charles Henry Ambler, *Sectionalism in Virginia from 1776 to 1861* (Chicago, 1910), 16-23; H. J. Eckenrode, *The Revolution in Virginia* (Boston and New York, 1916), 1-57; and Merrill Jensen, *The Articles of Confederation* (Madison, 1940), 21-25. Carl Bridenbaugh, *Seat of Empire: The Political Role of Eighteenth-Century Williamsburg*, new ed. (Williamsburg, 1958), 54-71, and Meade, *Patrick Henry*, are more moderate and more recent statements of the same view. None of these writers, however, produce detailed evidence to substantiate their case, and the recent tendency has been to minimize the importance of this conflict. See David J. Mays, *Edmund Pendleton, 1721-1803, A Biography* (Cambridge, Mass., 1952), I; Charles S. Sydnor, *Gentlemen Freeholders: Political Practices in Washington's Virginia* (Chapel Hill, 1952), 104-108; and Alden, *South in the Revolution*, 143-145. In this connection, see also the statement by a contemporary observer, St. George Tucker, that he had never witnessed anything in the House of Burgesses "that bore the appearance of *party spirit*." Tucker to William Wirt, Sept. 25, 1815, *Wm. and Mary College Qtly.*, 1st Ser., XXII (1913-14), 251-257.

[61] These appear mostly in Purdie and Dixon's *Virginia Gazette*, July-Oct. 1766.

of the Treasurer's office and the Speakership.[62] There were additional minor disturbances as well, among them one over the admission to bail of John Chiswell, a member of the gentry accused of murder.[63] As Fauquier observed, the Stamp Act may have left Virginia easily aroused to factional quarrels; but none of them survived for long or created a clear division among Patriots. On only one later occasion, the closing of the courts, in 1774, did Virginians appear close to splitting, and then the minority quickly bowed to the popular decision.[64]. Nearly all the various committees and delegations elected in Virginia—the Committee of Correspondence of 1773, the first Committee of Safety, the members of the First Continental Congress—included men labeled both radical and conservative by modern scholars. As the Revolutionary controversy progressed, potential conflicts among the Patriots lessened rather than increased.[65]

What remains as the fundamental issue in the coming of the Revolution, then, is nothing more than the contest over constitutional rights. None of the other potential issues seems to have applied in Virginia at the opening of the struggle. Perhaps after all the Virginians had stated their grievances reasonably accurately. In 1763 there was a tradition of jealously guarded rights and privileges, but no lingering issues capable in themselves of instigating new conflicts. The Revolution did not open in force until the announcement of the Stamp Act. From then until the beginning of armed conflict with Dunmore in the fall of 1775 political or constitutional issues were the occasion for every outbreak of protest within the colony. The Virginians reacted, moreover, to actions affecting other colonies—the suspension of the New York legislature, the threat to Massachusetts after the Circular Letter, the Gaspee incident in Rhode Island—almost as readily as to measures that applied directly to their own colony. They were apparently moved as much by the over-all conflict as by local considerations.

[62] The best treatment of the Robinson affair is Mays, *Edmund Pendleton*, I, 174-208.

[63] This affair can be traced in Purdie and Dixon's *Virginia Gazette*, July-Oct. 1766. See also Robert Carter to Thomas Bladen, July 26, 1766, Robert Carter Letter book, Colonial Williamsburg, Inc., and William Nelson to John Norton, Sept. 6, 1766, William Nelson Letter book, Va. State Lib.

[64] Edmund Pendleton to Ralph Wormeley, July 28, 1774, Ralph Wormeley Papers, Alderman Library; James Parker to Charles Steuart, postcript of June 17, 1774, to letter of June 7, 1774, Steuart Papers.

[65] Sydnor, *Gentlemen Freeholders*, 106-108.

Insofar as other issues of a more local character concerned Virginia Patriots, they crowded in during the last years of controversy, when, as Edmund Randolph noted, "a deeper tone broke forth."[66] The closing of the courts by the summer of 1774 and complaints against the merchants suggest that the personal debts of the planters might then have become involved in the political conflict. Western lands, on which there was new restrictive action in 1774, aroused the colony as it had not done before. By 1775 Lord Dunmore's personality and conduct became a further irritant. Nevertheless, without the constitutional struggle that had gone before, these issues would not have been productive of revolution.

Earlier local disputes, moreover, were not able of themselves to generate the conflict. The Parsons' Cause, for instance, arose within the colony, not in response to any imperial policy; and, when it did become a matter of concern to the home government, the action taken in the long run failed to constitute a clear invasion of what Virginians held to be colonial rights. The dispute over establishing an Anglican episcopate, which had a brief revival in 1770-71, was not really serious, in part because it, too, was not actually considered and not actively promoted by imperial officials.[67]

In its concentration upon the broader aspects of the constitutional conflict with the mother country, the Revolutionary movement in Virginia appeared lacking in local issues of prime relevance. Yet local conditions and circumstances in Virginia, as well as elsewhere, almost certainly gave distinctive characteristics to the development of this common issue. One such influence was the structure and distribution of political power within the colonies. The Revolution marked not only a clash of constitutional theories but also a contest between rival blocs of power, the British seeing a need to extend their control over the colonies and the Americans determined to preserve the degree of autonomy they had enjoyed. As early as May 1764, Richard Henry Lee referred to the "iron hand of power" raised against the colonies.[68] Although Virginians may have

103

---

[66] Randolph, History of Virginia.

[67] On this point see Arthur Lyon Cross, *The Anglican Episcopate and the American Colonies* (Cambridge, Mass., 1924), 226-240, and George W. Pilcher, "Virginia Newspapers and the Dispute over the Proposed Colonial Episcopate, 1771-1772," *The Historian*, XXIII (1960-61), 98-113.

[68] Richard Henry Lee to ———, May 31, 1764, in Ballagh, ed., *Letters of Richard Henry Lee*, I, 5. See also the first paragraph of the Association of 1774 of the Virginia Convention, in Boyd, ed., *Papers of Jefferson*, I, 137.

exaggerated in charging that the ministerial policies represented a determined system to reduce them to slavery, they correctly assessed the intent of Great Britain as an over-all decrease in colonial political power. Indeed, American constitutional theories were to some extent a rationalization of the power struggle, not in the sense of attempting to hide narrow self-interest but in the sense of explaining why some degree of political power was essential for the protection of liberty.

The operation of the British challenge upon the structure of power in Virginia did as much as anything to shape the Revolutionary controversy there. The nature of political control within the colony is generally familiar. The catch phrase is planter aristocracy. Historians have described a small, able ruling group, largely members of the planter class and frequently related by family ties. These men governed both through the Council and to an even larger extent through the House of Burgesses, and their dominance of the county courts and the Anglican parish vestries provided additional bases of local power. A further concentration of influence in the hands of a few leading Burgesses meant that a dozen or so men might dominate the government of the colony. At the same time a relatively wide franchise for the election of Burgesses prevented the ruling elite from completely ignoring the will of the populace and suggested a wide assent to the government of the colony.[69]

In this situation there was little chance for factionalism to arise among the Patriots—the unanimity with which Virginians acted was largely unavoidable. Since there were no separate sources of local power, the Revolutionary movement most 'likely was directed from the center outward to the counties. The county conventions and other local activities need more study. In all likelihood, those who participated in them may have simply been adopting resolutions and policies that the leaders of the colony wanted rather than instructing the Patriot high command. Moreover, the situation in Virginia left no room for the development of native Loyalist leadership. Loyalist claimants for British compensation after the Revolution numbered only thirteen persons born in Virginia. Even the Council, drawn from the same planter class as the Burgesses, was far from being a center of royalist sympathies. Several councilors were outspoken Patriots, and the others were more properly neutralist

[69] Sydnor, *Gentlemen Freeholders*, 60-119; Jack P. Greene, "Foundations of Political Power in the Virginia House of Burgesses, 1720-1776," *Wm. and Mary Qtly.*, 3d Ser., XVI (1959), 485-506.

than Loyalist. The real explanation for the weakness of Loyalism within the colony may lie deeper than in the common assumption that Dunmore's antics alienated strong potential support for the Crown. It may be attributable instead to the lack of an avenue to political power other than the one already monopolized by the planters.[70]

This combination of unanimity and concentration of political power probably accounts for many characteristic features of the Revolution in Virginia—features that have, at least, given a distinctive coloration to the central issue of political and constitutional rights. For example, the emphasis upon interference with the colonial legislatures in the charges against George III is perhaps a clue to the Virginians' preoccupation with threats to a political power that was centered in the House of Burgesses. Similarly, it suggests less concern about the rights of the individual than we commonly associate with the American Revolution. This may seem a risky supposition to make in the face of George Mason's classic defense of individualism in the Virginia Declaration of Rights, but Virginians may very well have thought they possessed individual liberty in sufficient degree and that their rights were endangered only to the extent that colonial self-government itself was in danger. Certainly, the changes that occurred in Virginia, with the exception of the achievement of religious freedom, had little to do with the extension of individual liberty. The two great consequences of the Revolution within Virginia were the elimination of all British control and the further predominance of the legislative branch of government.

The Virginia leaders, then, did not go far wrong in their attribution of the fateful dispute with Great Britain to an invasion of constitutional rights. The one thing they might perhaps have added, though for them it could hardly have needed to be made explicit, was that the new turn in imperial policy directly challenged an established ruling class who would not lightly give up its power and privileges of self-government. If one is seeking the material and substantial interests that represent the reality behind constitutional principle, this political power is substance enough.

[70] On the weakness of Loyalism in Virginia see Berwick, Loyalties in Crisis, 51-58.

New York's Radicals and the Coming of Independence

ROGER J. CHAMPAGNE

THE British-American skirmishes at Lexington and Concord and the consequent siege of British forces in Boston were responsible for creating a Continental Army and the extralegal political machinery to direct a military defense of individual liberty and freedom. Lexington and Concord also placed new and heavy responsibilities upon Whigs everywhere: manpower had to be mobilized, supplies and money obtained, and time given to the myriad details of war. With the emergence in each colony of a quasi-revolutionary government by the spring of 1775, the older tactics of the Sons of Liberty became obsolete and the radical Whig leaders were put to a severe test. In most cases unprepared by training or experience for anything more than managing newspaper propaganda, mass meetings, and street brawling, their continued usefulness would depend upon their adaptation to the changing times which they had in part created. What happened to these radical leaders, whether they continued to shape the future as they had the past, varied in each colony.

The response of New York's radical triumvirate of Isaac Sears, John Lamb, and Alexander McDougall was perhaps uniquely different from developments elsewhere. Identified since 1765 as leaders of New York's Sons of Liberty, Sears, Lamb, and McDougall, merchants of modest fortune and middle age, had an off again-on again personal relationship that was largely determined by their involvement in the rivalry of the Livingston and DeLancey factions for political power in the colony. Coming together under the Livingston banner in late 1769 during New York's political crisis over the Quartering Act, the popular trio was firmly joined in the American defense as the critical year of 1775 opened.[1] They soon found themselves,

Mr. Champagne is assistant professor of history in Illinois State University, Normal, Illinois.

[1] Daniel C. Haskell, "Alexander McDougall," *Dictionary of American Biography* (21 vols., New York, 1928-1944), XII, 21-22; Clarence H. Vance, "Isaac Sears," *ibid.*, XVI,

however, drifting apart under the pressure of changing conditions following Lexington and Concord. When the military events of 1776 forced the issues of independence and state-making, New York's extremist leadership had already been shattered, permitting other men mainly of aristocratic origins and inclinations to make the fateful decisions. Thus the responses made by Sears, Lamb, and McDougall to the transitional problems of 1775-1776 sheds light upon the revolutionary outcome in New York.

News of Lexington and Concord reached New York City on the morning of April 23, and as people gathered on street corners for additional news, they were swept first one way and then another by numerous stories. Isaac Sears and John Lamb were apparently delighted with a development that permitted them to end all pretense of loyalty to the British government. Parading the town with "drums and colors flying," they called upon the people to arm themselves in defense of the "injured rights and liberties of America." During the afternoon of April 23, two ships heavy with provisions for General Thomas Gage at Boston were unloaded by a boisterous gang directed by Sears, Lamb, Peter R. Livingston, John and Joshua Hett Smith, Anthony Lispenard, and Leonard Lispenard, Jr. That evening Sears and Lamb broke open the City Hall and seized five hundred muskets and quantities of gunpowder. As Judge Thomas Jones recorded years later, the city had indeed become "one continued scene of riot, tumult, and confusion."[2]

The turmoil reigned for nearly a week and thoroughly disrupted the city's normal routine. Commercial transactions had practically ceased, courtrooms were empty, armed parties appeared on the streets at all hours, and taverns were unusually crowded at night.[3] Although Sears and Lamb drilled their followers every day (to conservatives they resembled an armed mob) the extremist leaders found time to harass individuals. James Rivington, Loyalist printer, was openly threatened and fled to the safety of a warship, while Myles Cooper, president of Kings College, and other An

539-40; Isaac Q. Leake, *Memoir of the Life and Times of General John Lamb* (Albany, 1850). For the involvement of Sears, Lamb, and McDougall in New York politics, see Roger Champagne, "Family Politics versus Constitutional Principles: The New York Assembly Elections of 1768 and 1769," *William and Mary Quarterly*, XX (Jan. 1963), 57-79.
  [3] William H. W. Sabine, ed., *Historical Memoirs, from 16 March 1763 to 9 July 1776, of William Smith, Historian of the Province of New York* . . . (New York, 1956), 222; Thomas Jones, *History of New York during the Revolutionary War* . . . , Edward Floyd DeLancey, ed. (2 vols., New York, 1879), I, 39-40; Peter Force, ed., *American Archives*, Fourth Series (6 vols., Washington, 1837-1843), II, 364; Robert R. Livingston to Robert Livingston, April 23, 1775, Robert R. Livingston Papers (New-York Historical Society).
  [3] Sabine, ed., *Historical Memoirs of William Smith*, 222.

glican clergyman critical of the first Congress went into hiding.[4] At week's end the extremists reached the limits of their frenzied activity. On April 28, customs collector Andrew Elliot, confronted by 350 armed men led by Sears, was forced to surrender the customs house keys; Sears then declared the port of New York closed, and terror-stricken merchants could only "sigh or complain in whispers." Shortly thereafter Sears returned the keys to Elliot with orders that no ships were to be cleared for Boston or Halifax.[5] The city soon received another shock when Oliver DeLancey, Henry White, John Watts, and Myles Cooper were accused by a Philadelphia newspaper of requesting the use of royal troops to quell the Whigs. Although affidavits testifying to their innocence were collected by the accused, it was only the influence of aristocrats like William Smith, Jr., Robert R. Livingston, James Duane, and John Jay that prevented an angry mob from holding a lynching party.[6]

The chaotic condition of the city, reminiscent of Stamp Act days and as terrifying to Livingston aristocrats as it was to those now called Tories, forced the Whig party to take steps to restore order and to organize better the revolutionary movement. At first Sears tried by means of a mass meeting to give new powers to the city's sixty-man committee of inspection, but most members, like merchant Philip Livingston, opposed this irregular method.[7] The Committee of Sixty recommended instead the formation of a committee of one hundred persons, to be selected by a city election. More significant was the decision to convene a provincial congress to obtain the "united aid and counsel" of the counties on measures for the common safety. It was proposed that twenty deputies represent New York City, and the counties were urged also to send large delegations.[8] Sears and Lamb and the mechanics prepared for the election by reviving the Sons of Liberty and nominating a committee slate and twenty deputies, as did another group,

[4] Sears and Lamb held a mass meeting on April 24 and obtained signatures to a military association. Robert R. Livingston to Robert Livingston, April 22, 1775, Robert R. Livingston Papers; Isaac N. Stokes, comp., *The Iconography of Manhattan Island* . . . (6 vols., New York, 1915-1928), IV, 896; Colden to Earl of Dartmouth, June 7, 1775, *The Colden Letter Books* (2 vols., New York, 1876-1877), II, 421-22; Force, ed., *American Archives*, II, 547-48.

[5] Sabine, ed., *Historical Memoirs of William Smith*, 222; Colden to Dartmouth, May 3, 1775, Edmund B. O'Callaghan, ed., *Documents Relative to the Colonial History of the State of New York* (11 vols., Albany, 1853-1861), VIII, 571-72.

[6] Force, ed., *American Archives*, II, 25, 445-46; Sabine, ed., *Historical Memoirs of William Smith*, 222-23; Robert R. Livingston to his wife, May 3, 1775, Livingston Family Papers (New York Public Library).

[7] It seemed to Philip Livingston that the mass meeting intended to turn the city committee of inspection into a war council, for which he did not feel qualified. Committee notes, April 24, 1775, Alexander McDougall Papers (New-York Historical Society).

[8] Force, ed., *American Archives*, II, 400, 428.

unnamed but presumably consisting of aristocrats.[9] Election day, April 29, was a quiet affair and the outcome an aristocratic victory; whatever Sears may have thought, he did not command the city, nor would the Sons of Liberty or the mechanics' committee control the new city committee. Only sixteen of the new committee's membership can be identified as mechanics by occupation, the majority consisting of merchants and lawyers.[10]

Following the election Livingston aristocrats turned their attention to restoring peace in the city. While they probably did not believe that Sears and Lamb intended a random attack upon property, they were unsure of the city's rougher elements, encouraged as the toughs were by the talk and deeds of the extremists. Moreover, with Lt. Gov. Cadwallader Colden frankly admitting the helplessness of the local and provincial governments, quick action was clearly required if property was to be protected.[11] At a mass meeting engineered by aristocrats on election day, a city "association" drafted by Duane, Jay, and Peter Van Schaack was approved. While the declared intent of the agreement was to assure the execution of measures proposed by the Continental Congress and Provincial Convention, the last article revealed the associators' true purpose: "and that we will, in all things follow the advice of our general committee, respecting the purposes aforesaid, the preservation of peace and good order, and the safety of individuals, and private property."[12] It was hoped that the local association would accomplish two interrelated objects: regularize Whig activity by restricting it to those plans sanctioned by the intercolonial and provincial congresses, and thereby condemn the measures promoted by Sears and Lamb, which were outside the view of the extralegal agencies. By this association the Livingstons made it plain that they had as much distaste for demagogues within the Whig party as they had for their DeLancey opponents who condemned the revolutionary movement.[13]

[9] See the electioneering broadsides, "The Following Persons are Recommended to the Public, as Proper to be Elected for a General Committee for the City and County of New York . . . April 27, 1775," and "The Following Persons are Nominated by the Sons of Liberty, to Represent them in the Committee for the City and County of New York . . . April 28, 1775." Broadsides and pamphlets used are available in the Readex Microprint edition of the *Early American Imprints* published by the American Antiquarian Society.

[10] Sabine, ed., *Historical Memoirs of William Smith*, 223; Force, ed., *American Archives*, II, 459. Occupational identification of committee members was made by use of the New-York Historical Society *Collections* publication, *The Burghers of New Amsterdam and the Freemen of New York, 1765-1866* (New York, 1885), *passim.*

[11] Colden to Dartmouth, May 3, 1775, O'Callaghan, ed., *New York Colonial Documents*, VIII, 571-72.

[12] Isaac Low was chairman of the meeting and first to sign the "association"; Robert R. Livingston was second signer. Jones, *New York during the Revolutionary War*, I, 41-44. The association is in New York *Journal*, May 4, 1775.

[13] Robert R. Livingston optimistically reported that the association put the committee

McDougall kept conspicuously aloof from the commotion raised by his extremist friends. The Loyalist judge, Thomas Jones, who delighted in recording the demagoguery of the three popular leaders, does not mention that McDougall shared the military ardor of Sears and Lamb, or that he participated in the customs house raid and the removal of cannon from the Battery. Jones assigned a different role to McDougall. On the day that most aristocrats signed the new association, one figure was missing: William Smith, Jr., longtime strategist for the Livingston faction. Smith's failure to appear disturbed many Livingston leaders and McDougall was sent to learn the reasons for his tardiness. Smith explained that he had not signed the agreement because it would mean the end of his political usefulness, as a member of the governor's council, to the Livingston party. Impressed by this argument, McDougall then convinced his mechanic friends that Smith was still a friend of American liberty.[14] The episode is interesting for it reveals McDougall's essential attitude of moderation, which was to become more pronounced in the months ahead. Had he been of the same mind as Sears and Lamb, he would have placed the extremist cause before an agreement designed to promote peace and order. Thus, if Jones's account is true, McDougall was already closer to men of conservative temper than to Sears and Lamb, and this represented a crack in the solidarity of the popular leadership.

While the Whigs waited for the Provincial Congress to assemble on May 22, the new city committee of one hundred met practically every day to organize the city's defenses against the expected arrival of royal troops.[15] Supplies of arms and ammunition in the city were inventoried, a subcommittee was appointed to consider how more supplies could be obtained, orders were issued forbidding the sale of arms to Tories, militia companies in each ward were told to organize, and a military night watch was established.[16] In all these "regular" military preparations, McDougall played a leading role. He was also instrumental, along with John Morin Scott and Van Schaack, in the committee's acceptance of Samuel Broome's company of armed men for use in enforcing the April 29 city association.[17] Whether

and congress system "into a regular form of government," thus ending "the power of our demagogs." To his wife, May 3, 1775, Livingston Family Papers. See also Sabine, ed., *Historical Memoirs of William Smith*, 223.

[14] Jones, *New York during the Revolutionary War*, I, 44-45.

[15] Force, ed., *American Archives*, II, 387.

[16] *Ibid.*, 470-71, 481, 529-30, 617-18, 636-37, 670-71.

[17] Militia companies commanded by John Lasher, Rudolpha Ritzma, Andrew Stockholm, Christopher Banker, Edward Fleming, and Abraham P. Lott were used for the same purpose. *Ibid.*, 468-69, 534-35. See also, Address of the New-York Association to Colden, May 11, 1775, O'Callaghan, ed., *New York Colonial Documents*, VIII, 583-85.

all these military activities of the One Hundred would be enough to prevent the landing of British troops was never seriously considered, but it
was clear that general tumult and disorder, of the variety promoted earlier
by Sears, would not be allowed to develop again if the aristocrats could
help it.

The Provincial Congress which convened in New York City on May 22
marked a significant change in the revolutionary movement, overshadow-
ing the capital's committee system. Hitherto, opposition to British policy
and imperial rule had been initiated, promoted, and largely confined to
the provincial capital; with the Intolerable Acts, however, the colony
as a whole became more directly concerned in defending American rights.   *111*
Lexington and Concord, and the desire to make common military preparations, forced the revolutionary leaders in New York City to take an even
larger view of their activities. Just as it was obvious in the fall of 1774
that uniformity was necessary to make nonimportation effective, it was
equally apparent in the spring of 1775 that leadership in an armed conflict
could not be left to local committees: the problems of recruiting, supplying,
and financing an army could only be done by national and provincial congresses. Sears, Lamb, and McDougall, like many men in other places, were
ill-prepared for the new responsibilities, and the months to come would
determine whether they would remain local politicians or become provincial statesmen.

New York's revolutionary congress faced many immediate problems.
Local volunteer companies had to be knit into regiments, supplies of muskets and gunpowder had to be collected and new stocks ordered, and, above
all, consideration had to be given to ways and means of paying for the
army.[18] These were knotty, troublesome matters that grew worse as the
months passed and the urgency of New York's preparedness and the demands of the Continental Congress became greater. By the fall of 1775,
when the invasion of Canada began, recruiting had slowed down peril-
ously; military supplies were extremely scarce; and the revolutionary treasury was empty.[19] The faltering military preparations of New York Whigs
did not result from a lack of energy or effort. Perhaps not as enthusiastic
about war as Whigs elsewhere, the Livingstons did conscientiously try to
carry New York's share of the overall American defense. New York's
military problems stemmed from the fact that the colony was divided

[18] For a general discussion of the military problems early in the war, see John R. Alden,
The American Revolution, 1775-1783 (New York, 1954), 26, 29-30, 48-49.
[19] Force, ed., *American Archives*, II, 1137-38; *Journals of the Provincial Congress, Provincial Convention, Committee of Safety and Council of Safety of the State of New York*
(2 vols., New York, 1842), I, 85, 212, 239.

against itself, that Whig leaders, either by means of the Provincial Congress or local committees, were unable to establish themselves firmly as the new provincial rulers and to dominate thoroughly the colony. Basic to the Whig party's lack of control were the steady growth of Loyalism and the presence within the party of radicals who still insisted upon following a course of violence. Caught between the grinding action of these two extremes, the aristocratic Whig leadership barely survived.

Criticism of Whig measures had, of course, started months before Lexington and Concord, but the extent of anti-Whig sentiment was not fully known.[20] When the Provincial Congress directed local committees to obtain signatures to the Association as a test of political affiliation, it was found by the end of summer that Loyalists were a majority on Long Island and in parts of Westchester and Albany counties, and very numerous in New York City.[21] Loyalists were troublesome in many ways to the Whig party. They prevented local committees from collecting arms, secretly or openly supplied the British with provisions and information, prevented the election of deputies in Queens and Richmond counties, and gleefully singled out the foibles and blunders of the revolutionary leaders. It was an intolerable situation, causing some Whigs to "make long faces";[22] it also later gave hope to royal officials that the revolutionary movement would collapse.

Loyalism drew strength by the fall of 1775 from a variety of sources. Royal officials encouraged the anti-Whig opposition; merchants with more to gain in the empire than out of it wanted no part of what appeared to be an independence movement. Tenant farmers on the manors thought they would get free lands if they supported the king; others remained loyal because they disliked their landlords who were Whigs.[23] Many aristocrats would simply not associate with men like Sears and Lamb, whom they regarded as "rabble" and troublemakers, while some DeLancey politicians were too stubborn to admit they had made political blunders.[24] And me-

[20] The Rev. Samuel Seabury's pamphlets, under pseudonym of a "Westchester Farmer," achieved the greatest notoriety: *Free Thoughts, on the Proceedings of the Continental Congress* . . . (New York, 1774); *The Congress Canvassed; or, An Examination into the Conduct of the Delegates, at their Grand Convention* . . . (New York, 1774); *A View of the Controversy Between Great-Britain and Her Colonies* . . . (New York, 1774); *An Alarm to the Legislature of the Province of New York, occasioned by the Present Political Disturbances* . . . (New York, 1775).
[21] Carl L. Becker, *The History of Political Parties in the Province of New York, 1760-1776* (Madison, 1909), 215.
[22] McDougall to Jay, Oct. 30, 1775, John Jay Papers (Special Collections, Columbia University Library).
[23] Robert R. Livingston to Jay, July 17, 1775, *ibid.*
[24] Guy Johnston to Schuyler, July 8, 1775, Philip Schuyler Papers (New York Public

chanics and artisans followed the advice and lead of their employers and refused to aid the Whig cause. In addition to these somewhat personal reasons was the fear among aristocrats and men of middling status, whatever their economic interests, that the military policies of the Continental Congress would inevitably take the colonies out of the empire.[25]

The Whig party was in part responsible for the congenial environment in which Loyalism flourished. Time and again such conservative Whigs as Duane and Gouverneur Morris revealed that they were close in sentiment to Tories.[26] But it was the moderate if not timorous attitude of most aristocratic Whigs that gave encouragement to Loyalists and thereby sapped the strength of New York's military program. Whig moderation was founded upon a desire for reconciliation with the mother country and a fear that British forces would retaliate if any move was made against royal officials or Loyalists. The result was a cautiousness that encouraged Loyalists, infuriated Whig extremists, and finally invited outside interference.

113

Reconciliation was a frequently discussed subject after the first Continental Congress. New York's newspapers carried plans for an imperial settlement, while the private letters of provincial leaders often referred to the need of an accommodation of differences and occasionally approved of Joseph Galloway's plan of union.[27] The matter came to a head when Lord North in the House of Commons on February 27, 1775, offered to exempt any colony from taxation if it would provide funds for the common defense and support of civil government.[28] Lord North's plan of conciliation reached New York while the city was in the throes of the Lexington-Concord crisis, thereby frustrating Lt. Gov. Colden's hope that North's proposal might be considered by the General Assembly. Disorder in the provincial capital intensified the conservative desire for reconciliation, however, and the general question was brought before the Provincial Congress near the end of May.[29] The report on reconciliation, largely written by

Library). The obstinacy of the DeLanceys is analyzed in John Jones to Duane, July 13, 1775, James Duane Papers (New-York Historical Society).

[25] Tryon to Dartmouth, Aug. 7, 1775, O'Callaghan, ed., *New York Colonial Documents*, VIII, 603-04.

[26] For a revealing commentary on Duane, see McDougall to Samuel Adams, Jan. 29, 1775, McDougall Papers; on Gouverneur Morris, see his letter to [John?] Penn, May 20, 1774, Jared Sparks, *The Life of Gouverneur Morris* (3 vols., Boston, 1832), I, 23-26.

[27] *New York Mercury*, Sept. 12, 19, and 26, 1774; Philip Livingston approved Galloway's plan of union in *The Other Side of the Question: or, A Defence of the Liberties of North America* (New York, 1774); James Duane to Samuel Chase, Dec. 29, 1774, Duane Papers; Robert R. Livingston to Robert R. Livingston, Jr., May 5, 1775, Bancroft Collection, Livingston Papers (New York Public Library).

[28] Merrill Jensen, ed., *English Historical Documents. IX: American Colonial Documents to 1776* (New York, 1955), 839-40.

[29] Force, ed., *American Archives*, II, 460; *Journals . . . Provincial Congress . . . New York*, I, 8-9, 20, 26, 46, 50.

Gouverneur Morris, was not extraordinary for New York. It simply re-
stated constitutional principles held by aristocrats since the Stamp Act
crisis: Britain had the right to regulate imperial commerce but not internal
colonial affairs. A modified version of Galloway's American Congress was
also suggested.[10] Thus while other colonies steadily moved toward ultimate independence, the Livingston Whig leaders clung to the hope of an
imperial settlement. Unable to think of themselves as anything but British
subjects living under British law in a society essentially British, they rejected the idea of leaving the empire. It was, however, a difficult position
for the Livingston Whigs to maintain, convinced as they were that the
Intolerable Acts and subsequent British measures presented a real threat
to their liberty and to colonial rights.[11] Consequently, they followed the
tortuous policy of disavowing independence while supporting the war
measures of the Continental Congress.

Aristocratic caution was also dictated by an overpowering fear that New
York City would become a scene of battle.[12] While the provincial capital
was the center of revolutionary activity, it was also the weakest link in the
chain of defense: caught between large Tory parties in Westchester County
and Long Island, New York City was open to attack from the always present warships in its harbor. Although probably not informed of specific
naval orders—Captain George Vandeput of the *Asia* had instructions to
shell the houses of Sears and other prominent extremists if the city denied
provisions to his ship[13]—the Livingstons were nonetheless impressed by the
city's danger and openly placated royal officials and tolerated the Loyalist
opposition. An incident in late August 1775 demonstrated the Livingston
anxiety. In its search for cannon the Provincial Congress decided to strip
the Battery of royal artillery and assigned the job to Lamb. On August 23,
as Lamb's company moved the cannon, a small boat from the *Asia* came
close to shore to observe the operation, exchanging several musket volleys
with Lamb's party which resulted in the death of one sailor. When the
naval party returned, Captain Vandeput opened fire upon the Battery to
prevent the removal of crown property.[14] It seemed that the dread day had

[10] *Journals . . . Provincial Congress . . . New York*, I, 52-53, 54, 58. Morris thought
the plan would be rejected because New York also insisted that colonial legislatures be
limited to three-year terms. British officials, he claimed, would never give up their right
to alter colonial constitutions, and consequently there would be no reconciliation. Morris
to Jay, June 30, 1775, Jay Papers.
[11] Robert R. Livingston to Robert R. Livingston, Jr., May 5, 1775, Bancroft Collection,
Livingston Papers.
[12] Robert Cambridge Livingston to Robert Livingston, May 29 and 31, 1775, Livingston-
Redmond Papers (Franklin D. Roosevelt Library, Hyde Park, New York).
[13] Becker, *New York Political Parties*, 226.
[14] Before withdrawing, Lamb was able to remove twenty-one cannon. New York *Journal*,
Aug. 24, 1775.

come and Whig aristocrats willingly accepted Governor William Tryon's suggestion the next day to leave the Battery cannon alone and to continue to supply the *Asia* with provisions.[35] Meanwhile alarmed townspeople took flight. Philip Livingston and Duane ordered their personal and household goods shipped up the Hudson River, and Peter Van Brugh Livingston, president of the Provincial Congress, took his family upriver and never returned.[36]

If moderation was prudent and reasonable to aristocratic Whigs, it was deadening to radicals within the party. Never noted for their self-restraint under the royal government, Sears, Lamb, Marinus Willet, and even Scott could find no justification for forbearance under the rule of extralegal agencies. Unable to budge the city committee and the Provincial Congress from their middle course, extremists took action on their own initiative against royal officials and Tories. On June 6, 1775, Willet, contrary to explicit directions of the New York Congress and the personal efforts of aristocrats, raided the baggage train of the loyal royal garrison as it embarked for England.[37] A royal ordnance warehouse was looted on the night of July 12.[38] The next night a royal barge used by the *Asia* was burned, and when the Whig party approved the construction of a replacement, the new one was sawed to pieces by the tireless extremists.[39] One important project was frustrated by the moderates. When Sears contemplated seizing Governor Tryon, recently returned from England, Philip Schuyler's position as commanding general in New York and General Washington's written orders persuaded him to drop the idea.[40] While the activities of radicals during the summer months hardly compared to the turmoil and violence of

[35] Tryon to Dartmouth, Sept. 5, 1775, O'Callaghan, ed., *New York Colonial Documents,* VIII, 631-32. The New York Congress ordered an investigation, but nothing decisive resulted. Force, ed., *American Archives,* III, 550.

[36] Becker, *New York Political Parties,* 226-27.

[37] For a full account of the raid, see Major Isaac Hamilton to Colden, June 8, 1775, *The Letters and Papers of Cadwallader Colden* (9 vols., New York, 1918-1937), VII, 300-01. See also, Colden to Mayor Whitehead Hicks and to Major Hamilton, June 9, 1775, *Colden Letter Books,* II, 426, 427-28; Richard Montgomery to Robert R. Livingston, June 7, 1775, Bancroft Collection, Livingston Papers; Dorothy Dillon, *The New York Triumvirate: A Study of the Legal and Political Careers of William Livingston, John Morin Scott, and William Smith, Jr.* (New York, 1949), 135-36; Force, ed., *American Archives,* II, 1282-83.

[38] Report of Francis Stephens, Storekeeper of Royal Ordnance, July 21, 1775, O'Callaghan, ed., *New York Colonial Documents,* VIII, 599-600.

[39] Tryon to Dartmouth, Aug. 7, 1775, *ibid.,* 597; *Journals . . . Provincial Congress . . . New York,* I, 81, 97-98.

[40] Sabine, ed., *Historical Memoirs of William Smith,* 232. Sears was not the only one who thought Tryon should be seized and sent to Connecticut. See Richard Montgomery to Robert R. Livingston, July 1, 1775, and to Robert Livingston, Aug. 6, 1775, Bancroft Collection, Livingston Papers.

former occasions, the situation nonetheless represented a challenge to aristocratic control of the revolutionary movement. As Colden reported conditions, conservative Whig leaders "did not expect that their authority would meet with a public contempt, which demonstrated how inadequate they were to the government or protection of the people."[41]

Radical leaders like Sears and Lamb were obviously out of step with aristocratic Whigs, and under the pressure of conflicting interests, Sears, Lamb, and McDougall began to drift apart. Sears, already disillusioned by the timid Livingstons, was the first to leave his old friends. His first departure came over a trivial matter, the arrival of a suspicious newcomer, Patrick Sinclair, who was found to be the new governor of Michilimackinack.[42] Sears demanded that the Provincial Congress send Sinclair to Hartford for imprisonment, but the Livingstons would not permit such severe punishment for no particular reason; instead, Sinclair was ordered to stay on Long Island until further notice.[43] Following this apparent backsliding, Sears left for New Haven on August 5 and remained there until late September.[44] But conditions were unchanged upon his return and he soon found added proof of Whig irresolution. When the Continental Congress suggested that all crown military stores in New York City be seized, the New York Congress informed its Philadelphia delegates that it had no intention of risking the city's safety for a trifle.[45] The Continental Congress had also recommended the seizure and imprisonment of persons inimical to America, including royal officials, but the Whig majority promptly assured Governor Tryon that he would be safe in New York City.[46] In both cases Sears wanted positive action in defiance of the threat of naval bombardment, while the moderates, this time including McDougall, refused to jeopardize the revolutionary movement for what seemed dubious advantages. Nothing would soothe Sears, who withdrew from New York's Whig party during the first week of November. Aristocrats heaved a sigh of relief: "Sears . . . is so highly offended with this congress for acting so that he is set out for Connecticut and swears he

[41] Colden to Dartmouth, June 7, 1775, O'Callaghan, ed., *New York Colonial Documents,* VIII, 579-83.

[42] Sinclair's arrest was the work of the New York City committee. Force, ed., *American Archives,* III, 15.

[43] Apparently there was a heated argument over Sinclair: John DeLancey called John Morin Scott a scoundrel and attempted "to run his fist in his face." *Journals . . . Provincial Congress . . . New York,* I, 100-01.

[44] Sears' explanation of his absence is in a letter to the New York Congress, Aug. 8, 1775, Emmet Collection, No. 6922 (New York Public Library).

[45] John Patterson to Robert Livingston, Nov. 6, 1775, Livingston-Redmond Papers.

[46] O'Callaghan, ed., *New York Colonial Documents,* VIII, 638, 639, 645; Becker, *New York Political Parties,* 225-26.

won't return—meaning to punish the city by absenting himself from it. All people seem to wish he may persevere in such a punishment."[47]

Undoubtedly Lamb was also disenchanted with the Livingston Whigs, but unlike Sears he found an outlet for his revolutionary enthusiasm in a military career. Lamb's new role contributed as much to the radical triumvirate's expiration as did Sears' retirement to Connecticut. Although many former Liberty Boys organized or joined volunteer companies after Lexington-Concord, none exceeded Lamb's zeal in recruiting, equipping, and training his artillery company.[48] After he received a captaincy in the New York militia on June 30, he entered the regular service, and in early August upon his request his company was attached to General Philip Schuyler's force preparing for the Canadian invasion. At first Lamb tried to play an independent role in the war. He objected to being assigned to a specific regiment, disliked the pay arrangements, and complained of being "degraded" and "deprived" of a proper military rank. The Provincial Congress met his pay and rank demands and ordered him to Ticonderoga from whence he participated in the siege of St. John's in September.[49] Lamb distinguished himself in battle, but continued to give his superiors trouble. General Richard Montgomery, Schuyler's successor, described him as active, spirited, industrious, bad tempered, turbulent, and troublesome.[50] Lamb's service came to a temporary en'd at Quebec on December 31. Leading his company of mechanics and artisans in an assault upon Quebec's citadel, he received a severe facial wound and was captured. During his six months' imprisonment, a fellow prisoner performed a crude operation to relieve Lamb's pain, but his speech was permanently impaired. As a reward for his service, the Continental Congress promoted Lamb to major and artillery commander in Canada, a promotion he never enjoyed. He was finally paroled on August 2, 1776, and later returned to active military duty.[51]

The breakup of the radical leadership was not entirely the result of Sears' exasperation or Lamb's soldiering; McDougall, last of the popular trio, underwent a change that fundamentally separated him from his old

[47] John Patterson to Robert Livingston, Nov. 6, 1775, Livingston-Redmond Papers.
[48] Lamb offered his services to the New York Congress on June 2, 1775. Force, ed., *American Archives*, II, 891.
[49] Lamb's commission is in the John Lamb Papers (New-York Historical Society). See also *Journals . . . Provincial Congress . . . New York*, I, 81, 114; New York Congress to General Schuyler, Aug. 8 and Sept. 1, 1775, Schuyler Papers; Force, ed., *American Archives*, III, 445, 563; Leake, *Life of John Lamb*, 111.
[50] Richard Montgomery to Schuyler, Nov. 20, 1775, Force, ed., *American Archives*, III, 1684; Leake, *Life of John Lamb*, 118-19.
[51] Leake, *Life of John Lamb*, 131, 133-34, 145; Richard Smith, "Diary," Jan. 9, 1776, Edmund C. Burnett, ed., *Letters of Members of the Continental Congress* (8 vols., Washington, 1921-36), I, 304.

friends. He came to see what they could not, that the American cause could also be served by a policy of patience and adherence to rules laid down by aristocrats. While Sears fumed and fussed over the condemnation of those who destroyed an unimportant royal barge and over the mild treatment accorded a luckless royal official, McDougall, adjusting to his role as legislator, worked to reverse the decisions of the Provincial Congress.[52] And the difference was to become doubly significant as the months passed, for the longer McDougall checked his eagerness to drive out America's enemies, the more he became infected with the moderate spirit of the Livingstons. While he never accepted their views on reconciliation, he was nonetheless persuaded as they were that New York was not united against Britain as was Massachusetts or Virginia, and that even if it were, the colony's vulnerability to attack and its poor defenses still made a policy of moderation a prudent one. As he explained to General Charles Lee, "Our neighbours are not sufficiently informed of the condition of the colony, and some of our zealous friends in it, were urging to measures without the necessary means to carry them into execution in all their extent, regardless of the most probable & dangerous consequences."[53]

McDougall's commitment to the Livingston tactics of appeasement was a difficult part to play, and the popular leader had much to complain of. When the New York Congress dissolved itself on October 18, the election on November 7 of a new one was greeted by rank and file Whigs with a dulling apathy. Richmond County did not even hold an election, and in Queens the vote was 700 to 500 against sending deputies. After the elections, it took three weeks for enough delegates to straggle into Congress to make a quorum on December 6, 1775.[54] Even with a quorum, revolutionary affairs suffered from a shortage of leaders: some were in Philadelphia attending the Continental Congress, others were on military duty, and "Mr. V. B. Livingston has not attended Congress since the firing of *Asia*; Mr. Scott has been very ill for six weeks, Mr. Tho' Smith often out of town; many of the warm Whigs removed to Connecticut; others of them make long faces, & the Tories impudent."[55] Outsiders censured New York's indifference, singling out McDougall's failure to join the Canadian invasion, which only added to his despair since John Jay and Philip Schuyler

118

[52] McDougall was able to eliminate the harsh language in Isaac Low's motion condemning those responsible for burning the *Asia's* barge. *Journals . . . Provincial Congress . . . New York*, I, 102.
[53] McDougall to Lee, Dec. 20, 1775, McDougall Papers.
[54] Becker, *New York Political Parties*, 227–34; McDougall to Schuyler, Dec. 7, 1775, McDougall Papers.
[55] McDougall to Schuyler, Nov. 14, 1775, McDougall Papers.

had both urged him to remain in New York City to watch over public affairs.[54]

Frustrated by his party's listlessness and harassed by Tories and outsiders, McDougall also had to deal with the troublesome Sears, who neither forgave nor forgot his old enemies. Sears was barely settled in New Haven[57] when he collected ninety-six mounted men and set out for New York City to deal with Loyalist printer James Rivington and the Rev. Samuel Seabury. Reaching the city at noonday on November 23, his troop paraded down Broadway and drew up in close order before Rivington's printing shop. Within an hour Rivington's equipment was destroyed and Sears departed, it was said, to the tune of Yankee Doodle. On the way back to New Haven, a stop was made at the Borough of Westchester where Seabury and Nathaniel Underhill, borough mayor, were seized. Six miles farther, Jonathan Fowler, prominent Loyalist and Superior Court judge, was also captured. On November 28 Sears reached New Haven and jailed his prized catches.[58] It was a bold and brazen foray, perfectly in keeping with Sears' character but the more outrageous because Sears had used Connecticut men. "For my own part," Jay wrote from Philadelphia, "I do not approve the feat, and think it neither argues much wisdom nor much bravery; at any rate, if it was to have been done, I wish our own people, and not strangers, had taken the liberty of doing it."[59] Several days later the city committee petitioned the Provincial Congress to prevent future interventions in the colony's internal affairs.[60] It was a delicate point: if the convention denounced Sears, Connecticut might refuse to grant New York assistance when and if the Loyalists or the British attacked; but if Sears' escapade was ignored, the way would be opened to perhaps more serious intrusions. Without mentioning Sears, the Provincial Congress straddled

119

[54] For criticism of McDougall, see Duane to McDougall, Nov. 15, 1775 and Feb. 25, 1776; Schuyler to McDougall, Nov. 28, 1775 and Feb. 15, 1776; Jay to McDougall, Dec. 22, 1775, ibid.; McDougall to Duane, Feb. 13, 1776, Duane Papers. Jay's insistence that McDougall stay in New York City is in McDougall to Schuyler, Nov. 14, 1775, McDougall Papers.

[57] The Connecticut assembly appointed Sears and David Waterbury to examine the possibility of converting several merchant vessels into privateers; Sears was also to supervise the construction of a warship and collect naval stores. Louis F. Middlebrook, History of Maritime Connecticut during the American Revolution 1775-1783 (2 vols., Salem, 1925), I, 43, 146; James H. Trumbull and Charles J. Hoadly, eds., Public Records of the Colony of Connecticut, 1636-1776 (15 vols., Hartford, 1850-1890), XV, 200-01, 222, 232, 247, 254-55.

[58] Force, ed., American Archives, III, 1707-08; Jones, New York during the Revolutionary War, I, 65-67; Tryon to Dartmouth, Dec. 6, 1775, O'Callaghan, ed., New York Colonial Documents, VIII, 645-46; John Jones to Duane, Dec. 7, 1775, Duane Papers.

[59] Jay to New York Congress, Nov. 26, 1775, Force, ed., American Archives, IV, 410; Jay to McDougall, Dec. 4, 1775, McDougall Papers.

[60] Force, ed., American Archives, IV, 185-86.

the issue by requesting Governor Jonathan Trumbull of Connecticut to restrain the patriotic zeal of his people; the matter would also be taken before the Continental Congress to get a ruling on the question of jurisdiction.[61] The long-suffering McDougall thought that the problem had been
handled well, but John Jay replied that it was the "first instance of cen-
suring the followers without reprehending the leader."[62]

The storm created by Sears' raid had hardly blown over when another
loomed on the horizon for McDougall. Governor Tryon, in a public letter
dated December 4, placed the revolutionary movement in jeopardy by re-
opening the divisive question of Lord North's plan of conciliation. Expressing sorrow over provincial disorder, the governor claimed he was unable to judge the public's true reaction to Lord North's proposal and expressed hope that some means would be found to end the growing rebellion.[63] Thus encouraged, Loyalists and fainthearted Whigs cultivated
the seeds of peace planted by Governor Tryon. At a private meeting on
December 7, a dozen members of the New York Congress met with
Thomas and William Smith to explore the possibility of a General Assembly session to petition once more the King and Parliament.[64] The next
day Thomas Smith asked the New York Congress to request a meeting of
the assembly to disclaim independence and to safeguard Governor Tryon.
Caught flatfooted, the Whigs barely gained a postponement of Smith's
motion. McDougall, joined by John Morin Scott, tried to salvage something from their predicament. Realizing that many deputies leaned toward
Smith's proposals, they insisted that if the General Assembly was to meet a
new one should be elected, which would give them an opportunity to select
men friendly to the American cause. On that basis Thomas Smith's motion
was rejected, and Governor Tryon faced the unpleasant alternatives of convening an assembly on Whig terms or of dropping his attempt to discredit the revolutionary party.[65] Unwilling to admit defeat, Governor Tryon,
advised by William Smith, prepared secretly to dissolve the old Assembly
and once more surprise the Whigs, but the scheme was poorly guarded.[66]

[61] *Ibid.*, 393, 400-01, 422-23, 1033-34.
[62] McDougall to Jay, Dec. 14, 1775, Jay Papers; Jay to McDougall, Dec. 22, 1775, Mc-
Dougall Papers.
[63] Force, ed., *American Archives*, IV, 173-74.
[64] Sabine, ed., *Historical Memoirs of William Smith*, 252-53.
[65] *Journals . . . Provincial Congress . . . New York*, I, 210-11, 217-19; McDougall to
Jay, Dec. 18, 1775, Jay Papers; Sabine, ed., *Historical Memoirs of William Smith*, 252-53.
[66] William Smith to Tryon, Dec. 17, 1775, O'Callaghan, ed., *New York Colonial Documents*, VIII, 653-54; Sabine, ed., *Historical Memoirs of William Smith*, 255-56. One possible reason for Tryon's dissolution of the assembly in the face of a probable Whig victory
was his desire to have an assembly of any political hue in order to wean the people away
from the Provincial Congress. Hugh Hughes to Adams, Jan. 8, 1776, Samuel Adams
Papers (New York Public Library).

McDougall learned of the governor's intention and sounded the alarm: election broadsides appeared, John Holt's New York *Journal* was filled with Tory-baiting propaganda, and letters were sent to county committees warning them of Tryon's plot.[67] When election day came on February 1, 1776, an aroused Whig party routed the Loyalists.[68]

An election victory, however, offered only a temporary relief. The focal point of radical troubles in New York was the unwillingness of moderates to deal harshly with Loyalists determined to return the colony to its old allegiance. Extremists like McDougall could do little until Loyalism was put in full retreat, but he knew first hand that the Provincial Congress would reject an offensive into Loyalist strongholds.[69] If anything was to be done, outside assistance was necessary. Writing to John Jay at Philadelphia in November and again in December 1775, McDougall urged that Jersey or Pennsylvania troops be stationed in New York, warning Jay that unless quick action was taken Kings County on Long Island would fall.[70] Alarmed by reports from New York, the Continental Congress directed Nathaniel Hurd of New Jersey and David Waterbury of Connecticut to disarm the disaffected of Queens County and to arrest the Tory ringleaders. Waterbury was unable to carry out his orders, but in late January 1776 Hurd landed with twelve hundred men, disarmed six hundred Loyalists, and marched seventeen Tory leaders off to Philadelphia.[71]

Seeking outside help, while satisfactory in getting an urgent job done, had disadvantages. It was an admission of weakness, but more important, it was an invitation for others to give assistance that was unwanted. To McDougall's embarrassment, and all New York Whigs, that situation developed in February 1776. General Lee, member of Washington's general

121

[67] McDougall to Charles Lee, Dec. 29, 1775, McDougall Papers; Alexander Hamilton to Jay, Dec. 31, 1775, Jay Papers; Force, ed., *American Archives*, IV, 1020-21; for electioneering broadsides see, "To the Freeholders and Freemen of New York, December 29, 1775," and "To the Citizens of New York, December 30, 1775."

[68] Whig tactics and the party's slate of Philip Livingston, John Jay, John Alsop, and Alexander McDougall are discussed in Duane to Robert Livingston, Jan. 5, 1776, Duane Papers; McDougall to Schuyler, Jan. 17, 1776, McDougall Papers. Election results are in Becker, *New York Political Parties*, 242.

[69] As a member of the Provincial Committee of Safety, McDougall had ordered a militia battalion to disarm Queens County Tories, but at the last moment he was "restrained by authority." Force, ed., *American Archives*, III, 795; McDougall to Charles Lee, Dec. 20, 1775, McDougall Papers.

[70] McDougall to Jay, Nov. 15, 26, and Dec. 24, 1775, Jay Papers; Jay to McDougall, Dec. 8, 1775, McDougall Papers. A short time later McDougall indicated that New York City was practically defenseless. McDougall to Stamford, Conn. Committee of Inspection, Dec. 30, 1775, *ibid.*

[71] Richard Smith, "Diary," Jan. 3 and 6, 1776, Burnett, ed., *Letters of Continental Congress*, I, 294-95, 300; Tryon to Dartmouth, Feb. 7, 1776, O'Callaghan, ed., *New York Colonial Documents*, VIII, 663; Jones, *New York during the Revolutionary War*, I, 108-09.

staff and self-appointed guardian of American Liberty, had for some months been "uneasy" about New York's lukewarm patriotism.[72] Lee's opinions coincided with those of Sears and it was perhaps inevitable that the two should meet and plan a military expedition against Long Island Loyalists. Writing to Washington on January 5, 1776, Lee insisted that New York required immediate attention: if the British army, preparing to leave Boston, should attempt a landing on Long Island, the absence of defenses and the activity of Tories would make it a success. He advised that troops be sent to New York, and Washington approved the project when Lee and Sears assured him that only Connecticut volunteers would be used. Governor Trumbull readily gave Sears permission to recruit a force of 1,500 men.[73] Although Washington informed the New York Congress of the coming expedition, rumors flew in New York City. The Provincial Committee of Safety on January 21, directed by McDougall and Scott, demanded that Lee state his intentions and advised him to halt at the Connecticut border if he was coming with an army.[74] Blandly assuring the Committee that he had no hostile plans, Lee also wrote to Washington that he thought New Yorkers breathed the spirit of procrastination, timidity, and hysteria, and that he expected little cooperation.[75] He nonetheless proceeded with his plans, gratuitously naming Sears as his assistant deputy Adjutant General with the rank of lieutenant colonel, while confiding to Washington that "the man was much tickled, and it added spurs to his head. He is a creature of much spirit and public virtue, and ought to have his back clapped."[76]

New York's delegation at Philadelphia soon heard rumors of Lee's expedition and requested the appointment of a congressional investigating committee, which could if necessary assist in managing Lee's campaign and settle points of jurisdiction. Congress consequently appointed Thomas Lynch, Benjamin Harrison, and Andrew Allen, who arrived in New York City at the end of January[77] just as General Lee, Sears, and Colonel David Waterbury neared New York with 700 Connecticut troops. Frantic conferences were held between McDougall and Scott and the congressional committee. McDougall, as ranking militia colonel, wanted the troops to remain in Connecticut until it was settled whether the New York Congress

[72] Lee had earlier acted against the Tories of Newport, Rhode Island. Charles Lee to Robert Morris, Jan. 3, 1776, Bancroft Collection, Revolutionary Papers (New York Public Library).
[73] Force, ed., American Archives, IV, 582-83, 595-96, 604-05, 683-84, 1145.
[74] Ibid., 605-06, 807-08, 1062.
[75] Ibid., 830-31, 839.
[76] Ibid., 1145.
[77] Ibid., 839, 1091-92.

would have primary supervision of the force. Scott would admit Lee's army and settle the matter of jurisdiction afterward. But the congressional committee rejected both views, insisting that the troops were under the direction of the Continental Congress.[78]

The worst fears of conservatives and moderates alike were realized on February 4 when General Lee entered New York City at the same time that visiting British general Henry Clinton arrived aboard a frigate, accompanied by a troop transport. Lee promptly set the tone of his stay in New York. If the warships opened fire because of his presence in the city, he promised to use the first burning building as a funeral pile for one hundred Tories.[79] Townspeople immediately started a general evacuation of the city. Those who had money bought farms or houses in the country; many moved to nearby Jersey towns; the poor merely trudged out to await the outcome. Even John Alsop in Philadelphia, hearing some days later of the situation, asked McDougall to look after his house if he had time.[80] The incident was merely a sample of things to come. Lee soon halted all communications with British ships, his troops fired upon suspicious colonial boats moving in the harbor, and Governor Tryon's servant, ashore once a week with laundry, was seized and jailed.[81]

But it was Lieutenant Colonel Isaac Sears who caused his old friend McDougall the most anguish. Swaggering about town, Sears denounced the New York Congress "in the most harsh, disrespectful and abusive terms."[82] He swept through Queens County administering a test oath and arresting those who refused to take it.[83] Local committees were outraged and many complained to the Provincial Congress that Sears only converted Whigs into Tories instead of the other way around. On March 12 the Congress debated whether Sears should appear to explain his activities, but McDougall opposed the move because the colony was already under a cloud of suspicion.[84] Besides, Sears had taught the weak-kneed Whigs a good les-

123

[78] *Ibid.*, 1096, 1098, 1100. Thomas Lynch wrote that everything was wanting in New York. "The strong apathy that holds Congress in fetters is still more forcible here." *Ibid.*, 943.
[79] *Ibid.*, 942; Tryon to Dartmouth, Feb. 8, 1776, O'Callaghan, ed., *New York Colonial Documents*, VIII, 666-67.
[80] Charles Inglis to Col. C. Colden, Feb. 5, 1776, John McKesson Papers (New-York Historical Society); John Henry Livingston to Robert R. Livingston, Jr., Feb. 13, 1776, Bancroft Collection, Livingston Papers; Alsop to McDougall, Feb. 12, 1776, McDougall Papers.
[81] Becker, *New York Political Parties*, 240.
[82] *Journals . . . Provincial Congress . . . New York*, I, 333, 335, 343.
[83] Force, ed., *American Archives*, V, 75; Sears to Lee, March 7, 1776, Isaac Sears Papers (New-York Historical Society). The test oath used by Sears was probably the same that Lee administered to Rhode Island Tories. Jones, *New York during the Revolution*, I, 572.
[84] *Journals . . . Provincial Congress . . . New York*, I, 355. Sears later asked that the

son: "I am persuaded," McDougall wrote to Jay, "it will be the last instance of their passivity on a point of so much importance to the liberty of
a freeman."[85]

General Lee's transfer to another command brought a sense of relief
to New Yorkers, but not an end to Continental Army activity in the colony.
Lord Sterling of New Jersey, promoted to brigadier general, assumed
command of militia units in New York City, totalling 9,000 men by the
time of General Washington's arrival on April 13. Lord Sterling also continued the construction of land defenses begun by Lee.[86] McDougall,
colonel of New York's first militia battalion, was drawn into these military
activities, which became ever more important when Washington took personal command of the army.[87] In the face of the enemy's imminent arrival,
revolutionary politics became secondary to the popular leader; in fact, Mc-
Dougall was so determined to serve in the coming battle that he made no
effort to retain his seat in the Provincial Congress.[88] When McDougall failed
of election on April 16, a surprised Jay hurried home from Philadelphia to
manage affairs in the New York Congress.[89]

McDougall's withdrawal from the political arena and the beginning of
his military career ended the old leadership of the extremist wing of the
revolutionary movement. With Lamb in a British prison, Sears busy in
Connecticut, and McDougall on active military service, the popular triumvirate which for so many years had played the game of local politics and
had vigorously promoted opposition to Britain was now gone. It was indeed
an irony of events that the three men, who more than any others had paved
the way for New York's independence, should be out of public life when
separation from Britain and a new form of government became the burning issues of the day. The consequences were important: at a critical
moment, the Sons of Liberty lost their old leaders, a void which new men,
especially Daniel Dunscomb and William Goforth, could not immediately
fill. Thus New York's lower class was deprived of access, through the

expenses of his trip through Long Island be paid by the colony, but his request was simply
"filed." *Ibid.*, 386; Force, ed., *American Archives*, V, 511.
   [85] McDougall to Jay, March 20, 1776, Jay Papers.
   [86] *Journals . . . Provincial Congress . . . New York*, I, 343, 356-57; Christopher Ward,
The War of the Revolution (2 vols., New York, 1952), I, 205-07.
   [87] Lord Sterling's promotion miffed McDougall, but Jay soothed him by explaining that
it was for political reasons, not merit. McDougall to Schuyler, March 14, 1776, Jay to
McDougall, March 23, 1776, McDougall Papers; McDougall to Jay, March 20, 1776, Jay
Papers.
   [88] McDougall to Schuyler, March 14, 1776, McDougall Papers.
   [89] Becker, *New York Political Parties*, 256-58; McDougall probably did not tell Jay
that he wanted out of politics and therefore Jay could not understand why he was not
re-elected. Jay to McDougall, April 27, 1776, McDougall Papers.

old radicals, to aristocratic decision-makers when the Provincial Congress in May began considering the principles and structure of government. This loss, coupled with the British invasion and occupation of the provincial capital, had the ultimate effect of giving the Livingston aristocrats virtually a free hand in establishing New York's independence.

The Colonial Agents, English Politics, and the American Revolution

Michael G. Kammen*

A T the conclusion of the Seven Years' War the North American colonies had been maintaining agents in London for more than a century. These quasi-representatives, however, rapidly acquired new significance after 1763. Simultaneously their task of lobbying and conciliating became increasingly complex and difficult. The heightened importance of the agents as well as the new problems they faced were outgrowths of the prolonged crisis in British imperial relations which culminated in American independence.

When successive ministries in the 1760's attempted to tighten a framework of colonial administration that had been lax for decades, they constricted a system unaccustomed to such pressure. In consequence the formal and traditional mechanisms of Anglo-American government began to give way. As Governor Francis Bernard remarked, "the present disunion has broke thro' many respectable forms."[1] Under these circumstances an extraconstitutional institution such as the colonial agencies might have served as an adhesive element. After the accession of George III, in fact, the agents found themselves in positions of considerable responsibility, sometimes to such an extent that it unnerved them. During the Seven Years' War they had co-operated with the Treasury in handling the apportionment of parliamentary funds for colonial military expenses. Perhaps on the basis of this experience George Grenville indicated a willingness to work through the agents in 1764-65 as an alternative to more orthodox channels of communication. By the same token, the

* Mr. Kammen, a member of the Department of History, Harvard University, read this paper in a different form to the Colonial Society of Massachusetts, Apr. 23, 1964.
[1] Francis Bernard to Henry S. Conway, June 28, 1766, Bernard Manuscripts, IV, 228, Houghton Library, Harvard University. See also Samuel Adams to Dennys De Berdt, Jan. 30, 1768, in Henry Alonzo Cushing, ed., *The Writings of Samuel Adams*, I (New York, 1904), 177-178.

provincial representatives undertook to commit their constituents to a compromise affecting paper currency in 1764. The Stamp Act crisis, above all, proved just how aggressive and effective the North American lobby could be; it showed that the agents were critically needed while revealing their potential value.[2] But the successes that the lobbyists achieved during the brief Rockingham regime produced in some quarters expectations which were soon to be disappointed. Like other components of the old imperial system, the agencies underwent a gradual decline.

Nevertheless, close scrutiny of their institutional deterioration can broaden our understanding of the coming of the American Revolution. The causes of the agents' plight are to be found in their various relationships: to each other, to their traditional allies in lobbying, to their constituents, to the progress of the constitutional debate, and, most of all, to the English politicians—the hands and servants of power, as Jasper Mauduit called them.[3] An examination of these relationships suggests the way colonial affairs were handled in London during the years before independence, for the process by which the agencies declined is symptomatic of the way an entire network of formal and informal lines of transatlantic communication suffered under the strain placed upon them by the factional nature of English politics, the intransigence of the colonists, and the need for financial and administrative reform.

A major element in reducing the agents' effectiveness was the mutability of English public life. Until the accession of George III eighteenth-century politics had been notable for nothing so much as stability; but after 1760 ministries rose and fell in rapid succession, and with them often tumbled the bureaucratic hierarchy that managed the concerns of the kingdom. These were years of transition. Four and one-half decades of Whig preponderance were giving way to nearly half a century of Tory

[2] Lawrence Henry Gipson, *The Triumphant Empire: Thunder-Clouds Gather in the West, 1763-1766* (New York, 1961), 45-51; Edmund S. Morgan and Helen M. Morgan, *The Stamp Act Crisis, Prologue to Revolution* (Chapel Hill, 1953), 64-66; Lewis B. Namier, *England in the Age of the American Revolution*, 2d ed. (New York, 1961), 252-253; D. H. Watson, Barlow Trecothick and Other Associates of Lord Rockingham During the Stamp Act Crisis, 1765-66 (unpubl. M.A. thesis, Sheffield University, 1957); B. R. Smith, The Committee of the Whole House to Consider the American Papers (January and February 1766) (unpubl. M.A. thesis, Sheffield University, 1956).

[3] Mauduit to Samuel White, Feb. 19, 1765, in Alden Bradford, ed., *Speeches of the Governors of Massachusetts, from 1765 to 1775.* . . . (Boston, 1818), 31; *Jasper Mauduit. Agent in London for the Province of the Massachusetts-Bay, 1762-1765,* in Massachusetts Historical Society, *Collections,* LXXIV (Boston, 1918), 168n.

reign. Agents attempting to lobby under such conditions found their task becoming progressively more unmanageable. For several generations the operations of their institution had been facilitated by connections which were permanently situated and reliable.[4] Suddenly all aspects of political life became uncertain. As Benjamin Franklin, agent for several colonies, complained to the Pennsylvania Committee of Correspondence, " 'tis a kind of Labour in vain to attempt making Impressions on such moveable Materials; 'tis like writing on the Sand in a windy Day."[5]

The agents were acutely conscious of how the permutations of British ministries served to frustrate their purposes and complicate their work. After the Earl of Bute's administration had given way to Grenville's in 1763, Richard Jackson, agent for Connecticut and Pennsylvania, warned Eliphalet Dyer against making hasty "Applications, as it is very uncertain

[4] For the development of the agencies in the 17th and 18th centuries there is a considerable literature available. The general studies include Lillian M. Penson, *The Colonial Agents of the British West Indies* . . . (London, 1924); Mabel P. Wolff, *The Colonial Agency of Pennsylvania, 1712-1757* (Philadelphia, 1933); James J. Burns, *The Colonial Agents of New England* (Washington, 1935); Edward P. Lilly, *The Colonial Agents of New York and New Jersey* (Washington, 1936); Ella Lonn, *The Colonial Agents of the Southern Colonies* (Chapel Hill, 1945); Harold W. Currie, Massachusetts Politics and the Colonial Agency, 1762-1770 (unpubl. Ph.D. diss., University of Michigan, 1960); Edwin P. Tanner, "Colonial Agencies in England During the Eighteenth Century," *Political Science Quarterly,* XVI (1901), 24-49; Beverly W. Bond, Jr., "The Colonial Agent as a Popular Representative," *ibid.,* XXXV (1920), 372-392; Samuel J. Ervin, "The Provincial Agents of North Carolina," *James Sprunt Historical Publications,* XVI (Chapel Hill, 1919), 63-77; Marguerite Appleton, "The Agents of the New England Colonies in the Revolutionary Period," *New England Quarterly,* VI (1933), 371-387. Some of the better biographical studies include Appleton's "Richard Partridge: Colonial Agent," *ibid.,* V (1932), 293-309; Robert J. Taylor, "Israel Mauduit," *ibid.,* XXIV (1951), 208-230; Lewis B. Namier, "Charles Garth, Agent for South Carolina," *English Historical Review,* LIV (1939), 632-652; Malcolm Freiberg, "William Bollan, Agent of Massachusetts," *More Books,* XXIII (1948), 43-54, 90-100, 135-146, 168-182, 212-220; Charles L. Sanford, The Days of Jeremy Dummer, Colonial Agent (unpubl. Ph.D. diss., Harvard University, 1952); Alfred Owen Aldridge, "Benjamin Franklin as Georgia Agent," *Georgia Review,* VI (1952), 161-173; J. J. Zimmerman, Benjamin Franklin: A Study of Pennsylvania Politics and the Colonial Agency, 1755-1775 (unpubl. Ph.D. diss., University of Michigan, 1956); Ross J. S. Hoffman, *Edmund Burke, New York Agent* . . . (Philadelphia, 1956); Leonard W. Cowie, *Henry Newman: An American in London, 1708-43* (London, 1956); D. H. Watson, "Barlow Trecothick," British Association for American Studies, *Bulletin,* New Ser. (Sept. 1960), 36-49, (Mar. 1961), 29-39; Nicholas Varga, "Robert Charles: New York Agent, 1748-1770," *William and Mary Quarterly,* 3d Ser., XVIII (1961), 211-235.

[5] June 10, 1766, in *Pennsylvania Magazine of History and Biography,* V (1881), 355.

at present who will be the persons in Power after the Sitting of the Parliament . . . as the present Ministry are not Suposed to be permanent." Seven weeks later the situation was no more settled, and Jackson informed Franklin that "affairs here never were so mutable." A year and a half later Franklin found colonial affairs "at a total Stop here, by the Present unsettled State of the Ministry." When the Grenvillites in turn gave way to the Rockinghams in 1765, Jackson observed that "one hardly knows who to apply to on any occasion in any department except the Treasury which is the only one fixed, and even there the hurry of business yet so new to Gentlemen little acquainted with business in general leaves little leisure for new subjects of application."[6]

129

Rockingham and his followers made their exit during the summer of 1766, causing Franklin to comment that "all ministerial Dispositions are extremely fluctuating. . . . all American Affairs, even the Granting of Lands, are now at a Stand." In August the Duke of Grafton headed a new government; and, although he remained nominal leader of his ministry until North replaced him early in 1770, his unwieldy coalition underwent numerous shifts and changes.[7] These vicissitudes continually slowed the mechanics of colonial administration and the operations of those charged with expediting such affairs.[8] Late in 1766 Franklin reported a

---

[6] Dyer to Jared Ingersoll, Nov. 3, 1763, in Franklin B. Dexter, ed., "A Selection from the Correspondence and Miscellaneous Papers of Jared Ingersoll," in New Haven Colony Historical Society, *Papers,* IX (New Haven, 1918), 287; Jackson to Franklin, Dec. 27, 1763, in Carl Van Doren, ed., *Letters and Papers of Benjamin Franklin and Richard Jackson, 1753-1785* (Philadelphia, 1947), 121; Franklin to Hugh Roberts, July 7, 1765, in Albert Henry Smyth, ed., *The Writings of Benjamin Franklin* (New York, 1905-7), IV, 386; Franklin to Cadwallader Evans, July 13, 1765, Franklin Manuscripts, American Philosophical Society Library, Philadelphia; Jackson to Andrew Oliver, July 26, 1765, Letter book 1763-1773, pp. 100-101, Massachusetts Archives, State House, Boston.

[7] Franklin to Pa. Committee of Correspondence, June 10, 1766, in *Pa. Mag. of Hist. and Biog.,* V (1881), 355; Franklin to Joseph Galloway, Aug. 22, 1766, Mason-Franklin Collection, Yale University Library, New Haven.

[8] Charles Garth lamented to his South Carolina constituents that the "Fluctuation of Counsels and of Ministers in this Country is a truly unhappy Circumstance for the People in all Parts of the Dominions; The Ground of Yesterday is no longer to Morrow." Garth to South Carolina Committee of Correspondence, Aug. 14, 1768, in "Garth Correspondence," *South Carolina Historical and Genealogical Magazine,* XXX (1929), 218-223. By 1769 William Samuel Johnson believed England was on the verge of "some very decisive political revolution , , , in the very fluctuating condition we are now in, affairs are every day almost varying, and assuming new appearances." Johnson's alarm intensified as he stayed on in London, watching "their intestine divisions and party squabbles, which . . . actually seem to threaten a dis-

"Ferment at Court; every Day producing Changes or Resignations . . . so that little else has been attended to." The following April he found "daily apprehensions of new changes make it extremely difficult to get forward with business." And in May he remarked that "the ministry . . . has not been looked upon, either by itself or others, as settled, which is another cause of postponing every thing not immediately necessary to be considered."[9]

A series of cabinet resignations and replacements late in 1767 brought about a "fluctuation in the Ministry, during which time no business was done." At this juncture the Southern Department under Lord Shelburne relinquished stewardship of the colonies. "All American affairs will now be thrown into an entire new channel," Connecticut's agent, William Samuel Johnson, observed; "all is to begin anew with Lord Hilsborough; new negotiations are to be commenced, new connections formed, etc., which is an unhappy delay to all who have any affairs of that country [America] to solicit." Johnson had been on the verge of concluding some business with the Southern Department. Now the whole would have to be arranged again with Hillsborough. "Thus it is in all affairs," Johnson wrote. "When you have pursued them almost to a Close and think you are pretty sure of your point some change of System intervenes and oversets all your plans. So unsteady are their Counsels, so uncertain the Tenure of those in Power!"[10]

This instability and uncertainty had unfortunate effects beyond the obvious stoppage of political and administrative business. The agents began to regard these conditions as normal. Some developed a tendency to procrastinate in presenting petitions or to delay applying for redress

solution of the whole political system, and the ruin of the empire." Johnson to William Pitkin, Sept. 18, 1769, in *The Trumbull Papers*, Mass. Hist. Soc., *Colls.*, 5th Ser., IX (Boston, 1885), 362; Johnson to Jonathan Trumbull, Oct. 16, 1769, *ibid.*, 376.

[9] Franklin to Galloway, Dec. 13, 1766, Apr. 14 and May 20, 1767, William Clements Library, Ann Arbor, Michigan; Franklin to John Ross, Apr. 11, 1767, in Smyth, ed., *Writings of Franklin*, V, 23; Franklin to Cadwallader Evans, May 5, 1767, *ibid.*, 25.

[10] De Berdt to Samuel Dexter, Dec. 23, 1767, in "Letters of Dennys De Berdt, 1757-1770," in Colonial Society of Massachusetts, *Publications*, XIII (Boston, 1912), 328; Johnson to William Pitkin, Dec. 26, 1767, in *Trumbull Papers*, 252; Franklin to Galloway, Feb. 17, 1768, in Smyth, ed., *Writings of Franklin*, V, 97; Garth to South Carolina Committee of Correspondence, Jan. 27, 1768, in "Garth Correspondence," 183-184; Johnson to Dyer, Jan. 22, 1768, in Julian P. Boyd, ed., *The Susquehanna Company Papers* (Wilkes-Barre, 1930-33), III, 8.

in anticipation of a governmental shift favorable to the colonies. Ministries, for their part, became "afraid of changing anything in settled measures," Franklin wrote, "lest something should go wrong, and the opposition make an advantage of it against them." This applied with particular force in 1768 and 1769 after the Bedford faction, least sympathetic to the American view, joined Grafton's administration. Composed of incompatible and mutually mistrustful men, his Majesty's government was weak.[11]

If ministries were frail in these years, their fragmented opposition—relied on heavily by the colonists and their agents—was even weaker. The great breach in the ranks of those who had united to conciliate America during the Stamp Act crisis first appeared during the winter of 1766-67. At that time Edmund Burke, soon to be New York's agent, and the Rockinghams formally went into opposition, while Henry Conway and other Chathamites chose to remain in office. Early in 1769 William Samuel Johnson learned that the several factions then out of office wished to raise the American question in Westminster but were unable to agree on the best way. By 1771 Henry Marchant, Rhode Island's agent, found it "amazing into how many Parties the political World are divided. The Administration side seem not to be Cordial Friends to One Another—The City are in three or four Divisions, greatly detrimental to the General good—and the Opposition in the Higher Spheres have different Ends in View, —... Their Jealousy destroys One Another—"[12]

Even such a singular organization as the radical Bill of Rights Society in which Arthur Lee, deputy agent of Massachusetts Bay, participated was riven with dissension and unable to settle on the best policies to pursue. If Lee sided with any group in the Society he alienated the rest. Late in 1774 Lee took the petition of the Continental Congress to Chatham for the Great Commoner's approbation. "My object," Lee declared, "Is to unite the heads of opposition under one uniform large ground." He failed. Rockinghams and Chathamites could only join in

[11] De Berdt to Thomas Cushing, Feb. 1, 1769, in "Letters of Dennys De Berdt," 356; Franklin to William Franklin, Nov. 13, 1767, in Clarence Walworth Alvord and Clarence Edwin Carter, eds., *Trade and Politics, 1767-1769* (Springfield, Ill., 1921), 104-105; Franklin to ?, Mar. 18, 1770, in Smyth, ed., *Writings of Franklin*, V, 251-253.

[12] Johnson to Ingersoll, Mar. 8, 1769, Johnson Manuscripts, Box 1, Connecticut Historical Society, Hartford; Carl B. Cone, *Burke and the Nature of Politics: The Age of the American Revolution* (Lexington, Ky., 1957), 213-215; Marchant to Ezra Stiles, Sept. 21, 1771, Stiles Manuscripts, Yale Univ. Lib.

castigating the unwise policies of North's administration. Whereas Burke and his cohorts upheld the constitutional supremacy of Parliament, Chatham supported the American denunciation of parliamentary taxation.[13]

Gradually the agents came to realize that their so-called "friends" among the opposition minorities were often motivated by principles and pressures quite removed from any intrinsic sympathy for colonial aspirations. Arthur Lee wrote his brother that Shelburne was the "only one attached to us from principle." The rest were merely "against opposing us." As William Samuel Johnson cynically but astutely observed, the Rockinghams really did not seem so very enthusiastic to repeal the Townshend Revenue Act,

but rather that it should remain to embarrass the present Ministers, and as a means of their destruction, to whom they hope to succeed. They had rather have the honor of doing it themselves, and mean in their turn to govern the Colonies, though in a different way. . . . Indeed, this must be the case with every party, in some degree; the Colonies, therefore, if they are wise, will take care not to become the dupes of any party, nor connect themselves too deeply with any set of men in this country; but, conscious of their own importance, and attentive to their own rights and true interest, will avail themselves, as they may, of the divisions here as they arise, make use of each party in their turns as they find it expedient, but be absolutely subservient to none, and in the end it is not improbable they may be courted by every party, and eventually gain an ascendant over them all.[14]

Inscrutable party alignments in the 1760's and the uncertainty of factional ambitions had a peculiarly devastating effect on the functioning of agents because they occurred just when Parliament assumed a major

[13] Lee to Samuel Adams, June 14, 1771, Apr. 7, 1772, Adams Manuscripts, New York Public Library; Franklin to Joseph Smith, Feb. 6, 1772, Mason-Franklin Collection; Lee to Richard Henry Lee, Dec. 26, 1774, in Peter Force, comp., *American Archives*, 4th Ser., I (Washington, 1837), 1058-1059; Cone, *Burke and the Nature of Politics*, 280-281.

[14] Lee to Richard Henry Lee, Sept. 18, 1769, in Richard Henry Lee, *The Life of Arthur Lee* . . . (Boston, 1829), I, 191; Johnson to William Pitkin, Apr. 11, 1767, Apr. 26, 1769, in *Trumbull Papers*, 226, 338-339. Early in 1767 Rockingham hoped to form an administration that would include both George Grenville and Charles Townshend! (See Lewis B. Namier and John Brooke, eds., *The History of Parliament: The House of Commons, 1754-1790*, II [New York, 1964], 148.) See also William Lee to Samuel Adams, Mar. 4, 1775: "you will readily perceive how little essential good, you are to expect . . . from the opposition here." (Adams MSS.)

role in formulating colonial policy. Heretofore Commons and Lords had viewed imperial government primarily as one aspect of a mercantile mechanism overseen by the Secretary of State for the Southern Department and the Board of Trade. But after 1763, as legislative decisions became more important than executive administration, opportunities for individual negotiation and favor lessened. For nearly a century the agencies had institutionalized accommodating relationships with the various governmental boards and civil servants. After 1763, however, traditional modes of lobbying in Georgian England were wrenched into new and unfamiliar forms. The measure of an agent's capacity and shrewdness became his ability to discern the proper points and persons where pressure could best be applied. As never before the place was Westminster;[15] and in the eighteenth century the House of Lords, where bills were frequently initiated, was quite as important as its elected counterpart. Thus the lobbyist's field of operations broadened greatly, and with it the complexity of achieving Anglo-American understanding.[16]

133

The agents' mission in identifying and influencing the decisive men in Parliament and the shifting ministries was itself difficult enough. But they were also faced in both Westminster and Whitehall with widespread ignorance of the colonies, with general indifference to provincial conditions, and with increasing hostility to America. Henry Cruger, Jr., spent three weeks in London in 1766, "every Day with some one Member of Parliament, talking as it were for my own Life. It is surprising," he observed, "how ignorant some of them are of *Trade* and *America*." "The affairs of America seem very little understood and not all attended to,"

---

[15] Thus in 1767 Henry Eustace McCulloh reported to North Carolina that "a vast struggle for Power, is expected this Winter." McCulloh had learned there would be a concerted effort "to take the Affairs of the Colonies out of the hands of the Parliament and place them in their old Channel, that is, under the direction of the Crown, and the Great Boards,—by repealing the restrictive Acts." McCulloh to John Harvey, Sept. 13, 1767, in William L. Saunders, ed., *The Colonial Records of North Carolina*, VII (Raleigh, 1890), 517. Nevertheless the legislators clung tenaciously to the responsibilities they had assumed after the war. When Arthur Lee applied to the Secretary of State for the Colonies in 1773, he found Lord Dartmouth had "no power to relieve us in anything. The means of redress for the rest of our complaints, he [said], only parliament can minister." Lee to Samuel Adams, Dec. 22, 1773, Adams MSS.

[16] A. S. Turberville, *The House of Lords in the Eighteenth Century* (Oxford, 1927), passim. For a discussion of these alterations in general terms by a political sociologist, see Samuel E. Finer, *Anonymous Empire: A Study of the Lobby in Great Britain* (London, 1958), 21-23.

complained Henry Eustace McCulloh, North Carolina's agent. And William Samuel Johnson heard "a respectable Counsellor at Law ask Mr. [Richard] Jackson gravely in the Hall whether Philadelphia was in in [*sic*] the E. or West Indies and said he had a Notion it was upon the Coast of Sumatra. Such is their Knowledge of America." After Johnson returned to Connecticut Thomas Pownall warned him not to expect any action to be taken regarding the colonies "because few think and of those who do think on these matters 'tis by piece meal and not upon system." The ultimate indictment came in 1773 from a frustrated Franklin: "The great Defect here is, in all sorts of People, a want of attention to what passes in such remote Countries as America; an Unwillingness even to read any thing about them if it appears a little lengthy, and a Disposition to postpone the Consideration even of the Things they know they must at last consider, that so they may have Time for what more immediately concerns them, and withal enjoy their Amusements, and be undisturbed in the universal Dissipation."[17]

Difficulties the agents encountered in London as a result of English ignorance of America were compounded by the suspicion with which the successors to the Rockingham ministry viewed them. In 1768 Dennys De Berdt, agent for Massachusetts Bay, reported that the Grafton ministry found the concerted efforts of the North American lobby "disagreeable." The next year he communicated to the same confidant Hillsborough's "disapprobation to all Agents"; and Franklin noted "the Plan here at present being, to have as little to do with Agents as possible." In 1771, early in North's government, Franklin related to his constituents a still more serious development. "Under the present American administration, [agents] are rather looked on with an evil eye, as obstructors of ministerial measures; and the Secretary would, I imagine, be well pleased to get rid of them, being, as he has sometimes intimated, of opinion that agents are unnecessary, for that, whatever is to be transacted

[17] Henry Cruger, Jr., to Henry Cruger, Feb. 14, 1766, in *Commerce of Rhode Island, 1726-1800* (Mass. Hist. Soc., *Colls.*, 7th Ser., IX [Boston, 1914]), I, 139; McCulloh to John Harvey, July 15, 1768, in Saunders, ed., *Col. Recs. of N. C.*, VII, 757; entry for Nov. 27, 1769, in William Samuel Johnson's London journal, Johnson Manuscripts, Conn. Hist. Soc.; Pownall to Johnson, July 31, 1772, Johnson MSS., Box 2; Franklin to Samuel Cooper, July 7, 1773, in Smyth, ed., *Writings of Franklin*, VI, 93. See also John Wentworth to Daniel Peirce, Feb. 15, 1766: "It is notorious, that we are scarcely known and not considered but in the most diminutive way." (Peirce Papers, Portsmouth Athenaeum, Portsmouth, N. H.) Wentworth was then in London as New Hampshire's agent.

between the assemblies of colonies and the government here, may be
done through and by the governor's letters, and more properly than by
any agent whatever."[18]

By the beginning of the 1770's the provincial representatives were also
meeting with heightened resistance in other spheres of British life. Such
traditional allies in lobbying as the editors, publishers, merchants, and some
important Dissenters became more and more reluctant to commit themselves to a cause that seemed politically hopeless and intellectually unreasonable.[19] The problem was succinctly evoked in a letter to John
Adams from a relative abroad: "I agree with you, sir, absolutely that
America suffers to an inexpressible degree for want of proper connections in England. But when you ask me to procure you a friend or an
acquaintance here, you put me, sir, to a very difficult task indeed." This
dilemma is central to the coming of the Revolution, and the circumstances
of the agents are a significant manifestation of the problem. Through
them it is possible to observe and gauge the waning influence of America
and Americans in London. Relying on information from New York
based on Edmund Burke's letters, Adams noted in his diary that the
English "Nation is against us, that we cannot depend upon any Support
of any kind from thence, that the Merchants are very much against us,"
and so on.[20]

Among the interest groups lost to the lobbyists, none was so sorely
missed as the British mercantile community. The briefly joined alliance
of West Indian and North American merchants that was so instrumental
in procuring repeal of the Stamp Act collapsed in 1766. After 1770 the
colonial nonimportation agreements lost their political and economic
leverage and it became apparent that the American commercial classes
could not sustain the boycott without breaches that undermined its ef-

[18] De Berdt to Richard Cary, Nov. 15, 1768, Mar. 29, 1769, in "Letters of Dennys
De Berdt," 342, 370; Franklin to Joseph Galloway, Jan. 9, 1769, in Carl Van Doren,
ed., Benjamin Franklin's Autobiographical Writings (New York, 1945), 186; Frank-
lin to Thomas Cushing, Feb. 5, 1771, in Smyth, ed., Writings of Franklin, V, 295;
Letter from the Provincial Agent, Apr. 3, 1769, in Allen D. Candler, ed., The
Colonial Records of the State of Georgia, XV (Atlanta, 1907), 26-27.

[19] See Michael G. Kammen, The Colonial Agents, English Politics and the American Revolution (unpubl. Ph.D. diss., Harvard University, 1964), chaps. 11 and 12.

[20] Isaac Smith, Jr., to Adams, Sept. 3, 1771, in Lyman H. Butterfield and others,
eds., Adams Family Correspondence, I (Cambridge, Mass., 1963), 79-80; Entry Aug.
22, 1774, in Lyman H. Butterfield and others, eds., Diary and Autobiography of
John Adams, II (Cambridge, Mass., 1961), 107.

fectiveness. By the end of the 1760's British trade no longer depended upon North America as it had earlier. New markets opened to the East and the depression that unsettled Britain after the Seven Years' War disappeared.[21] Therefore the ultimate crisis initiated by the Boston Tea Party in 1773-74 found many of Britain's merchants unresponsive to the agents' efforts to activate them. "It is a capital mistake of our American friends to expect insurrections here," wrote Samuel Curwen from London. "The manufactories are in full employ, and one of the warmest of the friends of America told me that letters from Manchester expressed joy that no American orders had been sent, otherwise there must have been disappointment somewhere."[22]

136

As antipathies toward America grew and colonial allies in and out of Parliament defected or became powerless in the decade before the Revolution, the agents met with one obstruction after another in their attempts to perform their traditional functions. Members of Parliament and ministers reacted to American resistance by making themselves less available to the agents and by invoking procedural technicalities to inhibit the agents' activities. For generations before the Seven Years' War there had been many accessible and often corrupt means of circumventing orthodox lines of procedure. But between 1766 and 1775 the system of colonial administration developed a disconcerting devotion to proprieties. All manner of long forgotten and ignored regulations were invoked in order to suppress the provincial voice in the Great Debate. In Westminster standing orders of the Houses of Parliament were revived to obviate the agents' petitions; and in Whitehall the various departmental heads relied upon quibbling points to invalidate the agents' requests for hearings. As Franklin was prompted to observe, refusing to hear "complaints, from punctilios about form, had always an ill effect, and gave great handle to those turbulent, factious spirits who are ever ready to blow the coals of dissention."[23]

[21] Lucy S. Sutherland, "Edmund Burke and the First Rockingham Ministry," *Eng. Hist. Rev.*, XLVII (1932), 46-70; Charles M. Andrews, "The Boston Merchants and the Non-Importation Movement," in Col. Soc. Mass., *Publs.*, XIX (Boston, 1918), 250 ff.; Johnson to Jonathan Trumbull, Dec. 5, 1769, in *Trumbull Papers*, 384-385.

[22] Quoted in Namier, *England in Age of American Revolution*, 254-255; see also Edmund Burke to Rockingham, Aug. 23, 1775, in George H. Guttridge, ed., *The Correspondence of Edmund Burke*, III (Chicago, 1961), 191.

[23] Franklin to William Franklin, Nov. 9, 1765, Mason-Franklin Collection. For the ease with which lobbying was facilitated in the 17th and 18th centuries, see

A strong feeling developed within governmental circles that for any business there was a "regular official Method" of effecting it. Ministers and their myrmidons frowned upon any alternative as "irregular and disrespectful." Before 1766, for example, issues of prime importance might be managed by the First Lord of Trade independently of his board. This permitted the lobbyist to avoid excessive red tape and hindrances. After that date, however, it became increasingly difficult to avoid procedural problems in search of prompt solutions to pressing questions.[24] When Hillsborough refused to recognize the authority of agents chosen by assemblies alone, Edmund Burke lamented to his New York employers: "this I consider in Effect, as a destruction of one of the most necessary Mediums of Communication between the Colonies and the parent Country. The provinces ought in my opinion to have *a direct* intercourse with Ministry and Parliament here, by some person who might be truely confidential with them who appoint him. Who might be entrusted with the strength and weakness of their Cause in all controverted points; and who might represent their own Sentiments in their own way."[25]

137

Factions and coalitions hostile to the colonies had at their disposal various ways of making life miserable for the agents and effective lobbying all but impossible. The Grenvillites, for example, even while in opposition, could stir up in Parliament a "general rage" against America. Thus a politician's views on provincial questions became "one of the distinctions of party here," Franklin remarked. Members of the opposition who stood against measures to tax the colonies "would be stigmatized as Americans, betrayers of Old England, etc." When Tories out of office seized upon reports of the disreputable "conduct of the Assemblies of

---

Increase Mather, *A Brief Account Concerning Several of the Agents of New-England, Their Negotiation at the Court of England* . . . (London, 1691); entry for Nov. 6, 1735, in Beverly McAnear, ed., "An American in London, 1735-1736," *Pa. Mag. of Hist. and Biog.,* LXIV (1940), 387; Stanley N. Katz, An Easie Access: Anglo-American Politics in New York, 1732-1753 (unpubl. Ph.D. diss., Harvard University, 1961).

[24] Franklin and others to Edward Biddle, Dec. 24, 1774, in *Boston Gazette and Country Journal,* Mar. 27, 1775; Aldridge, "Franklin as Georgia Agent," 168; Franklin to Charles Thomson, Feb. 5, 1775, in Smyth, ed., *Writings of Franklin,* VI, 303; Lord Hyde to Lord Dartmouth, Aug. 13, 1765, Dartmouth Manuscripts #78, William Salt Library, Stafford, England; Privy Council, Class 2, Vol. 114, pp. 212-213, 225-226, 229, 234-235, 245-246, 248-249, Public Record Office, London.

[25] Burke to James De Lancey, Dec. 4, 1771, in Lucy S. Sutherland, ed., *The Correspondence of Edmund Burke,* II (Chicago, 1960), 291. Italics are Burke's.

New York and Boston . . . in order to distress the friends of America in the present ministry, nothing so little interesting to them as our application can get forward," Franklin wrote.[26]

The mildest means a ministry might employ was simply to ignore agents and unpleasant issues they raised. The Grafton-Chatham coalition squelched Jackson, De Berdt, and Johnson in this fashion in 1767 when they sought favor for the New England fishery interest. Again in 1768, Charles Garth, South Carolina's agent, related that administration refusal to push repeal of the Currency Act brought lobbying to a halt: "Paper Currency they decline meddling with, the Agents dare not stir in it, unless the Ministry will adjust in promoting the Measure."[27]

After 1770 the new North ministry anxiously sought to achieve permanence and power. Therefore it became critically important to by-pass imperial questions that might be unsettling.[28] Very soon after taking office North's government attempted to intimidate the agents by warning them "that any further opposition to the Ministry will induce the Government to withdraw the several bounties paid for the encouragement of American produce or importation to Great Britain." The admonition was repeated whenever the situation seemed to warrant, and it undoubtedly put a damper upon excessive prodding of North and his cabinet by the agents.[29]

[26] Benjamin Franklin to Joseph Galloway, May 20 and Aug. 8, 1767, William Clements Library; Smyth, ed., *Writings of Franklin*, V, 41-42; Franklin to John Ross, Apr. 11, 1767, *ibid.*, 23.

[27] Johnson to Pitkin, Mar. 19, 1767, in *Trumbull Papers*, 219-220; Garth to South Carolina Committee of Correspondence, Jan. 27, 1768, in "Garth Correspondence," 183-184.

[28] William Samuel Johnson warned Connecticut's governor in 1771 that "the general state of things here is extremely calm. The Ministry, in perfect plenitude of power, seem to wish for nothing so much as to possess that power in peace, and to continue undisturbed in their offices. To this end, they avoid, as far as possible, everything that may tend to awaken the attention, to unite the force, or increase the strength of that Opposition they have so surprisingly and so unexpectedly vanquished and dissipated." Johnson to Trumbull, Mar. 15, 1771, in *Trumbull Papers*, 476; see also Arthur Lee to Samuel Adams, Oct. 13, 1773, in Lee, *Life of Arthur Lee*, I, 236; Garth to South Carolina Committee of Correspondence, May 4, 1773, Garth Letter book, South Carolina Archives, Columbia, S. C.

[29] *Boston Evening Post*, May 28, 1770, Nov. 1, 1773. In 1774 stories persisted that the administration unjustly persecuted friends of the colonies. A year later Arthur Lee reported the rumor in London "that if any one is proceeded against here for corresponding with the people of America, or befriending them here, [the Continental Congress] will immediately seize upon all those in America who correspond with or act for the Ministry. Without such a declaration their friends, and especially

Apart from these assorted pressures, ministerial politicians consistently relied on four weapons to keep the agents in check after 1767. Parliament could exclude them from the galleries, and it could avoid hearing remonstrances they tried to present. Administrations could refuse to recognize the legitimacy of an agent's appointment, and they could gain access to his mail through spies and control of the postal system.[30] These weapons used in combination proved effective in undermining lobbying and restricting the efforts of the agents toward conciliation.

. Early in 1773 Franklin wrote his son that he had grown weary of endless ministerial obstacles to negotiation and accommodation. He wanted to return to Philadelphia. A year later, after his public condemnation by Alexander Wedderburn in the Cockpit, the Doctor poured out his irritation and discouragement to Thomas Cushing, Speaker of the House in Massachusetts Bay.

139

When I see that all petitions and complaints of grievances are so odious to government, that even the mere pipe which conveys them becomes obnoxious, I am at a loss to know how peace and union are to be maintained or restored between the different parts of the empire. Grievances cannot be redressed unless they are known; and they cannot be known but through complaints and petitions. If these are deemed affronts, and the messengers [i.e., agents] punished as offenders, who will henceforth send petitions? And who will deliver them? It has been thought a dangerous thing in any state to stop up the vent of griefs. Wise governments have therefore generally received petitions with some indulgence, even when but slightly founded. Those who think themselves injured by their rulers are sometimes, by a mild and prudent answer, convinced of their error. But where complaining is a crime, hope becomes despair.[31]

By 1775 the agents found they must operate only through the Secretary of State for the Colonies, "that being the regular official method, and the

---

their Agents here, will be at the mercy of the most unprincipled Administration that ever disgraced humanity." Lee to Francis L. Lee, Apr. 2, 1774, in Force, comp., *American Archives*, 4th Ser., I, 237; Lee to ?, Sept. 5, 1775, Lee Manuscripts, II, #62, Houghton Library.

[30] For illustrations and the development of these sanctions, see Kammen, Colonial Agents and the American Revolution, 205-227.

[31] Franklin to William Franklin, Mar. 15, 1773, in John Bigelow, ed., *The Complete Works of Benjamin Franklin* . . . (New York, 1887-88), V, 116-117; Franklin to Cushing, Feb. 15, 1774, *ibid.*, 302-303.

only one in which we might on occasion call for an Answer." Yet by
that time responsibility for colonial administration had shifted from the
ineffectual Lord Dartmouth to other hands.[32]

The impediments encountered by the agents and the handicaps under
which they operated were not entirely the making of English politics,
however. The agencies as an institution suffered from inherent weak-
nesses which were exacerbated by the deepening crisis in imperial relations. Their effectiveness as a pressure group was governed as much by
the demands and attitudes of their constituents as by the political scene
in London where they functioned. In the seventeenth and eighteenth
centuries the agencies had developed—and logically so—as discrete
extensions of each colony's government in Britain. The lobbyist was conscious only of a relationship to his particular employers; and when the
interests of two colonies came into conflict, as over a boundary, the
representatives of these colonies customarily re-enacted the dispute in
London, like marionettes responding to some remote manipulators. The
agencies were indeed provincial. Their frailties partially grew out of the
fact that their fealties had long been parochial and local. Too often their
own personal concerns and those of their respective colonies barred the
way to co-ordinated efforts.

Nevertheless, between 1763 and 1770 they nearly transcended the
limitations of their institutional background. During these years they
averaged one joint consultation per month (exclusive of the holiday and
adjournment seasons of government). During the next three years, however, they hardly conferred at all; and the last two years before independence saw only moderate improvement.[33] "*Juncta juvant*," wrote William
Bollan, agent for the Council of Massachusetts Bay, in 1773, "and when

[32] Franklin to Charles Thomson, Feb. 5, 1775, in Smyth, ed., *Writings of
Franklin*, VI, 303; John Pownall to William Knox, July 23, 1773, Oct. 10, 1775,
in Historical Manuscripts Commission, *Report on Manuscripts in Various Collections*,
VI (Dublin, 1909), 110, 122.

[33] This calculation discounts those occasions when administrative boards required the presence of the agents at a hearing. Only meetings initiated by the
agents and attended by more than three have been included. Undoubtedly conferences occurred that went unrecorded in diaries, letters, and public documents.
But I believe the trend indicated here is essentially accurate. Charles Garth's communications with the South Carolina Committee of Correspondence faithfully
span these years and provide a rough measure in gauging the lobbyists' decline as
a unified pressure group. Garth's Letter book is in the South Carolina Archives. Part
of it has been printed in the *S. C. Hist. and Gen. Mag.*, XXVIII-XXXIII.

vested with ample authority I have gone in to the Lords of the Treasury at the head of seven or eight agents of so many colonies, but now they seem a rope of sand."[34]

As the character of American radicalism became transformed after 1766, many of the agents who were English by birth and residence found themselves out of sympathy with the constitutional claims of their constituents. Others who were ardent colonials were forced to recognize the devastating impact political controversy and rigid constitutional positions could have on their attempts at expedient mollification and adjustment. As the preplexed agents seemed to be achieving less than the colonists hoped for, the latter in certain cases became disenchanted with the institution. The representatives, in turn, discovered that they were increasingly hampered by their employers' inadequate support. Without sufficient authority and funds, the lobbyists' effectiveness was considerably reduced.[35]

141

Caught between their constituents and the imperial government, the agents were hamstrung by the attendant inflexibility on both sides. The truculent positions maintained by the colonies as the Great Debate progressed proved to be dangerous stumbling blocks for lobbyists whose sole concern was with practical achievements. On countless occasions the agents might have successfully pressured for repeal of undesirable legislation; but they were tightly bound by instructions sent by men who would only accept their goals cloaked in the guise of "inalienable right." William Knox, formerly agent for Georgia, summed up the problem lucidly in 1768. "I have been told that the colony agents were sent for lately by Lord Hillsborough, and acquainted that if they would wave the point of right, and petition for a repeal of the duties as *burdensome and grievous,* Administration were disposed to come into it. The agents, however, declared they could not leave out the point of right, consistent with their present instructions, but should inform their respective colonies, and so it rests."[36] In 1769 Dennys De Berdt remarked to his employers that "in the repeal of the Stamp Act it was a very different application from the present, in the former the whole Ministry were on our side but now it is the reverse[.] when ever these Acts are repealed, the question of right

[34] Bollan to James Bowdoin, Sept. 29, 1773, in *The Bowdoin and Temple Papers,* in Mass. Hist. Soc., *Colls.,* 6th Ser., IX (Boston, 1897), 320. See also De Berdt to Richard Cary, Feb. 2, 1769, in "Letters of Dennys De Berdt," 358.

[35] Kammen, Colonial Agents and the American Revolution, 149-158, 161-165.

[36] Knox to George Grenville, Dec. 15, 1768, Additional Manuscripts 42086, fol. 167, British Museum, London.

must be kept out of sight . . . and the repeal must be on the foot of inexpediency."[37]

Those agents who wholeheartedly supported the colonial constitutional position responded to the hardening of British attitudes toward America by undergoing a deepening disaffection from imperial authority and from England herself. These provincial representatives were repelled by what Franklin considered "the extream Corruption prevalent among all Orders of Men in this old rotten State. . . . Here Numberless and needless Places, enormous Salaries, Pensions, Perquisites, Bribes, groundless Quarrels, foolish Expeditions, false Accounts or no Accounts, Contracts and Jobbs, devour all Revenue, and produce continual Necessity in the Midst of natural Plenty."[38] The lobbyists vocally conveyed such sentiments to their correspondents; and by injecting these harangues into the hostile climate of colonial opinion, reinforced the agitated provincials' sense of alienation from Britain—an important ingredient of the rapidly developing patriotism in America.[39] In John Adams's words, a "Period shall arrive that an entire Allienation of Affection and a total Opposition of Interests shall take Place, And War and Desolation shall close the melancholly Prospect."[40]

After 1770 many of the agents began urging their constituents to look to their own strengths and be self-sustaining in every way. As James Bowdoin put it, the colonists had been induced "to think that they had nothing to hope for but from themselves." In 1773 Arthur Lee in-

[37] De Berdt to Thomas Cushing, Jan. 2, 1769, in "Letters of Dennys De Berdt," 350-351.

[38] Franklin to Joseph Galloway, Feb. 25, 1775, in Smyth, ed., Writings of Franklin, VI, 311-312. See also Franklin to Galloway, Apr. 20, 1771, Mason-Franklin Collection.

[39] See, for examples, the diatribes Henry Marchant sent his friends in Rhode Island. In the metaphor he devised, London was swelling like the head of a rickety child, while the body was fast wasting. "Thus the Head feeding upon the Body, without procuring any supplies to it, will sooner or later become all Head and no Body, when Louis Baboon and his Continental brothers will make a Foot Ball of it for their Cubs." "What a pity it is," he regretted, that "our Americans stay in England too long." Marchant to Ezra Stiles, May 14, 1772, Stiles MSS.; entry for Jan. 29, 1772, in Franklin Bowditch Dexter, ed., The Literary Diary of Ezra Stiles . . . (New York, 1901), I, 315. See also entries Jan. 18 and 25, 1772, Marchant's London "journell," owned by Miss Alice Clarke (copy in the Rhode Island Historical Society, Providence); Marchant to William Greene, Feb. 25, 1772, Peck Manuscripts, III, R. I. Hist. Soc.

[40] Adams to Isaac Smith, Jr. [1771?], in Butterfield, ed., Adams Family Correspondence, I, 82.

structed his correspondents from London not to trust "the persons who may be in power here." "Happily America is capable of working her own salvation," he added two years later, "or the influence of corruption and dissipation here would render her escape from the hand of Tyranny extremely doubtful."[41]

The differences that developed between the patriot agents and their more moderate and conservative colleagues, like Richard Jackson, Charles Garth, Edward Montagu of Virginia, the Mauduit brothers, and others, demonstrate many of the cleavages that divided political society on both sides of the Atlantic. By emphasizing and exemplifying the most divisive elements within the Empire, the agents revealed that their institution offered no hope of averting the ultimate breach. Prodded by their representatives the colonists looked inward, their backs up and wills stiffened. Henceforward they would cultivate the seeds of independence that had been stimulated, if not planted, by a group of North American agents in London.

143

Through one of those coruscations of irony that makes history fascinating, a root was already growing where life ebbed steadily from an old plant. The expiring agency was nourishing its progeny, the foreign service of a new nation.[42] The beginnings of American lobbying are not to be found in the national period, but before the Revolution when lobbying and diplomacy were intimately related. Just as Samuel was simultaneously the last of the Biblical judges and the first of the prophets, so Arthur Lee was the last of the colonial agents and the first national diplomat. As the agencies became consolidated into the hands of a few, these patriots ceased to be parochial "men of business" and became in embryo exactly what Whitehall had proclaimed eighty years earlier they must not be, namely, "plenipotentiaries from a sovereign state." In 1771

[41] Bowdoin to Alexander MacKay, Nov. 29, 1770, in *Bowdoin and Temple Papers*, 243; Lee to Thomas Cushing, June 10, 1773, Colonial Office Papers, Class 5, Vol. 118, foll. 90-91, Public Record Office; Lee to Benjamin Franklin, July 6, 1775, Franklin Manuscripts, Amer. Phil. Soc. See also William Lee to Josiah Quincy or Samuel Adams, Apr. 6, 1775, Adams MSS.

[42] Almost no author who has treated the history of the United States diplomatic corps has probed previous to the Revolution in search of origins. See, e.g., Tracy Hollingsworth Lay, *The Foreign Service of the United States* (New York, 1925); William Barnes and John Heath Morgan, *The Foreign Service of the United States* . . . (Washington, 1961); for a weak exception see Carl Russell Fish, *American Diplomacy*, 4th ed. (New York, 1923), 21-22.

Franklin had notified his Massachusetts Bay constituents that when the colonies "come to be considered in the light of *distinct states,* as I conceive they really are, possibly their agents may be treated with more respect, and considered more as public ministers." Eighteen months later the Doctor confided to his son that "several of the foreign ambassadors have assiduously cultivated my acquaintance, treating me as one of their *corps,* partly I believe from the desire they have, from time to time, of hearing something of American affairs, an object become of importance in foreign courts." Early in 1774 the Earl of Buckinghamshire remarked that Franklin "was here [in England], not as an agent of a province, but as an ambassador from the states of America. That he could not compare his embassy to any thing but that sent by Louis XIV. to the republic of Genoa, commanding the doge to come and prostrate himself at Versailles, to appease the resentment of the grand monarque."[43]

In the last year of America's subordination to Britain, Franklin, Lee, and Bollan looked about. They saw that nearly half the colonies now lacked agents, and that most of the remainder refused to participate in the final negotiations between Britannia and her offspring. Then the realization came that each agent must serve for and in liaison with *all* and not just his own particular colony. America, and not merely Massachusetts or Pennsylvania, had become their constituency. In consequence they sent a copy of their letters to every colony so that each would be apprized of proceedings in Westminster and Whitehall.[44]

When the Olive Branch negotiations collapsed in the late summer of 1775, Arthur Lee became the confidential correspondent in London of the Continental Congress, and later their secret envoy in Paris. The whole irony turned back on itself following American independence. When an exchange of ministers was proposed to George III, he rejected the suggestion outright: "As to the question whether I wish to have a Minister

[43] "Extract from the History of the New-England Colonies, concerning the Charter of William and Mary," in Mass. Hist. Soc., *Colls.,* 1st Ser., IX (Boston, 1804), 273; Franklin to Thomas Cushing, Feb. 5, 1771, in Smyth, ed., *Writings of Franklin,* V, 295; Franklin to William Franklin, Aug. 19, 1772, *ibid.,* 414; Arthur Lee to Samuel Adams, Feb. 8, 1774, in Lee, *Life of Arthur Lee,* I, 241.

[44] See, e.g., their general letter to the speakers of the colonial assemblies, dated Dec. 24, 1774. Franklin's draft is in his manuscripts (#268) in the Library of Congress, Washington. The agents' circular letter of Feb. 5, 1775, was also given wide distribution in America. For an anticipation of this development see Dennys De Berdt's letter to George Wyllys, Jan. 16, 1766, in "Letters of Dennys De Berdt," 311.

accredited from America, I certainly can never say that it will be agreeable to Me, and I should think it wisest for both parties if only Agents were appointed."[45]

[45] George III to Charles James Fox, Aug. 7, 1783, in Sir John Fortescue, ed., *The Correspondence of King George the Third . . .*, VI (London, 1928), 430. See also Charles R. Ritcheson, *British Politics and the American Revolution* (Norman, Okla., 1954), 274.

145

Patterns of Massachusetts Colonial Politics: The Writs of Assistance and the Rivalry between the Otis and Hutchinson Families

John J. Waters and John A. Schutz*

FROM ordinary and peaceful pursuits in 1760 the younger James Otis became the foe of British trade regulation and, in the opinion of many historians, an early advocate of revolution. To explain his sudden and dramatic denunciation of the Writs of Assistance, historians have referred to his unbalanced mind in later stages of the American Revolution and to his intense hatred of Thomas Hutchinson.[1] Otis was a turbulent person who could easily fly into rage, give fighting language, and leave a lasting impression of his actions, but he was not insane in these years; rather he was a brilliant lawyer who was admired and feared in the Boston community. His famous courtroom appearance against the Writs was a tactical·maneuver in which he pressed Chief Justice Hutchinson to rule on the legality of the Writs.[2] Though failing in his strategy when Hutchinson sought a decision from London, Otis had succeeded so completely, nevertheless, in associating Hutchinson with these unwise methods of law enforcement that the chief justice could not escape being implicated.[3]

* Mr. Waters is a member of the Department of History, The University of Rochester. Mr. Schutz is a member of the Department of History, the University of Southern California.

[1] See Lawrence H. Gipson, *The Coming of the Revolution, 1763-1775* (New York, 1954), 38-39; Clifford K. Shipton, "James Otis," *Sibley's Harvard Graduates* (Boston, 1873—), XI, 247-286. John J. Waters, who catalogued and first utilized the Otis Manuscripts and the Gay Papers of Columbia University's Butler Library, presented the argument that this essay explores in The Otis Family in Provincial and Revolutionary Massachusetts (unpubl. Ph.D. diss., Columbia University, 1965).

[2] Thomas Hutchinson, *The History of the Colony and Province of Massachusetts-Bay,* ed. Lawrence Shaw Mayo (Cambridge, Mass., 1936), III, 67-69. Bernard's son claimed that Hutchinson received his appointment because of his known views in favor of the Writs of Assistance. See Thomas Bernard, *The Life of Sir Francis Bernard* (London, 1790), 43-44.

[3] The legislature tried to substitute another writ, but Bernard rejected the bill in a ceremony before the Council. See Hutchinson to William Bollan, Mar. 6, 1762,

The focus of historians on the Otis-Hutchinson controversy has usually been on the years 1760 and 1761. Little consideration is given to relations between the families or to the reaction of other Otises to the bold assault on Hutchinson. Nor has the dispute been seen in the light of the colony's politics during the governorships of William Shirley and Thomas Pownall and in terms of Hutchinson's political aspirations. Some of this information has not been previously available, and it is only within the decade that a large collection of the Otis Papers has been opened to historians. These documents suggest the need for a long-range approach to the Hutchinson-Otis family dispute. They argue for shifting the historical focus from the traditional explanation of a fight over trade regulation to a broader consideration of the social and political fortunes of these two families.[4]

147

Both families migrated early to New England. The Otises in leaving Somerset about 1621 had moved to Devon in search of improved income before crossing the Atlantic a decade later. Settling first at Hingham (called Bear Cove) in Massachusetts Bay and then at Scituate and Barnstable in Plymouth Colony, these Otises cut trees, piled stones into walls, planted crops, opened a store, and served frequently as selectmen of their towns. Time and fortune were on the side of John Otis I and II. They moved in company with fellow town leaders, married their children well, and were respected and law abiding people. Though they were highly regarded by their countrymen, they were not deeply involved in church affairs and took their time about gaining full communion in the Congregational Church. The first Otis to exert his influence county wide was John III (1657-1727), whose many farms and flourishing businesses released him from much toil. He became free to accept responsibilities in the House of Representatives, then in the Council and the Common Pleas Court of Barnstable.[5] As province matters

---

Massachusetts Archives, XXVI, 8-9, Massachusetts State House, Boston, and Bernard to Barrington, May 1, 1762, Bernard Letterbooks, II, 188, Houghton Library, Harvard University, Cambridge, Mass.

[4] The Butler Library, Columbia University, New York, acquired and opened for use the long missing Otis Manuscripts in 1959. They supplement Otis papers at the Massachusetts Historical Society, Boston, and the Massachusetts Archives.

[5] Horatio N. Otis, "Genealogical and Historical Memoir of the Otis Family," New England Historic and Genealogical Society, Register, II (1848), 281-296; William Tudor, The Life of James Otis of Massachusetts (Boston, 1823), 5-9, 496-498.

demanded more of his time, family and relatives were drawn into the management of his personal affairs. Together with his growing sons, the Littles, Russells, and Bacons handled the local problems or accompanied him to Boston where they looked after patronage opportunities. Since provincial connections often made business flourish, John III took care that his sons John IV and Solomon were Harvard educated and prepared to step into his governmental positions. Another son James I (1702-1778) was apprenticed to a merchant, perhaps in Boston, and given training in exporting. At John III's death in 1727, he had established himself as Barnstable's political leader. His six children were married into prominent families, almost all had offices in county and local government, and most had modest wealth.[6]

For reasons not altogether clear John IV (1687-1758) did not succeed to his father's positions. He may have been discouraged by the harsh politics of William Burnet's administration, then by the bitter wrangling of Jonathan Belcher's, and let others assume the burdens of office. A quiet man, not personally aggressive, he busied himself with his wife's estate. It is possible, too, that his father and Belcher had been political rivals in the 1720's, and Belcher's administrative favors in the 1730's were given to the Bourne, Russell, and Gorham families in retaliation. When John and his brother-in-law, Isaac Little, were nominated to the Council by colleagues in the House of Representatives, they were rejected by Belcher.[7] Significantly, Little was approved for council membership by Governor Shirley in 1743. During these years the family held on to some local offices, and James, who had been handling legal cases along with management of the family businesses, was rising in county affairs. In spite of a rustic education, James picked up useful legal principles and developed a courtroom manner that swayed local juries. Rough and tumble encounters in court gave him wide acquaintances with such influential men as James Warren of Plymouth, Samuel White, and Jeremiah Gridley, the dean of the Boston bar, and they encouraged him to stand for the House of Representatives.[8] Taking

148

[6] *Ibid.*, 7-8; George Lincoln, ed., *History of the Town of Hingham* (Hingham, Mass., 1893), III, 101-103; Shipton, "Solomon Otis," *Sibley's Harvard Graduates*, VI, 200-201.

[7] Massachusetts Historical Society, *Journals of the House of Representatives of Massachusetts* (Boston, 1919—), XVIII, 8; XIX, 7-8.

[8] See Warren's testimony in *Otis* v. *Cornelius and Peter Drew*, Jan. 21, 1734/5,

advantage of the war crisis of 1745 to enter the House, apparently as a supporter of Shirley's Louisburg expedition, he stepped readily into committee vacancies left by the departure of military leaders. Within four years Otis successfully garnered and retained appointments on the committees dealing with the war effort, currency, Indian policy, and supply.[9] As his talents in the House were being relied upon to mobilize support for the administration, he became a familiar figure at the governor's mansion, often in company with Speaker of the House Thomas Hutchinson.

The Hutchinson family traced its origins to Alford, Lincolnshire, where William had been an enterprising businessman and his wife, Anne Marbury, had studied Puritan theology while giving birth to and raising fourteen children. In 1634, with other Puritans seeking religious refuge, they crossed the Atlantic to settle in Boston. However, before William and Anne could establish themselves in the new community, Anne involved them in the monumental Antinomian religious controversy that resulted in the exile of their immediate family, their son-in-law and daughter, John and Bridget Sanford, and a vast number of friends. Edward (1613-1676) stayed in Boston, together with some grown or married Hutchinsons, while Richard left for London and a career as a merchant.

Though William and Anne would soon die in exile, Edward and his brothers and brothers-in-law became merchants of Boston; their families prospered and multiplied. Over the years, in cooperation with Richard, John and Peleg Sanford of Portsmouth, and Sanfords in Barbados, they created a vast system of commercial alliances which brought huge risks as well as comparable profits. In 1676 Elisha succeeded to his father Edward's business, becoming an influential leader of the merchant community. He held in time offices in the Boston government, seats in the House of Representatives and Council, and power sufficient to challenge the governor's policies. With unusual care he arranged the marriage of

149

Suffolk Court Files, 269, 48-49, Suffolk County Court House, Boston; Samuel White to James Otis, Sr., May 29, 1741, Miscellaneous Bound Manuscripts, XI, Mass. Hist. Soc.; Jeremiah Gridley to James Otis, Sr., Dec. 5, 1743, Otis Papers, I, 51.

[9] Mass. Hist. Soc., *Mass. House Journals* are full of examples of Otis's work on committees: XXII, 4, 17, 19, 20, 56, 73, 75; XXIII, 6, 13, 17, 19, 21; XXIV, 5, 6, 12, 16.

son Thomas I (1676-1739) to Sara Foster, daughter and heiress of a rich Boston merchant. Marriage brought Thomas additional wealth. It also increased his responsibilities. He had to manage a large family business as well as meet the social demands of his relatives who were conscious of their positions as judges, legislators, and town officials. His beautiful mansion now became the meeting place of the elite. Until his death in 1739 he was himself either a member of Boston's government, a representative, or a councillor, but he was always a steadfast supporter of the town's charitable and religious foundations.[10] Upon his son Thomas II (1711-1780), destined to inherit most of the family fortune, he lavished attention by securing tutors, providing money for a Harvard College education, giving opportunity for local travel, and sharing advice on the proper conduct of a wealthy merchant's son. As the favorite son Thomas II was pushed by the family. He entered Harvard before he was twelve years of age, succeeded in a merchant venture at twenty-one, and won election to the House of Representatives at twenty-six. In 1734, he married Margaret Sanford, daughter of the deceased Rhode Island merchant and relative who had long been associated with his father and grandfather. His friend Andrew Oliver, nephew of Governor Belcher, wed the sister in the same year. The two marriages were social events of significance in Boston and tied the fortunes of three families together.[11]

As the son of an influential father, Thomas moved in the highest political company and committed himself to Belcher's policies. In supporting the governor's hard money policies, he became involved in a bitter dispute that divided the politicians and wrecked the administration. While Belcher purged the government of enemies and pushed many to the point of desperation, Hutchinson journeyed to London as the governor's agent. His efforts to save the governor eventually proved

150

[10] "Memoir of Governor Hutchinson," New Eng. Hist. and Gen. Soc., Reg., I (1847), 297-310; Malcolm Freiberg, "Thomas Hutchinson: The First Fifty Years (1711-1761)," William and Mary Quarterly, 3d Ser., XV (1958), 35-36; Hutchinson, History of Massachusetts-Bay, ed. Mayo, has many references to the author's family in the three volumes.

[11] Shipton, "Thomas Hutchinson," Sibley's Harvard Graduates, VIII, 149-214; Peter Oliver, Origin and Progress of the American Rebellion, a Tory view, eds. Douglass Adair and John A. Schutz (Stanford, Calif., 1967), x-xi; Boston Weekly News-Letter, May 23, 1734; New-England Weekly Journal, May 20, 28, 1734. The Hutchinson-Sanford marriage was given priority in the newspapers over that of the Princess Royal in England!

to be futile, and a group hostile to him had assumed power when he returned to Boston in 1741.[12]

The new political order of which James Otis and Thomas Hutchinson found themselves members was managed by William Shirley, an English-born attorney who had ventured to Massachusetts in 1731 and had become a pivotal factor in Belcher's removal. Shirley drew his following at first from critics of the old governor, from county families like the Choates, Hales, Stoddards, and Waldos, and from some Boston families who were recent arrivals in America or Anglican in religion, like the Apthorps, Hancocks, Kilbys, and Eliakim Hutchinsons (Thomas's distant relatives). To attract these people the governor successfully exploited the resources of his office—his English connections and patronage opportunities. He had the facility, moreover, to forget past political alliances and sought to broaden the base of support. Over the years he traded favors for legislative help, and he gratified those who were willing to cooperate with commissions in the militia, judiciary, and local government.[13] As the intercolonial wars with Spain and France expanded in the early 1740's, he used the military contracts and favors to reward friends.

151

With James Otis working for Shirley, the ascendance of the family in Barnstable was assured. Solomon continued as notary and Joseph held the post of excise collector, while John IV became a member of the Council and a justice of the Common Pleas Court of Barnstable and James a colonel of the militia. James's son Joseph, his nephew John V, and his brother-in-law James Allyne were named to captaincies, while he had Shirley's promise of a major's rank for his political protégé and cousin, Edward Bacon.[14] Even more important were the benefits of a

---

[12] John A. Schutz, "Succession Politics in Massachusetts, 1730-1741," *Wm. and Mary Qtly*, 3d Ser., XV (1958), 508-520; Hutchinson to Josiah Willard, July 31, 1741, Mass. Archives, XXV, 1-6.

[13] John A. Schutz, *William Shirley: King's Governor of Massachusetts* (Chapel Hill, 1961), chaps. III, IV, V. Hutchinson was again elected to the House of Representatives as one of Boston's members in 1742 and immediately assumed a position of influence. See Mass. Hist. Soc., *Mass. House Journals*, XX, 15, 17, 18, 57, 58, 395, 396.

[14] William H. Whitmore, *The Massachusetts Civil List for the Colonial and Provincial Periods, 1630-1774* (Albany, 1870), 104, 145-146; *Boston News-Letter*, Jan. 15, 1774; James Otis, Sr., to Joseph Otis, Feb. 13, 1756, and Otis, Sr., to Edward Bacon, Mar. 1, 1756, Otis MSS, I, 34, 36.

larger law practice, the military contracts for food and services that were passed to family and friends, and the esteem of being associated with official Boston. His son James II (1725-1783), who had graduated from Harvard College in 1743, studied with the influential Jeremiah Gridley, was admitted to the bar in Plymouth County, practiced there for two years, and then moved to Boston where at first he handled his father's legal business. Then, as a bright, well-connected young man, he entered into merchant affairs, soon to wed Ruth Cunningham, the daughter of an affluent merchant, and to establish himself as a Bostonian.[15]

152   Fortune also smiled upon Hutchinson. He was often with the governor, on a junket into Maine, in frequent legislative conferences, and as a guest in the home of brother-in-law Andrew Oliver. While he had to overcome personal hostility towards Shirley, their ideas on the use of paper money were not far apart, as were their thoughts of colonial defense and loyalty to the Crown. When former Governor Belcher finally left Massachusetts for England, their relations warmed considerably; when war brought the need of arms and the Olivers became suppliers, they worked closely for favorite policies. Signs of changing relations came when Andrew Oliver was appointed a councillor, his brother Peter, a justice of the peace and justice of the Common Pleas Court of Plymouth County, and Thomas, in a contest with brother-in-law Oliver, was given Shirley's approval as speaker of the House of Representatives.[16]

Further opportunity for advancement came in 1748 when both families benefitted from the turmoil that shook the administration over the governor's financial and military policies. For years Shirley (through his son-in-law William Bollan in London) had been trying to secure a reimbursement for the Louisburg campaign. The money was intended for setting up a hard currency in the colony. Arguments over accounting the expenditures and the nature of the payment alienated many people, particularly the colonial agent Christopher Kilby, who was offended by

[15] Tudor, *Otis*, 19-21; James Otis, Jr., to James Otis, Sr., Sept. 10, 1750, Otis MSS., I, 31; William Bourn to James Otis, Jr., Mar. 1, 1754, Suffolk Court Files, 445, 04; James Otis, Jr., receipt for Samuel Watts, Oct. 8, 1756, Chamberlain Manuscripts A. 4. 22, Boston Public Library.
[16] Thomas Hutchinson, *The Diary and Letters of His Excellency Thomas Hutchinson . . .* , ed. Peter O. Hutchinson (London, 1883-86), I, 52; Mass. Hist. Soc., *Mass. House Journals*, XXIII, 5, 8.

the governor's interference, and some legislative leaders who favored inflation. In this crisis Hutchinson and Otis moved quickly to aid the governor by backing a plan for currency reform. Their help was decisive in the bloody legislative encounter that immediately took place in 1749 and led to other battles over ancillary issues. The first victim of the fight was Hutchinson who was ousted from his House seat by the voters of Boston.[17] He was, however, promptly brought into the Council through the help of Shirley and Otis. In retaliation, they turned upon agent Kilby, replacing him in the agency with William Bollan. The give and take of these encounters intensified feeling, and the House, swayed by two or three new members, ordered an investigation of military accounting and the governor's part in it. The newspaper publicity and the hostility of some politicians convinced the governor that it was best for him to argue his case before the British government. He deflected the attack rather easily, but his leave of absence lengthened into three years of service in London and Paris. In the meantime, his position as governor was occupied by Spencer Phips who was cautioned to follow Hutchinson's advice, and Shirley, in securing the arrangement, left his son-in-law Eliakim Hutchinson in Boston as his personal representative. Eliakim was also related to the lieutenant governor.[18]

153

During the governor's absence legislative leaders completed the process of withdrawing the old paper currency. So that the inflationary interests would not seize control of the House, laws had to be passed and precautions taken. This was a great responsibility, but James Otis apparently handled the critics with consummate skill, especially the tactics of James Allen of Boston who shouted insults, apologized, and

[17] In a report to his friend Israel Williams, Hutchinson described his defeat: "You have heard my Fate. I could make but about 200 Votes in near 700. They were the principal Inhabitants, but you know we are govern'd not by Weight but by Numbers," May 19, 1749, Williams Papers, II, 139, Mass. Hist. Soc. See also Schutz, *Shirley*, 140-148.
[18] Shipton, "Eliakim Hutchinson," *Sibley's Harvard Graduates,* VIII, 726-729. Thomas Hutchinson, however, had a powerful voice in Phips's administration. In a letter of Nov. 28, 1749, Shirley advised the colony's secretary, Josiah Willard, to consult in the Council with Hutchinson "as a gentleman in whom I have entire confidence" and in the House of Representatives with John Choate whose "fidelity and attachment" were beyond question. It is interesting that Choate outranked Otis in Shirley's estimation. In 1750, when Choate lost his seat in the spring elections, Otis had an unrivaled position of confidence. See Shirley's letter in Bancroft Transcripts, Massachusetts Papers, 63, New York Public Library.

repeated them in displays of emotion. While Allen was a force to approach with care, he met his equal in Otis who spoke the farmer's language, giving perhaps the tonal sound and idiom, too, and was not above using threats and calling upon members at their boarding houses. During these tense years he and the Hutchinsons and Olivers conferred often, sometimes turning from strategy sessions to the relaxation of the punch bowl. A letter Peter Oliver sent to Otis in 1750 revealed the warmth of their association. Otis's lack of formal education and his rough and tumble behavior seemed of no consequence to the aristocratic Oliver. "Your son tells me," he wrote, "that Mrs. Otis has some expectation of seeing Mrs. Oliver this summer at Barnstable; since which Mrs. Winslow and I have almost agreed on a visit. We propose to set out the beginning of the week after next, so that if nothing more than common prevents, we shall have the pleasure of seeing you then; but I should be glad you would not let our visit interfere with any business you may have from home."[19]

154

Adding a slight reference at the close of the letter to paper money, Oliver playfully predicted that the "Golden Age" was returning to the colony. "We shall all be kings, priests, and anything else we incline to." The "Blessed Times" of the interim period saw the younger James Otis become a respected, influential Boston lawyer, with excellent social ties, a commission as acting king's attorney, and all the legal work he could handle. His father was House "whip" for the Phips administration, well received in Boston, and manager of Barnstable business in the capital. Both Otises had also a growing law practice with Boston's trading people. They lived well, but not in the style of their friends the Hutchinsons and Olivers, who had their town houses and country homes where they idled away their time gardening, riding over their fields, and collecting books and art objects. Thomas Hutchinson had a magnificent home at Milton, Peter Oliver had one at Middleborough, and Eliakim Hutchinson lived in the Shirley mansion at Roxbury. Compared with the rustic life of Barnstable, these seats were palaces. The degree of luxury surrounding the families was also reflected in their progress in public affairs. Thomas Hutchinson was appointed in 1752 judge of the Probate Court and associate justice of the Suffolk Common Pleas Court, while his relative Eliakim Hutchinson became its chief

[19] Oliver to Otis, Aug. 3, 1750, Otis Papers, I, 105.

justice. Retaining his post as councillor, Thomas was one of its active members and was frequently called upon to serve in positions of great distinction.[20] Notwithstanding these marks of prominence, Thomas dreamed of the future, his childrens' education, their marriages, and his own prestige, and no doubted welcomed in 1752 the marriage of nephew Andrew Oliver with Mary Lynde, daughter of the Superior Court justice.

It would be difficult to balance the fortunes of the Otises and Hutchinsons with precision, but the Hutchinsons would seem to have had wealth, honor, and numbers on their side. Most Otises were still in Barnstable as local officeholders and country folk. Except for the two Jameses and John IV, who did his duty in the Council without much fanfare, the family had only the potential of greatness, not the prestige and distinction of the Hutchinsons.

When Shirley returned to the colony in 1753, the Otises did not fare any better. The governor's homecoming coincided with the resumption of hostilities with France. Since he favored a renewal of the war, he backed policies which extended Massachusetts's authority into the frontier and drew people to him who had interests in Maine and western Massachusetts. Men like Israel Williams, Oliver Partridge, John Erving, Robert Temple, and James Bowdoin wielded considerable power, and leaders of the 1740's like John Choate and Robert Hale, who had been out of office since Shirley's departure for England, resumed their former places of prominence.

In domestic affairs Otis had trouble managing the representatives, who refused to vote an expense allowance for the governor and were sharply critical of other recommendations. Outspoken in leading the opposition was again James Allen of Boston, who exploited feeling over declining trade to arouse hostility to the governor's financial measures and kept the House on edge with his unpredictable maneuvers.[21] Until

155

[20] Lawrence H. Gipson would give Hutchinson an even greater role in the writing of the Albany Plan of Union than has been traditionally allotted. See his "Thomas Hutchinson and the Framing of the Albany Plan of Union, 1754," *Pennsylvania Magazine of History and Biography,* LXXIV (1950), 5-35.

[21] Mass. Hist. Soc., *Mass. House Journals,* XXX, 16, 132, 153, 181, 187, 195; XXXI, 23, 24, 28, 31, 32, 205; *Boston News-Letter,* Jan. 9, 1755. See also Schutz, *Shirley,* 170-176, 179-180.

his death in January 1755 he gave the House a political force of independence and daring that was not cajoled by contracts and honors. In the background, also, was a cluster of men surrounding Sir William Pepperrell who were hoping for a change in governors, but not one of them, including Thomas Hancock, Samuel Waldo, and Christopher Kilby, enjoyed the prestige to bring it off. They had grown wealthy contracting for the military and imagined one of their number would guarantee them continuance of their prosperity if he. were the colony's governor. While Shirley was well aware of this group, he upstaged them by joining personally in an expedition to Maine and making his own politics. His adventure was popular with the land speculators and lessened, too, his dependence upon any one leader of the House.[22]

156

As the war intensified, Shirley had again contracts and honors to distribute. For a time in 1755 and 1756 he was commander-in-chief of British forces, and Boston became the center of army financial services. In helping these British officials, the Otises had a minor part, while most of the work fell to John Erving, Jr. (Shirley's new son-in-law), Eliakim Hutchinson, the Olivers, and to others like Charles Apthorp who had long shared in the governor's spoils. The elder Otis, however, was expected during the governor's absences to use all of his influence to push the unpopular war measures. In Barnstable County he was the driving force that produced full military musters, and he rightly expected some public honor as recognition. Though he longed for a seat on the Council, and possibly the Superior Court, he was persuaded by the governor in 1756 that his services in the House were irreplaceable. He was assured that there would be opportunity enough to give him preferment when the war crisis passed. A token honor, nonetheless, was conferred upon the family when the younger James was named a justice of the peace for Suffolk County. In marked contrast, not long afterward, the Oliver brothers gained much more prestige when Peter

---

[22] In making appointments, however, Shirley seemed warmer towards Israel Williams, Hutchinson's friend, than he did toward James Otis. He appointed a half-brother Ephraim Williams as commandant of Fort Massachusetts in place of the stranger Elisha Chapin. When James Otis wanted to fill an administrative vacancy in Barnstable, he was told to name three men, and Shirley even rejected one nominee "by reason of the near connection—and appearance of partiality." See James Otis, Jr., to James Otis, Sr., July 24, 1756, Otis MSS., I, 39.

became an associate justice of the Superior Court and Andrew the acting secretary of the colony.[23]

In the midst of the war crisis Britain removed Shirley as commander-in-chief and governor of Massachusetts and put the direction of the war in the hands of the Earl of Loudoun, who transferred the military headquarters to New York and thus unsettled patronage relationships. In Massachusetts the administration fell momentarily into the feeble hands of Spencer Phips, then suffering his last illness. His impotence in office and the patronage crisis naturally caused much uneasiness. When his death occurred six months later without a successor being designated, politicians were in a state of fervid excitement. Hutchinson, with visions of the governorship flashing through his mind, made the acquaintance of Loudoun, lent his skill in ghostwriting the general's address to the Massachusetts legislature, and offered to recommend people for administrative posts in the colony pending the appointment of a new governor.[24] Pepperrell, as the highest ranking councillor, undertook a tour of the colony's defenses and assumed the bearing of a governor. Hancock and Waldo, contriving through their English friend Kilby, worked anxiously to save their military provisioning by getting a subcontract for the Boston market.

The Otises also moved to strengthen their position. Because John Otis IV was in declining health, James planned to succeed his brother as councillor before the new governor came. In preparing for the election, which would be unusual without a governor present to approve the House election, he relinquished his Barnstable post in the House in favor of his relative and protégé Edward Bacon, who campaigned for him, and he sought the good will of the commander-in-chief. He counted on his popularity, his friend's help, and the rather usual patronage right of succeeding a brother. To his amazement and that of his friends and family, he lost the vote of the House.[25] News of this bitter

[23] Peter Oliver won the vacancy on the Superior Court. Some additional favors, however, were passed out to the Otis family in the form of contracts for whale boats and food supplies. See James Otis, Sr., to Joseph Otis, Feb. 13, 1756, Otis MSS., I, 34; Hannah Nicolson to James Otis, Sr., Mar. 27, 1756, Otis Papers, I, 132.

[24] Hutchinson to Loudoun, Jan. 21, Mar. 7, Apr. 6, July 6, 1757, and Loudoun to Commissioners, Jan. 29, 1757, Loudoun Papers, Huntington Library, San Marino, Calif.

[25] Lynde diary notation, May 25, 1757, in Fitch Edward Oliver, ed., *The Diaries of Benjamin Lynde and of Benjamin Lynde, Jr.* (Boston, 1880), 186.

blow spread wide, even as far as St. Eustatius, and was recorded in the diaries of politicians.[26] Otis wanted no sympathy, only an explanation for his failure to win election. By August 1757 he had an answer and did something very unusual for a man of his nature—he wrote himself a memo. It followed a reported conversation of Thomas Hutchinson in the council chamber. Its point was that his standing in the administration rested on "doing little low dirty things for Governor Shirley, such as persons of worth refuse to med[d]le with and that Shirley made use of . . . [him] only as a tool for his purposes."[27] This cruel appraisal cut James deeply; he wondered now whether his services were not being appropriated for the gratification of others. His bitterness spread to Hutchinson and the Olivers as successors of the Shirley administration, and even to Shirley himself, and determination deepened for obtaining honor.

158

About the time that Otis wrote his memo Governor Thomas Pownall arrived in Boston. As a staff member of the general and brother of the secretary of the Board of Trade, he had powerful credentials that attracted the Bostonian merchants. The first to make his acquaintance were the Otises, possibly because the younger Otis was nearly Pownall's age and had interests in the classics and philosophy that were similar to the governor's. Within a few weeks the governor reviewed the patronage aspirations of the Otises and urged the younger James to accept the post of acting advocate general, a flattering position of prestige and utility in the merchant community. Apparently the elder James was promised a seat on the Superior Court bench when a vacancy occurred. Equally friendly were Pownall's relations with the Hutchinsons and the Olivers. He approved of Hutchinson's appointment as lieutenant governor and Andrew Oliver's permanent commission as the colony's secretary. He even nominated Foster Hutchinson as Thomas's successor in the Suffolk County Court of Common Pleas. Pownall's relations cooled later, however, when he was instructed in political matters by Hancock, Waldo, Pepperrell, and the Otises.[28]

[26] William Fletcher to James Otis, Sr., Nov. 6, 1757, Otis Papers, I, 172.
[27] [Aug. 15, 1757], Otis MSS., I, 44.
[28] Malcolm Freiberg believes that Pownall's letter to Lord Halifax, the president of the Board of Trade, Sept. 4, 1757, was sufficient to make Hutchinson lieutenant governor. See his "Thomas Hutchinson: The First Fifty Years," 53-54. Otis's bitterness toward the old Shirley party developed in the fall of 1757. He told

In developing his following, Pownall relied mainly upon the Otises and Thomas Hancock and gravitated towards Shirley's old enemies in seeking advisors. Probably, too, he viewed Hutchinson's power as a threat and limitation upon his freedom of movement. Whatever his thoughts, he was delighted when Hancock agreed to enter the Council as a supporter, and he welcomed Samuel Waldo's friendship, which included participation in the government and a gift of real estate in Maine. Even the powerful Sir William Pepperrell, who wanted the governorship himself, offered his military advice and political help. In this realignment of politicians, the younger James Otis forsook his former friends who had so little respect for his father and joined Pownall. Their first bit of maneuvering was an attack on William Bollan, both the advocate general and the colony's agent. Otis may have been motivated by revenge, for Bollan was a close political friend of Thomas Hutchinson, but he may also have had designs on the advocacy by ridding himself of a superior who was sharing the honor and fees of office. The governor, however, considered Bollan as a representative of the Shirley faction and the agency as patronage. With the agency in the hands of his brother John, he could control the colony's relations with London. The process of undermining Bollan's reputation in England went along so well by 1759 that Pownall could point to Bollan's inability to operate the agency.[29]

While Bollan had his critics, often because of his arrogant treatment of the legislature, he had been most successful in representing the colony in London. The purge particularly disturbed Hutchinson who said later that it was the single cause of his estranged relations with Pownall. In letters of the day, however, Hutchinson revealed that they quarreled over many things, and particularly over patronage distribution. Sometimes the governor picked men of little social rank and many times he neglected to seek the advice of leaders. Hutchinson found himself excluded from the inner councils of the administration and sent off to the country on recruiting missions when others were allowed

---

William Fletcher apparently that Pownall's tenure promised much for the colony—this coming from one who had been a leader of the old administration. See Fletcher to Otis, Nov. 6, 1757, Otis Papers, I, 172.

[29] Hutchinson to Israel Williams, Mar. 28, Oct. 28, 1759, Mar. 4, 1760, Williams Papers, II, 145, 152, 153.

to remain at the seat of authority. These relations with Pownall were galling because they revealed his weakness in the administration and lengthened the shadows between his place and the governorship, which he aspired to have more than anything else.[30]

The contest over the agency was principally between Pownall and Hutchinson because none of the Otises were then in the legislature. But William Brattle in the Council and friends like John Choate in the House represented their interests and assisted Pownall in his maneuvering. The governor, however, was not able to count upon a majority except in military affairs, where his influence meant sterling exchange for the colony. He lost heavily in 1759 when Pepperrell and Waldo both died suddenly, and he had been unable to keep Hancock in the Council. He sacrificed prestige, too, when he failed to make the elder Otis a councillor while the Hutchinson faction had the votes to nominate Peter Oliver and Chambers Russell as councillors.[31]

One of the last acts Pownall performed as governor in 1760, for he had been rescued from these political difficulties by his transfer to the Carolina governorship, was the approval of the elder Otis as speaker of the House; and almost the first business of the House while Hutchinson served as acting governor was Bollan's reelection to the agency.[32] Though Bollan was chosen by a slight vote scattered among weak candidates, Otis and other Bollan enemies may have withheld their fire in anticipation of support from Governor Francis Bernard, who was a county man and recent confidant of the Pownalls. Need of strong leadership, too, was most urgent and Bollan's election may have represented a pause in the warfare. The old Shirley party was now splintered into factions and some of its powerful leaders were aged, retired, or dead, and many of the ties that had held them together were worn thin. Shirley's popular policies of American participation in the British trading and military system were radically changed by the Seven Years' War when the British government took over the direction of the war and deprived the governor of much independent military spending. Though Pownall longed for these same advantages, he had been re-

160

[30] Hutchinson to William Bollan, Apr. 24, Nov. 15, 1762, Mass. Archives, XXVI, 12, 30.

[31] James Otis, Sr., to Joseph Otis, June 13, 1759, Otis MSS., I, 74.

[32] *Boston Gazette*, July 14, 1760; Mass. Hist. Soc., *Mass. House Journals*, XXXVII, Pt. i, 34.

strained by military regulations and given little or no initiative in formulating military plans. Without hope of a command, he settled down uneasily to the life of a civilian official and spun philosophical theories on the relations of the governor and legislature to the people in an attempt to create popular support for his administration. An advocate of Whig principles of government, he lectured the legislature on its position as "Voice of the People" and spoke glibly of their liberties. It is not too much to imagine Pownall sitting with the younger Otis, Samuel Cooper, James Bowdoin, and other like spirits debating the rights and responsibilities of man and musing on the aristocratic behavior of the Hutchinsons. Pownall had some harsh words to say on the ruling group, none more pointed than that the rich took the profits of war and let the poor do the fighting.[33]

161

The transition between administrations in 1760 was completed in August when the new governor finally received his commission and formally entered the colony. The general impression on all sides was favorable for an easy succession. Hutchinson, as acting governor during the interim, was in a commanding position to influence policy, but James Otis, Sr., as speaker of the House, was also prominent. The Otises, nonetheless, were busy with shipping problems and with answering solicitations from clients about favors from the new governor.[34] Younger James Otis was acting upon an order from Bollan to look into violations of the trade laws and take steps in line with an order from the secretary of state to apprehend the offenders. Chief Justice Stephen Sewall had also requested Otis to study ways of using search warrants in harmony with English liberties. Both of these investigations were reinforced by Governor Bernard who was related to Secretary at War Lord Barrington and was anxious not only to do his duty but to participate in the prize money of any condemnation. Customs officials had already aroused opposition among the merchants, and Pownall had in the last days of his administration come under severe criticism for permitting this activity. But Pownall had been willing like Shirley before him to overlook most violations and deal with offenders by compro-

[33] John A. Schutz, *Thomas Pownall: British Defender of American Liberty* (Glendale, Calif., 1951), 102, 140, 154, 167-174.
[34] Enoch Freeman to James Otis, Sr., Aug. 15, 1760, and James Warren to James Otis, Sr., Jan. 14, 1762, Otis Papers, II, 39, 64; Governor Bernard to Lord Barrington, Aug. 7, 1760, Bernard Letterbooks, I, 272.

mise.[35] Bollan, however, had prosecuted vigorously in the early 1740's and was known for his tough methods of enforcement. When he went to England as a special agent in 1745, Shirley had relieved himself of much antagonism but sacrificed for merchant friendship the revenue from condemnations. Those who acted in Bollan's place, including the younger James Otis, followed the Shirley policy of applying self-regulating rules to trade. When Governor Bernard reversed this policy in compliance with his British instructions, customs officials had already apprehended the elder John Erving of the Council as a smuggler, and their spying had unsettled the whole merchant community. This new policy thrust a great burden upon Otis as admiralty court prosecutor because many of his friends and clients were involved in the proscribed commerce. But just as he became embroiled, a significant event occurred.

162

In September 1760 Stephen Sewall died unexpectedly. On hearing the news, young James petitioned Bernard to appoint his father to the court and recalled in a private meeting with Hutchinson, who was intimate with the governor, the promises Shirley and Pownall had made to the family. They discussed patronage matters, agreeing on some joint action, and spoke also about the governor's absorption with trade regulation.[36]

Bernard was interested in the fees from confiscations which could double his yearly salary and help solve his family problems. Weighing heavily on his mind then, and for years to come,[37] were the burdens of educating his sons, the expenses of securing his commissions and moving the family to Boston, and his future in America. He had spoken to the late chief justice about law enforcement and undoubtedly repeated

[35] Bernard to Thomas Pownall, Aug. 28, 1761, *ibid.*, II, 9.
[36] Both Otis and Hutchinson agree that in this meeting patronage considerations were discussed, but they disagree about the understanding reached. From Aug. 21 to Nov. 13 when Hutchinson was appointed chief justice, Hutchinson, his relatives, and a few other administrators were the only members of the Council present at business meetings to advise Bernard. With Hutchinson the Olivers were powerful during these first days of the Bernard administration, and they were interested in having him join them on the bench.
[37] The financial opportunities of the Massachusetts government were a frequent topic of Bernard's letters. Samuel Allyne Otis in a letter to his brother, Oct. 20, 1761, Otis Papers, II, 56, wrote that Bernard should say openly that "he is poor and wants to make what money he can of us." Yet ought he "to oppress the industrious merchant to fill his own pockets and gild his own Chariot with anothers gold: or aggrandize his famili with the neighbours property?"

his conversation to Hutchinson and Otis. The chief justice, in turn, had
followed up the matter by discussing the legality of the Writs of Assistance with the younger Otis.

The death of the chief justice offered a new occasion for Bernard to
re-emphasize the need for law enforcement. Calling members of the
Superior Court to his office, he sought their advice on Sewall's successor
and even had solicited Hutchinson's opinion. Apparently he decided
that Hutchinson was the best available man for chief justice. His decision raised then as now questions about his motives. Did he name
Hutchinson in exchange for a promise of rigorous law enforcement?[38]
Did the old Shirley party on the court and the Hutchinson relatives—
the two Olivers and Lynde—make Hutchinson appear to be the only
person equipped for the position? Was this privately a move by the
Hutchinson-Oliver family to keep the Otises again from a position of
prestige? It could have been retaliation for their attack on Bollan and
Pownall's exclusion of Hutchinson from the inner councils of the late
administration. It seems clear, however, that Bernard did not seriously
consider the aspirations of the Otises or reflect on the political repercussions of the appointment. His remarks about the Hutchinson appointment give the impression that he may have been deceived by the
maneuvering.[39]

163

[38] Bernard had two motives in wanting smuggling curbed. He was anxious to
please the British government which had ordered rigorous enforcement of the trade
laws, and he wanted to share in the lucrative fees from seizures. Bernard could have
first asked Otis to enforce the trade laws (Otis had been requested by the late
chief justice to look into the legality of the Writs of Assistance) and, upon an unsatisfactory response, then asked Hutchinson to be chief justice on condition that he
would support the Writs and severe enforcement. Hutchinson's willingness to
cooperate with the governor may explain his appointment in place of Eliakim
Hutchinson, for example, who was chief justice of the Suffolk Court of Common
Pleas.

[39] Confirmation of Hutchinson's appointment on Nov. 13, 1760, was made by
a minority of the Council (13 out of 28). Bernard reported the action to Lord
Halifax on Nov. 17, 1760, in this casual manner: "No public business of consequence has been moved of late, except . . . the filling up the place of Chief
Justice." Apparently the patronage aspirations of the Otises were not seriously
presented to him or their claims were put forth in such a way as to seem unimportant. In short, James Otis was made to appear unsuitable for the position—the
spirit of the Otis memo of 1757 and of Peter Oliver's famous description of him
in the *Origins and Progress of the American Rebellion*. Besides James Otis, there
was also Colonel William Brattle who, according to Clifford Shipton, wanted to
be considered for the position and was equally disappointed with the results.

Hutchinson's behavior in accepting the appointment is curious. With three of the surviving justices relatives and the fourth a close friend (Chambers Russell), there would be no question of any control of the court. Hutchinson was the first chief justice, moreover, who was taken from outside its ranks, and the court had plenty of talent. Two of its members when Hutchinson became chief justice would eventually serve in that capacity. Either Hutchinson had decided in 1760 that the governorship was beyond his reach, and the Superior Court was balm for disappointment; or he was revealing his own hatred of the Otises, and his move to the court was an act of desperation in halting their rise to prominence. For Hutchinson had risen from speaker of the House to the Council and his present eminence! One wonders what Hutchinson said to the governor as they discussed the court vacancy and later when he accepted the honor.[40] Sometime later, when Bernard and Otis were conferring on admiralty affairs, the governor undoubtedly pressed for prosecution of smugglers and may have solicited a promise from Otis to make peace with Bollan in the agency dispute. The result of these talks was a blistering exchange between Otis and the governor in which Hutchinson's preferment, Bollan's agency, and the trade laws were denounced by Otis. In the end he refused to continue in office and "swore revenge."[41]

164

Brattle had opposed Bollan in 1759 and was an enemy of the Hutchinsons and Olivers. Unlike the Otises he was related to important Bostonians and long a member of the ruling elite. Refusal of Brattle and, undoubtedly, of others would indicate that Hutchinson took the court position to stop hostile politicians from gaining power. His determination in holding on to his other posts would indicate also that he was blocking the aspirations of others. See Massachusetts Council Records, XIV, 263-264, 267-268, 279, 288, Mass. State House; Bernard to Lord Halifax, Nov. 17, 1760, Bernard Letterbooks, I, 283; Shipton, "William Brattle," *Sibley's Harvard Graduates*, VII, 17.

[40] Some commentators on Hutchinson and the court appointment make the point that he did not apply for the post. They fail to note that Bernard apparently solicited Hutchinson's opinion on the Writs of Assistance; that Hutchinson was almost daily or weekly at the governor's side from Aug. to Nov. when many councillors were absent from Boston; that the Olivers were interested in Hutchinson's appointment; and, finally, that the governor's son wrote years later that Hutchinson asked his father for the post. See Mass. Hist. Soc., *Mass. House Journals*, XXXVII, Pt. i, x; Mass. Council Records, XIV, 263-268, 279, 288; Bernard, *Sir Francis Bernard*, 43-44.

[41] Otis resigned sometime between Nov. 13, 1760, and Jan. 13, 1761, when he undertook the defense of Harrison Gray. Hutchinson repeated the threat Otis

Otis's break with the governor was quickly evident in Boston when he joined merchant friends in objecting to admiralty search and seizure. He first assisted William Barrons, an admiralty official and former colleague, who had attempted to protect an illegally entered vessel and was suspended arbitrarily from his post. For months Otis helped Barrons file charges against customs officials, but he then took the issue to the House of Representatives and raised a storm over admiralty seizures. This fierce opposition was most upsetting to Bernard who complained mournfully of the furor to his English friend John Pownall. "Mr. Barrons had plaid the Devil in this town. He has put himself at the head of a combination of merchants all raised by him with the assistance of two or three others to demolish the Court of Admiralty . . . because I endeavoured to prevent Mr. Barrons raising this flame and afterwards expressed my Disapprobation of his proceedings, he and his emissaries have turned the fury of his party against me."[42]

165

While Otis was coaching Barrons in court and making Bernard's life miserable, he was occupied also with another issue that brought him directly into conflict with Hutchinson. The Writs of Assistance that were gaining much importance under Bernard's policy of law enforcement had to be renewed because of the death of George II in October 1760. Many Boston and Salem merchants had been objecting to these general search warrants by the admiralty and were ready to use this opportunity of the king's death to contest their legality. A case finally reached Chief Justice Hutchinson and his associates, with the younger James Otis as principal critic of the Writs. His four-hour address in the small chamber of the court house made a lasting impression on a few hearers and established him as a daring opponent of the admiralty. His immediate reward was an election to one of the four Boston seats in the House of Representatives.[43]

In the courtroom Otis had denounced the Writs as a violation of human rights. His eloquent remarks have fire even in our day as he spoke of the "freedom of one's house" and home as a man's "Castle."[44] But Otis knew, as did Hutchinson, that the Writs had been used in

---

is said to have made against him on Jan. 21, 1761; see Thomas Hutchinson to Israel Williams, Williams Papers, II, 155.

[42] Bernard to John Pownall, Jan. 19, 1761, Bernard Letterbooks, I, 296.

[43] Common Place Book, Joseph Hawley Papers, II, 8-14, N. Y. Pub. Lib.

[44] Ibid., 12. Compare "Adams' Minutes of the Argument," Feb. 24, 1761, in

England since the days of Charles II and were considered to be legal. However, they were relatively novel in Massachusetts. But Otis chose to denounce arbitrary methods of the hated admiralty court and, more, he was forcing Hutchinson to adjudge them legal. He was trying, further, to associate Hutchinson in the public mind with the aggressive policies of the admiralty officials. While the chief justice had referred the question of the Writs' legality to London, he was expected to announce a decision in their favor.[45]

166

The legality of the Writs became the business of the House of Representatives in 1761 and 1762. Otis and his friends knew what they wanted and drew up a writ to replace the Writs of Assistance. As Thomas Hutchinson noted, this new writ would have restrained the "Superior Court from issuing Writs of Assistance except upon special information to a customs house officer—the oath being made first, the informer mentioned, and the person supposed to own the goods and the place where they are suspected to be concealed."[46] These limitations would obviously tie the hands of the customs people, and their opposition put great pressure upon Bernard, who hated to be involved in partisan politics. In the meantime, the Superior Court had rescheduled the case against the Writs, reheard the arguments, and announced its decision. The court's verdict in favor of the Writs led directly to the passage of the bill and to its veto by Governor Bernard. Emotion in Boston rose to a high point and bitterness towards Hutchinson was great.

Otis, in taking advantage of this situation, assailed Hutchinson in many other ways and had some success in separating him from the "American" part of the Boston community. In general, Hutchinson was criticized for holding too many offices and for disturbing the balance of authority by having legislative, executive, and judicial positions. Otis tried unsuccessfully to strike at this multiple officeholding by excluding judges from the legislature, but won a small cut in judicial salaries as a

---

L. Kinvin Wroth and Hiller B. Zobel, eds., *The Legal Papers of John Adams,* in L. H. Butterfield, ed., *The Adams Papers,* Ser. III (Cambridge, Mass., 1965), II, 123-134.

[45] The battle over the Writs of Assistance, it should be noted, began in the courts, not in the House of Representatives, and the repercussions of the dispute only became apparent when Otis joined the representatives in May 1761. See *ibid.,* 106-123. (There are some errors in this discussion of the Writs.)

[46] Thomas Hutchinson to William Bollan, Mar. 6, 1762, Mass. Archives, XXVI, 8-9.

token of disapproval. A newspaper campaign finally turned the dispute into a series of personal exchanges that invited public debate and others took up the issue of multiple officeholding.[47]

Otis's most telling attack, however, was upon Hutchinson's friend, William Bollan. Without any scruple, Otis accused the agent of plotting to destroy the Congregational Church in New England. This curious charge was inspired by a wave of emotion sweeping the colony because of the activities of East Apthorp. The young clergyman seemed to be part of an English conspiracy to establish the national church in Massachusetts. Recently returning to the colony after an absence of years, he erected an Anglican mission in Cambridge and was proselytizing students and townsmen. His disregard for local prejudices aroused the clergy, who soon were debating his theological positions in the newspapers. East was the son of Charles Apthorp, the recently deceased, wealthy merchant of Boston, who had long been a Shirley supporter. East was also the grandson of the former governor, having married a daughter of Eliakim Hutchinson. By this distant connection Bollan's relations with Apthorp were noted and became his undoing. A bitter assault on him brought the help of the clergy, the merchants who hated him as advocate general, and the representatives who resented his dealings as colonial agent.[48]

167

Bollan's removal revealed how effectively Otis had woven his campaign against Hutchinson into the popular emotion. The governor, helpless in stopping the wave of prejudice, sacrificed Bollan without raising a hand, and Hutchinson had to look on as a majority in both houses swept away all opposition in favor of a new agent who was ill and unknown.[49] Hutchinson called the proceedings "mad," but Otis's will prevailed. The committee that instructed the new agent, furthermore, put into an official document the natural rights philosophy that Otis had been spreading since his denunciation of the Writs.

---

[47] *Boston Gazette*, Feb. 28, Apr. 4, May 16, 1763; *Boston News-Letter*, Apr. 7, 1763; *Boston Evening-Post*, Apr. 25, 1763; [Edward Bacon], "Philo-Politae," *ibid.*, Oct. 24, 1763; Ellen Brennan, *Plural Office-Holding in Massachusetts, 1760-1780* (Chapel Hill, 1945), 41-73.

[48] Wendell D. Garrett, *Apthorp House 1760-1960* (Cambridge, Mass., 1960), 8-12; Hutchinson to William Bollan, Apr. 24, 1762, Mass. Archives, XXVI, 12.

[49] Bernard to John Pownall, Apr. 25, 1762, Bernard Letterbooks, II, 183-184; Hutchinson to Israel Williams, Nov. 17, 1763, Williams Papers, II, 157.

Although Otis often drew on the philosophy of natural rights to make his points against Crown and governor, he was being pulled simultaneously in various directions. Born and educated in an eighteenth-century society of patronage, he and his family sought the rewards of position and wealth. At the same time their friends were confronted by challenges to colonial liberty, to which he was impelled to seek an answer in the natural rights philosophy, particularly in the proposition that there was a higher law than Parliament's governing the actions of men. In developing this philosophy, he found himself in the peculiar position of being a leader of Boston's merchants and trades-men, far removed from the country folk of Barnstable who sent his father and grandfather to Boston. He was an opposition leader in the tradition of Elisha Cooke and James Allen. His conduct like theirs was wild and explosive, often unpredictable, spreading fear to enemy and friend alike, but his maneuvering won the left-handed praise of Thomas Hutchinson who called him a "clever fellow" who could readily adjust to the political situation.[50] Unlike Cooke he did not feign drunkenness to oppose the governor, or unlike Allen he was not expelled from the House; he was a brilliant speaker whose knowledge of the classics, the law, and language made him the object of admiration.[51] He craved honor for the family; he wanted to surpass his father; and he was also the leader of an opposition force that was being called into existence by conflicts with Britain.

The power of his position, nonetheless, had induced Governor Bernard in 1762 to approve his father as a councillor and to appoint his brother Joseph as sheriff of Barnstable. This initial success pleased the family, except that the Otis brothers did not like James's tactics, which aroused feeling in the conservative community of Barnstable, separated them from boyhood friends, and made the Boston Otises dependent upon the city's tradesmen for political support. Samuel Allyne Otis, who had opened a store in Boston, wanted better relations with the administration so that he could marry the daughter of the colony's treasurer, Harrison Gray.[52] Joseph, as the sheriff of Barnstable, did not appreciate the political confusion as did his Sturgis family in-laws. Some

168

[50] Hutchinson to Thomas Cushing, Jan. 3, 1763, Mass. Archives, XXVI, 38.
[51] See Wroth and Zobel, eds., *Legal Papers of John Adams*, II, 106-107.
[52] Samuel Allyne Otis to Joseph Otis, May 31, 1762, Otis MSS., II, 94.

of the family's rural cousins like Edward Bacon were frankly opposed to the radical turn of the Boston Otises and were perplexed by James's behavior. In Boston itself, Samuel Allyne Otis, aware of the instability of Massachusetts politics, which he styled as a "wild democracy," cautioned against radicalism. He did not intend to provide an opportunity for the "many who wish both here and else where to tread down every branch of our family."[53]

Otis opposition certainly did not shake Hutchinson's control of his many offices. As chief justice, member of the Council, and lieutenant governor, he was personally powerful and had the additional help of relatives who were councillors and justices. He had been separated, however, from many colleagues and branded a Tory. Instead of being Shirley's successor, as he surely wanted to be, he was leader of a faction that was labeled as defenders of British, high church, and admiralty interests, and he was handicapped by a weak governor. He considered leaving Boston for a time and serving as a colony agent in London; he weighed the cost in power of resigning his commissions.[54] His critics predicted, however, that a trip to the capital would find him returning as royal governor.

169

The Otises were fully aware of these calculations and never let their opposition towards Bernard become too bitter.[55] Young James, even at the height of his attack upon the admiralty court, seconded the governor's salary bill, and secured him a land grant in Maine. The governor responded as graciously in approving the elder James as a member of the Council and Joseph as sheriff of Barnstable. In fact, Bernard had so much trouble on all sides, including plots against his position, that he may have approached the Otises suggesting peace. Sometime in 1763 he, Hutchinson, and the Otises apparently agreed to disagree and a partial reconciliation occurred. Colonel Otis became chief justice of the Barnstable Court of Common Pleas and justice of the Probate Court. He had returned the family to father's eminence, except that son James was leader of an opposition in Boston which would challenge this order of honor, office, and patronage.

[53] Samuel Allyne Otis to Joseph Otis, Mar. 2, [1762?], Gay Papers.

[54] Hutchinson to William Bollan, Feb. 7, 1764, Mass. Archives, XXVI, 77; Hutchinson to [unknown], July 11, 1764, *Jasper Mauduit* (Massachusetts Historical Society, *Collections*, LXXIV [Boston, 1918]), 163-164.

[55] James Otis, Jr., to Jasper Mauduit, Oct. 28, 1762, *ibid.*, 78.

The Otis-Hutchinson rivalry presents a fascinating pattern of Massachusetts politics. The Otises, a provincial outport family, ever after a Boston foothold, struggled with the Hutchinsons, an urban, mercantile, and metropolitan family. Influence, patronage, position, and family, not ideological abstractions, were the propellants of their politics. At this juncture younger James was no torchbearer of revolution but a zealous seeker of those prizes and rewards of colonial life. Thomas Hutchinson, irritated over the pretensions of these country folk, was blocked at the same time from the governorship by Pownall, Bernard, and uncertainty. Inconsiderate of Otis feeling, he raised a storm when he accepted the appointment of chief justice of the Superior Court in order to safeguard family prestige and stop the Otises. The storm that broke over the Writs of Assistance in 1761 ruined his friends and separated him from the society he wanted to dominate.

170

Jack Tar in the Streets:
Merchant Seamen in the Politics of
Revolutionary America

Jesse Lemisch*

HERE comes Jack Tar, his bowed legs bracing him as if the very Broadway beneath his feet might begin to pitch and roll.[1] In his dress he is, in the words of a superior, "very nasty and negligent," his black stockings ragged, his long, baggy trousers tarred to make them waterproof.[2] Bred in "that very shambles of language," the mer-

* Mr. Lemisch is a visiting member of the Department of History, Northwestern University. An earlier version of this article was read at a meeting of the Organization of American Historians, Cincinnati, Ohio, April 1966. A grant and a fellowship from the American Council of Learned Societies aided the research.

[1] His walk was sometimes described as a "waddle," *New-York Gazette; or the Weekly Post-Boy*, Sept. 3, 1759. Seamen were often called Jack Tar in England and in the colonies, for example, *ibid.*, Oct. 15, 1770. The term was used more or less interchangeably along with "seaman," "sailor," and "mariner," with the latter frequently connoting "master" (as in Panel of Jurors [n.d.], New York Supreme Court, Pleadings P-2689, Office of County Clerk, Hall of Records, New York City, where seven of ten "mariners" are identifiable as captains by comparison with such sources as *The Burghers of New Amsterdam and the Freemen of New York, 1675-1866* [New-York Historical Society, *Collections*, XVIII (New York, 1886)], *passim; N.-Y. Gaz.; Weekly Post-Boy, passim;* and the especially valuable list of privateer captains in Stuyvesant Fish, *The New York Privateers, 1756-1763* [New York, 1945], 83-90). In this article Jack Tar is a merchant seaman, a "sailor" is in the Royal Navy, and a "mariner" is the captain of a merchant vessel. If a source calls a man a "mariner" or a "sailor" I have had to have evidence that he was in fact a merchant seaman before I would count him as one. For a useful discussion of terms see I. M. V., "Note," *Mariner's Mirror*, VII (1921), 351.

[2] [George Balfour], "Memorandum," *Mariner's Mirror*, VIII (1922), 248. For the seaman's dress see *Abstracts of Wills on File in the Surrogate's Office, City of New York* (N.-Y. Hist. Soc., *Coll.*, XXV-XLI [New York, 1893-1909]), VI, 111; descriptions of dress scattered throughout Admiralty Group, Class 98, Piece 11-14, Public Record Office. Hereafter cited as Adm. 98/11-14: *N.-Y. Gaz.; Weekly Post-Boy*, Dec. 10, 1759, Oct. 14, Dec. 16, 1762, Nov. 3, 1763, Mar. 6, June 26, 1766, Oct. 1, 1767, Jan. 29, 1770, July 6, 1772; Samuel Eliot Morison, *John Paul Jones* (Boston, 1959), 72. A pair of useful illustrations appears in *Mariner's Mirror*, IX (1923), 128.

chant marine, he is foul-mouthed, his talk alien and suspect.[3] He is Jolly Jack, a bull in a china shop, always, in his words, "for a Short Life and a Merry one," and, in the concurring words of his superiors, "concerned only for the present . . . incapable of thinking of, or inattentive to, future welfare," "like froward Childeren not knowing how to judge for themselves."[4]

Clothes don't make the man, nor does language; surely we can do better than these stereotypes. Few have tried. Maritime history, as it has been written, has had as little to do with the common seaman as business history has had to do with the laborer. In that *mischianza* of mystique and elitism, "seaman" has meant Sir Francis Drake, not Jack Tar; the focus has been on trade, exploration, the great navigators, but rarely on the men who sailed the ships.[5] Thus we know very little about Jack. Samuel Eliot Morison is one of the few who have tried to portray the common seaman. In an influential anecdote in *The Maritime History of Massachusetts* Morison has described a "frequent occurrence" in early New England. A farmer's boy, called by the smell or the sight of the sea, suddenly runs off; three years later he returns as a man, marries the hired girl, and lives "happily ever after." This experience, Morison tells us, was "typical of the Massachusetts merchant marine," where the "old salt" was almost non-existent and where there never was "a native deep-sea prole-

---

[3] J. R. Hutchinson, *The Press-Gang, Afloat and Ashore* (New York, 1913), 29. See *The Acts and Resolves . . . of the Province of Massachusetts Bay . . .* (Boston, 1869-1922), III, 318-319, for an act of Feb. 10, 1747, prescribing the stocks and whipping for seamen guilty of "profane cursing or swearing." For a landsman's version of some seamen's dialogue, see *N.-Y. Gaz.; Weekly Post-Boy*, Dec. 10, 1767.

[4] Robert E. Peabody, "The Naval Career of Captain John Manley of Marblehead," Essex Institute, *Historical Collections,* XLV (1909), 25; Ralph D. Paine, *The Ships and Sailors of Old Salem* (New York, 1909), 23; John Cremer, *Ramblin' Jack . . .,* ed. R. Reynell Bellamy (London, 1936), 38-39; Congressman Edward Livingston, Apr. 10, 1798, United States, Congress, *Debates and Proceedings in the Congress of the United States . . .* (Washington, D. C., 1834-1856), 5th Cong., 2d sess., 1388. Hereafter cited as *Annals of Congress;* Colvill to Admiralty, Nov. 12, 1765, Adm. 1/482.

[5] The bibliography is endless: a typical recent instance is Edmund O. Sawyer, *America's Sea Saga* (New York, 1962), foreword, 185, "a tale of unending courage" by a retired lieutenant colonel who now lives in Hollywood where he "plays an active role in the relentless crusade against the Communist conspiracy." Although there is much of use in *American Neptune,* the magazine's definition of maritime history has been too genteel, dwelling too often on such matters as ship design and construction, yachting, reminiscences, and model-building. On the other hand, even the W. P. A. Writer's Program neglected the seamen in *Boston Looks Seaward* (Boston, 1941) and in *A Maritime History of New York* (Garden City, N. Y., 1941).

tariat." The ships were sailed by wave after wave of "adventure-seeking boys," drawn by high wages and *wanderlust*. If they recovered, they took their earnings, married, and bought a farm; if not, these "young, ambitious seamen culled from the most active element of a pushing race" stayed on and rose to become masters in a merchant marine distinguished from its class-ridden European counterparts by easy mobility.[6]

There is much to support Morison's *tableau*. Even if the mystique of the sea has been no more than mystique, still it has existed and exerted a powerful force. Washington, Franklin, and thousands of others did suffer attacks of "sea fever."[7] Seamen were, as Morison says, young men, averaging in one sample slightly over twenty-four, with many like John Paul Jones who went to sea at thirteen and even some who went at eight.[8] Many of them "hove in hard at the Hause-hole"[9] and became masters of their own vessels; later, while their sons and grandsons added to their wealth, they retired, perhaps to their farms, and wrote proud histories of their successes.[10] Some, like Nicholas Biddle, found the navy a better outlet for their ambitions than the merchant service.[11] Others, following Morison's pattern, quit the sea early and turned to farming.[12] For many

173

[6] Samuel Eliot Morison, *The Maritime History of Massachusetts* (Boston, 1921), 105-107, 111; see also Morison, *John Paul Jones*, 22-23.

[7] Mason L. Weems, *The Life of Washington*, ed. Marcus Cunliffe (Cambridge, Mass., 1962), xxxv, 27; Douglas S. Freeman, *George Washington* (New York, 1948-1957), I, 190-199; Jesse Lemisch, ed., *Benjamin Franklin: The Autobiography and Other Writings* (New York, 1961), 23; Elmo Paul Hohman, *Seamen Ashore* (New Haven, 1952), 217, calls this kind of motivation "positive"; see *ibid.*, for "negative" motives.

[8] Morison, *John Paul Jones*, 11; sixty-one American seamen of ascertainable age listed in *Muster Rolls of New York Provincial Troops: 1755-1764* (N.-Y. Hist. Soc., *Coll.*, XXIV [New York, 1892]), *passim*, average 24.3 years; Cremer, *Ramblin' Jack*, ed. Bellamy, 38.

[9] The phrase appears in Cremer, *Ramblin' Jack*, ed. Bellamy, 31-32, and in Morison, *Maritime History*, 107.

[10] See for example, Mary Barney, ed., *A Biographical Memoir of the Late Commodore Joshua Barney* (Boston, 1832); Thomas Dring, *Recollections of the Jersey Prison-Ship*, ed. Albert G. Greene (Providence, 1829); Ebenezer Fox, *The Adventures of Ebenezer Fox in the Revolutionary War* (Boston, 1847?); Christopher Hawkins, *The Adventures of Christopher Hawkins* (New York, 1864); Paine, *Ships and Sailors of Salem*, 100, 117-119; James A. Henretta, "Economic Development and Social Structure in Colonial Boston," *William and Mary Quarterly*, 3d Ser., XXII (1965), 76.

[11] Joseph Galloway to Benjamin Franklin, Apr. 23, 1771, Franklin Papers, III, 50, American Philosophical Society, Philadelphia.

[12] "In America . . . all sorts of people turn farmers—where no mechanic or

there was mobility between generations and between trades.[13] Seamen and landsmen might be distinct classes in Europe, but in America, men such as Albert Gallatin who knew both the Old World and the New found no "material distinction."[14] So Jack Tar seems to have been simply the landsman gone to sea, indistinguishable from his fellows ashore, and, together with them, on his way to prosperity.

If the seaman was a clean young farm-boy on the make—and likely to succeed—why was Josiah Franklin so apprehensive lest young Benjamin "break loose and go to sea"? Why did Josiah fight his son's "strong inclination to go to sea" by frantically trying to make of him a joiner, a bricklayer, a turner, a brazier, a tallow-chandler, a cutler, a printer—anything, so long as it would keep him on land?[15] Why did Washington's uncle suggest that young George would better become a planter or even an apprentice to a tinker, while explicitly urging that he not become a seaman?[16]

"All masters of vessels are warned not to harbor, conceal, or employ him, as they will answer for it, as the law directs."[17] To a fleeing apprentice, dissatisfied with the "bondage" of work ashore,[18] to a runaway slave,

174

---

artizan—sailor—soldier—servant, etc. but what, if they get money, take land, and turn farmers." Harry J. Carman, ed., *American Husbandry* (New York, 1939), 124.

[13] The sons of captains might find themselves apprenticed to gentlemen or to butchers or barbers as well as to other mariners. See, for example, *Burghers of New Amsterdam*, 577-578, 617, 620; *Indentures of Apprentices, 1718-1727* (N.-Y. Hist. Soc., *Coll.*, XLII [New York, 1910]), 122-123, 140, 142-143, 150, 155, 166, 169, 181, 188, 189, 193, 195.

[14] Albert Gallatin, Apr. 10, 1798, *Annals of Congress*, 5th Cong., 2d sess., 1392; J. Hector St. John de Crevecoeur, *Letters from an American Farmer* (New York, 1957), 122, has similar observations about American "sea-faring men," but he seems to be describing only whalers.

[15] Lemisch, ed., *Franklin*, 23, 25-26. History apparently repeated itself in the next generation. Franklin's son William "left my house unknown to us all, and got on board a privateer, from whence I fetched him." Benjamin Franklin to Jane Mecom [June ? 1748], Leonard W. Labaree et. al., eds., *The Papers of Benjamin Franklin* (New Haven, 1959—), III, 303.

[16] Freeman, *Washington*, I, 198-199. For some other instances of opposition by families of young men who expressed the intention of going to sea, see Barney, ed., *Memoir*, 3-4, and Fox, *Adventures*, 29, 36, 40.

[17] This is a composite of advertisements appearing in almost every colonial newspaper. See, for example, *N.-Y. Gaz.; Weekly Post-Boy*, May 17, 24, 1764, June 27, 1765.

[18] The term is used by Fox, *Adventures*, 18, describing his situation in 1775. In an interesting passage *ibid.*, 17-19, he sees in the movement for independence a cause of a general "spirit of insubordination" among American youth at the time. For another runaway, see Bushnell, *Adventures of Hawkins*, 10, 60-61.

the sea might appear the only real shelter. Men with no experience at sea tried to pass for seamen and before long discovered that they had indeed become seamen. Others *were* seamen, apprenticed in one vessel and fled to another. Still others, deserted soldiers, bail-jumpers, thieves, and murderers, had gotten into trouble with the law.[19] And others went to sea entirely unwillingly, originally impressed—perhaps from jail—into the navy, or tricked into the merchant service by crimps.[20] These were the floaters who drifted and slipped their moorings, the suicides, the men whose wives—if they had wives—ran off with other men; the beneficiaries in their wills—when they left wills—were innkeepers.[21] Hitherto, argued a proponent of a United States navy in 1782, the merchant marine had been "the resource of necessity, accident or indulgence."[22]

175

The merchant marine was a place full of forces beyond the seaman's control: death and disease, storms, and fluctuations in employment. Indeed, the lack of "old salts" in Morison's merchant marine might reflect a sombre irony: was the average seaman young because mobility rapidly brought him to another trade or because seamen died young?[23] A man in

[19] See *N.-Y. Gaz.; Weekly Post-Boy*, Sept. 3, Dec. 10, 1759, Oct. 14, Dec. 16, 1762, July 21, Oct. 6, Nov. 3, 1763, Mar. 29, May 10, 24, July 19, Sept. 6, 20, 1764, Apr. 4, 18, June 27, 1765, June 29, July 6, 1772; *New-York Journal: or the General Advertiser*, May 13, 1773. For a Negro seaman see log of *Hunter*, Sept. 8, 1758, Adm. 51/465. Some Negro seamen were free and some received their freedom as a reward for service in warships. Benjamin Quarles, *The Negro in the American Revolution* (Chapel Hill, 1961), 84; Robert McColley, *Slavery and Jeffersonian Virginia* (Urbana, 1964), 89. But Negroes also served at sea and in related maritime trades as part of their bondage and were sometimes advertised as "brought up from his Infancy to the sea." William Waller Hening, *The Statutes at Large . . . of Virginia* (Richmond, 1809-1823), XI, 404; *N.-Y. Gaz.; Weekly Post-Boy*, Mar. 26, 1761, July 7, Aug. 18, Nov. 17, 1763; Samuel Hallett in American Loyalists: Transcripts of the Commission of Enquiry into the Losses and Services of the American Loyalists . . . 1783-1790, XIX, 207, New York Public Library; George William Edwards, *New York as an Eighteenth Century Municipality, 1731-1776* (New York, 1917), 178.

[20] For crimps, see Hutchinson, *Press-Gang*, 48-49. Hohman, *Seamen Ashore*, 273-274, dates the development of crimping in America between 1830 and 1845, but there were crimps in Norfolk in 1767. See Captain Jeremiah Morgan to Governor Francis Fauquier, Sept. 11, 1767, Adm. 1/2116, Library of Congress transcript.

[21] *N.-Y. Gaz.; Weekly Post-Boy*, Sept. 30, 1773; *The King* v. *Jane the Wife of Thomas Dun*, Indictment for Bigamy, filed Oct. 26, 1763, N. Y. Supreme Court, Pleadings K-41. Although no statistical conclusions are possible, to a surprising extent the beneficiaries in a sample of seamen's wills are not wives but rather brothers and sisters, friends and innkeepers, *Abstracts of Wills*, VI, 111, 226; VII, 12, 38, 148, 397; VIII, 98; XI, 194.

[22] *Independent Chronicle* (Boston), Sept. 5, 1782.

[23] For some reflections on mortality in the merchant marine see Ralph Davis, *The

jail, said Dr. Johnson, was at least safe from drowning, and he had more room, better food, and better company. The Quaker John Woolman was one of the few sensitive enough to see that if the "poor bewildered sailors" drank and cursed, the fault lay not so much in themselves as in the harsh environment and the greed of employers. Nor was the road up through the hawse-hole so easy as Morison asserts. That the few succeeded tells us nothing of the many; only the successful left autobiographies.[24] Perhaps the sons of merchants and ship-masters made it, along with the captain's brother-in-law[25] and those who attended schools of navigation,[26] but what of the "poor lads bound apprentice" who troubled Woolman, those whose wages went to their masters? What of the seamen in Morison's own Boston who died too poor to pay taxes and who were a part of what James Henretta has called "the bottom" of Boston society?[27] What of those who went bankrupt with such frequency in Rhode Island?[28] Why,

---

Rise of the English Shipping Industry in the Seventeenth and Eighteenth Centuries (London, 1962), 156. As late as the 1840's Massachusetts seamen, with an average age at death of 42.47 years, died younger than farmers, clergymen, lawyers, physicians, blacksmiths, carpenters, merchants, and laborers. Only painters, fishermen, manufacturers, mechanics, and printers are listed as having shorter lives in Lemuel Shattuck *et al., Report of the Sanitary Commission of Massachusetts, 1850* (Cambridge, Mass., 1948), 87. For employment see *N. Y. Journal or Gen. Adv.,* Oct. 5, 1775; Thomas Paine, *The Complete Writings,* ed. Philip S. Foner (New York, 1945), I, 33; in addition, a kind of unemployment is built into the profession; a seaman ashore is generally unemployed. See Hohman, *Seamen Ashore,* 209.

[24] Quoted in Davis, *Rise of English Shipping,* 154; John Woolman, *The Journal of John Woolman and A Plea for the Poor* (New York, 1961), 206, 192-193, 196. For comments on elitism in the writings of Morison and of other historians of early America, see Jesse Lemisch, "The American Revolution Seen from the Bottom Up," in Barton J. Bernstein, ed., *Towards a New Past: Dissenting Essays in American History* (New York, 1968), 3-45.

[25] Barney, ed., *Memoir,* 10. For the relative prospects of the sons of merchants and masters as opposed to others in the English merchant marine, see Davis, *Rise of English Shipping,* 117.

[26] For such schools see Boston Registry Department, *Records Relating to the Early History of Boston* (Boston, 1876-1909), XIII, 2, 204; Carl Bridenbaugh, *Cities in Revolt* (New York, 1955), 377.

[27] Woolman, *Journal,* 195; *Bethune* v. *Warner,* May 27, 1724, Admiralty Court, Boston, Minute Book II (1718-1726), 177, Office of Clerk, Supreme Judicial Court, Suffolk County, Mass.; Boston Reg. Dept., *Records of Boston,* XIV, 88-89, 94-95; Henretta, "Economic Development," 85; see also Jackson T. Main, *The Social Structure of Revolutionary America* (Princeton, 1965), 74.

[28] Only three occupational groups exceeded "mariners" in the number of insolvency petitions filed with the Rhode Island legislature from 1756 to 1828. See Peter J. Coleman, "The Insolvent Debtor in Rhode Island, 1745-1828," *Wm. and*

at the other end of the colonies, did Washington's uncle warn that it would be "very difficult" to become master of a Virginia vessel and not worth trying?[29]

The presence of such men, fugitives and floaters, powerless in a tough environment, makes *wanderlust* appear an ironic parody of the motives which made at least some men go to sea. Catch the seaman when he is not pandering to your romanticism, said former seaman Frederick Law Olmsted a century later, and he will tell you that he hates the sight of blue water, he hates his ship, his officers, and his messmates—and he despises himself. Melville's Ishmael went to sea when he felt grim, hostile, and suicidal: "It is a way I have of driving off the spleen." No matter what we make of Ishmael, we cannot possibly make him into one of Morison's "adventure-seeking boys." Others, perhaps, but not Ishmael. The feelings of eighteenth-century Americans toward seafaring and seamen, and what evidence we have of the reasons men had for going to sea indicate that there were many like Ishmael in the colonial period, too, who left the land in flight and fear, outcasts, men with little hope of success ashore. These were the dissenters from the American mood. Their goals differed from their fellows ashore; these were the rebels, the men who stayed on to become old salts.[30]

Admiralty law treated seamen in a special way, as "wards." Carl Ubbelohde says that seamen favored the colonial Vice Admiralty Courts as "particular tribunals in case of trouble," and Charles M. Andrews and Richard B. Morris agreed that these courts were "guardians of the rights of the seamen." The benefits of being classified as a "ward" are dubious, but, regardless of the quality of treatment which admiralty law accorded

---

Mary Qtly., 3d Ser., XXII (1965), 422n. Mr. Coleman has stated in conversation with the author that the "mariners" appear to be predominantly common seamen.

[29] Freeman, *Washington*, I, 199.

[30] Frederick Law Olmsted, *A Journey in the Back Country* . . . (New York, 1860), 287. Morison, *Maritime History*, offers no evidence for the assertion that his anecdote of the adventurous farm-boy is "typical" and that Massachusetts "has never had a native deep-sea proletariat." In the absence of such evidence and in the light of the evidence offered above for the existence of a very different type there is no basis for a claim that either group was "typical." My contention about the nature of the merchant marine is limited and negative. The presence of runaway slaves, thieves, murderers, fugitives, and floaters, *in addition to* Morison's adventure-seekers prevents any statement about typicality until we can offer quantitative evidence. Meanwhile all that we can say is that both types existed and that it is misleading to view the colonial merchant marine as a homogenous entity.

to seamen, it certainly does not follow that, all in all, the colonial seaman was well treated by the law. Indeed, if we broaden our scope to include colonial law generally, we find an extraordinarily harsh collection of laws, all justifying Olmsted's later claim that American seamen "are more wretched, and are governed more by threats of force than any other civilized laborers of the world."[31] There are laws providing for the whipping of disobedient seamen and in one case for their punishment as "seditious"; laws prohibiting seamen in port from leaving their vessels after sundown and from travelling on land without certificates of discharge from their last job; laws empowering "every free white person" to catch runaway seamen.[32] We find other laws, less harsh, some seeming to protect the seaman: laws against extending credit to seamen and against arresting them for debt, and against entertaining them in taverns for more than one hour per day; laws against selling them liquor and prohibiting them from playing with cards or dice; laws waiving imprisonment for seamen convicted of cursing; laws requiring masters to give discharge certificates to their seamen and laws prohibiting hiring without such certificates.[33] Finally, there are laws which clearly do help the

178

[31] Carl Ubbelohde, *The Vice-Admiralty Courts and the American Revolution* (Chapel Hill, 1960), 20, 159-160; Charles M. Andrews, introduction to Dorothy S. Towle, ed., *The Records of the Vice Admiralty Court of Rhode Island, 1716-1752* (Washington, 1936), 60; Richard B. Morris, *Government and Labor in Early America* (New York, 1946), 232, 256; Olmsted, *Journey,* 287. Ubbelohde, Morris, and Andrews do not contend that the seaman was well treated by the law in an overall sense. Ubbelohde and Morris show that the seaman was better treated in Vice Admiralty Courts than in courts of common law; but when the focus moves to colonial legislation the hostility of the law emerges as the central fact for the seaman.

[32] Hening, *Statutes of Virginia,* IV, 107-108; VI, 26; E. B. O'Callaghan, ed., *Laws and Ordinances of New Netherland, 1638-1674* (Albany, 1868), 11-12. This law also prevented landsmen from going aboard vessels without authorization from the director of the West India Company. On June 13, 1647, two seamen convicted of tearing down a copy of this law attached to their vessel's mainmast were sentenced to be chained to a wheelbarrow and employed at hard labor on bread and water for three months. I. N. P. Stokes, *The Iconography of Manhattan Island, 1498-1909* (New York, 1915-1928), IV, 87. Thomas Cooper, ed., *The Statutes at Large of South Carolina* (Columbia, 1836-1841), III, 736.

[33] See the laws cited in Morris, *Government and Labor,* 230, n. 2; *Minutes of the Common Council of the City of New York, 1675-1776* (New York, 1905), I, 223, 372; *Acts and Resolves,* I, 142, 560; III, 318-319; IV, 73; James T. Mitchell and Henry Flanders, eds., *Statutes at Large of Pennsylvania from 1682 to 1801* (Harrisburg, 1896-1908), II, 239-240; Albert S. Batchellor and Henry H. Metcalf, *Laws of New Hampshire* (Manchester, 1904-1922), I, 691; J. Hammond Trumbull and C. J. Hoadly, eds., *The Public Records of the Colony of Connecticut (1636-1776)* (Hartford, 1850-1890), III, 54; *Charters and General Laws of the Colony and Province*

seaman: laws requiring masters to provide "good and sufficient diet and accommodation" and providing for redress if the master refused; laws providing punishment for masters who "immoderately beat, wound, or maim" their seamen; laws providing that seamen's contracts be written.[34]

These harsh or at best paternalistic laws[35] add up to a structure whose purpose is to assure a ready supply of cheap, docile labor.[36] Obedience, both at sea and ashore, is the keystone.[37] Charles Beard at his most rigidly mechanistic would doubtless have found the Constitution merely mild stuff alongside this blatantly one-sided class legislation. Today's historians of the classless society would do well to examine the preambles of these laws, written in a more candid age, by legislatures for which, even by Robert Brown's evidence, most seamen could not vote.[38] Again and again these laws aim to inhibit acts of seamen which may do "prejudice to

179

---

of Massachusetts (Boston, 1814), 185; Cooper, ed., Statutes of South Carolina, III, 735, 736; Hening, Statutes of Virginia, IV, 108-110; VI, 25, 28.

[34] Hening, Statutes of Virginia, IV, 109-110, VI, 27. Colonial Laws of New York from the Year 1664 to the Revolution . . . (Albany, 1894-1896), IV, 484-485; Morris, Government and Labor, 230, n. 5 and 7.

[35] Eugene T. Jackman, "Efforts Made Before 1825 to Ameliorate the Lot of the American Seaman: With Emphasis on his Moral Regeneration," American Neptune, XXIV (1964), 109, describes legislation for seamen after the Revolution as "paternalistic." As late as 1897 the Supreme Court declared that "seamen are treated by Congress, as well as by the Parliament of Great Britain, as deficient in that full and intelligent responsibility for their acts which is accredited to ordinary adults." Hohman, Seamen Ashore, 214.

[36] Morris, Government and Labor, 230, agrees with this statement in a somewhat more limited form.

[37] See Deposition of Commander Arthur Tough [1742], Gertrude MacKinney, ed., Pennsylvania Archives, 8th Ser. (Harrisburg, 1931-1935), IV, 2993.

[38] Robert E. Brown, Middle-Class Democracy and the Revolution in Massachusetts, 1691-1780 (Ithaca, 1955), 27-30, acknowledges that the "city proletariat" constituted "the largest disfranchised group" and strongly implies that itinerant seamen could not vote. Even so, Brown has stated the case too optimistically. By including propertied captains under the ambiguous label "mariner," he has disguised the fact, legible in his own evidence, that the "mariners" who could vote were captains and the common seamen could not. See John Cary, "Statistical Method and the Brown Thesis on Colonial Democracy, With a Rebuttal by Robert E. Brown," Wm. and Mary Qtly., 3d Ser., XX (1963), 257. For Brown's acknowledgement of the error see ibid., 272. Arthur M. Schlesinger, The Colonial Merchants and the American Revolution, 1763-1776 (New York, 1918), 28, includes seamen in a list of those who were "for the most part, unenfranchised." For an assertion that "sailors" could vote based on evidence that masters could compare Jacob R. Marcus, Early American Jewry (Philadelphia, 1953), II, 231, and B. R. Carroll, ed., Historical Collections of South Carolina (New York, 1836), II, 441.

masters and owners of vessells" or constitute a "manifest detriment of . . . trade."[39] The seamen's interests are sacrificed to the merchants', and even the laws which seem friendly to the seaman benefit the master. Laws against giving credit, arresting, and suing aim to keep the seaman available rather than involved in a lawsuit or imprisoned; the certificates and written contracts seek to prevent desertion and to protect the master against what would today be called a "strike";[40] the laws protecting seamen against immoderate punishment and requiring adequate food and accommodation are implicitly weak in that they require that dependents make open complaint against their superiors.[41] Sometimes this limitation is made explicit, as in a South Carolina law of 1751 whose stated purpose is "TO DISCOURAGE FRIVOLOUS AND VEXATIOUS ACTIONS AT LAW BEING BROUGHT BY SEAMEN AGAINST MASTERS AND COMMANDERS."[42]

Thus if we think of Jack Tar as jolly, childlike, irresponsible, and in many ways surprisingly like the Negro stereotype, it is because he was treated so much like a child, a servant, and a slave. What the employer saw as the necessities of an authoritarian profession were written into law and culture: the society that wanted Jack dependent made him that way and then concluded that that was the way he really was.[43]

180

<hr>

[39] Trumbull and Hoadly, *Public Records of Connecticut*, III, 54; Cooper, ed., *Statutes of South Carolina*, II, 54; III, 735; for other legislation containing similar phrases see Batchellor and Metcalf, *Laws of New Hampshire*, I, 691; *Minutes of the Common Council of New York*, I, 223; *Colonial Laws of New York*, IV, 483; Hening, *Statutes of Virginia*, IV, 107.

[40] For instance, *Colonial Laws of New York*, IV, 484 (later disallowed), required a written contract in order to end such practices as this: "very often when Ships and vessels come to be cleared out . . . the Seamen refuse to proceed with them, without coming to new agreements for increasing their wages and many of them will Leave their Ships and Vessels and not proceed on their voyages which puts the owners of such ships and vessels to Great Trouble and Charges." The act also mentions subterfuges of seamen but fails to acknowledge the possibility that masters might also use subterfuge. For a "mutiny" which clearly expressed a labor grievance see below, 406.

[41] See the procedure provided in Hening, *Statutes of Virginia*, IV, 109-110. See also Morris, *Government and Labor*, 268.

[42] Cooper, ed., *Statutes of South Carolina*, III, 735.

[43] For examples of the similarity between life at sea and life on the plantation compare Morris, *Government and Labor*, 230, 247, 256, 262, 274, and McColley, *Slavery and Jeffersonian Virginia*, 103. For Frederick Olmsted's comments on the similarity, based on his own experience at sea in 1843-1844, see *The Cotton Kingdom*, ed. Arthur M. Schlesinger (New York, 1953), 453. For the image of the sea-

II

Constantly plagued by short complements, the Royal Navy attempted to solve its manning problems in America, as in England, by impressment.[44] Neil Stout has recently attributed these shortages to "death, illness, crime, and desertion" which were in turn caused largely by rum and by the deliberate enticements of American merchants.[45] Rum and inveiglement certainly took a high toll, but to focus on these two causes of shortages is unfairly to shift the blame for impressment onto its victims. The navy itself caused shortages. Impressment, said Thomas Hutchinson, caused desertion, rather than the other way around.[46] Jack Tar had *181* good reasons for avoiding the navy. It would, a young Virginian was warned, "cut him and staple him and use him like a Negro, or rather,

---

man in literature see Harold F. Watson, *The Sailor in English Fiction and Drama, 1550-1880* (New York, 1931), 159-160, and *passim*.

[44] For shortages which led to impressment see, for example, Capt. Thos. Miles to Admiralty, Jan. 31, 1705/6, Adm. 1/2093; Lord Cornbury to Lords of Trade, Oct. 3, 1706, E. B. O'Callaghan, ed., *Documents Relative to the Colonial History of the State of New York* (Albany, 1853-1887), IV, 1183-1185; Captain A. Forrest to Lt. Gov. Spencer Phips, Oct. 26, 1745, Adm. 1/1782. For a detailed record of such shortages see items headed "The State and Condition of His Majesty's Ships and Sloops" appearing frequently, scattered throughout Admirals' Dispatches, Adm. 1/480-486. For impressment in the colonies see Neil R. Stout, "Manning the Royal Navy in North America, 1763-1775," *American Neptune*, XXIII (1963), 174-185, and Neil R. Stout, The Royal Navy in American Waters, 1760-1775 (unpubl. Ph.D. diss., University of Wisconsin, 1962), 359-395; R. Pares, "The Manning of the Navy in the West Indies, 1702-63," Royal Historical Society, *Transactions*, 4th Ser., XX (1937), 31-60; Dora Mae Clark, "The Impressment of Seamen in the American Colonies," in *Essays in Colonial History Presented to Charles McLean Andrews by his Students* (New Haven, 1931), 198-224; Jesse Lemisch, Jack Tar vs. John Bull: The Role of New York's Seamen in precipitating the Revolution (unpubl. Ph.D. diss., Yale University, 1962), 12-51. Two useful accounts primarily dealing with impressment in England may be found in Hutchinson, *Press-Gang, passim*, and Daniel A. Baugh, *British Naval Administration in the Age of Walpole* (Princeton, 1965), 147-240.

[45] Stout, "Manning the Royal Navy," 176-177, suggests the possibility of other causes when he notes that desertion was high "whatever the causes," but he mentions no cause other than rum and inveiglement. The Admiralty made the seamen's "natural Levity" another possible reason for desertion. Admiralty to Gov. Thomas on Impressments, 1743, *Pennsylvania Archives*, 1st Ser. (Philadelphia, 1852-1856), I, 639; see also Massachusetts Historical Society, *Journals of the House of Representatives of Massachusetts* (Boston, 1919—), XX, 84, 98; Colvill to Admiralty, Aug. 8, 1765, Adm. 1/482; Pares, "Manning the Navy," 31, 33-34.

[46] Hutchinson to Richard Jackson, June 16, 1768, G. G. Wolkins, "The Seizure of John Hancock's Sloop 'Liberty,'" Massachusetts Historical Society, *Proceedings*, LV (Boston, 1923), 283.

like a dog"; James Otis grieved at the loss of the "flower" of Massachusetts's youth "by ten thousands" to a service which treated them little
better than "hewers of wood and drawers of water." Discipline was harsh
and sometimes irrational, and punishments were cruel.[47] Water poured
into sailors' beds, they went mad, and died of fevers and scurvy.[48] Sick-
ness, Benjamin Franklin noted, was more common in the navy than in
the merchant service and more frequently fatal.[49] In a fruitless attempt to
prevent desertion, wages were withheld and men shunted about from
ship to ship without being paid.[50] But the accumulation of even three or
four years' back wages could not keep a man from running.[51] And why
should it have? Privateering paid better in wartime, and wages were
higher in the merchant service; even laborers ashore were better paid.[52]

182

[47] Freeman, *Washington*, I, 199; James Otis, *The Rights of the British Colonies
Asserted and Proved* (Boston, 1764) in Bernard Bailyn, ed., *Pamphlets of the American Revolution, 1750-1776* (Cambridge, Mass., 1965), I, 464. Flogging was universal
and men received as many as 600 and 700 lashes. Colvill to Admiralty, Nov. 12,
1765, Adm. 1/482. For obscenity the tongue was scraped with hoop-iron. There were
punishments for smiling in the presence of an officer. One captain put his sailors'
heads in bags for trivial offenses. Hutchinson, *Press-Gang*, 31-36. And, of course,
the captain might go mad, as did Captain Robert Bond of *Gibraltar*. Admiral Gambier to Admiralty, Oct. 10, 1771, Adm. 1/483, log of *Gibraltar*, Feb. 10, 14, 1771,
Adm. 51/394.
[48] Log of *Arethusa*, Dec. 28, 1771, Adm. 51/59; Petition of Jeremiah Raven,
[fall 1756], Letters as to Admission of Pensioners to Greenwich Hospital, 1756-
1770, Adm. 65/81, an excellent source for the discovery of the effects of service in
the navy on health. See also the items headed "Weekly Account of Sick and
Wounded Seamen" in Admirals' Dispatches, for example, Admiral Gambier to Admiralty, May 6, June 10, July 20, 27, 1771, Adm. 1/483; Nov. 9, 1771, Aug. 29,
1772, Adm. 1/484.
[49] Remarks on Judge Foster's Argument in Favor of . . . Impressing Seamen,
Jared Sparks, ed., *The Works of Benjamin Franklin*, II (Boston, 1844), 333. Sparks
gives this no date; John Bigelow, ed., *The Complete Works of Benjamin Franklin*
(New York, 1887-1888), IV, 70, dates it 1767; Helen C. Boatfield of the Papers of
Benjamin Franklin, Yale University, dates it post-1776.
[50] Pares, "Manning the Navy," 31-38; Roland G. Usher, Jr., "Royal Navy Impressment during the American Revolution," *Mississippi Valley Historical Review*,
XXXVII (1950-1951), 686. At the time of the Mutiny at the Nore the crew of one
ship had not been paid in 15 years, Hutchinson, *Press-Gang*, 44.
[51] Mr. William Polhampton to Lords of Trade, Mar. 6, 1711, O'Callaghan, ed.,
Docs. Rel. Col. Hist. N. Y., V, 194. A seaman who deserted his ship would leave an
"R"—for "run"—written against his name in the ship's book. See Hutchinson, *Press-
Gang*, 151, for a song which urges seamen to flee the press-gang and "leave 'em
an R in pawn!"
[52] Peter Warren to Admiralty, Sept. 8, 1744, Adm. 1/2654; Mr. William Polhampton to Lords of Trade, Mar. 6, 1711, O'Callaghan, ed., *Docs. Rel. Col. Hist.
N. Y.*, V, 194; Admiralty to Thomas, 1743, *Pa. Arch.*, 1st Ser., I, 638-639; Morris,

Thus Stout's claim that the navy was "forced" to press is only as accurate as the claim that the South was forced to enslave Negroes. Those whose sympathies lie with the thousands of victims of this barbaric practice—rather than with naval administrators—will see that the navy pressed because to be in the navy was in some sense to be a slave, and for this we must blame the slave owners rather than the slaves.[53]

Impressment angered and frightened the seamen, but it pervaded and disrupted all society, giving other classes and groups cause to share a common grievance with the press-gang's more direct victims: just about everyone had a relative at sea.[54] Whole cities were crippled. A night-time _183_ operation in New York in 1757 took in eight hundred men, the equivalent of more than one-quarter of the city's adult male population.[55] Impressment and the attendant shortage of men may have been a critical factor in the stagnancy of "the once cherished now depressed, once flourishing now sinking Town of Boston."[56] H.M.S. _Shirley_'s log lists at

---

Government and Labor, 247-248. The navy's most imaginative response to the problem was sporadic and abortive attempts to limit the wages given to merchant seamen, but the inviting differential remained. When the navy offered bounties for enlistment, this merely served to induce additional desertions by men who could pick up a month's pay simply by signing up. Pares, "Manning the Navy," 33-34; Hutchinson, _Press-Gang_, 22, 48-49; Remarks on Judge Foster's Argument, Sparks, ed., _Works of Franklin_, II, 333; _N.-Y. Gaz.; Weekly Post-Boy_, Mar. 31, Apr. 21, 1755, Mar. 11, 1771.

[53] Stout, "Manning the Royal Navy," 182. England abolished the press-gang in 1833, Hutchinson, _Press-Gang_, 311. Parliament abolished slavery in the British colonies in the same year.

[54] At least in Pennsylvania and New Jersey, according to the _Independent Chronicle_ (Boston), Sept. 5, 1782.

[55] Three thousand men participated in this massive operation. Three or four hundred of those seized were released. Lord Loudoun to Pitt, May 30, 1757, Gertrude S. Kimball, ed., _Correspondence of William Pitt_ (New York, 1906), I, 69; Paul L. Ford, ed., _The Journals of Hugh Gaine, Printer_ (New York, 1902), II, 8-9; May 20, 1757, _The Montresor Journals_ (N.-Y. Hist. Soc., _Coll._, XIV [New York, 1882]), 150-151; Benjamin Cutter, _History of the Cutter Family of New England_ (Boston, 1871), 67; Evarts B. Greene and Virginia D. Harrington, _American Population before the Federal Census of 1790_ (New York, 1932), 101, 1756 census.

[56] Boston is so described in a petition of the town meeting to the House of Representatives, Mar. 11, 1745/6, Mass. Hist. Soc., _Mass. House Journals_, XXII, 204. This petition is but one of many attributing the depletion of Boston's population in part to impressment. For a table indicating a downward trend in Boston's population after 1743 see Stuart Bruchey, ed., _The Colonial Merchant: Sources and Readings_ (New York, 1966), 11. I am indebted to Joel Shufro, a graduate student at the University of Chicago, for the suggestion of a connection between impressment and the decline of Boston.

least ninety-two men pressed off Boston in five months of 1745-1746; *Gramont* received seventy-three pressed men in New York in three days in 1758; *Arethusa* took thirty-one in two days off Virginia in 1771.[57] Binges such as these left the communities where they occurred seriously harmed. Preachers' congregations took flight, and merchants complained loudly about the "many Thousands of Pounds of Damage."[58] "Kiss my arse, you dog," shouted the captain as he made off with their men, leaving vessels with their fires still burning, unmanned, finally to be wrecked.[59] They took legislators and slaves, fishermen and servants.[60] Seamen took to the woods or fled town altogether, dreading the appearance of a man-of-war's boat—in the words of one—as a flock of sheep dreaded a wolf's appearance.[61] If they offered to work at all, they demanded inflated wages

184

[57] Log of *Shirley*, Dec. 25, 1745-May 17, 1746, Adm. 51/4341; log of *Gramont*, Apr. 25-27, 1758, Adm. 51/413; log of *Arethusa*, Mar. 19-20, 1771, Adm. 51/59. *Shirley's* haul was not mentioned in the *Boston Evening Post* or in the records of any American governmental body. Here is but one instance in which the serious grievance of 92 Americans has previously gone unnoticed. Such grievances are nonetheless real and play a causal role despite their invisibility to historians. On the other hand, overdependence on British sources is apt to be extremely misleading. Either because of sloppiness or because of the clouded legality of impressment, official records seem more often to ignore the practice or to distort it than to complement information from American sources. Admiral Charles Hardy neglected to mention the massive press in New York in 1757 in his correspondence with the Admiralty. See May-June 1757, Adm. 1/481. The absence of impressment in *Triton's Prize's* log in 1706, Adm. 51/1014, is contradicted in Lord Cornbury to Lords of Trade, Oct. 3, 1706, O'Callaghan, ed., *Docs. Rel. Col. Hist. N. Y.*, IV, 1183-1185. Sometimes logs show what seems to be purposeful distortion: *Diana*, whose log, Apr. 15, 1758, Adm. 51/4162, reveals only that she "saluted with 9 Guns" *Prince of Orange* privateer, in fact pressed her hands, *Montresor Journal*, 152. In another instance *St. John* "received on board a Boat Load of Ballast," log, July 16, 1764, Adm. 51/3961, which seems in fact to have consisted of hogs, sheep, and poultry stolen from the people of Martha's Vineyard, *Newport Mercury*, July 23, 1764. See below n. 69.

[58] *Boston Evening Post*, Sept. 3, 1739, July 6, 1741.

[59] Deposition of Nathaniel Holmes, July 18, 1702, Deposition of John Gullison, July 17, 1702, Lt. Gov. Thomas Povey to Lords Commissioners for Trade and Plantations, July 20, 1702, Colonial Office Group, Class 5, Piece 862, Public Record Office. Hereafter cited as C.O. 5/862; *Boston Evening Post*, Dec. 14, 1747; *N.-Y. Gaz.; Weekly Post-Boy*, Jan. 14, 1771.

[60] Peter Woodbery and John Tomson to Governor William Phips, July 1, 2, 1692, C.O. 5/751; James and Drinker to [?], Oct. 29, 1756, James and Drinker Letterbook 1, Historical Society of Pennsylvania, Philadelphia; *Boston Evening Post*, Dec. 9, 1745; Mass. Hist. Soc., *Mass. House Journals*, II, 300-301, XXXIII, Pt. ii, 433; *N.-Y. Gaz.; Weekly Post-Boy*, July 12, 1764.

[61] Mass. Hist. Soc., *Mass. House Journals*, XXXV, 267; William Shirley to Gideon Wanton, June 6, 1745, Charles H. Lincoln, ed., *Correspondence of William Shirley*

and refused to sail to ports where there was danger of impressment.[62] "New York and Boston," Benjamin Franklin commented during the French and Indian War, "have so often found the Inconvenience of . . . Station Ships that they are very indifferent about having them: The Pressing of their Men and thereby disappointing Voyages, often hurting their Trade more than the Enemy hurts it." Even a ferryboat operator complained as people shunned the city during a press; food and fuel grew short and their prices rose.[63]

From the very beginning the history of impressment in America is a tale of venality, deceit, and vindictiveness. Captains kept deserters and dead men on ships' books, pocketing their provision allowances. In 1706 a captain pressed men and literally sold them to short-handed vessels; his midshipman learned the business so well that after his dismissal he became a veritable entrepreneur of impressment, setting up shop in a private sloop. Another commander waited until New York's governor was away to break a no-press agreement and when the governor returned he seriously considered firing on the Queen's ship.[64] In Boston in 1702 the lieutenant-governor *did* fire, responding to merchants' complaints. "Fire and be damn'd," shouted the impressing captain as the shots whistled through his sails. The merchants had complained that the press was illegal under 1697 instructions which required captains and commanders to

185

(New York, 1912), I, 227; Mr. Colden to Lords of Trade, Aug. 30, 1760, O'Callaghan, ed., *Docs. Rel. Col. Hist. N. Y.,* VII, 446; Andrew Sherburne, *Memoirs of Andrew Sherburne* (Utica, 1828), 68.

[62] Mass. Hist. Soc., *Mass. House Journals,* XXXV, 267; James and Drinker to Nehemiah Champion, July 13, 1757, James and Drinker Letterbook, I, 145.

[63] Franklin to Joseph Galloway, Apr. 7, 1759, Labaree *et al.,* eds., *Papers of Benjamin Franklin,* VIII, 315-316; Morris, *Government and Labor,* 274; Mr. Colden to Lords of Trade, Aug. 30, 1760, O'Callaghan, ed., *Docs. Rel. Col. Hist. N. Y.,* VII, 446; Mass. Hist. Soc., *Mass. House Journals,* XVIII, 202; XX, 84; Boston Reg. Dept., *Records of Boston,* XVII, 125. See also Gerard G. Beekman to William Beekman, July 3, 1764, Philip L. White, ed., *The Beekman Mercantile Papers, 1746-1799* (New York, 1956), I, 469.

[64] William Polhampton to the Lords of Trade, Mar. 6, 1711, Lord Cornbury to Lords of Trade, Oct. 3, Dec. 14, 1706, O'Callaghan, ed., *Docs. Rel. Col. Hist. N. Y.,* V, 194; IV, 1183-1184, 1190-1191. The captain later publicly declared that he hated the whole province and would not help a New York vessel in distress at sea if he met one. Lord Cornbury to Lords of Trade, July 1, 1708, *ibid.,* V, 60. It seems increasingly to have become common practice to press after a public declaration that there would be no press, for example, *Boston Evening Post,* Dec. 9, 23, 1745; log of *Shirley,* Dec. 25, 1745-May 17, 1746, Adm. 51/4341.

apply to colonial governors for permission to press.[65] These instructions, a response to complaints of "irregular proceedings of the captains of some of our ships of war in the impressing of seamen," had clearly not put an end to irregularities.[66] In 1708 a Parliament fearful of the disruptive effect of impressment on trade forbade the practice in America. In the sixty-seven years until the repeal in 1775 of this "Act for the Encouragement of the Trade to America" there was great disagreement as to its meaning and indeed as to its very existence. Did the Sixth of Anne, as the act was called, merely prohibit the navy from impressing and leave governors free to do so? At least one governor, feeling "pinioned" under the law, continued impressing while calling it "borrowing."[67] Was the act simply a wartime measure, which expired with the return of peace in 1713?[68] Regardless of the dispute, impressment continued, routine in its regularity, but often spectacular in its effects.[69]

186

[65] Lieutenant Governor Thomas Povey to Lords Commissioners for Trade and Plantations, July 20, 1702, Memorial of Thomas Povey, [July, 1702], Deposition of Nathaniel Holmes, July 18, 1702, Deposition of John Arnold and John Roberts, July 18, 1702, C.O. 5/862.

[66] For instructions to royal governors giving them sole power to press in their province see Leonard W. Labaree, ed., *Royal Instructions to British Colonial Governors, 1670-1776* (New York, 1935), I, 442-443; Instructions for the Earl of Bellomont, Aug. 31, 1697, Copy of . . . Lovelace's Instructions, n.d., O'Callaghan, ed., *Docs. Rel. Col. Hist. N. Y.*, IV, 287; V, 101. See also Clark, "Impressment of Seamen," in *Essays to Andrews*, 202-205.

[67] *Calendar of Council Minutes, 1668-1783* (New York State Library, *Bulletin 58* [Mar. 1902]), 229, 230; Stokes, *Iconography of Manhattan*, IV, 465, 973; V, 99-101; Chief Justice . . . Opinion, June 30, 1709, Report of the Councill, July 3, 1709, Governor Hunter to Secretary St. John, Sept. 12, 1711, O'Callaghan, ed., *Docs. Rel. Col. Hist. N. Y.*, V, 100, 102, 254-255.

[68] In 1716 the attorney-general declared, "I am of Opinion, that the whole American Act was intended . . . only for the War," *Massachusetts Gazette* (Boston), June 17, 1768. Governor Shirley of Massachusetts agreed in 1747, despite the fact that, along with other colonial governors, he was still instructed to enforce the Sixth of Anne and had indeed sworn to do so, The Lords Justices to William Shirley, Sept. 10, 1741, Lincoln, ed., *Correspondence of Shirley*, I, 74-76; Stout, Royal Navy, 391. Twenty-two years later Governor Hutchinson feared that John Adams might publicize the act. The Admiralty continued to instruct American commanders to obey the act after Queen Anne's War, for example, see Admiralty to Captain Balcher, Mar. 9, 1714, Adm. 2/48, but ceased so to instruct them in 1723, Clark, "Impressment of Seamen," in *Essays to Andrews*, 211. Of course, the act's repeal in 1775 indicated that it had been on the books, if no place else, all that time.

[69] Stout's claim in Royal Navy, 366, that the navy began pressing again only in 1723 illustrates again the dangers of over-reliance on British sources in such controversial matters. That the Admiralty continued to instruct commanders not to press does not mean that they did not in fact press. *Shark* pressed in Boston in 1720,

Boston was especially hard-hit by impressment in the 1740's, with frequent incidents throughout the decade and major explosions in 1745 and 1747. Again and again the town meeting and the House of Representatives protested, drumming away at the same themes: impressment was harmful to maritime commerce and to the economic life of the city in general and illegal if not properly authorized.[70] In all this the seaman himself becomes all but invisible. The attitude towards him in the protests is at best neutral and often sharply antagonistic. In 1747 the House of Representatives condemned the violent response of hundreds of seamen to a large-scale press as "a tumultuous riotous assembling of armed Seamen, Servants, Negroes, and others . . . tending to the Destruction of all Government and Order." While acknowledging that the people had reason to protest, the House chose to level *its* protest against "the most audacious Insult" to the governor, Council, and House. And the town meeting, that stronghold of democracy, offered its support to those who took "orderly" steps while expressing its "Abhorence of such Illegal Criminal Proceedings" as those undertaken by the seamen "and other persons of mean and Vile Condition."[71]

Protests such as these reflect at the same time both unity and division in colonial society. All kinds of Americans—both merchants and seamen—opposed impressment, but the town meeting and the House spoke for the merchant, not the seaman. They opposed impressment not for its effect on the seaman but for its effect on commerce. Thus their protests express antagonism to British policy at the same time that they express class division. These two themes continue and develop in American opposition to impressment in the three decades between the Knowles Riots of 1747 and the Declaration of Independence.

During the French and Indian War the navy competed with privateers for seamen.[72] Boston again protested against impressment, and then

187

Mass. Hist. Soc., *Mass. House Journals,* II, 300-301; interestingly, her log for Oct.-Nov. 1720, Adm. 51/892, contains no mention of the fact.

[70] See, for example, Mass. Hist. Soc., *Mass. House Journals,* XVIII, 202; XX, 98-99; XXII, 76-77, 204-205.

[71] *Ibid.,* XXIV, 212; Boston Reg. Dept., *Records of Boston,* XIV, 127. Bridenbaugh, *Cities in Revolt,* :17, sees the law of 1751 for suppressing riots as in part a response to the Knowles Riots; he calls the law "brutal" even for its own day and a "triumph for the reactionaries."

[72] See, for example, : ord Loudoun to Pitt, Mar. 10, May 30, 1757, Kimball, ed., *Correspondence of Pitt,* I, 19, 69; Lieutenant-Governor De Lancey to Secretary Pitt, Mar. 17, 1758, O'Callaghan, ed., *Docs. Rel. Col. Hist. N. Y.,* VII, 343.

considered authorizing the governor to press, "provided said Men be impressed from inward-bound Vessels from Foreign Parts only, and that none of them be Inhabitants of this Province."[73] In 1760 New York's mayor had a naval captain arrested on the complaint of two shipmasters who claimed that he had welched on a deal to exchange two men he had pressed for two others they were willing to furnish.[74] With the return of peace in 1763 admirals and Americans alike had reason to suppose that there would be no more impressment.[75] But the Admiralty's plans for a large new American fleet required otherwise, and impressment began again in the spring of 1764 in New York, where a seven-week hot press was brought to a partial stop by the arrest of one of the two offending captains.[76] In the spring and summer a hunt for men between Maine and Virginia by four naval vessels brought violent responses, including the killing of a marine at New York; another fort, at Newport, fired on another naval vessel.[77]

Along with the divisions there was a certain amount of unity. Seamen who fled after violently resisting impressment could not be found—probably because others sheltered them—and juries would not indict them. Captains were prevented from impressing by the threat of prosecution.[78]

[73] Mass. Hist. Soc., *Mass. House Journals*, XXXIII, Pt. ii, 434; XXXIV, Pt. i, 134; Boston Reg. Dept., *Records of Boston*, XIX, 96-97; log of *Hunter*, Aug. 31, 1758, Adm. 51/465. The Council voted such authorization, but the House did not concur.

[74] Capt. George Ant. Tonyn to Admiralty, Mar. 1, 1760, Depositions of Peter Vail and Singleton Church, Jan. 15, 16, 1760, Adm. 1/2588.

[75] Admiral Colvill, Journal, Mar. 19, 1764, Adm. 50/4; Colvill to Admiralty, May 19, 1764, Adm. 1/482; *N.-Y. Gaz.; Weekly Post-Boy*, July 18, 1765.

[76] Stout, *Royal Navy*, 72-73, citing Admiralty to Egremont, Jan. 5, 1763, State Papers Group, Class 42, Piece 43, Public Record Office. Hereafter cited as S.P. 42/43; Captain Jno. Brown to Admiralty, May 16, 1764, Adm. 1/1494; log of *Coventry*, Mar. 31, 1764, Adm. 51/213, indicates impressment on that date; compare Stout, *Royal Navy*, 379, 393n.

[77] Admiral Colvill, Journal, June 4, 1764, Adm. 50/4; Colvill to Admiralty, June 18, 1764, Adm. 1/482. On the violence at New York see log of *Jamaica*, June 8, 1764, Adm. 51/3874; *N.-Y. Gaz.; Weekly Post-Boy*, July 12, 1764; Report of the Grand Jury, Aug. 2, 1764, New York Supreme Court Minute Book (July 31, 1764-Oct. 28, 1764), 7. On the violence at Newport see log of *St. John*, July 10, 1764, Adm. 51/3961; Captain Smith to Colvill, July 12, 1764, in Colvill to Admiralty, Aug. 24, 1764, Adm. 1/482; John Temple to Treasury, Sept. 9, 1765, Treasury Group, Class 1, Piece 442, Library of Congress transcript.

[78] *The King* v. *Osborn Greatrakes* and *The King* v. *Josiah Moore*, Oct. 24, 28, 30, Nov. 11-17, 1760, New York Supreme Court Minute Book (1756-1761), 1-6, 200, 209, 215; Henry B. Dawson, *The Sons of Liberty in New York* (New York, 1859), 53; *N.-Y. Gaz.; Weekly Post-Boy*, July 12, 1764; Report of Grand Jury, Aug.

And in 1769 lawyer John Adams used the threat of displaying the statute book containing the Sixth of Anne to frighten a special court of Admiralty into declaring the killing of an impressing lieutenant justifiable homicide in necessary self-defense.[79]

There were two kinds of impressment incidents: those in which there was immediate self-defense against impressment, usually at sea, and those in which crowds ashore, consisting in large part of seamen, demonstrated generalized opposition to impressment. This is what the first kind of incident sounded like: a volley of musketry and the air full of langrage, grapeshot, round shot, hammered shot, double-headed shot, even rocks. "Come into the boat and be damned, you Sorry Son of a Whore or else Ile breake your head, and hold your tongue." Small arms, swords and cutlasses, blunderbusses, clubs and pistols, axes, harpoons, fishgigs, twelve-pounders, six-pounders, half-pounders. "You are a parsill of Raskills." Fired five shots to bring to a snow from North Carolina, pressed four. "You have no right to impress me . . . If you step over that line . . . by the eternal God of Heaven, you are a dead man." "Aye, my lad, I have seen many a brave fellow before now."[80]

Here is hostility and bloodshed, a tradition of antagonism. From the beginning, impressment's most direct victims—the seamen—were its most active opponents. Bernard Bailyn's contention that "not a single murder resulted from the activities of the Revolutionary mobs in America" does

189

2, 1764, New York Supreme Court Minute Book (July 31, 1764-Oct. 28, 1767), 7; Colvill to Admiralty, Aug. 5, 1766, Adm. 1/482.

[79] Charles Francis Adams, ed., *The Works of John Adams* (Boston, 1850-1856), II, 225n-226n, and "The Inadmissable Principles of the King of England's Proclamation of October 16, 1807, Considered" [1809], IX, 317-318; Thomas Hutchinson, *The History of the Colony and Province of Massachusetts-Bay*, ed. Lawrence S. Mayo (Cambridge, Mass., 1936), III, 167n; log of *Rose*, Apr. 22, 1769, Adm. 51/804; Admiral Hood to Admiralty, May 5, 1769, Adm. 1/483.

[80] *The King* v. *Ship Sampson*, Examination of Hugh Mode, Pilot, taken Aug. 19, 1760, N. Y. Supreme Court, Pleadings K-304; *N.-Y. Gaz.; Weekly Post-Boy*, May 1, 1758, Aug. 7, 1760; Captain J. Hale to Admiralty, Aug. 28, 1760, Adm. 1/1895; William McCleverty to Admiralty, July 31, 1760, Adm. 1/2172; Howard Thomas, *Marinus Willett* (Prospect, N. Y., 1954), 3-4; Deposition of John Gullison, July 17, 1702, Deposition of Woodward Fay, July 17, 1702, C.O. 5/862; log of *Magdelen*, Apr. 6, 1771, Adm. 51/3984, describing the loss during a press "by Accident" of a sword and musquet—apparently a common accident; see also log of *Arethusa*, Apr. 18, 1772, Adm. 51/59; Weyman's *New-York Gazette*, Aug. 25, 1760; Admiral Hood to Admiralty, May 5, 1769, Adm. 1/483; paraphrase of log of *Shirley*, Jan. 17, 1746, Adm. 51/4341; "Inadmissable Principles" [1809], Adams, ed., *Works of Adams*, IX, 318.

not hold up if extended to cover resistance to impressment; there were murders on both sides. Perhaps the great bulk of incidents of this sort must remain forever invisible to the historian, for they often took place out of sight of friendly observers, and the only witness, the navy, kept records which are demonstrably biased and faulty, omitting the taking of thousands of men.[81] But even the visible records provide a great deal of information. This much we know without doubt: seamen did not go peacefully. Their violence was purposeful, and sometimes they were articulate. "I know who you are," said one, as reported by John Adams and supported by Thomas Hutchinson. "You are the lieutenant of a man-of-war, come with a press-gang to deprive me of my liberty. You have no right to impress me. I have retreated from you as far as I can. I can go no farther. I and my companions are determined to stand upon our defence. Stand off."[82] (It was difficult for Englishmen to fail to see impressment in such terms—even a sailor *doing* the pressing could feel shame over "fighting with honest sailors, to deprive them of their liberty.")[83]

Ashore, seamen and others demonstrated their opposition to impressment with the only weapon which the unrepresentative politics of the day

190

[81] Bailyn, ed., *Pamphlets*, I, 581. Six Englishmen of varying ranks were killed while pressing in the 1760's. In addition to the incidents just discussed in which a lieutenant of marines was murdered on June 8, 1764, while pressing at New York and in which John Adams's clients-to-be, accused of murdering a lieutenant off Cape Ann Apr. 22, 1769, got off with justifiable homicide in self-defense, four sailors were shot to death at New York, Aug. 18, 1760. Cadwallader Colden to Lords of Trade, Aug. 30, 1760, O'Callaghan, ed., *Docs. Rel. Col. Hist. N. Y.*, VII, 446; *The King* v. *Osborn Greatrakes* and the *King* v. *Josiah Moore*, Oct. 24, 28, 30, Nov. 11-17, 1760, New York Supreme Court Minute Book (1756-1761), 1-16, 200, 209, 215; *The King* v. *Ship Sampson*, Examination of Hugh Mode, Pilot, taken Aug. 19, 1760, N. Y. Supreme Court, Pleadings K-304; Capt. J. Hale to Admiralty, Aug. 28, 1760, Adm. 1/1895; Weyman's *N.-Y. Gaz.*, Aug. 25, 1760; Dawson, *Sons of Liberty*, 51-54. Governor Cadwallader Colden called the last incident murder, but the jury refused to indict. For some instances of Americans killed while resisting impressment see deposition of William Thwing, Nathaniel Vaill, and Thomas Hals, July 15, 1702, C.O. 5/862; Governor Hunter to Secretary St. John, Sept. 12, 1711, O'Callaghan, ed., *Docs. Rel. Col. Hist. N. Y.*, V, 254-255 (conviction of murder); Bridenbaugh, *Cities in Revolt*, 114-115; *N.-Y. Gaz.; Weekly Post-Boy*, Aug. 7, 1760. There is every reason to suppose that this list is partial. See above n. 57.

[82] "Inadmissable Principles" [1809], Adams, ed., *Works of Adams*, IX, 318, quotes Michael Corbet, commenting that Corbet displayed "the cool intrepidity of a Nelson, reasoned, remonstrated, and laid down the law with the precision of a Mansfield." Hutchinson, *History of Massachusetts-Bay*, ed. Mayo, III, 167*n*, notes that Corbet and his companions "swore they would die before they would be taken, and that they preferred death to slavery."

[83] "Inadmissable Principles" [1809], Adams, ed., *Works of Adams*, IX, 317-318.

offered them—riot. In Boston several thousand people responded to a nighttime impressment sweep of the harbor and docks with three days of rioting beginning in the early hours of November 17, 1747. Thomas Hutchinson reported that "the lower class were beyond measure enraged." Negroes, servants, and hundreds of seamen seized a naval lieutenant, assaulted a sheriff and put his deputy in the stocks, surrounded the governor's house, and stormed the Town House where the General Court was sitting. The rioters demanded the seizure of the impressing officers, the release of the men they had pressed, and execution of a death sentence which had been levied against a member of an earlier press-gang who had been convicted of murder. When the governor fled to Castle William— some called it "abdication"—Commodore Knowles threatened to put down what he called "arrant rebellion" by bombarding the town. The governor, who, for his part, thought the rioting a secret plot of the upper class, was happily surprised when the town meeting expressed its "Abhorence" of the seamen's riot.[84]

191

After the French and Indian War press riots increased in frequency. Armed mobs of whites and Negroes repeatedly manhandled captains, officers, and crews, threatened their lives, and held them hostage for the men they pressed. Mobs fired at pressing vessels and tried to board them; they threatened to burn one, and they regularly dragged ships' boats to the center of town for ceremonial bonfires. In Newport in June 1765, five hundred seamen, boys, and Negroes rioted after five weeks of impressment. "Sensible" Newporters opposed impressment but nonetheless condemned this "Rabble." In Norfolk in 1767 Captain Jeremiah Morgan retreated, sword in hand, before a mob of armed whites and Negroes. "Good God," he wrote to the governor, "was your Honour and I to prosecute all the Rioters that attacked us belonging to Norfolk there would not be twenty left unhang'd belonging to the Toun."[85] According

[84] Hutchinson, *History of Massachusetts-Bay*, ed. Mayo, II, 330-331, 333; Mass. Hist. Soc., *Mass. House Journals*, XXIV, 212; Bridenbaugh, *Cities in Revolt*, 115-117; Boston Reg. Dept., *Records of Boston*, XIV, 127; William Shirley to Lords of Trade, Dec. 1, 1747, Lincoln, ed., *Correspondence of Shirley*, I, 412-419, is the best single account. Shirley says that only the officers responded to his call for the militia.

[85] *Newport Mercury*, June 10, 1765; Captain Jeremiah Morgan to Governor Francis Fauquier, Sept. 11, 1767, Adm. 1/2116; log of *St. John*, July 10, 1764, Adm. 51/3961; Remarks of Thomas Hill in Colvill to Admiralty, July 26, 1764, Colvill to Admiralty, Jan. 12, Sept. 21, 1765, Adm. 1/482; log of *Maidstone*, June 5, 1765, Adm. 51/3897; Captain Smith to Colvill, July 12, 1764 (extract) in Colvill to Admiralty, Aug. 24, 1764, Adm. 1/482; *N.-Y. Gaz.*; *Weekly Post-Boy*, July 12, 1764;

to Thomas Hutchinson, the *Liberty* Riot in Boston in 1768 may have been as much against impressment as against the seizure of Hancock's sloop: *Romney* had pressed before June 10, and on that day three officers were forced by an angry crowd "arm'd with Stones" to release a man newly pressed from the Boston packet.[86] *Romney* pressed another man, and on June 14, after warding off "many wild and violent proposals," the town meeting petitioned the governor against both the seizure and impressment; the instructions to their representatives (written by John Adams) quoted the Sixth of Anne at length. On June 18 two councillors pleaded with the governor to procure the release of a man pressed by *Romney* "as the peace of the Town seems in a great measure to depend upon it."[87]

Thomas Laugharne to Admiral Colvill, Aug. 11, 1764 (extract) in Colvill to Admiralty, Aug. 24, 1764, Adm. 1/482; Stout's contention, "Manning the Royal Navy," 185, that "there is no recorded case of impressment on shore during the 1760's and 1770's, although the Navy did capture some deserters on land" is inaccurate. See Captain Jeremiah Morgan to Governor Francis Fauquier, Sept. 11, 1767, Adm. 1/2116, and *Pennsylvania Chronicle and Universal Advertiser* (Philadelphia), Oct. 26, 1767.

[86] For impressment by *Romney*, see log, June 10, 1768, Adm. 51/793; Mayo, ed., *Hist.*, III, 139. Oliver M. Dickerson, *The Navigation Acts and the American Revolution* (Philadelphia, 1951), 238, sees the riot as growing out of the seizure and has the support of most sources. Massachusetts Council to Governor Gage, Oct. 27, 1768, Bowdoin-Temple Papers, I, 120, Massachusetts Historical Society, Boston; Admiral Hood to Admiralty, July 11, 1768, Adm. 1/483; Hutchinson, *History of Massachusetts-Bay*, III, 136. On the other hand Thomas Hutchinson also spoke of impressment as adding "more fewel to the great stock among us before." Mass. Hist. Soc., *Proceedings, 1921-1922* (Boston, 1923), 283. Clark, "Impressment of Seamen," in *Essays to Andrews*, 219, describes the rioting as a response to impressment alone by a mob "which seemed to be always ready to resent any infringement of American liberties." Dickerson, *Navigation Acts*, 219-220, attributes the burning of a boat belonging to the customs collector to the mob's failure to locate *Romney's* press boat. In 1922 G. G. Wolkins, "Seizure of Liberty," 250, speculated that "impressment of seamen, rather than the seizure of John Hancock's goods, was perhaps the genesis of what happened." L. Kinvin Wroth and Hiller B. Zobel, eds., *Legal Papers of John Adams* (Cambridge, Mass., 1965), II, 179n, summarize: "Boston's position was that the employment of the *Romney*, already despised for the impressment activities of her captain, brought on the riot of 10 June." The riot seems to have been caused by a combination of factors among which impressment has been given too little attention.

[87] Boston Reg. Dept., *Records of Boston*, XX, 296; [Thomas Hutchinson], State of the Disorders, Confusion and Misgovernment, which have lately prevailed . . . in . . . Massachusetts, June 21, 1770, C.O. 5/759, Pt. 4; Report of Resolves Relating to Riot of June 10, June 14, 1768, James Bowdoin and Royall Tyler to Jno. Corner, June 18, 1768, Bowdoin-Temple Papers, I, 102, 104; *Mass. Gaz.* (Boston),

There were other impressment riots at New York in July of 1764 and July of 1765;[88] at Newport in July of 1764;[89] at Casco Bay, Maine, in December 1764.[90] Incidents continued during the decade following, and impressment flowered on the very eve of the Revolution. Early in 1775 the practice began to be used in a frankly vindictive and political way—because a town had inconvenienced an admiral, or because a town supported the Continental Congress.[91] Impresses were ordered and took place from Maine to Virginia.[92] In September a bundle of press warrants arrived from the Admiralty, along with word of the repeal of the Sixth of Anne. What had been dubious was now legal. Up and down the coast, officers rejoiced and went to work.[93]

Long before 1765 Americans had developed beliefs about impressment, and they had expressed those beliefs in words and deeds. Impressment was bad for trade and it was illegal. As such, it was, in the words of the Massachusetts House in 1720, "a great Breach on the Rights of His Majesties Subjects." In 1747 it was a violation of "the common Liberty of the Subject," and in 1754 "inconsistent with Civil Liberty, and the Natu-

193

Nov. 10, 1768. For Adams's authorship, see L. H. Butterfield *et al.*, eds., *Diary and Autobiography of John Adams* (New York, 1964), III, 291; Adams, ed., *Works of Adams*, III, 501.

[88] *N.-Y. Gaz.; Weekly Post-Boy*, July 12, 1764, July 18, 1765; Thos. Laugharne to Admiral Colvill, Aug. 11, 1764 (extract) in Colvill to Admiralty, July 26, Aug. 24, 1764, Adm. 1/482; Weyman's *N. Y. Gaz.*, July 18, 1765.

[89] Captain Smith to Colvill, July 12, 1764 (extract) in Colvill to Admiralty, Aug. 24, 1764, Adm. 1/482; Remarks of Thomas Hill in Colvill to Admiralty, July 26, 1764, Adm. 1/482; log of *Squirrel*, July 10, 1764, Adm. 51/929; log of *St. John*, July 10, 1764, Adm. 51/3961; *Newport Mercury*, July 16, 1764.

[90] Colvill to Admiralty, Jan. 12, 1765, Adm. 1/482; log of *Gaspee*, Dec. 8, 10, 12, 1764, Adm. 51/3856.

[91] Graves to Admiralty, Feb. 20, 1775, Adm. 1/485; *N. Y. Journal or Gen. Adv.*, Feb. 23, 1775; Margaret Wheeler Willard, ed., *Letters on the American Revolution, 1774-1776* (Boston, 1925), 65-66.

[92] Graves to Admiralty, Apr. 11, 1775, Mowat to Graves, May 4, 1775, in Graves to Admiralty, May 13, 1775, Barkley to Graves, June 5, 1775, in Graves to Admiralty, June 22, 1775, Montagu to Graves, June 17, 1775, in Graves to Admiralty, July 17, 1775, Adm. 1/485; log of *Scarborough*, May 14, 1775, Adm. 51/867; log of *Fowey*, July 16, 23, 1775, Adm. 51/375. Despite the troubles at Marblehead in February, *Lively* was still pressing there in May, Graves to Admiralty, May 13, 1775, Adm. 1/485.

[93] Admiralty to Graves, June 24, Sept. 29, 1775, Adm. 2/549, 550; Graves to Admiralty, Sept. 12, 1775, List of . . . Press Warrants, Jan. 27, 1776, in Graves to Admiralty, Jan. 1776, Adm. 1/486; Shuldham to Arbuthnot, June 5, 1776, in Shuldham to Admiralty, July 24, 1776, Adm. 1/484.

ral Rights of Mankind."[94] Some felt in 1757 that it was even "abhorrent to the English Constitution."[95] In fact, the claim that impressment was unconstitutional was wrong. (Even *Magna Charta* was no protection. *Nullus liber homo capiatur* did not apply to seamen.)[96] Instead impressment indicated to Benjamin Franklin "that the constitution is yet imperfect, since in so general a case it doth not secure liberty, but destroys it." "If impressing seamen is of right by common law in Britain," he also remarked, "slavery is then of right by common law there; there being no slavery worse than that sailors are subjected to."[97]

194   For Franklin, impressment was a symptom of injustice built into the British Constitution. In *Common Sense* Tom Paine saw in impressment a reason for rejecting monarchy. In the Declaration of Independence Thomas Jefferson included impressment among the "Oppressions" of George III; later he likened the practice to the capture of Africans for slavery. Both "reduced [the victim] to . . . bondage by force, in flagrant violation of his own consent, and of his natural right in his own person."[98]

Despite all this, and all that went before, we have thought little of impressment as an element in explaining the conduct of the common man in the American Revolution.[99] Contemporaries knew better. John Adams

[94] Mass. Hist. Soc., *Mass. House Journals*, II, 300-301; Freeman, *Washington*, I, 199; *N.-Y. Gaz.; Weekly Post-Boy*, Aug. 12, 1754.

[95] Mass. Hist. Soc., *Mass. House Journals*, XXXIII, Pt. ii, 434.

[96] Hutchinson, *Press-Gang*, 5-7.

[97] Sparks, ed., *Works of Franklin*, II, 338, 334. For opposition to impressment on the part of the Genevan democrat, Jean Louis De Lolme, and by the British radical John Wilkes, see Robert R. Palmer, *The Age of the Democratic Revolution* (Princeton, 1959), 148. *N.-Y. Gaz.; Weekly Post-Boy*, Dec. 31, 1770; *Annual Register . . . for 1771* (London, 1772), 67, 68, 70-71; R. W. Postgate, *That Devil Wilkes* (New York, 1929), 182; Percy Fitzgerald, *The Life and Times of John Wilkes* (London, 1888), II, 120.

[98] Paine, *Writings*, ed. Foner, I, 11. For later attacks on impressment by Paine see *ibid.*, I, 449, II, 476. The complaint in the Declaration of Independence alludes to impressment after the outbreak of fighting: "He has constrained our fellow Citizens taken Captive on the high Seas to bear Arms against their Country, to become the executioners of their friends and Brethren, or to fall themselves by their Hands." Carl L. Becker, *The Declaration of Independence* (New York, 1958), 190, 156, 166. Thomas Jefferson to Dr. Thomas Cooper, Sept. 10, 1814, Andrew A. Lipscomb and Albert Ellery Bergh, eds., *The Writings of Thomas Jefferson*, XIV (Washington, 1907), 183.

[99] James Fulton Zimmerman, *Impressment of American Seamen* (New York, 1925), esp. 11-17, treats the practice as almost non-existent before the Revolution, giving the pre-revolutionary phenomenon only the briefest consideration, and concluding, on the basis of speculative evidence, that impressment was rare in the colonies. The author does not understand the Sixth of Anne and thinks it was re-

felt that a tactical mistake by Thomas Hutchinson on the question of impressment in 1769 would have "accelerated the revolution. . . . It would have spread a wider flame than Otis's ever did, or could have done."[100] Ten years later American seamen were being impressed by *American* officers. The United States Navy had no better solution for "public Necessities" than had the Royal Navy. Joseph Reed, President of Pennsylvania, complained to Congress of "Oppressions" and in so doing offered testimony to the role of *British* impressment in bringing on revolution. "We cannot help observing how similar this Conduct is to that of the British Officers during our Subjection to Great Brittain and are persuaded it will have the same unhappy effects viz., an estrangement of the Affections of the People from the Authority under which they act which by an easy Progression will proceed to open Opposition to the immediate Actors and Bloodshed."[101] Impressment had played a role in the estrangement of the American people from the British government. It had produced "Odium" against the navy, and even six-year-olds had not been too young to have learned to detest it.[102] The anger of thousands of victims did not vanish. Almost four decades after the Declaration of Independence an orator could still arouse his audience by tapping a folk-memory of impressment by the same "haughty, cruel, and gasconading nation" which was once again trying to enslave free Americans.[103]

195

pealed in 1769. Clark, "Impressment of Seamen," in *Essays to Andrews*, 202; Paine, *Ships and Sailors of Salem*, 65; George Athan Billias, *General John Glover and his Marblehead Mariners* (New York, 1960), 31; Bridenbaugh, *Cities in Revolt*, 114-117, 308-310; Bernhard Knollenberg, *Origin of the American Revolution: 1759-1766* (New York, 1961), 12, 179-181, all see impressment as contributing in some way to the revolutionary spirit.

[100] Adams, ed., *Works of Adams*, II, 226n. Neil Stout, "Manning the Royal Navy," 182-184, suggests that impressment did not become a "great issue" of the American Revolution because American "radicals" did not *make* an issue of it and especially because of the failure of John Adams's attempt to make a *"cause celebre"* in 1769. Stout's approach sides with the navy and minimizes the *reality* of impressment as a grievance. Its implication is that the seaman had in fact no genuine grievance and that he acted in response to manipulation.

[101] Pres. Reed to Pres. of Congress, 1779, Oct. 21, 1779, *Pa. Archives*, 1st Ser., VII, 762. Reed renewed his complaint of these "Opressions" in the following year, Reed to Pennsylvania Delegates in Congress, 1780, *ibid.*, 1st Ser., VIII, 643.

[102] Colvill to Admiralty, Aug. 8, 1765, Adm. 1/482; Sherburne, *Memoirs*, 68.

[103] William M. Willett, *A Narrative of the Military Actions of Colonel Marinus Willett, Taken Chiefly from his own Manuscript* (New York, 1831), 149-151. On the level of leadership impressment was not a major cause of the American Revolution. But the extent to which the articulate voice a grievance is rarely an adequate measure of the suffering of the inarticulate. Since it is unrealistic to suppose that

III

The seamen's conduct in the 1760's and 1770's makes more sense in the light of previous and continued impressment. What may have seemed irrational violence can now be seen as purposeful and radical. The pattern of rioting as political expression, established as a response to impressment, was now adapted and broadened as a response to the Stamp Act. In New York General Gage described the "insurrection" of October 31, 1765, and following as "composed of great numbers of Sailors." The seamen, he said, were "the only People who may be properly Stiled Mob,"
196 and estimates indicate that between a fifth and a fourth of New York's rioters were seamen. The disturbances began among the seamen—especially former privateersmen—on October 31. On November 1 they had marched, led primarily by their former captains; later they rioted, led by no one but themselves. Why? Because they had been duped by merchants, or, if not by merchants, then certainly by lawyers. So British officials believed—aroused by these men who meant to use them, the seamen themselves had nothing more than plunder on their minds. In fact, at that point in New York's rioting when the leaders lost control, the seamen, who were then in the center of town, in an area rich for plunder, chose instead to march in an orderly and disciplined way clear across town to do violence to the home and possessions of an English major whose provocative conduct had made him the obvious political enemy. Thus the "rioting" was actually very discriminating.[104]

---

the victims of impressment forgot their anger, the question becomes not, why was impressment irrelevant to the American Revolution—for it had to be relevant, in this sense—but, rather, why were the articulate not *more* articulate about the seamen's anger? In part, perhaps, because much impressment took place offshore and was invisible to all but the seamen directly involved. But the leaders had always perceived even visible impressment more as an interference with commerce than as a form of slavery. As the Revolution approached, impressment as human slavery interested them even less than Negro slavery did; the gap between Jack Tar and the men who made laws for him continued. The failure of the elite to see impressment more clearly as a political issue means only that they failed, as we have, to listen to the seamen.

[104] General Gage to Secretary Conway, Nov. 4, Dec. 21, 1765, Clarence Edwin Carter, ed., *The Correspondence of General Thomas Gage . . . 1763-1775* (New Haven, 1931), I, 70-71, 79; *N.-Y. Gaz.; Weekly Post-Boy,* Nov. 7, 1765, estimates that there were four to five hundred seamen in the mob; Nov. 1, 7, 1765, *Montresor Journal,* 336, 339, estimates the total mob at "about 2000" and is the only source describing the participation of a professional group other than seamen, estimating 300 carpenters; R. R. Livingston to General Monckton, Nov. 8, 1765, Chalmers

Seamen and non-seamen alike joined to oppose the Stamp Act for many reasons,[105] but the seamen had two special grievances: impressment and the effect of England's new attitude toward colonial trade. To those discharged by the navy at the end of the war and others thrown out of work by the death of privateering were added perhaps twenty thousand more seamen and fishermen who were thought to be the direct victims of the post-1763 trade regulations.[106] This problem came to the fore in the

Manuscripts, IV, New York Public Library, for a note signed "Sons of Neptune"; Lieutenant-Governor Colden to Secretary Conway, Nov. 5, 9, 1765, O'Callaghan, ed., *Docs. Rel. Col. Hist. N. Y.*, VII, 771-774; *New York Mercury*, Nov. 4, 1765. For additional information on the leadership of privateer captains, especially Isaac Sears, see William Gordon, *History of the Rise, Progress, and Establishment of the United States of America* (London, 1788), I, 185-186. The navy continued to press during the crisis. See log of *Guarland*, Apr. 22, 1766, Adm. 51/386; Apr. 21, 1766, *Montresor Journal*, 361. Impressment also limited the navy's activities against the rioting. "As most of our men are imprest," wrote a captain in answer to a governor's request for men to put down a mob, "there is a great risque of their deserting." Marines were needed as sentries to keep the men from deserting. Archibald Kennedy to Cadwallader Colden, Nov. 1, 1765, *The Letters and Papers of Cadwallader Colden* (N.-Y. Hist. Soc., *Coll.*, L-LVI [New York, 1918-1923]), VII, 85-86.

[105] For a fuller account of the seamen's opposition to the Stamp Act see Lemisch, "Jack Tar vs. John Bull," 76-128.

[106] *N.-Y. Gaz.; Weekly Post-Boy*, May 19, 1763; "Essay on the trade of the Northern Colonies," *ibid.*, Feb. 9, 1764. Even admirals were worried about the prospects of postwar unemployment, Colvill to Admiralty, Nov. 9, 1762, Adm. 1/482. During the French and Indian War 18,000 American seamen had served in the Royal Navy, *Annual Register . . . for 1778* (London, 1779), 201, and a large additional number had been privateersmen. Fifteen to twenty thousand had sailed in 224 privateers out of New York alone, 5670 of them in 1759, Fish, *New York Privateers*, 4, 54-82; Bridenbaugh, *Cities in Revolt*, 62. A New York merchants' petition of Apr. 20, 1764, expressed the fear that seamen thrown out of work by the Sugar Act might drift into foreign merchant fleets, *Journal of the Votes and Proceedings of the General Assembly of the Colony of New York* (New York, 1764-1766), II, 742-743. On the eve of the Revolution maritime commerce employed approximately 30,000-35,000 American seamen, Carman, ed., *American Husbandry*, 495-496; John Adams to the President of Congress, June 16, 1780, Francis Wharton, ed., *The Revolutionary Diplomatic Correspondence of the United States* (Washington, 1889), III, 789. I am presently assembling data which will allow more detailed statements on various demographic matters involving seamen, such as their numbers, comparisons with other occupations, their origins and permanence. For some further quantitative information on seamen in various colonial ports, see in addition to the sources cited immediately above, Evarts B. Greene and Richard B. Morris, *A Guide to the Principal Sources for Early American History (1600-1800) in the City of New York*, 2d ed., rev. (New York, 1953), 265; E. B. O'Callaghan, ed., *The Documentary History of the State of New York*, I (Albany, 1849), 493; Governor Clinton's Report on the Province of New York, May 23, 1749, Report of Governor Tryon on the Province of New York, June 11, 1774, O'Callaghan, ed., *Docs.*

weeks following November 1, 1765, when the Stamp Act went into effect. The strategy of opposition chosen by the colonial leadership was to cease all activities which required the use of stamps. Thus maritime trade came to a halt in the cities.[107] Some said that this was a cowardly strategy. If the Americans opposed the Stamp Act, let them go on with business as usual, refusing outright to use the stamps.[108] The leaders' strategy was especially harmful to the seamen, and the latter took the more radical position— otherwise the ships would not sail. And this time the seamen's radicalism triumphed over both colonial leadership and British officials. Within little more than a month the act had been largely nullified. Customs officers were allowing ships to sail without stamps, offering as the reason the fear that the seamen, "who are the people that are most dangerous on these occasions, as their whole dependance for a subsistence is upon Trade," would certainly "commit some terrible Mischief." Philadelphia's customs officers feared that the seamen would soon "compel" them to let ships pass without stamps. Customs officers at New York yielded when they heard that the seamen were about to have a meeting.[109]

Customs officers had worse luck on other days. Seamen battled them throughout the 1760's and 1770's. In October 1769 a Philadelphia customs officer was attacked by a mob of seamen who also tarred, feathered, and nearly drowned a man who had furnished him with information about

198

Rel. Col. Hist. N. Y., VI, 511, VIII, 446; Main, *Social Structure,* 38-39; Benjamin W. Labaree, *Patriots and Partisans* (Cambridge, Mass., 1962), 5; John R. Bartlett, ed., *Records of the Colony of Rhode Island and Providence Plantations* . . . (Providence, 1856-1865), VI, 379.

[107] See, for example, James and Drinker to William Starkey, Oct. 30, 1765, James and Drinker Letterbook; *N.-Y. Gaz.; Weekly Post-Boy,* Dec. 19, 1765.

[108] See, for example, *N.-Y. Gaz.; Weekly Post-Boy,* Nov. 28, Dec. 5, 1765. For a fuller account of this dispute, see Jesse Lemisch, "New York's Petitions and Resolves of December 1765: Liberals vs. Radicals," New-York Historical Society, *Quarterly,* XLIX (1965), 313-326.

[109] Edmund S. and Helen M. Morgan, *The Stamp Act Crisis* (Chapel Hill, 1953), 162. For a fuller account of the nullification of the Stamp Act, see *ibid.,* 159-179. The seamen's strategy may have been more effective in bringing about repeal than was the strategy of the leaders. Commenting on Parliament's secret debates, Lawrence Henry Gipson, "The Great Debate in the Committee of the Whole House of Commons on the Stamp Act, 1766, as Reported by Nathaniel Ryder," *Pennsylvania Magazine of History and Biography,* LXXXVI (1962), 10-41, notes that merchant pressure was only the "ostensible cause" of repeal and that many members were influenced by the violent resistance in America. I am indebted to E. S. Morgan for calling Ryder's notes to my attention.

illegally imported goods. A year later a New Jersey customs officer who approached an incoming vessel in Delaware Bay had *his* boat boarded by armed seamen who threatened to murder him and came close to doing so. When the officer's son' came to Philadelphia, he was similarly treated by a mob of seamen; there were one thousand seamen in Philadelphia at the time, and according to the customs collector there, they were "always ready" to do such "mischief."[110] This old antagonism had been further politicized in 1768 when, under the American Board of Customs Commissioners, searchers began to break into sea chests and confiscate those items not covered by cockets, thus breaking an old custom of the sea which allowed seamen to import small items for their own profit. Oliver M. Dickerson has described this new "Invasion of Seamen's Rights" as a part of "customs racketeering" and a cause of animosity between seamen and customs officers.[111]

Many of these animosities flared in the Boston Massacre. What John Adams described as "a motley rabble of saucy boys, negroes and molattoes, Irish teagues and out landish jack tarrs," including twenty or thirty of the latter, armed with clubs and sticks, did battle with the soldiers. Their leader was Crispus Attucks, a mulatto seaman; he was shot to death in front of the Custom House.[112] One of the seamen's rea-

199

110 John Swift to Commissioners of Customs, Oct. 13, 1769, Customs Commissioners to Collector and Comptroller at Philadelphia, Oct. 23, 1769, John Hatton, A State of the Case, Nov. 8, 1770, John Hatton to John Swift, Nov. 9, 1770, Customs Commissioners at Boston to Collector and Comptroller at Philadelphia, Jan. 1771, John Swift to Customs Commissioners, Feb. 11, 1772, John Swift to Customs Commissioners, Nov. 15, 1770, Collector and Comptroller at Philadelphia to Customs Commissioners, Dec. 20, 1770, Philadelphia Custom House Papers, X, 1205, 1209, 1286, 1288; XI; XII; X, 1291-1292; XI, Hist. Soc. Pa. Swift made the customary contention that the seamen rioted because their captains told them to. For a qualification of this contention see Arthur L. Jensen, *The Maritime Commerce of Colonial Philadelphia* (Madison, 1963), 152. For a mob which attacked a collector of customs and others at the time of the Stamp Act and which may have been led by a seaman, see Morgan and Morgan, *Stamp Act Crisis*, 191-194; log of *Cygnet*, Aug. 29, 30, 1765, Adm. 51/223; Captain Leslie to Admiral Colvill, Aug. 30, 31, 1765, Adm. 1/482.

111 Dickerson, *Navigation Acts*, 218-219. On seamen's right to import, see Morris, *Government and Labor*, 238-239.

112 On the participation of seamen in the Boston Massacre see testimony of Robert Goddard, Oct. 25, 1770; Ebenezer Bridgham, Nov. 27, 1770; James Bailey, Nov. 28, Dec. 4, 1770; James Thompson, Nov. 30, 1770; all in Wroth and Zobel, eds., *Legal Papers of Adams*, III, 57-58, 103-106, 114-115, 115n-120n, 188, 189n, 268-269; also Frederick Kidner, *History of the Boston Massacre, March 5, 1770* (Albany,

sons for being there has been too little explored. The Massacre grew
out of a fight between workers and off-duty soldiers at a ropewalk two
days before.[113] That fight, in turn, grew out of the long-standing practice in the British army of allowing off-duty soldiers to take civilian employment. They did so, in Boston and elsewhere, often at wages which
undercut those offered to Americans—including unemployed seamen
who sought work ashore—by as much as 50 per cent.[114] In hard times
this led to intense competition for work, and the Boston Massacre was in
part a product of this competition. Less well known is the Battle of
Golden Hill, which arose from similar causes and took place in New
York six weeks before. In January 1770 a gang of seamen went from
house to house and from dock to dock, using clubs to drive away the
soldiers employed there and threatening anyone who might rehire
them.[115] In the days of rioting which followed and which came to be
called the Battle of Golden Hill, the only fatality was a seaman, although many other seamen were wounded in the attempt to take vengeance for the killing.[116] The antipathy between soldiers and seamen was
so great, said John Adams, "that they fight as naturally when they meet,
as the elephant and Rhinoceros."[117]

1870), 288. For Adams's description, see Wroth and Zobel, eds., *Legal Papers of
Adams*, III, 266. For Attucks see testimony of James Bailey, Nov. 28, 1770, of Patrick
Keeton, Nov. 30, 1770, *ibid.*, III, 114-115, 115n-120n, 191-192, 262, 268-269; Kidder,
Boston Massacre, 29n-30n, 287; Hutchinson, *History of Massachusetts-Bay*, ed. Mayo,
III, 196; *Boston Herald*, Nov. 19, 1890 [sic.]; John Hope Franklin, *From Slavery to
Freedom* (New York, 1956), 127.
    [113] Lt. Col. W. Dalrymple to Hillsborough, Mar. 13, 1770, C.O. 5/759, Pt. 3,
Library of Congress photostat; Capt. Thos. Rich to Admiralty, Mar. 11, 1770, Adm.
1/2388; Morris, *Government and Labor*, 190-192.
    [114] *The Times*, Broadsides, 1770-21, New-York Historical Society, New York
City; Morris, *Government and Labor*, 190n.
    [115] *N.-Y. Gaz.; Weekly Post-Boy*, Feb. 5, 1770, reports on the gang of seamen
which went from dock to dock turning out soldiers. *The Times*, N.-Y. Hist. Soc.
Broadsides, 1770-21 describes what could only be the same group and adds the
threat of vengeance.
    [116] *N.-Y. Gaz.; Weekly Post-Boy*, Jan. 22, Feb. 5, 1770; Dawson, *Sons of Liberty*,
117n; William J. Davis, "The Old Bridewell," in Henry B. Dawson, *Reminiscences
of the Park and its Vicinity* (New York, 1855), 61. Thomas Hutchinson noted the
death of the seaman and believed that the Battle of Golden Hill "encouraged"
Boston, thus leading to the Boston Massacre, Hutchinson, *History of Massachusetts-
Bay*, ed. Mayo, III, 194.
    [117] Wroth and Zobel, eds., *Legal Papers of Adams*, III, 262. See also John Shy,
Toward Lexington (Princeton, 1965), 309.

IV

To wealthy Loyalist Judge Peter Oliver of Massachusetts, the common people were only "Rabble"—like the "Mobility of all Countries, perfect Machines, wound up by any Hand who might first take the Winch." The people were "duped," "deceived," and "deluded" by cynical leaders who could "turn the Minds of the great Vulgar." Had they been less ignorant, Americans would have spurned their leaders, and there would have been no Revolution.[118] I have tested this generalization and found it unacceptable, at least in its application to colonial seamen. Obviously the seamen did not cause the American Revolution. But neither were they simply irrational fellows who moved only when others manipulated them. I have attempted to show that the seaman had a mind of his own and genuine reasons to act, and that he did act—purposefully. The final test of this purposefulness must be the Revolution itself. Here we find situations in which the seamen are separated from those who might manipulate them and thrown into great physical danger; if they were manipulated or duped into rebellion, on their own we might expect them to show little understanding of or enthusiasm for the war.

To a surprising extent American seamen remained Americans during the Revolution. Beaumarchais heard from an American in 1775 that seamen, fishermen, and harbor workers had become an "army of furious men, whose actions are all animated by a spirit of vengeance and hatred" against the English, who had destroyed their livelihood "and the liberty of their country."[119] The recent study of loyalist claimants by Wallace Brown confirms Oliver Dickerson's earlier contention that "the volumes dealing with loyalists and their claims discloses an amazing absence of names" of seamen. From a total of 2786 loyalist claimants whose occupations are known Brown found only 39, 1.4 per cent, who were seamen (or pilots). (It is possible to exclude fishermen and masters but not pilots from his figures.) In contrast, farmers numbered 49.1 per cent, artisans 9.8 per cent, merchants and shopkeepers 18.6 per cent, professionals 9.1 per cent, and officeholders 10.1 per cent. Although as Brown states, the poor may be underrepresented among the claimants,

201

---

[118] Douglass Adair and John A. Schutz, eds., *Peter Oliver's Origin and Progress of the American Rebellion: A Tory View* (San Marino, Calif., 1961), 65, 94-95, 48, 158, 39, 162, 165.

[119] Louis de Loménie, *Beaumarchais and His Times*, trans. Henry S. Edwards (London, 1856), III, 110. See also Paine, *Writings*, ed. Foner, I, 33.

"the large number of claims by poor people, and even Negroes, suggests that this is not necessarily true."[120]

An especially revealing way of examining the seamen's loyalties under pressure is to follow them into British prisons.[121] Thousands of them were imprisoned in such places as the ship *Jersey*, anchored in New York harbor, and Mill and Forton prisons in England. Conditions were abominable. Administration was corrupt, and in America disease was rife and thousands died.[122] If physical discomfort was less in the English prisons than in *Jersey*, the totality of misery may have been as great, with prisoners more distant from the war and worse informed about the progress of the American cause. Lost in a no-man's land between British refusal to consider them prisoners of war and Washington's unwillingness in America to trade trained soldiers for captured seamen, these men had limited opportunities for exchange. Trapped in this very desperate situation, the men were offered a choice: they could defect and join the

202

[120] Dickerson, *Navigation Acts*, 219, offers no explanation of the extent or method of his search. Wallace Brown, *The King's Friends* (Providence, 1965), 263, 287-344. Although Brown states that those listed pages 261-263 "make up 100 per cent of the claimants," he has excluded those whose occupations are unknown without noting the exclusion. He has also made some minor errors in his calculations, *ibid.*, 261-263, 295, 300, 313. The figures given in the text are my own computations based on corrected totals. I would like to thank Mr. Brown for his assistance in clearing up some of these errors. My own examination of New York materials in Loyalist Transcripts, I-VIII, XLI-XLVIII, and Lorenzo Sabine, *Biographical Sketches of Loyalists of the American Revolution with an Historical Essay* (Boston, 1864), turned up very few loyalist seamen, some of whom were obviously captains. See for example, Alpheus Avery and Richard Jenkins, Loyalist Transcripts, XVIII, 11-15, XLIII, 495-504. Brown, *King's Friends,* 307-308, also finds five out of a total of nine New York loyalist "seamen" are masters.

[121] See Morison, *John Paul Jones*, 165-166. "The unpleasant subject of the treatment of American naval prisoners during the war afforded fuel for American Anglophobes for a century or more, and there is no point in stirring it up again." For a plea that the horrors of the prisons not be forgotten see *New Hampshire Gazette* (Portsmouth), Feb. 9, 1779. The following brief account of the prisons in England and America summarizes my full-length study, "Jack Tar in the Darbies: American Seamen in British Prisons during the Revolution," to be completed shortly.

[122] On the prison ships the standard work at present is James Lenox Banks, *David Sproat and Naval Prisoners in the War of the Revolution with Mention of William Lenox, of Charlestown* (New York, 1909). This contains many useful documents, but the commentary is a one-sided whitewash written by a descendant who was not above ignoring evidence that Sproat elicited favorable accounts of conditions in *Jersey* through threats and bribery. Compare *ibid.*, 12-14, 81-84, with Danske Dandridge, *American Prisoners of the Revolution* (Charlottesville, 1911), 419-423.

Royal Navy. To a striking extent the prisoners remained patriots,[123] and very self-consciously so. "Like brave men, they resisted, and swore that they would never lift a hand to do any thing on board of King George's ships."[124] The many who stayed understood the political significance of their choice as well as the few who went. "What business had he to sell his Country, and go to the worst of Enemies?"[125] Instead of defecting they engaged in an active resistance movement. Although inexperienced in self-government and segregated from their captains, on their own these men experienced no great difficulties in organizing themselves into disciplined groups. "Notwithstanding they were located within the absolute dominions of his Britanic majesty," commented one, the men "adventured to form themselves into a republic, framed a constitution and enacted wholesome laws, with suitable penalties."[126] Organized, they resisted, celebrating the Fourth of July under British bayonets, burning their prisons, and escaping. Under these intolerable conditions, seamen from all over the colonies discovered that they shared a common conception of the cause for which they fought.[127]

203

[123] For instance, computations based on a list of prisoners in Mill Prison from May 27, 1777, to Jan. 21, 1782, from the *Boston Gaz.*, June 24, July 1, 8, 1782, indicate that 7.7% of 1013 men entered the king's service. This figure may be slightly distorted by the presence of a small number of non-Americans, but there is almost precise confirmation in Adm. 98/11-14 which lists only 190 out of a total of 2579 Americans, 7.4%, entered from all English prisons. This figure is slightly inflated. See Adm. 98/13, 108. See also, John Howard, *The State of the Prisons in England and Wales*, 3d ed. (Warrington, Eng., 1784), 185, 187, 188, 192, 194. I am indebted to John K. Alexander, a graduate student at the University of Chicago, for these figures and for valuable assistance in connection with the prisons.

[124] Charles Herbert, *A Relic of the Revolution* (Boston, 1847), 157. See also entry for Aug. 19, 1778, in Marion S. Coan, "A Revolutionary Prison Diary: the Journal of Dr. Jonathan Haskins," *New England Quarterly*, XVII (1944), 430. Clearly there is plagiarism here, as there is in many other, but by no means all, entries in the two journals. For a contention that Haskins is the plagiarist, see John K. Alexander, "Jonathan Haskins' Mill Prison 'Diary': Can it be Accepted at Face Value?" *ibid.*, XL (1967), 561-564.

[125] William Russell, "Journal," Dec. 31, 1781, Paine, *Ships and Sailors of Salem*, 155.

[126] Sherburne, *Memoirs*, 81. For a prisoners' committee in Forton Prison see Jan. 27, 1779, Adm. 98/11, 442-444; for a trial in Mill Prison for "the crime of profanely damning of the Hon:bl. Continental Congress," see Mar. 4, 1778, in Coan, "Revolutionary Prison Diary," 305. For self-government in *Jersey*, see Dring, *Recollections*, ed. Greene, 84-86.

[127] For example, Dring, *Recollections*, ed. Greene, 97-116; Herbert, *Relic of the Revolution*, 142; Russell, July 4, 1781, Paine, *Ships and Sailors of Salem*, 142. For a celebration of the British defeat at Yorktown, see Benjamin Golden to Benjamin Franklin, Dec. 2, 1781, Franklin Papers, XXIII, 94.

At the Constitutional Convention Benjamin Franklin spoke for the seamen:

It is of great consequence that we shd. not depress the virtue and public spirit of our common people; of which they displayed a great deal during the war, and which contributed principally to the favorable issue of it. He related the honorable refusal of the American seamen who were carried in great numbers into the British prisons during the war, to redeem themselves from misery or to seek their fortunes, by entering on board of the Ships of the Enemies to their Country; contrasting their patriotism with a contemporary instance in which the British seamen made prisoners by the Americans, readily entered on the ships of the latter on being promised a share of the prizes that might be made out of their own Country.[128]

204

Franklin spoke *against limiting* the franchise, not *for broadening* it: he praised the seamen, but with a hint of condescension, suggesting that it would be prudent to grant them a few privileges. A decade later a French traveller noticed that "except the laborer in ports, and the common sailor, everyone calls himself, and is called by others, a *gentleman*."[129] Government was still gentleman's government: more people were defined as gentlemen, but Jack Tar was not yet among them.

V

Bernard Bailyn has recently added needed illumination to our understanding of pre-Revolutionary crowd action. Bailyn has disagreed with Peter Oliver and with modern historians who have concurred in describing pre-Revolutionary rioters as mindless, passive, and manipulated: "far from being empty vessels," rioters in the decade before the outbreak of fighting were "politically effective" and "shared actively the attitudes and fears" of their leaders; theirs was a " 'fully-fledged political movement' "[130] Thus it would seem that Bailyn has freed himself from

[128] Max Farrand, ed., *The Records of the Federal Convention of 1787*, rev. ed. (New Haven, 1937), II, 204-205.

[129] Duke de la Rochefoucauld Liancourt, *Travels through the United States of North America* . . . , trans. H. Neuman (London, 1799), II, 672, quoted in Staughton Lynd and Alfred Young, "After Carl Becker: The Mechanics and New York City Politics, 1774-1801," *Labor History*, V (1964), 220.

[130] Bailyn, ed., *Pamphlets*, 581-583, 740, n. 10; Bailyn quotes the last phrase from George Rudé, "The London 'Mob' of the Eighteenth Century," *Historical Journal*, II (1959), 17. Bailyn is here contending that the post-1765 crowd was more highly

the influential grasp of Gustave Le Bon.[181] But Bailyn stopped short of total rejection. Only in 1765, he says, was the colonial crowd "transformed" into a political phenomenon. Before then it was "conservative"— like crowds in seventeenth- and eighteenth-century England, aiming neither at social revolution nor at social reform, but only at immediate revenge. Impressment riots and other "demonstrations by transient sailors and dock workers," Bailyn says, expressed no "deep-lying social distress" but only a "diffuse and indeliberate antiauthoritarianism"; they were "ideologically inert."[182]

Other historians have seen the colonial seamen—and the rest of the lower class—as mindless and manipulated, both before and after 1765.[133] The seeming implication behind this is that the seamen who demonstrated in colonial streets did so as much out of simple vindictiveness or undisciplined violence as out of love of liberty. Certainly such motiva-

---

developed than its English counterpart which was, according to Rudé, not yet "a fully-fledged political movement." See also Gordon S. Wood, "A Note on Mobs in the American Revolution," *Wm. and Mary Qtly.*, 3d Ser., XXIII (1966), 635-642.

131 See Gustave Le Bon, *The Crowd* (New York, 1960). For a critique of interpretations of the American Revolution which seem to echo Le Bon, see Lemisch, "American Revolution," in Bernstein, ed., *Towards a New Past, passim.* Two useful discussions which place Le Bon and those he has influenced in the context of the history of social psychology (and of history) are George Rudé, *The Crowd in History* (New York, 1964), 3-15, and Roger W. Brown, "Mass Phenomena," in Gardner Lindzey, ed., *Handbook of Social Psychology* (Cambridge, Mass., 1954), II, 833-873. Both Rudé and Brown describe Le Bon's bias as "aristocratic." Also relevant are some of the studies in Duane P. Schultz, ed., *Panic Behavior* (New York, 1964), especially Alexander Mintz, "Non-Adaptive Group Behavior," 84-107.

132 Bailyn, ed., *Pamphlets,* 581-583, citing Max Beloff, *Public Order and Popular Disturbances, 1660-1714* (London, 1938), 33, 153, 155, calls Beloff "the historian of popular disturbances in pre-industrial England," thus bypassing at least one other candidate for the title, George Rudé, whom he describes as "an English historian of eighteenth-century crowd phenomena." Rudé has shown in *The Crowd in History* and elsewhere that the crowd was purposeful, disciplined, and discriminating, that "in the eighteenth century the typical and ever recurring form of social protest was the riot." Rudé finds in Beloff echoes of Burke and Paine. Thus, the European foundation for Bailyn's interpretation of the pre-1765 American crowd is somewhat one-sided. Compare with Bailyn R. S. Longley's extremely manipulative "Mob Activities in Revolutionary Massachusetts," *New Eng. Qtly.*, VI (1933), 108: "Up to 1765, the Massachusetts mob was not political. Even after this date, its political organization was gradual, but it began with the Stamp Act."

133 For a further discussion see Lemisch, "American Revolution," in Bernstein, ed., *Towards a New Past, passim.* Bailyn, ed., *Pamphlets,* 581, is not entirely clear on the situation *after* 1765. He denies that "Revolutionary mobs" in America were in fact "revolutionary" and questions their "meliorist aspirations."

tion would blend well with the traditional picture of the seaman as rough and ready. For along with the stereotype of Jolly Jack—and in part belying that stereotype—is bold and reckless Jack, the exotic and violent.[134] Jack *was* violent; the conditions of his existence were violent. Was his violence non-political? Sometimes. The mob of seventy to eighty yelling, club-swinging, out-of-town seamen who tried to break up a Philadelphia election in 1742 had no interest in the election; they had been bought off with money and liquor.[135]

Other violence is not so clear-cut. Edward Thompson has seen the fighting out of significant social conflict in eighteenth-century England "in terms of Tyburn, the hulks and the Bridewells on the one hand; and crime, riot, and mob action on the other."[136] Crime and violence among eighteenth-century American seamen needs reexamination from such a perspective. Does "mutiny" adequately describe the act of the crew which seized *Black Prince,* re-named it *Liberty,* and chose their course and a new captain by voting? What shall we call the conduct of 150 seamen who demanded higher wages by marching along the streets of Philadelphia with clubs, unrigging vessels, and forcing workmen ashore? If "mutiny" is often the captain's name for what we have come to call a "strike," perhaps we might also detect some significance broader than mere criminality in the seamen's frequent assaults on captains and thefts from them.[137] Is it not in some sense a political act for a seaman to

206

---

[134] For rough and ready Jack see Watson, *Sailor in English Fiction,* 45, 159-160; Hohman, *Seamen Ashore,* 217.

[135] *Pa. Archives,* 8th Ser., IV, 2971, 2987, 2995-2998, 3009; "Extracts from the Gazette, 1742," Labaree *et al.,* eds., *Papers of Benjamin Franklin,* II, 363-364. Yet even these men can be shown to have had some ideas; their shouts, which included attacks on "Broad-brims," "Dutch dogs," and "You damned Quakers, . . . Enemies to King GEORGE," are similar to those of the European "Church and King" rioters. See Rudé, *Crowd in History,* 135-148; E. J. Hobsbawm, *Primitive Rebels* (New York, 1965), 110, 118, 120-123.

[136] E. P. Thompson, *The Making of the English Working Class* (New York, 1964), 60.

[137] Deposition of Thomas Austin, Dec. 10, 1769, in Hutchinson to Hillsborough, Dec. 20, 1769, C.O. 5/759, Pt. 2, Library of Congress Transcript; *Pennsylvania Packet* (Philadelphia), Jan. 16, 1779; *Colonial Records of Pennsylvania 1683-1790* (Harrisburg, 1852-1853), XI, 664-665; J. Thomas Scharf and Thompson Westcott, *History of Philadelphia, 1609-1884* (Philadelphia, 1884), I, 403. For some crimes of seamen against masters see *The King* v. *John Forster,* Indictment for Petty Larceny, filed Oct. 23, 1772, N. Y. Supreme Court, Pleadings K-495; Deposition of Cap. Elder and Examination of John Forster, sworn Oct. 20, 1772, N. Y. Supreme Court, Pleadings K-457; *N.-Y. Gaz.; Weekly Post-Boy,* Feb. 2, 1764.

tear off the mast a copy of a law which says that disobedient seamen will be punished as "seditious"?

Impressment meant the loss of freedom, both personal and economic, and, sometimes, the loss of life itself. The seaman who defended himself against impressment felt that he was fighting to defend his "liberty," and he justified his resistance on grounds of "right."[138] It is in the concern for liberty and right that the seaman rises from vindictiveness to a somewhat more complex awareness that certain values larger than himself exist and that he is the victim not only of cruelty and hardship but also, in the light of those values, of injustice. The riots ashore, whether they be against impressment, the Stamp Act, or competition for work express that same sense of injustice. And here, thousands of men took positive and effective steps to demonstrate their opposition to both acts and policies.

Two of England's most exciting historians have immensely broadened our knowledge of past and present by examining phenomena strikingly like the conduct and thought of the seamen in America. These historians have described such manifestations as "sub-political" or "pre-political," and one of them has urged that such movements be "seriously considered not simply as an unconnected series of individual curiosities, as footnotes to history, but as a phenomenon of general importance and considerable weight in modern history."[139] When Jack Tar went to sea in the American Revolution, he fought, as he had for many years before, quite literally, to protect his life, liberty, and property. It might be extravagant to call the seamen's conduct and the sense of injustice which underlay it in any fully developed sense ideological or political; on the other hand, it makes little sense to describe their ideological content as zero. There are many worlds and much of human history in that vast area between ideology and inertness.

207

---

[138] See above, 390.
[139] Thompson, *Making of the English Working Class*, 55, 59, 78; Hobsbawm, *Primitive Rebels*, 2, 7, 10.

Maryland's Impulse Toward Social Revolution: 1750-1776

DAVID CURTIS SKAGGS

IN the third quarter of the eighteenth century Maryland's form of government was a medieval relic in an age of enlightenment. A dissolute proprietor ruled the colony *in absentia* through a governor, a council, and a centralized civil and religious bureaucracy. The revenue that supported the bureaucratic establishment came from a mandatory poll tax levied on all males over sixteen and on all female slaves of the same age, and from the fees paid to the various governmental officials for the performance of their duties. The minimum charges in both cases were regulated by legislative enactment. Any change in their amount was subject to proprietary veto.

The complexity of the problems in Maryland was increased by the colony's social and economic heterogeneity. German immigration from Pennsylvania into Baltimore and Frederick counties (comprising the northwestern half of the colony) resulted in a population that engaged in tenant farming and that was not particularly interested in politics because it was denied the privilege of holding office, although it could vote. Completely excluded from voting were the Roman Catholics, who comprised a twelfth of the population and were concentrated in the southern part of the Western Shore. An additional 5 percent were Negro freedmen who possessed few political rights or social privileges. Only New Jersey, New York, and Pennsylvania had more heterogeneous populations; only Virginia, Pennsylvania, and Massachusetts were more populous in 1776.[1]

Mr. Skaggs is assistant professor of history in Bowling Green State University.

[1] The best treatments of Maryland population and government are found in Arthur E. Karinen, "Numerical and Distributional Aspects of Maryland Population, 1631-1840" (doctoral dissertation, University of Maryland, 1958); American Council of Learned Societies, "Report of Committee on Linguistic and National Stocks in the Population of the United States," *Annual Report of the American Historical Association for the Year 1931* (3 vols., Washington, 1932), I, 124; Charles Albro Barker, *The Background of the Revolution in Maryland* (New Haven, 1940); John V. L. McMahon, *An Historical View of the Government of Maryland* (Baltimore, 1831); Newton D. Mereness, *Maryland as a Proprietary Province* (New York, 1901).

TABLE I

PERCENTAGE OF WHITE ADULT FREEMEN
WHO WERE LANDOWNERS, 1756*

County	Total Pop. 1756	Adult Freemen 1756	Landowners 1756	% Landowners
Baltimore	18,000	2,400	1,096	45.7
Prince George's	14,500	1,934	752	38.9
Queen Anne's	11,500	1,533	780	50.9
Talbot	8,500	1,133	451	39.8
Total	52,500	7,000	3,079	44.0

209

The level of economic welfare of Maryland's citizens was among the lowest in British America. A study of landholding in Baltimore, Prince George's, Queen Anne's, and Talbot counties reveals that about 40 percent of the white freemen owned land. As Tables I and II illustrate, land ownership in these representative counties became increasingly more restrictive in the years under investigation. In 1756, 44 percent of the white adult freemen owned land in these counties. By 1771 the percentage of freemen to landowners dropped to 37 percent. Except in Baltimore County, the size of the

TABLE II

PERCENTAGE OF WHITE ADULT FREEMEN
WHO WERE LANDOWNERS, 1771*

County	Total Pop. 1771	Adult Freemen 1771	Landowners 1771	% Landowners
Baltimore	28,000	3,733	1,531	41.0
Prince George's	18,400	2,453	775	31.6
Queen Anne's	13,800	1,840	813	44.2
Talbot	11,500	1,533	419	27.3
Total	71,700	9,560	3,538	37.0

* The population statistics are taken from Karinen, "Numerical and Distributional Aspects," (pp. 115–30). The number of adult freemen is derived from the assumption that 20 percent of the population was adult male and that one third of these were either slaves or servants. The number of landowners is derived from the quitrent Debt Books for these counties for 1756 and 1771 (1769 in the case of Queen Anne's County where the 1770 and 1771 records are missing) located in the Maryland Land Office, Annapolis.

TABLE III

MEDIAN LANDHOLDING ACREAGE IN
FOUR MARYLAND COUNTIES*

County	Median Acreage Owned 1756	Median Acreage Owned 1771
Baltimore	186	157
Prince George's	200	205
Queen Anne's	190	200
Talbot	199	209

210

* The median landholdings are derived from an analysis of the freeholdings recorded in the quitrent Debt Books for these counties for 1756 and 1771 (1769 in the case of Queen Anne's County where the later records are missing) located in the Maryland Land Office.

median farm holding (between 160 and 210 acres) rose in the period. The sale of lots in Baltimore Town accounts for the slight reduction in that particular county. These figures in Table III do not indicate that the small planter was becoming a larger one but that land steadily fell into the hands of a few large planters.

For that three fifths of the white male population disqualified from voting for not having a fifty-acre freehold, there was the possibility that they might qualify by having a "visible estate" of £40 sterling. The Prerogative Court records indicate that approximately 29 percent of all freemen (almost all of whom were nonlandholders) who died in Baltimore and Talbot counties, 1750-1773, did not meet this qualification. An additional 6 percent of the landowners were not qualified to vote because they did not have the requisite fifty acres of land, and a further 8 percent were denied the franchise because of their Roman Catholicism. These figures indicate that between 33 and 40 percent of Maryland's white freemen were disfranchised.[2]

[2] This conclusion can be confirmed in another way. Only 55 percent of the nonfreeholders listed in the Baltimore and Talbot county inventories were qualified because they had sufficient personal estate. If this figure is projected over the four representative counties and if the estimate of 7,000 adult freemen therein in 1756 is valid, then 2,156 of the 3,921 nonlandowners were qualified. Add to this figure the 94 percent of the 3,079 landowners possessing the requisite fifty acres and one has 2,956 more qualified voters for a total of 5,112. Of this number approximately 8 percent must be subtracted because their Catholicism disqualified them. This decreases the number of voters by 409 to 4,703 or 69 percent of the freemen. If one uses the 1771 figures and the same methodology, the percentage so qualified drops to just less than 64 percent. Personal estate figures are based on the author's investigation of the Baltimore and Talbot County Prerogative Court Records, Inventories, 1750-1773 (Maryland Hall of Records, Annapolis, Maryland).

Actually, the number of qualified voters was probably less than indicated by these percentages. First, because the figures from the quitrent Debt Books and Prerogative Court Records include many women and a few businesses which did not possess the franchise and, second, because many freemen died without any property worthy of an inventory, the percentage of eligible voters was less than 60 percent. This is corroborated by a commentator in 1776 who claimed that the election requirements of the convention era, which by this time allowed Roman Catholics to vote, excluded at least half of the freemen from the suffrage. Philip A. Crowl estimated that the broadened franchise requiréments of the 1776 convention permitted only 55 percent of the white male freemen to vote in 1790.[3]

Social and economic mobility was also limited. A recent survey of the value of estates in the colony between 1690 and 1759 found movement up the economic scale to be glacially slow.[4] Baltimore Town was just beginning its rise to economic importance. His Lordship's land policy prohibited much of the opportunity traditionally associated with the American frontier. Most of the lands in Frederick County (the western third of the colony) were in the hands of the same landed gentry who controlled the political, economic, and social life in the eastern portion of the province. Thirteen nonresident landlords owned some 250,000 acres, which constituted 21 percent of the total patented land in the county. Lord Baltimore retained an additional 148,000 acres of manor and reserve lands in the same county. There can be little doubt that such large-scale engrossment of the land in an area as small as the western end of the province, limited the amount of economic opportunity on the Maryland frontier. A rise in tenancy, not freeholding, characterized the pre-revolutionary years.[5]

One of the best contemporary views of this situation came from the pen of Joseph Mosley, a Jesuit missionary in St. Mary's and Talbot counties, who reported Marylanders "to be very poor, and not to be compared in riches to the rest of our colonies." He described how Maryland had "been a fine poor man's country, but now it is well peopled, the lands are all secured and the harvest for such is now over. The Lands are mostly worked

---

[3] "Watchman," Annapolis *Maryland Gazette*, Aug. 15, 1776; Philip A. Crowl, *Maryland During and After the Revolution: A Political and Economic Study* (Baltimore, 1943), 35-36.

[4] Aubrey C. Land, "Economic Base and Social Structure: The Northern Chesapeake in the Eighteenth Century," *Journal of Economic History*, XXV (Dec. 1965), 639-54.

[5] R. Bruce Harley, "The Land System in Colonial Maryland" (doctoral dissertation, State University of Iowa, 1948), 147-81, 245, 260; Clarence P. Gould, *The Land System in Maryland, 1720-1765* (Baltimore, 1913), 61-87; Paul H. Giddens, "Land Policies and Administration in Maryland, 1753-1769," *Maryland Historical Magazine*, XXVIII (June 1933), 142-71.

by the landlord's negroes, and, of consequence, white servants, after their bondage is out, are strolling about the country without bread."[6]

There is other evidence to indicate that gaining admission to the inner circle of ruling gentry was more difficult in the late colonial years. Few were able to engineer such social mobility without the active support of the absentee Lord Proprietor, who continually sent over his favorites to occupy the choicest patronage offices and to patent the best land. For the native Marylander of little social standing, such opportunities were seldom, if ever, offered.[7] This was hardly a middle-class democracy.

The House of Delegates was becoming increasingly more malapportioned. Each county regardless of its population had four delegates. In 1755 the typical Eastern Shore delegate had 2,400 constituents; his Western Shore colleague had 3,100. Twenty years later, the average Eastern Shore representative had 2,700 constituents; those on the opposite side of the Chesapeake had 4,100. Between individual counties, the disparity was even more apparent. The four Frederick County assemblymen of 1775 had 7,400 constituents each, and those from Caroline County each had but 2,000. The maintenance of an equal number of counties on each shore throughout the period resulted in a decided discrimination against the residents of the fast-growing western portion of the province.[8]

Political conflict was traditional in the colonies. Jonathan Boucher noted that the political battles were between "Placemen and their dependants" (the so-called "Court party") on the one hand and their opponents (the so-called "Country party") on the other. The proprietor acknowledged that he bought particular opposition leaders by offering them patronage plums. This practice caused another observer to say that assemblymen made "Patriotism their Plea, but Preferment their Design. . . ."[9]

Both the patronage plums and the elective offices went to the most af-

[6] Joseph Mosley to his sister, Sept. 1, 1759, Sept. 7, 1770, June 5, 1772, E. I. Devitt, ed., "Letters of Father Joseph Mosley, 1757-1786," *Woodstock Letters*, XXXV, No. 1 (1906), 40, 52, 54.

[7] For examples see: James High, "The Origins of Maryland's Middle Class in the Colonial Aristocratic Patterns," *Maryland Historical Magazine*, LVII (Dec. 1962), 334-45; Neil E. Strawser, "The Early Life of Samuel Chase" (master's thesis, George Washington University, 1958).

[8] Figures based on population statistics in Karinen, "Numerical and Distributional Aspects," 115-30.

[9] Jonathan Boucher, *Reminiscences of an American Loyalist, 1738-1789: Being the Autobiography of the Revd. Jonathan Boucher . . .* (Boston, 1925), 68-69; Cecilius Calvert to Horatio Sharpe, March 17, 1760, *Archives of Maryland*, IX, 376-80 (hereafter cited as *Archives*); R. Alonzo Brock, ed., "Journal of William Black, 1744," *Pennsylvania Magazine of History and Biography*, I, No. 1 (1877), 127.

fluent members of the community. A study of the land records and the officeholders in Baltimore, Prince George's, Talbot, and Queen Anne's counties indicates that three fourths of the public offices went to the one fourth of the gentry who owned the most land.[10] Maryland's politicians were mostly men of wealth, men of breeding, men of the established church, men who held common middle-class, mercantile, and Whig attitudes, and men who knew and respected each other, despite occasional partisan differences. They governed and expected to continue governing the colony in its orderly conduct as a member of the British Empire.

This gentry leadership was not solving the economic and social problems of the colony. Many individuals demonstrated their disapproval of the growing incidence of poverty and tenantry by emigrating to Carolina, where settlers found a less restrictive environment.[11] For the colonists who remained, the desire for a change was strong; but there had to be a spark to ignite their resentment. The preparation for such a conflagration came in the form of a breakdown of the traditional respect for established authority.

One such assault occurred in 1753 when Thomas Cradock, distinguished rector of St. Thomas Parish, Baltimore County, and schoolmaster for the more affluent of his fellow colonists, preached to a gathering in Annapolis. His doctrine was simply that public officials must be held accountable for their conduct. He directed his fire primarily against his fellow-Anglican priests, many of whom he felt were unworthy of their calling. His proposal denied the proprietor's right of patrimony and threatened the proprietary system. Its application to civil officers would institute a major revision in Maryland's government.[12]

During the conflict between the proprietor and the Assembly over the tax levy necessary to provide Maryland's support for the French and Indian War, severe attacks were made against the colony's charter. The document was held to deprive Marylanders of their rights as Englishmen.[13] The

213

---

[10] Based upon a comparison of the county Debt Books, Maryland Land Office, with the Vestry Proceedings of the appropriate parishes, the Commission Records (Hall of Records); Donnell M. Owings, *His Lordship's Patronage: Offices of Profit in Colonial Maryland* (Baltimore, 1953).

[11] Robert W. Ramsey, *Carolina Cradle: Settlement of the Northwest Carolina Frontier, 1747-1762* (Chapel Hill, 1964), 11-22, 200-04.

[12] Thomas Cradock, "Sermon Preached in Annapolis, 1753" (Maryland Historical Society, Baltimore).

[13] R [ichard] B [rooke], "Queries relative to the Constitution of Maryland," *Gentlemen's Magazine*, XXXIII (Nov. 1763), 541-44. For assembly debate on these issues see *Archives*, LV, xxiii-xxxii, 77, 119-29, 270-83, 443-61, 480-91, 542-45, 555-57, 567-72, 663, 674-77, 707-50; *ibid.*, LVI, xliii-lii, 26-27, 76-81, 176-83, 202-04, 222-24, 257-306; *ibid.*, LVIII, xxxviii-xlix, 5-7, 25-26, 56-64, 109-15, 138-43, 157-70.

Stamp Act crisis widened this controversy by bringing into question the nature of royal and parliamentary authority. Daniel Dulany's famous *Considerations on the Propriety of Imposing Taxes in the British Colonies for the Purpose of Raising a Revenue* became a classic legal argument against Parliamentary taxation. Although Dulany championed the colonial cause within the limitations of the law and remained outside the subsequent revolutionary movement, the *Considerations* did much to break down respect for order and stability.[14]

214

Moreover, before Parliament repealed the Stamp Act, several novel ingredients had been added to the Maryland political scene. On September 2, 1765, a mob of Annapolis rowdies, with Samuel Chase as one of its leaders, gathered outside an uninhabited house recently leased by Zachariah Hood, a stamp collector, destroyed the building, and forced Hood to leave the colony. This use of lower-class elements as a political force represented a radical departure from the past, when controversy was generally conducted on a more genteel plane.[15]

Another novel ingredient was the emergence of extralegal political organs to express discontent. The free*men*, not the free*holders*, of Talbot County assembled in the fall of 1765 and promised to risk "their lives and fortunes . . . by all lawful ways and means, to preserve and transmit to their posterity their rights and liberties." Here again was a form of political deviation. This same Talbot County group also declared dissent from their views to be inimical to American rights; and it resolved to "detest, abhor, and hold in utmost contempt" all persons connected with the stamp duties in any way. This prohibition included any agent, "Stamp-pimp, informer or favorer of said Act."[16] To enforce such ideas of mass conformity required the services of the "inferior" elements of society. Similar *ad hoc* committees and their enforcers became an increasingly important factor on the political scene.

Equally significant was a notable change occurring in the motivation of the Country party forces. Formerly, party rivalry had been between the

[14] Aubrey C. Land, *The Dulanys of Maryland: A Biographical Study of Daniel Dulany, The Elder (1685-1753) and Daniel Dulany, The Younger (1722-1779)* (Baltimore, 1955), 263-70; Edmund S. and Helen M. Morgan, *The Stamp Act Crisis: Prologue to Revolution* (Chapel Hill, 1953), 71-87; Bernard Bailyn, ed., *Pamphlets of the American Revolution 1750-1776* (4 vols., Cambridge, 1965-   ), I, 599-658.

[15] Sharpe to Lord Baltimore, Sept. 10, 1765, *Archives*, XIV, 223-24; Aubrey C. Land, ed., "Sharpe's Confidential Report on Maryland, 1765," *Maryland Historical Magazine*, XLIV (June 1949), 123-29. Sharpe to Gen. Thomas Gage, Sept. 6, 23, 1765, Thomas Gage Papers (William L. Clements Library, University of Michigan).

[16] Oswald Tilghman, *History of Talbot County, Maryland: 1661-1861* (2 vols., Baltimore, 1915), II, 44-45.

"ins" and the "outs." In 1768 Lord Baltimore offered Matthew Tilghman and his son-in-law Charles Carroll, barrister, influential posts on His Lordship's Council in an effort to secure their loyalty to the government. Their blunt refusal of his overtures was a slap in the proprietor's face.[17] By declining these appointments, Tilghman and Carroll served notice that the Country party now represented more than the desire for the fruits of patronage. No men of their stature subsequently accepted such appointments.

Finally, during this period, there was a decline in the traditional deference shown the gentry by the other freemen. A seemingly insignificant event in Trinity Parish, Charles County, is symptomatic of this trend. For years the congregation followed the English custom of recognizing social rank by reserving special pews for gentlemen and their families. When, in 1755, it was proposed to award pews by lot rather than by rank, the gentry protested, only to see themselves overruled at a mass meeting of the Protestant freeholders of the parish. In the years after the Stamp Act crisis such disputes became more frequent in parishes throughout the province.[18]

The most dramatic evidence of defiance was resistance by the vestry of Coventry Parish in 1766 to the proprietor's right to name their rector. The vestry demanded the right of patrimony on the grounds that they, not Lord Baltimore, were the real patrons of the parish. When Governor Horatio Sharpe refused to appoint their choice, the vestry allied themselves with "Swamp men and Shingle Makers, and the rest of their Banditti" to terrorize the countryside and to keep the governor's appointees from taking office. Three years passed before this Eastern Shore parish solved the impasse, and a new governor and the vestry agreed on a minister.[19]

Thus, by 1770, the citizens had openly denied the desires of the proprietor, the governor, and the council. To insure the success of their attacks on proprietary authority the opposition had begun to employ lower-class whites to intimidate the establishment. Under these circumstances, the

215

---

[17] Sharpe to Ld. Balto., Oct. 31, Nov. 28, 1768, *Archives*, XIV, 550-51, 557.

[18] J. N. Barry, "Trinity Parish, Charles County Maryland," *Maryland Historical Magazine*, I (Dec. 1906), 325; Vestry Proceedings, Chester Parish, Kent County, Feb. 18, 1766; Vestry Proceedings, Prince George's Parish, Frederick County, Aug. 4, Sept. 1, 1772; Vestry Proceedings, St. Luke's Parish, Queen Anne's County, Jan. 7, 22, 1773 (Hall of Records). For a detailed discussion of the pew controversies see Harold E. Hartdagen, "The Anglican Vestry in Colonial Maryland" (doctoral dissertation, Northwestern University, 1965), 105-14.

[19] "The Remonstrance of the Reverend Philip Hughes Rector of Coventry to Horatio Sharpe," *Archives*, XXXII, 222-24; "Vestry of Coventry Parish to Sharpe [Jan. 1767]," *ibid.*, XIV, 363-69; "Vestry of Coventry Parish of Worcester County to Governor Horatio Sharpe in Regard to the Appointment of a New Rector for That Parish," *ibid.*, LXI, lxii, 513-17; "Letters and Vestry Proceedings of the Year 1769 Relating to the Rev. Philip Hughes and Other Colonial Clergymen," *ibid.*, LXII, 463-66.

"Swamp men and Shingle Makers" emerged as a political force. The Coventry affair was but one in a series of episodes in which the proprietary government found itself embroiled after the Stamp Act crisis. They all resulted in a loss of prestige for the existing government and its leadership.

The proprietor and the religious establishment also came under vigorous attack from members of both the Court and Country parties as the result of several inappropriate appointments to Maryland curés. A lack of piety and an avaricious nature characterized Bennet Allen, a lackey of Lord Baltimore who was successively foisted upon the congregations of St. Anne's Parish, Annapolis, St. James Parish, Anne Arundel County, and All Saint's Parish, Frederick County. After installing himself in the last parish, Allen hired two curates to perform his duties; and he retired to Philadelphia to live off the £1,300 sterling annual income provided from taxes imposed on the hapless citizens of the frontier county. By combining the Coventry controversy and the Allen affair with the suspected, but unproved, murder of a slave by Parson Richard Brown of King and Queen Parish, St. Mary's County, there was enough scandal to unite the usually warring Court and Country factions behind the demand for a sweeping reform of the establishment. The assembly established a commission consisting of the governor, three Anglican clergymen, and three Anglican laymen to investigate charges of ministerial irregularity and to admonish, suspend, or totally deprive a guilty parson of his benefice. Of course, the clergy knew that such a commission would transform their church from "episcopal" to "presbyterian." Clerical remonstrances to the Bishop of London and the Board of Trade as well as in the Maryland press only brought the established church into greater disrepute with the populace in the years 1768-1775.[20]

At the same time that the religious establishment came under vigorous attack, the civil government virtually eliminated any popular support of its position during the Fee Controversy of 1770-1773. This *cause célèbre* emerged when the Tobacco Inspection Act of 1763 came up for renewal. Tied to this act were provisions regulating the fees to be paid to civil and clerical officers, and setting the rates at which tobacco would be commuted

216

[20] Boucher to John James, June 8, 1770, "Letters of the Rev. Jonathan Boucher," *Maryland Historical Magazine*, VIII (June 1913), 169; Sharpe to Hugh Hamersley, Nov. 27, 1767; Sharpe to Lord Baltimore, Feb. 9, May 15, 27, 1768, *Archives*, XIV, 460-61, 465, 494, 497, 499; *ibid.*, LXI, lxix-lxxi, 304-05, 315, 319, 361, 383, 400, 405, 406, 412, 420; *ibid.*, LXIII, xxxiii-xxxiv, 290-93; Nelson W. Rightmyer, *Maryland's Established Church* (Baltimore, 1955), 101-08. See also Jonathan Boucher, *A View of the Causes and Consequences of the American Revolution* (London, 1797), 89-150; for the paper war between Boucher and William Paca and Samuel Chase, see Annapolis *Maryland Gazette*, Dec. 31, 1772, Jan. 14, Feb. 4, April 1, 29, May 6, 1773.

into currency. Because increasing population brought a rapid increase in the amount of fees collected, the burgesses decided that these incomes were excessive and planned to reduce the rates. The proprietor's councilors, who held the most lucrative of these offices, opposed any change; and when the legislative session ended in stalemate, Governor Robert Eden issued a proclamation continuing the rates. The "patriots" immediately claimed that they were being taxed without legislative approval. Dulany found that his arguments on the governor's behalf in a newspaper exchange with Charles Carroll of Carrollton destroyed the last vestiges of his popular support. The affair ended with Dulany and the Court party in full retreat. The elections of 1773, a total victory for the Country faction, brought the permanent demise of the proprietary party. From this time forward, all political battles were within the old Country party, which was now torn between right and left wings—between the Whigs and the democrats.[21]

217

In the political vacuum created by the decline of proprietary authority and the failure of the royal government to assert itself in the midst of a rising colonial opposition to parliamentary control, Marylanders established a system of extralegal county meetings, committees of observation and correspondence, provincial conventions, and a council of safety. Until late 1775 most of these associations were headed by men of property and propriety who followed a policy of moderation and toleration.

When Parliament enacted the Coercive Acts, moderation quickly passed. To be effective, the American response had to appear united. To make it so required the use of coercion, but the gentry's control of the extralegal political machinery and mob activities was tenuous. There was no convenient anchorage upon which the moderate revolutionaries could depend while they assaulted British authority. Radicalism, therefore, became a genuinely significant factor in Maryland political life.

The colonial response to the Intolerable Acts took the form of a rigorously enforced nonimportation agreement, and commercial life on the Chesapeake dwindled. Baltimore's wheat prices, which had been at 7½ shillings currency per bushel in 1773, fell to 3½ shillings in the fall of

---

[21] Daniel Dulany's articles appeared in the Annapolis *Maryland Gazette* headed "A Dialogue Between Two Citizens," Jan. 7, and signed "Antilon," Feb. 18, April 8, June 3, 1773; Charles Carroll's signed "First Citizens," appeared on Feb. 4, March 11, May 6, July 1, 1773. Further arguments may be found in Attorney General John Hammond's defense of the governor, *ibid.*, July 29, 1773, and the reply of Chase, Thomas Johnson, and Paca, *ibid.*, Sept. 9, 1773. For assembly debates on the inspection and fee issue see *Archives*, LXII, 59-63, 82-83, 123, 212-16, 300-01, 349-53, 356-57, 360-63, 366-69, 383-84, 394-98, 401-02, 411-14, 422-26, 429-31; *ibid.*, LXIII, 42-65, 98, 109-11, 144-47, 152-54, 163-65, 169, 192-210, 219-33, 236-37, 388-89; *ibid.*, LXIV, xv-xvii, 12-13, 42-46, 77, 81, 86, 95-97, 116, 119-20, 151-92, 254-56.

1775. The price of corn, 5 shillings per bushel in 1772, dropped to 3 shillings in 1776. The effects of this economic stagnation and depression became apparent when the farmers "began to complain, and threaten to mob the merchants."[22] The traditional gentry leadership now found it hard to control the depressed populace. Open defiance of the gentry-controlled committees of observation emerged in late 1774.

When Thomas Charles Williams, an Annapolis merchant visiting in London, heard of the Maryland nonimportation agreements, he set out to defy them deliberately. He shipped seventeen chests of tea aboard the *Peggy Stewart*. The vessel, owned by James Dick and his son-in-law Anthony Stewart, arrived in mid-October. After Stewart had paid the duty on the tea and prepared to unload the ship, the Annapolis committee decided that the tea should be brought ashore and burned. Matthias Hammond, who with his brother Rezin led the radicals of Anne Arundel County, objected and asked for a general meeting of citizens to decide the issue. Carroll, barrister, the committee's chairman, felt that he could control any popular meeting; and Hammond's suggestion was adopted.

The meeting was attended not only by citizens of Anne Arundel County but also by delegations from surrounding areas. The latter groups constituted an important and volatile segment of the gathering. When Carroll asked for the sense of the meeting, he received overwhelming approval of the committee's proposal to burn the tea ashore. But dissident elements also demanded the burning on the vessel, so that the hated leaf would not contaminate Maryland soil. Although they constituted only a fourth of the people at the meeting, their threats against Stewart's store and against his home, where his wife lay seriously ill, forced him to burn the tea "voluntarily," and with it the brig, in the Annapolis harbor.[23] John Galloway expressed the dismay of the Maryland conservatives at the power of the public meeting: "I think Sir I went to Annapolis yesterday to see my liberty destroyed which was done when fire was put to the brig." Arthur M. Schlesinger aptly summarized the significance of the event when he wrote: "In a word, Annapolis had out-Bostoned Boston."[24]

218

[22] James High, ed., "Letters from the Reverend David Love to Horatio Sharpe, 1774-1779," *Historical Magazine of the Protestant Episcopal Church*, XIX (Dec. 1950), 365-66. For grain prices see John Armstrong Account Book (Manuscript Division, Library of Congress). For another account of emerging radicalism see William Eddis, *Letters from America . . . 1769, to 1777, Inclusive* (London, 1792), 169, 215-16.

[23] Annapolis *Maryland Gazette*, Oct. 20, 1774; Richard K. MacMaster and David C. Skaggs, eds., "The Letterbooks of Alexander Hamilton, Piscataway Factor: Part II, 1774-1775," *Maryland Historical Magazine*, LXI (Dec. 1966), 318-19; Eddis, *Letters from America*, 171-84; Fisher Transcripts, Vol. II (Maryland Historical Society).

[24] Arthur Meier Schlesinger. *The Colonial Merchants and the American Revolution,*

During the following year the Talbot County patriots refused to allow British ships to discharge their cargoes. Kent County ruffians expelled His Majesty's customs collector. And in July 1775, young radicals in southern Anne Arundel County defied the committee of observation and burned the British-owned ship *Totness*, which had run aground in Chesapeake Bay. The subterfuge of Stewart's voluntary burning was no longer used. A proprietary official wrote that this "second burnt-offering to liberty" and other "instances of popular fury" were "heartily condemned by very many, even of the patriotic party."[25]

Slowly but surely the revolutionary movement seemed to be slipping from gentry hands. In Charles and Baltimore counties mobs stormed the local jails and released men imprisoned for debts. The courts of Charles County were closed by debtors who did not or could not make payments on their obligations.[26] The gentry still controlled the Maryland convention, which governed the colony; but the 1775 elections brought radical leaders, like the Hammond brothers, into the body to contend with the traditional leadership for control.

219

More assaults on the established order came from a creature of the convention, the revolutionary militia. Militiamen demanded not only the right to select their company officers but also the privilege of electing regimental officers. When the convention of December 1775 named fifty of its eighty members to field-grade and general-officer ranks, the protest was immediate and loud. From the militia came one of the first outcries against the system of special privilege that heretofore had characterized proprietary and country politics in Maryland. In Queen Anne's County an unknown by the name of James O'Bryan usurped the colonelcy at a regimental meeting. The convention-appointed colonel wrote: "The people have been induced to believe they ought not to submit to any appointments, but those made by themselves. . . ."[27]

1763-1776 (New York, 1939), 392; "Account of the Destruction of the Brig 'Peggy Stewart,' at Annapolis, 1774," *Pennsylvania Magazine of History and Biography*, XXV, No. 2 (1901), 248-54.

[25] Eddis, *Letters from America*, 217-18; "Correspondence of Governor Eden," *Maryland Historical Magazine*, II (March 1907), 6-7; Annapolis *Maryland Gazette*, July 20, 1775.

[26] *Archives*, XI, 33; Richard K. MacMaster and David C. Skaggs, eds., "The Letterbooks of Alexander Hamilton, Piscataway Factor: Part III, 1775-1776," *Maryland Historical Magazine*, LXII (June 1967), 162. There were continued demands for conformity to the "Association of Freemen of Maryland," and Alexander Hamilton reported (Aug. 2, 1775) that the most "Unexceptionable Conduct will not screen any Man. The cry is now if they will not fight for us, they are against us, no neutrality now." *Ibid.*, 149.

[27] "Th. Wright to Council," Sept. 20, 1776, *Archives*, XII, 288; "Joseph Sims to Council," Sept. 23, 1777, *ibid.*, 296; "An American," *Maryland Journal and Baltimore Adver-

The by-now-frightened gentry saw that stable government must be restored in order to check the radical trend. The establishment of independence, but with a conservative constitution that retained all the old gentry privileges without the odious restrictions of proprietary control, seemed the politic course to pursue. Similarly, the radicals moved toward independence but with the hope of consolidating the gains that they had made. Thus, both factions could unite in support of separation from British control. When the Maryland convention finally resolved for independence in June 1776, the infighting turned toward the election of delegates to the state constitutional convention to be held in August.

220 Prior to the election the radicals made a series of demands—most of which were embodied in the resolutions drawn up by representatives of the Anne Arundel County militia. The radicals insisted on the supremacy of a popularly elected legislature over a plural executive, elective county governments and the decentralization of administration, lessening of gentry control over appointive offices by abolishing pluralism, ending of the oppressive fees and poll tax on all citizens, and a dramatic shift of the tax base to those most capable of bearing it—the large landowners.[28]

The June convention, which had resolved for independence, raised the voting qualifications for the constitutional convention to the proprietary level of a 50-acre freehold or £40 sterling visible estate. Since the earlier convention elections had allowed all freeholders to vote, the reimposition of the higher standards resulted in considerable discontent. Demands for wider manhood suffrage brought disturbances at polling places in Prince George's, Kent, Worcester, Queen Anne's, and Frederick counties. Although proper elections with the old qualifications were eventually held in all localities, the demand for wider suffrage continued.[29]

Vigorous approval of the popular demands appeared in an essay signed "Watchman," which was printed in the *Maryland Gazette* on August 15, 1776, the day after the constitutional convention opened. The author, who may have been Rezin Hammond, argued that all freemen should be allowed "the enjoyment of their inherent right of free suffrage." Continuing in this vein, he impugned the argument that only those who have a stake in society

tiser, July 3, 1776. James O'Bryan owned 185 acres in 1769 and ranked in the bottom half of Queen Anne's County landholders. Debt Books, Queen Anne's County, 1769, fol. 42 (Maryland Land Office, Annapolis).

[28] Annapolis *Maryland Gazette*, July 18, 1776.

[29] "Council to Maryland Deputies [in Congress]," Aug. 16, 1776, *Archives*, XII, 212; *Proceedings of the Convention of the Province of Maryland, Held in the City of Annapolis, on Wednesday, the Fourteenth of August, 1776* (Annapolis, 1776), 2-6.

should be entrusted with the suffrage: "Every poor man has a life, a personal liberty, and a right to his earnings: and is in danger of being injured by government in a variety of ways: therefore it is necessary that these people should enjoy the right of voting for representatives, to be the protectors of their lives, personal liberty, and their little property which, though small, is yet, upon the whole, a very great object to them." Each citizen of a state, Watchman concluded "who lends his aid to the support of it, has an equal claim to all the privileges, liberties and immunities with every of his fellow countrymen."

Watchman's essay, the riots at the polls, and the militia proposals represented more than political squabbles amongst the gentry. They were part of a conscious attempt to take the control of the province from the hands of the great planters who maintained town houses in Annapolis and who saw to it that they, their brothers, their cousins, and their in-laws received the most influential and lucrative offices. The demands by the radicals were not an attempt to secure a leveling of society; instead, they represented a desire for the creation of an environment in which a greater degree of social, political, and economic mobility might exist. Obviously, the shift from a stake-in-society suffrage system to one embodying manhood suffrage threatened traditional concepts and prerogatives which supported gentry control of the economic and political life of Maryland.

The gentry realized that these outbursts jeopardized their position. At no time did the threat to the established order become more apparent than in the election for delegates to the constitutional convention. All along the Western Shore, old-line Country party leaders like Thomas Stone (signer of the Declaration of Independence), Thomas Contee, Robert Tyler, Josias Beall, Walter Tolley, Jr., and John Moale lost their seats. The results in Anne Arundel County alone were enough to send tremors through the moderate camp. Thomas Johnson, Jr. (soon to be named first governor of the State of Maryland), William Paca (another future governor), and Carroll, barrister, were not returned. Chase barely escaped defeat. After evaluating the election results, an alarmed Council of Safety despaired that "there is a very great change in the members in all counties, according to the intelligence we have." Two thirds of the convention membership went to men who had not served in the lower house of the Maryland General Assembly.[30] Governor Eden's prediction, "Those who first encouraged the Opposition

221

---

[30] *Archives,* XII, 163, 186, 191, 234. Fifty of the seventy-six delegates had not served in the proprietary assembly. Paca was subsequently returned from Annapolis, and Thomas Johnson, Jr. was elected by Caroline County, where he held no property.

to Government, and set there on this licentious Behaviour, will probably be amongst the first to repent thereof," seemed about to be fulfilled.[21]

The democratically minded delegates comprised all or part of the membership from Baltimore, Harford, Calvert, Montgomery, and Anne Arundel counties. They were, however, unable to wring any important concessions from the traditional gentry leaders who represented Annapolis, Baltimore Town, and the Eastern Shore and who retained a majority in the convention. The old guard, led by a coterie of great landowners with long legislative experience, quickly gained control of the important offices and committee assignments. The voting requirement was lowered to £30 current money from the £40 sterling of the earlier period—a drop of over 50 percent. Still, the principle of a property qualification for voting was maintained. Although plural officeholding was prohibited and a semblance of local autonomy was extended when the shrievalty was made elective instead of appointive, all other county officers were appointed by the executive branch of the state government. Only the members of the House of Delegates were directly elected. The senators and the governor were selected by an indirect process. For the first time formal property qualifications—exceptionally high ones at that—were placed on officeholders.[22] Maryland's constitution of 1776 was one of the most conservative written in the Revolutionary era.

However, the defeat of the democrats in the constitutional convention does not permit the historian to disregard the existence in Maryland of a strong impulse toward radical social change. The fact that their ideas did not become political realities in Maryland until 1801 does not make them any less a part of the revolutionary heritage of the state. Even though it took several years after the fighting ended to achieve these goals, many of the men who fought in the War of the Revolution in this particular state did so because they desired to change the existing social order; to see the enactment of what has been termed an "internal revolution."

A study of the revolutionary movement in Maryland indicates that the

222

[22] *Proceedings of the Convention . . . of August, 1776,* 3, 19, 22-23, 27, 29, 34, 35, 37, 52-53, and *passim.* The constitutional convention did make some dramatic changes in the old order which met with little opposition: the Anglican church was disestablished, although the state would collect tithes for the denomination chosen by the tithe-payer; the old alien and religious voting restrictions were eliminated; and, despite the opposition of the Eastern Shore, Baltimore Town was given two seats in the new House of Delegates and two new counties were created on the Western Shore. It is interesting to note that the political divisions in the 1776 constitutional convention have decided similarities to those illustrated in Jackson Turner Main, "Political Parties in Revolutionary Maryland, 1780-1787," *Maryland Historical Magazine,* LXII (March 1967), 1-27.

most influential segment of society desired the preservation of the existing social, economic, and political order and that it was willing to exert extensive energies and talent to preserve that society from threats directed against it either by the British government or by domestic malcontents. Evidence also shows that in the years just prior to the Declaration of Independence, other social elements began to demand a more drastic revision of society than the gentry believed necessary to end parliamentary tyranny. Such demands demonstrate that many colonial Marylanders desired a more democratic social, political, and economic order than existed prior to 1776.

223

Representation, Taxation, and Tyranny in Revolutionary Massachusetts

John A. Schutz

The author is professor of history in the University of Southern California. This paper was his presidential address to the Pacific Coast Branch of the American Historical Association at its annual meeting in December 1973.

Aᴍᴇʀɪᴄᴀɴꜱ ʜᴀᴠᴇ ɴᴇᴠᴇʀ liked taxation, particularly the British taxes levied upon them in the decade before the American Revolution. They referred to those assessments with various impolite phrases, some not fit for mixed company, but the saying, "Taxation without representation is tyranny," became a famous slogan and is better remembered today than any other.[1] The Stamp Act, the Townshend Duties, and the Tea Act fell under the odium of being tyrannical and aroused emotions that are difficult to comprehend some two hundred years later when taxation has become a game of hide and cheat. Those feelings of 1776, however, were genuine, deepseated, and explosive. No one who has read the literature of the conflict will dispute the revolutionary nature of the reaction against taxation. And most will agree that the taking of any tax money in America, but especially in Massachusetts, caused acute pains, synonymous to blood letting, and caused men to wail like sinners at Jerusalem's Wall. Even for such worthy purposes as education, defense, and the promotion of trade, New Englanders wanted hard

---

[1] The slogan is attributed to James Otis, Jr., but American newspaper writers used variations in their columns as did both Edmund Burke and Charles Pratt, the Earl of Camden, in speeches to Parliament.

facts to be presented by the selectmen of the towns or their representatives in the assembly, then a public debate, and a vote of the people. For them, money in one's pocket was preferable to a public service rendered by officials in Boston or at Whitehall, where extravagance was likely to be tolerated.

Luxury in high places created its own special fears for colonials, and prayers were surely offered to God for the forgiveness of a society that permitted the frolicking of public officials at Boston, or Hartford, or Providence, not to mention at distant London. Luxury was the expenditure of money for unnecessary purposes, and tyranny was the nonecclesiastical term for this public offense. To end such luxury, New Englanders held close rein on their assemblies and sought to keep legislative initiative in local hands. In the Stamp Act crisis of 1765 they did not seek representation at Westminster, nor wish to exercise greater representation in their legislatures than they already enjoyed, but they assailed the purposes of taxation and the shift of the taxing authority to Westminster. The money, they believed, would be spent on luxury in the form of unnecessary imperial government, particularly in the expansion of a patronage system that would foster militarism and the violation of privacy. For Parliament to assume the taxing power would be to remove government from the locality, where it naturally belonged; and for Parliament to legislate for the whole empire would be to deprive subjects of appropriate representation. In short, parliamentary taxation with or without representation was tyranny.

225

In the early years of the conflict with Great Britain some theorists suggested colonial representation in the House of Commons as an expedient means of solving the constitutional issue of consent in voting taxes. By allowing consent they thought the levying of British taxes would become more palatable to colonials. Such distinguished Englishmen and Americans as Thomas Pownall and Benjamin Franklin pondered the feasibility of an imperial parliament, and Pownall openly advocated the idea in his famous book, *The Administration of the Colonies*.[2] However, most colonials quickly brushed aside the idea of parliamentary union because they considered it impolitic and immoral. Some objections touched such practical issues of representation as the distance of Westminster from the New England towns and the matter of legislative account-

[2] *The Administration of the Colonies* (London, 1768), 149–151, 163–164.

ability. But few critics were intrigued by the schemes of representation, or let their fancy dwell on a spacious empire of travelling delegates, or imagined themselves for a moment in the hallowed halls of the Commons or condoned plans for virtual representation. Critics who took the time to assail the proposal condemned participation in Parliament because they saw it as a way of legalizing imperial taxation. Particularly odious to them was the shifting of responsibility for American affairs to a distant land and the placing of local resources into the hands of outsiders.

226   The specter of an overseas government legislating for an empire frightened most colonials who could recall sufficiently their schoolboy history of ancient Rome with its corrupt politics and politicians. The history of Rome, they would readily admit, had some bright moments of courage, but it was full of crime, militarism, and combat. The British Empire, now the greatest of empires, was likewise corrupt, and many Britons were predicting the decline of the nation as a result of its waste of resources. But colonials also cited examples of American corruption. Their opposition to distant government applied as well to local colonial governments, where royal governors, sometimes with ruthless disregard for popular rights, used their prerogatives to force their will on the people. Sometimes governors, through the use of bribery, distributed rewards to officials who joined them in corruption. The only safe government, many people felt, was the local government of town meetings where men knew the candidates, their families, and friends and where political interests were uncomplicated by distance, city life, and capital politics. Colonials revered the natural life of farm and small town, the stone walls that fenced their farms, and the crops that gave sustenance. For the people, government meant the right to assemble in town meetings, to select officials, and to vote taxes.

Representative government in Massachusetts was generally defined in the Charter of 1691. It gave the colony a two-house legislature, courts, and a semipopular administration. The charter had a revered position similar to that of Magna Carta in England and was the fundamental law for Massachusetts. But there were other rights —the natural rights and the rights of Englishmen—that had an equal place of honor. These were often called to public notice in times of crisis, long before James Otis's famous declamation against the Writs of Assistance. Under the charter, male land owners in general won the right to vote, providing they lived in the townships that were awarded the privilege of sending delegates to the House of Representatives. Over the years the privilege was generously extended to most communities so that townships of less than a hundred farmers shared honors proportionally with larger centers of business and commerce. Representation traditionally was tied to residency in a township. Though the length of residency was no serious matter, residency was the determining factor. The requirement was rigorously enforced by the townsmen who insisted upon selecting a representative from the locality.[3]

In the town the privilege of representation was exercised at the May meeting. Those present selected the delegate, and he, standing before his fellow townsmen, reaffirmed his promises to back agreed-upon legislation. Specific issues disturbing the town were then discussed; resolutions were drawn and presented; and the votes taken. Whenever consensus could not be obtained, and consensus was a desired objective of many townsmen, then the wording of the instruction to the delegates became crucial.[4] Sometimes the instructions were such that the chosen representatives, one after another, resigned their posts. Other times debate over issues became so bitter that the town placed the powers of representation in the hands of a committee which served as its agent in Boston. In turning to this solution, the town gave its agents special power to bargain and negotiate, but it retained the initiative in other matters.[5]

When issues of local importance were not pressing, many towns refused or neglected to send representatives or agents to Boston. Some towns, it seems, never had issues that compelled them to send delegates, for many went twenty or thirty years without sending anyone to the capital. Other towns, in times of peace, chose people of limited talent or people expendable from town business.[6] The townspeople held the philosophy that the best government was per-

227

---

[3] Residency was established as a requirement of town elections shortly after the promulgation of the Charter of 1691. Nearly every session of the legislature made inquiries into local elections and the qualifications of legislators.

[4] *Records of Ye Towne Meetings of Lyn, 1742–1759* (Lynn, 1966), 38, 42, 51–52 (hereafter cited as *Lynn Records*).

[5] Agents handled such issues as town boundaries, relations with absentee proprietors who founded some towns, and quarrels over the location of the town's church and school.

[6] Frequently men who had not served in any town offices were chosen to represent the town in the legislature—perhaps because they were willing to serve or had personal business in Boston.

formed by those living in the town and that dependence upon a representative was at best a second-rate way of doing business.

But Americans were by no means against government itself. While a few would hold that less government was good government, their concern was primarily about unnecessary government and rule from distant places. In fact, in ordinary life men were greatly dependent upon each other and did not hesitate to make laws regulating human relations. On the town level they rarely thought of limiting government. Whatever seemed necessary for human welfare was voted even if it involved interference in personal affairs. Appropriate subjects of legislation were matters of guardianship, poor relief, public worship, education, habits of dress, and property use. When issues became too complex, then townsmen turned to the colonial legislature, where the coordination of town efforts, defense, and the protection of natural resources were considered and acted upon. In much the same manner the British government was expected to perform tasks not within the capacity of the colony. In theory, representatives should have gone to Westminster to handle those large problems, but the colonial legislatures preferred using agents because the people feared the consequences of a loss of local power.

Since the people thought government was best at the level closest to them, their representatives held the same prejudices. Most rural representatives stayed long enough in the capital to manage the town's business and do some personal shopping. When their business was completed, they hurried home. Their habits were shared by other rural represesatives, and thus the early and late days of a legislative session had few members present.[7]

This homeward look reveals the fountainhead of political power. Representatives left family, friends, and property to serve in the capital, but they left them only temporarily. They had resolved that they were accepting service for the year, with the opportunity between sessions of visits to the town. At home they enjoyed the privilege of being deacons, officers of the militia, and selectmen, or the prestige of being members of the town's leading families. In the capital they lived in boarding houses, were often strangers in the

---

[7] Both weather conditions in winter and town business in late March affected attendance. Governors frequently apologized for special sessions and for extending them into the planting or harvest months.

city, and suffered a loss of identity in the assembly where they joined a hundred or more delegates.

Wearing homespun, they presented a curious, rustic sight to the stylish Bostonians who poked fun at their folksy manners. One haughty chief justice of the superior court described them as "horse jockies," a special type of local yokel whose country bumpkin ways, language, and demeanor reflected his rural background.[8] Other critics took note of their humorless manners, their ignorance of provincial affairs, and their dependence upon town instructions for direction.[9] While these farmers may have recognized their provincialism, they preferred the customs of the town to those of the capital. They compared their homespun stockings, pants, and shirts with the imported fabrics worn by their urban colleagues, and took pride in their costumes.

While the representatives from seaboard communities dressed more stylishly than the rural members, they also regarded the home town rather than the capital as the center of their lives. Ties of family and fortune drew them to the town where they had their basis of power. Though they had much private business in the assembly which generated for them opportunities in land investment and commerce, they shared with their rural colleagues the suspicion of distant government. They felt more at home in the town and spent most of the year there managing their stores, warehouses, and docks. Like the rural representatives, they were reminded by the town's instructions of their political obligations to which they were strictly bound. Some were ordered to account for the days spent in legislative business and others were required to return salary for any time away from duty.[10]

This attitude of the urban towns towards the legislature should not be mistaken. Few of them sent more than one representative to the assembly, and some towns suffered fines rather than send even one representative. Instead, seaboard communities often availed themselves of the practice of using agents to handle important busi-

---

[8] *Peter Oliver's Origin & Progress of the American Rebellion*, ed. Douglass Adair and John A. Schutz (Stanford, 1967), 27.

[9] Thomas Hutchinson denounced this dependence upon instructions as unconstitutional because it made the representative little more than a figurehead. Hutchinson to William Bollan, Nov. 22, 1766, Hutchinson Papers, XXVI, 468, Massachusetts Historical Society.

[10] *Lynn Records, 1742–1759*, pp. 47, 65.

ness. Even so, the principle of representation in the assembly was an accepted objective of political maturity as new communities, one after another, applied for the privilege. The privilege was valued in principle, however, more than in practice. Only two thirds of the Massachusetts towns regularly sent representatives, and less than half of these members stayed for the entire session. The seaboard towns used the privilege of representation more than the interior towns, but the towns, wherever their location, usually turned to themselves rather than to the assembly to solve their problems.

230   The attitude of the towns toward representation was also revealed by their prejudice toward long service in the assembly. Of the approximately one thousand representatives who served in the Massachusetts House of Representatives between 1740 and the American Revolution only a score served as many as fifteen years. Until the decade before the Revolution, few men served more than five consecutive terms, while most preferred service in the township to that in the legislature.[11] Even those who served many years in Boston failed to develop a power base. Instead, they were in the capital on business and expanded some effort in behalf of the town by attending legislative sessions. Of course, men of ability, who were skilled in the law, in argumentation, and in politics, rose in legislative ranks, but skill, more than tenure, determined their position.

Colonial attitudes toward the legislature plainly gave it a different kind of position than we grant our present state assemblies. The colonial saying, "Taxation without representation is tyranny," obviously emphasized the process of government, not personal representation or the voting of people for assemblymen. Most colonials favored the assembly as a deliberative body; it was there to do the people's business when they required it. The people expected it to meet regularly, to process the hundreds of petitions, and to grant the multitudes of exceptions to the law. In fact, the people thought of legislators as magistrates, important members of society to be sure, but judges rather than legislators, petty administrators rather than powerful executives. Indeed, society's awarding of prestige to them is indicative of popular esteem.

---

11 Those who had long tenures as town clerks, treasurers, and selectmen rarely moved to the office of representative. Some townsmen interrupted local service or served simultaneously in local and colonial office, but few regarded local experience as a prerequisite for colonial service.

Legislators could serve ten years or more in the House of Representatives and never move in social rank.[12] They were called "Mister." But those who managed to win a position as justice of the peace became esquire as did those who became major or colonel in the militia. This differential society awarded honors to deacons, ministers, judges, and captains and even greater honors to those in the higher echelons of government, but representatives remained "Misters." This humble position was recognized in some wills when former legislators referred to themselves as yeomen. In the towns men apparently won prominence by performing the assigned tasks of elective offices over years of devoted service. To be elected a select- *231* man or deacon was a mark of high distinction; to be a member of the town's leading family brought with it a seat of honor in the meetinghouse; to have served long and well in the town was finally recognized with a sturdy headstone in the local cemetery.

Good men, nonetheless, were attracted to assembly service; and some became legislative experts. Even though the leadership changed from session to session, it adhered to British parliamentary procedures, or developed similar rules of its own. The House of Representatives was conducted like a town meeting where men came and went as issues rose and fell. In the hall there was not sufficient room for everybody: those who arrived early were seated; others took seats as they became vacant; but many stood at crowded sessions and spoke from wherever they had a place.

The assembly functioned like a large committee, like a board of equalization in our day, hearing its committee reports, calling witnesses, listening to evidence, and deliberating before reaching a decision. At times two-thirds of legislative business was in the form of petitions and private bills, in which exceptions were made to current laws. A town missed its annual election because of a heavy snow fall; an innkeeper failed to file his annual request for a license; beneficiaries of a will needed clarification of the law; or an Indian landowner asked for legislative approval to sell his land. Another kind of legislative work took members into the colony in the performance of special tasks. They became petty administrators, acting as referees of disputes in the towns, as surveyors of town lines, as

---

12 Since many legislators served also as justices of the peace or militia officers, they gained social rank while they served as representatives. Election to the House often brought with it a commission as justice of the peace.

messengers, as commissioners of Indian affairs. They opened new tracts of land, presided at initial meetings of new towns, collected taxes, and stepped in during emergencies to aid the governor in the tasks of higher administration.[13]

Despite the seriousness of the business being transacted by the legislature, New Englanders had a curious attitude towards it. This attitude raises critical questions about the legislature's place in American life. Why were Massachusetts colonials so hesitant about sending delegates to Boston? Why did they change their representatives frequently? Why did the representatives often leave the assembly before the business of the year was completed? An answer to these questions may lie in the fact that the assembly was only one center of the governmental process. Other centers of representation were sometimes more useful and responsive to immediate needs than the distant assembly. At the town center, action was taken on most issues of local concern. Education, religious observance, law and order, taxation, and zoning were always sources of serious debate. At the church meetings, issues of the present and eternity were debated, sometimes causing great bitterness as the opinions of minister and deacons were severely challenged. In addition, at the Commons militia training contributed to the general welfare of the community. In providing military training for defense and order, the militia was a popular organization whose badges of leadership were eagerly sought. In the isolated, wilderness towns, men depended more upon each other than did those in settled areas. The twenty families of some frontier towns were well aware of the outside world, but for everyday living they called upon the selectmen, church, and the militia to give them the security to survive and the hope for future happiness.

The county was also a center of power, especially for the organization of the regiments and courts. The regiments were formed by grouping the companies of the towns and advancing to regimental positions those captains who had shown natural talents of leadership. These men took pride in their titles, thought of themselves as

232

---

13 See *The Acts and Resolves, Public and Private, of the Province of the Massachusetts Bay . . .* (Boston, 1869–1922), XVIII. The session of 1766–1767 considered 227 resolves and private bills. Two-thirds dealt with some exception to the law and about one-fourth required personal action in some form from the representatives in enforcing the law.

important people, and became a county aristocracy of talent.[14] In their positions of prestige they were often called upon to preside at the town meetings of their home township, to chair important town committees, and to sit as members of the legislative council for the colony. As barons of a sort they held such positions of honor as grand juror, deacon, and sheriff. Even though the militia leaders were important, they had competition from the judges in the quest for power. The judges included a group of functionaries who ranged from the justices of the peace in the town to the superior court justices for the colony. The J.P.s held court in the towns, swearing in officials, performing marriages, and handling petty disputes. Some joined others in performing services in the general sessions where such administrative tasks as the licensing of innkeepers and tavernkeepers were transacted. They provided also first instance criminal court review, and bound over offenders for the county court. From their hands cases went to the county judicial tribunal, the inferior court of common pleas, which handled most cases of local importance. Appeals were then taken to the colony's superior court and the governor's council.

233

Since the New England colonists used the courts an extraordinary number of times during their lives, these tribunals had far greater importance in the ordinary business of the colonies than do today's courts in the lives of American citizens.[15] Most men appeared on their own behalf in lower court proceedings, and as the cases pressed higher the litigants secured the services of professional attorneys who acted as advisors and spokesmen. Court dockets were crowded, burdened by the resort to the bench, and by the unusual number of appeals. Government for many people had more meaning through the opportunity to fight in court than to have a representative in the legislature.

The courts, like the militia, tied the towns into regional and county units. Towns were never isolated as governmental agencies, but were parts of judicial and militia units. Acting in cooperation with towns, the counties provided a large amount of self-

---

14 Governors frequently gave these leaders responsibility in filling militia posts and often relied upon them for advice on county politics. For example, see Israel Williams to Thomas Hutchinson, March 5, 1772, Hutchinson Papers, XXV, 508.

15 During the governorship of William Shirley (1741–1756) bills were passed limiting the number of court appeals because litigants were making excessive use of the privilege.

government. Most issues of life, death, and taxes were resolved on this community level. If the New England towns had been quiet, pastoral centers of life, "peaceable kingdoms," perhaps there would have been no need for this complex system of local government, but townsmen were industrious, assertive, and quarrelsome and trespassed regularly on each other's interests. When local appeals to town and county were insufficient, then help was secured from the legislature.

Otherwise, colonials contented themselves with the problems of town and region. These required an unusual amount of time and effort, partly because there were few professional administrators and most business was done by committees. The tasks involved a large number of people, but the hard labor fell upon a handful of men who had time and interest. The services of these people were in constant demand; and they, almost as an act of survival, scheduled their time among the various committees and agencies of government. Like the rest of the community, moreover, they had their crops to plant, tend, and harvest; their families and home problems to oversee.

234

For New England, therefore, there emerged an annual schedule of meetings for town, county, and colony governments so that a kind of rhythm of seasons and duties was imposed upon the lives of everyone.[16] When townsmen met in mid-March to choose their score or more officials, their act opened the new year of business. The annual meeting of the town was a time for assigning duties, making judgments of power, and getting a new start. In May the representative was chosen or not chosen, depending upon the will of the town meeting. In the meantime, landholders had their names put into a ballot box for the process of selecting men to serve as petit jurors and grand jurors. Town meetings were held in summer, fall, and winter, at times when all could attend, while meetings of the selectmen, town comittees, and the officials were held as tasks compelled action.

The work of the justice of the peace was determined less by the rhythm of yearly meetings than by the ordinary drudgery of life. But

---

[16] The times of court sessions were occasionally adjusted to meet the needs of the office holders. In the 1769–1770 General Court, the judicial court sessions of Barnstable were moved from the first Tuesday in April to the third Tuesday because "sundry of the Justices and Officers of said Courts and others concerned in the business thereof are members of this Court [legislature]." *The Acts and Resolves*, XVIII, 403.

as the chief officer of the town in charge of swearing in officials, issuing marriage licenses, and carrying out tasks of the county officials, he had a pattern of responsibility in his life. He also had duties as a justice at general sessions of the peace, when he met with other justices, reviewed criminal cases, issued licenses, and supervised town matters. For the justice, the quarterly horseback ride to the neighboring town was a regular duty, marking the season and the movement of events.

The rhythm of events occurred for the meeting of the county courts. The inferior courts of common pleas met at times of the year determined by the legislature so that litigants, attorneys, and judges could be at hand. Usually these courts were scheduled so that the circuit time of the superior court would coincide with the completion of local business.   235

The legislature had its schedule too. Its first session of the year occurred in late May and June. Other sessions followed in October, January, and March. The interlacing of interests and duties of members forced the legislature to schedule its sessions so that its members who were judges, justices of the peace, selectmen, and militia officers were not burdened by conflicting schedules.

Probably no agency of Massachusetts government was more involved in this scheduling of meetings than the council. Its twenty-eight members were chosen primarily because of their contribution to colonial life. As selectmen, committeemen, justices of the peace and quorum, judges and officers of the militia, they represented a spectrum of interests. Perhaps no group in the colony had a greater representation of those sharing the vital offices of colonial life than the council. Except for a few Boston counselors who were rich merchants, most men gained membership in the council as recognition of their positions in town and county government, and most spent part of every year in their home towns. They timed their return home so that they could attend the annual town meetings and be available as moderators, so that they could rise at the end of the meeting and report on business in the capital.[17]

---

17 Many councilors, like Ebenezer Burrill, Sr., of Lynn, served in local offices, while younger members of the family held other prestigious positions in the town at the same time. The younger Ebenezer was town clerk, treasurer, and selectman. Sometimes the tenure of family members, because of similarity of names, is difficult to determine with absolute accuracy.

Their love of home, like that of other townsmen, reflected their English Whig bias for country living. Almost everywhere Puritan gentlemen were good Whig politicians in their respect and love for the home seat. In this feeling they shared the English esteem for home rule. Most had a vested interest in the process of self government and the right to order their own lives through institutions of local control. For them town and county government in Massachusetts met the ordinary needs of law and order.

These provincial attitudes toward the Boston government were modified by the political events of the 1750s and 1760s. The intermittent warfare against Spain and France after 1739 opened colonial eyes to the power of the governor and assembly. The organization of the Cape Breton expedition in 1745 proved immensely popular, and the skillful capture of Fort Louisbourg aroused a sense of excitement that few past events had ever brought. Massachusetts now had heroes, military plunder, and tales of grandeur that challenged the pastoral traditions of town life. It also had a group of merchant and military investors who depended for their livelihood on war profits.[18]

Even though the War of the Austrian Succession ended in 1748 with the return of Louisbourg, apparently New Englanders never forgot the earlier capture. Men proudly remembered the siege, counted their scars, and retold their acts of heroism. The fame of Louisbourg in their minds was probably never overshadowed by other battles, although younger men, in the Seven Years' War, remembered more vividly the Louisbourg victory of 1758 than that of 1745, the capture of Quebec and Montreal, and the sea battles in the St. Lawrence. Others remembered the military marches in New York, along the lakes to Crown Point, and beside the rivers of Maine.

The wars broke down the insularity of towns by encouraging men to return to the rich frontier country that they had seen as soldiers. The House of Representatives responded to the wishes of these restless people by creating new counties in western Massachusetts and eastern Maine, by granting town charters to scores of communities, and by sanctioning land-development organizations which

18 John A. Schutz, *William Shirley: King's Governor of Massachusetts* (Chapel Hill, 1961), chaps. V, VI.

founded the new towns of the 1770s and 1780s. The promoters looked to the legislature for help, and it generated the opportunities for land sales and profits.

The enlarged role of the legislature in colony affairs was reflected in the sessions of the 1750s that were longer than those of the 1740s. Business in some years multiplied by fifty to seventy-five percent.[19] On the surface the problems of the 1750s seemed to be primarily military, for the colony established forts and fortified places in western Massachusetts and eastern Maine. In actuality, promoters were laying plans for the large scale land developments of the 1760s and 70s. The creation of Berkshire, Cumberland, and Lincoln counties seemed premature in 1761, but those county organizations undoubtedly resolved many legal problems as the people rushed into these areas in the mid-1760s.

237

Probably the most impressive development in the legislature was the attraction to it of energetic and prominent men. The two James Otises, father and son, joined the House of Representatives in 1760.[20] The father was immediately elected speaker, a recognition of his long service as a political manager for Governor William Shirley. His return to top leadership after three years absence in Barnstable brought new policies to bear on House organization and conduct. Greater emphasis than before was placed upon the use of experienced representatives in House business, and the committee system was modified slightly to allow some committees to handle more than one issue.

The Otises more than any other leaders brought to prominence questions of assembly power, rights of privacy, and the concentration of administrative positions in the hands of a clique.[21] Their prominence as legislators contrasted sharply with past leadership. From the beginning of charter government in 1691, only a few men had gained much distinction in legislative service. Their reputations had usually been made as opponents of the governor and his friends, but it was difficult to penetrate the power of the administra-

---

19 A rough measure of size can be made from the published legislative record. Usually the business of most legislative years can be published in one volume, but for 1755–1756, 1756–1757, and 1760–1761 two volumes were required.

20 John J. Waters and John A. Schutz, "Patterns of Massachusetts Colonial Politics: The Writs of Assistance and the Rivalry between the Otis and Hutchinson Families," *William and Mary Quarterly*, XXIV (1967), 558–567.

21 John J. Waters, Jr., *The Otis Family in Provincial and Revolutionary Massachusetts* (Chapel Hill, 1968), chap. VII.

tion. To attract public attention they often had to speak brashly on the House floor and get themselves expelled from the House or make spectacles of themselves in taverns. While the Otises acted in the same fashion—and with some special peculiarities of their own—they also broke new ground as legislative leaders. They gathered to themselves a group of followers who provided opposition to various governmental acts from admiralty regulations to administrative policies. They also took their policies to a wide public audience by using newspapers and pamphlets.

238 To succeed, however, they had to attack the governor's administration, which was filled with his friends and supporters. His most powerful spokesman, Thomas Hutchinson, had long dominated the central administration and was then serving as lieutenant governor, chief of the superior court, and councillor. Hutchinson's brother-in-law was the colony's secretary and also a councillor. Other relatives held seats on the superior court bench, the probate court, and the Suffolk County bench in addition to other offices. By holding these positions, they effectively closed the administration to the new legislative politician, who, in disgust, now denounced them as the governor's corrupt placemen.[22]

For four years the Otises criticized the governor and his party with great vigor, but they suffered ridicule more than they won applause because they were not able to find a solid basis of opposition. In the meantime, the assembly's liberal land policies rewarded promoters who sought legislation for land development. New towns were admitted to assembly representation, and the number of representatives regularly attending legislative sessions grew slowly.

Finally, the Stamp Act controversy gave the Otises an issue—but the issue at first was better comprehended by their associates than by themselves. For a time they wavered between approving some form of British taxation and offering opposition. With the advice of Samuel Adams, Oxenbridge Thatcher, and James Bowdoin, they became less confused and approved a policy of direct assaults upon the opposition. Their attack took the form of two well-directed riots, in which some British property was burned. Thomas Hutchinson's home was also destroyed, but he escaped physical harm by hiding from the rioters. In the next elections the Otis party con-

22 *Boston Gazette*, Feb. 28, April 4, May 17, 1763; *Boston News-Letter*, April 7, 1763; *Boston Evening-Post*, April 25, 1763.

tinued its attack on Hutchinson and his friends by removing them from the council.[23] Over the next three years the party also succeeded in removing many of Hutchinson's supporters from the House of Representatives by advertising votes on sensitive issues and by convincing the town electorate to send other men. The House, thus purged, concentrated its energy upon making British taxation the political issue that would draw into Boston support from the towns.

But the towns associated the Otis opposition with Boston politics, the violence toward British property, and the hostility toward Hutchinson and his friends. While most towns supported the opposition toward British taxation, they worried about the reactions of the British government and the assault upon the property and person of distinguished colonials, and they held Boston responsible for the violence. Most towns refused to pay compensation to the riot victims. Although they granted the justice of the claims, they insisted that the Boston taxpayers alone compensate for the damage. But the towns also gave their support to the more pacific nonimportation agreements that were used to oppose the Townshend Duties. In addition, they sent circular letters urging other colonies to support the nonimportation agreements. When these letters were hostilely received by the British government, however, the towns hesitated to accept the Otis demand for an illegal legislative session, and a significant number of towns reassessed the measures of opposition.[24] A few towns even denounced the radical protests that appeared in the newspapers.

Through nonviolent means, many towns joined the attack upon the Stamp Act and Townshend Duties, but they were disturbed by the mob actions in Boston and other seacoast communities. Townspeople instructed their representatives to resist this kind of hostility toward Britain. Some conservative legislators even absented them-

239

---

[23] Hutchinson reflected the bitterness of the campaign in these words: "They [the opposition] have chosen four or five new ones [councillors] little better than the scum who I suppose the governor must negative though I have had no conversation with him about them." Hutchinson to unknown, May 29, 1766, Hutchinson Papers, XXVI, 233.

[24] Those representatives who came to Boston were unusually cautious, and some feared the consequences of the illegal assembly. Hutchinson described their hesitancy with contempt: "They met and spent a week and made themselves ridiculous and then dissolved themselves after a message or two to the Governor." Hutchinson to Thomas Whately, Oct. 5, 1768, *ibid.*, XXV, 281-282.

selves from the legislature rather than face the ridicule of the Otis opposition.[25] For most people the issue at Boston was not taxation without representation, but how to express legitimate opposition to Britain without destroying the empire. Many towns in bewilderment sent no representatives; others sent men who attended sessions only when issues directly affecting the town were discussed.

In spite of absenteeism and hesitancy the towns sent to Boston more representatives in the 1770s than in any previous decade. The tenure of members was also longer. The experience thus gained by legislators encouraged them to speak out on issues, and there developed regional leaders of great force and influence. Men like Joseph Hawley, the member from Northampton, who was particularly powerful with the Connecticut River representatives and those from seaport and market towns, also found their voices. Oratory became such a popular part of legislative business that a gallery was constructed in the House so that townsmen could hear speeches from the floor.[26] The gallery symbolized the change in House procedures. Instead of the routine transactions of committees, the House floor became more and more a center of debate and oratory—a place, too, for exercising leadership talents and demagogy.

The representatives spoke so much to their gallery of tradesmen and workers that the governor found an excuse for removing the legislature to Cambridge. Out at the college, in its rarefied pastoral setting, the governor hoped that the legislators would return to their older habits. Instead, they debated principles of legislative procedure and exchanged state papers with the governor and refused to transact business. The impasse lasted for months until a compromise was finally worked out. But when the House members returned to Boston, they opened the gallery to admirers.

As the crisis of the Revolution mounted, legislators used newspapers and pamphlets to express their positions, and some representatives spoke at patriotic organizations to spread their personal

---

25 John Worthington, a powerful and distinguished representative from Springfield, described his embarrassment in these words: "The Jealousy and Suspicion with which I seem'd to be Viewed by Most of the Members the last Session made my Scituation at Court very unpleasant." Worthington to Hutchinson, Sept. 15, 1770, *ibid.*, XXV, 427–428a.

26 The gallery was small, but it gave the speakers an opportunity to address the townsmen and thereby spread their opinions. It also officially opened the House floor to the public and broke down the traditional secrecy of legislative proceedings.

feelings. A few seaboard representatives dressed in homespun in order to gain popular esteem, thus joining the rural members in making the rustic dress a patriotic one. House leadership published votes of members on important issues, and those representatives who backed unfavorable positions found themselves sharply criticized in the press. The amazing fact, however, was the reluctance of the towns to enlarge substantially the base of representation in the House. They regularly sent only half to three-quarters of the potential numbers of representatives to Boston and even then they worried about the power of these men. To limit their initiative, the towns enlarged the practice of instructing the delegates.

241

Even though townspeople became increasingly angry over British policy in the 1770s, their anger did not immediately bring forth greater representation. When Britain threatened to pay executive and judicial officials, the attack on the independence of the bureaucracy was protested, strongly and solemnly. When the governor suspended legislative sessions or moved the legislature from the capital, the disturbance to ordinary business was memorialized in vigorous and, often, abusive language. When Britain ordered changes in the Charter of 1691 that threatened the whole fabric of liberty and constitutionalism, at that point representation in the legislature finally became an issue, and most towns responded affirmatively. Until this crisis when the Charter of 1691 was emasculated and the British Intolerable Acts were imposed upon the colony, the towns had contented themselves with appointing committees of correspondence, gathering arms, and taking measures to limit British imports.

In 1774 when the crisis became an open confrontation, with the charter shredded and the legislature moved to Salem, the towns looked upon representation in the legislature as a necessity for political existence. They answered the calls for provincial congresses in October 1774 and February and May 1775 with great seriousness. Towns, with or without legislative rights, sent delegates. Towns, without available delegates, recruited men from neighboring towns. In fact, many towns dispatched alternate delegates so that, if the regular representative was ill or out of the legislature on business, a substitute could stand in his place.[27]

In 1775, when the first independent House of Representatives

---

[27] Most towns also sent a full delegation. Representation, as a result, was nearly doubled.

met, bills for extending the privilege of representation were passed, thus qualifying most communities to send delegates. So many representatives were present in the sessions of the 1775 and 1776 legislatures that standing room only was available even on ordinary days.

The popularity of the legislature increased as it faced the problems of revolution. Those problems of defense and political reorganization were handled efficiently and with courage and determination. The legislature attracted talented men from the towns to fill administrative offices and raised money to pay the ordinary costs of government. Patriotic fervor in the towns supported these activities and most towns required assurances of loyalty from their citizens.

But the revolution had little effect on the administration in the towns. They continued past procedures, and the rhythm of life was generally uninterrupted; men were still concerned with problems of education, religion, land titles, fencing, and other day-to-day concerns. The appearance of peace and order was generally deceptive. Some men were away on military duty; the war brought a heavy burden of taxes; loyalty was imposed on belligerent persons. Men speculated, too, on the future political order, worried about the loosening of political ties, and criticized the wide enfranchisement of citizens and the extension of representation to small frontier towns.[28] Many men also agitated for a new charter, one as balanced and representative as that of 1691, and one that was reflective of the "natural rights" of the people. Some men also wanted continued freedom to live without much outside interference, but the towns, particularly those in eastern Massachusetts, recognized their dependence upon state government. They faced a dilemma: most preferred the rural life of British America under the Charter of 1691 with its semi-independent existence; but most also accepted the fact of revolution, with its greater involvement in state matters, and the need for a new constitution.

The political order, therefore, had to be delineated, and the towns, meeting in county congresses, applied pressure on the House of Representatives for a new document. In 1777 the legislature, meeting as a constitutional convention, drew up a document similar to the old British Charter of 1691, though it weakened those agen-

---

[28] See the "Resolutions of the Essex County Convention," April 25, 1776, in the Massachusetts Archives, CLVI, 192–193, State House, Boston; and Boston town records, 1770 through 1777, in *A Report of the Record Commissioners of the City of Boston* (Boston, 1887), 237–238.

cies that had been peculiarly British. The proposal was immediately rejected by the town meetings which insisted upon an elected convention to draw a constitution.[29] In 1778 the towns of Essex County, in a special congress, observed that representation in any constitution should be "fixed upon known and easy principles" that were "sacred and inviolable." They condemned proposals for a single legislative assembly, because it could be "influenced by the vices, follies, passions, and prejudices of an individual."[30] They urged, instead, the creation of a strong executive, a fair court system, and a popular administration. These agencies of government, whatever their powers, should be appropriately balanced one against the other. They also urged a bill of rights, guarantees against excessive use of power, and a government ever solicitous to the general interest. The Essex convention, it should be noted, regarded state government as a vital force in the lives of the people and insisted upon the calling of a constitutional convention.

243

The legislature finally obliged. In 1779 the people chose delegates for a convention, and the result, after much debate in town meetings, was the Massachusetts constitution of 1780. It was explicit in defining the powers of government, cautious in granting representation in the legislature, and careful in providing guarantees against abuse of power. It outlawed multiple office holding of the kind that had made Thomas Hutchinson powerful.[31] General satisfaction greeted the finished constitution. In 1780 the meetings of the new House of Representatives were full of new members, but some towns, as in colonial times, soon neglected to send representatives. Fifteen percent of the towns voted negative when the moderators of the town meetings asked the question: Shall the town be represented at Boston?

With the constitutional system again established and Boston again in good hands, townsmen once more turned inwardly. Happy in the thought that the crisis had ended, they returned to the rhythm of rural life: the annual elections of town officials, the debates over education, roadmaking, and taxes, and the pleasures of their private lives.

---

29 Most Massachusetts towns enclosed with their election returns a list of objections to the 1778 Constitution. See "Return of Lexington," June 15, 1778, Massachusetts Archives, CLX, 24–27.

30 Theophilus Parsons, Jr., *Memoir of Theophilus Parsons* (Boston, 1859), 359–402.

31 *Massachusetts Constitution of 1780*, Part I, Articles VIII and XXX.

New York Lawyers and the Coming of the American Revolution

By MILTON M. KLEIN

Neither their contemporaries nor historians have evaluated the role of lawyers in the American Revolution. Milton M. Klein, Professor of History at the University of Tennessee in Knoxville, analyzes that role and offers a hypothesis.

I N HIS famous Speech on Conciliation with America delivered in the House of Commons on March 22, 1775, Edmund Burke paid his respects to the colonial lawyers as one source of that "fierce spirit of liberty" which made the problem of easing the imperial crisis so difficult:

> In no country, perhaps, in the world is the law so general a study. The profession itself is numerous and powerful, and in most provinces it takes the lead. The greater number of deputies sent to the Congress were lawyers. But all who read, and most do read, endeavor to obtain some smattering in that science. I have been told by an eminent bookseller, that in no branch of his business, after tracts of popular devotion, were so many books as those on the law exported to the plantations.

Why, then, queried Burke, had not such knowledge taught the Americans more clearly the nature of their "obligations to obedience, and the penalties of rebellion"? Simply because Britain had not managed to win over such knowledge to the service of the Crown. Instead, study of the law rendered the colonists "stubborn and litigious . . . dextrous, prompt in attack, [and] ready in defence" of their legal rights. A citizenry so well versed in law and led by lawyers did not await grievances to assay the evil of the principles on which they were grounded; rather it anticipated the evils of the grievances to the degree that they violated the principles which Americans held dear. Such a people "augur misgovernment at a distance, and sniff the approach of tyranny in every tainted breeze."[1]

At the turn of the nineteenth century, George Otto Trevelyan, the Whig historian of the Revolution, encapsulated Burke's sentiments in a neater exposition. Lawyers, he observed, should have been loyalists by and large since many of them held positions under the Crown, and all who practiced in the courts were, in effect, public servants of the royal governments; but instead, he noted, "most lawyers were patriots, for the same reason that . . . every patriot was, or thought himself, a lawyer."[2]

Subsequent historians have not capitalized on either Burke's or Trevelyan's perceptive observations, nor have numerous schools of historians since rendered any more tribute to the legal profession than did the revolutionary generation itself. Participants in the Revolution gave the leading role to lawyers by naming thirty members of the bar to the First Continental Congress (out of a total delegation of fifty-six), by having twenty-five lawyers affix their signatures to the Declaration of Independence (about half that constellation of immortals), and by sending no less than thirty-one of the profession (about half of all the delegates) to sit in Philadelphia during the summer of 1787 and organize that "more perfect union" which marked the close of the revolutionary era. Yet the task of appraising their role in these events and of elucidating its meaning has thus far eluded historiographical treatment.

Revolutions, of course, are very complex affairs, and their precise political and social anatomy has defied analysis despite generations of scholarly postmortems. The study of leadership in the making and shaping of revolutions is no less fascinating but equally elusive. Those of our own day that go by the name of "black revolution" or "student revolution" are illustrative case studies in the complexity of the problem. Intuitive and superficial examinations produced the hasty conclusion that these disruptions in the social order were led by the most disadvantaged elements in those communities, those elements most disturbed by the material deprivations of the system and hence reacting on the most personal of grounds—self-interest.

245

---

[1] *The Writings and Speeches of Edmund Burke,* 12 vols. (Boston, 1901), II, 124–125.

[2] George O. Trevelyan, *The American Revolution,* new ed., 4 vols. (London, 1905–1913), I, 73.

Closer and more systematic analysis has disclosed a surprisingly different collective portrait—of individuals more rooted in the community than rootless, more prosperous than deprived, more fortunate than unsuccessful, and more disinterested than self-interested.

For that distant event called the American Revolution, we are indebted to two centuries of amateur and professional diagnosticians, but we are not much closer to concluding our postmortems as to the nature or the leadership of the affair. It is not likely that the approaching bicentennial celebration will complete the analysis or terminate the discussion; it will merely escalate the level of historiographical activity and proliferate the multiplicity of scholarly findings. Historians would not want it otherwise. How else would they find grist for their never-ending intellectual and literary mills? Carl Becker, who delighted in criticizing the historianship of others even more than he enjoyed writing history himself, once confessed that he secretly hoped the day would never come when "all fields of history having been 'definitely' done and presented in properly dull and documented monographs, the final synthesis could be made." What would historians do then, he worried?[3] If Thomas Jefferson's forewarning was at all omniscient, we need not worry about the historiography of the Revolution. Responding in 1815 to John Adams's query, "Who shall write the history of the American revolution? Who can write it? Who will ever be able to write it?" Jefferson said:

Nobody; except merely its external facts. All its councils, designs, and discussions, having been conducted by Congress with closed doors, and no members, as far as I know, having ever made notes of them, those, which are the life and soul of history must forever be unknown.[4]

Jefferson's gloomy forecast has not been entirely realized, although his warning may well give us pause as we immodestly attempt to confound it by the diligence and extent of our modern researches. But surely we have learned much about the American Revolution since its first chroniclers crudely narrated the event for posterity; and we are able with hind-

246

---

[3] Review of J. B. Black, *The Art of History, American Historical Review*, XXXII (1927), 295.

[4] John Adams to Thomas Jefferson, July 30, 1815, Jefferson to Adams, Aug. 10, 1815, *The Adams-Jefferson Letters*, ed. Lester Cappon, 2 vols. (Chapel Hill, 1959), II, 451–452.

Cadwallader Colden, by an unidentified artist. Courtesy of the New-York Historical Society, New York City.

sight to diagnose somewhat better its anatomy. Crane Brinton's effort in 1938 to do just that for the American, French, Russian, and English Revolutions concluded that, as to leadership, all four revealed an extraordinary degree of moderation but that the American Revolution, particularly, was led by men who were of "striking respectability and excellent social standards."[5] More sophisticated and recent attempts to construct a theory of revolution modify Brinton's generalizations considerably but help little in understanding the American Revolution. Its leadership was not that of an aggrieved peasantry, a millenarian and charismatic single figure, a palace guard, a jacquerie, a nostalgic group of reactionaries, or a militarized mass in insurrection.[6] Its roots seem to have been less economic, sociological, or psychological than political, and central to any political revolution—in the view of today's theorists—is the role of an elite which feels itself alienated from the existing political order.[7]

[5] Crane Brinton, *The Anatomy of Revolution* (1938; Vintage ed., New York, 1957), p. 107.
[6] Lawrence Stone, "Theories of Revolution," *World Politics,* XVIII (1966), 159–176, particularly 162–163. The typology summarized by Stone is that of Chalmers Johnson.
[7] On this, see Stone, "Theories of Revolution," p. 165; Harry Eckstein, "On the Etiology of Internal War," *History and Theory,* IV (1965), 133–163; and Isaac Kramnick, "Reflections on Revolution: Definition and Explanation in Recent Scholarship," *ibid.,* XI (1972), 26–63.

If it is the anomie of the elite which caused the American Revolution—or which was its underlying imperative—then an analysis of the composition, nature, and mentality of this elite should tell us much of the character of the Revolution itself. That the colonies had developed such "stable, coherent, effective, and acknowledged local political and social elites," with considerable experience, visibility, authority, and broad public support seems amply demonstrable.[8] That astute if biased observer of events in colonial New York, Cadwallader Colden, adumbrated the findings of later social psychologists in noting, in 1732, that "few instances can be given where great changes were brought to effect, in any state, but when they were headed by Rich and powerful men; any other commotions generally only produced short lived disorders and Confusions."[9] It is a commonplace, too, to distinguish certain professional and occupational groups among this American elite: the merchants, the planters, the newspaper printers and editors, the clergy, and the lawyers; but the role of each of these groups in the leadership of the Revolution is not equally well known. Almost fifteen years ago, I called attention to the fact that while there were excellent monographs on the part played by the merchants, the clergy, and the press in the coming of the Revolution, there were none on the lawyers.[10] Since that time, we have had two more published studies on the influence of religion and the clergy but not one on the lawyers.[11] The ne-

[8] See Jack Greene, "An Uneasy Connection: An Analysis of the Preconditions of the American Revolution," in Stephen Kurtz and James Hutson, eds., *Essays on the American Revolution* (Chapel Hill, 1973), pp. 35–36, and Greene, "Changing Interpretations of Early American Politics," in Ray A. Billington, ed., *The Reinterpretation of Early American History* (San Marino, Cal., 1966), pp. 171–177.

[9] "The State of the Lands in the Province of New York, in 1732," in E. B. O'Callaghan, ed., *Documentary History of the State of New York*, 4 vols. (Albany, 1849–1851), I, 385.

[10] Klein, "Prelude to Revolution in New York: Jury Trials and Judicial Tenure," *William and Mary Quarterly*, XVII (1960), 440. The monographs to which attention was called were Arthur M. Schlesinger, *The Colonial Merchants and the American Revolution* (New York, 1918); Alice M. Baldwin, *The New England Clergy and the American Revolution* (Durham, N. C., 1928); Philip Davidson, *Propaganda and the American Revolution* (Chapel Hill, 1941); and Schlesinger, *Prelude to Independence: The Newspaper War on Britain, 1764–1776* (New York, 1958).

[11] Carl Bridenbaugh, *Mitre and Sceptre: Transatlantic Faiths, Ideas, Personalities, and Politics, 1689–1775* (New York, 1962); and Alan Heimert, *Religion and the American Mind from the Great Awakening to the Revolution* (Cambridge, Mass., 1966).

glect is not surprising when it is learned that between 1861
and 1972, of all the dissertations completed during that century—and there were over 400,000, some 14,000 of them in
history—only 22 deal with law and lawyers and only 5 of them
with members of the colonial or revolutionary bar. One treats
of the relation of English law to the coming of the Revolution,
one deals with Virginia lawyers, two with the Massachusetts
bar, and only one covers the legal career of an early New York
lawyer.[12]

The myopia of later Americans was not shared by the earliest historians of the Revolution on this side of the Atlantic.
One of the first patriot accounts, that of David Ramsay,
emphasized how much the event was a lawyer affair:

249

> Of the whole number of deputies which formed the Continental Con-
> gress of 1774, one half were lawyers. Gentlemen of that profession
> had acquired the confidence of the inhabitants by their exertion in
> the common cause. The previous measures in the respective provinces
> had been planned and carried into effect, more by lawyers than by
> any other order of men. Professionally taught the rights of the people,
> they were among the foremost to decry every attack made on their
> liberties. Bred in the habits of public speaking, they made a distin-
> guished figure in the meetings of the people, and were particularly
> able to explain to them the tendency of the late acts of Parliament.
> Exerting their abilities and influence in the cause of their country, they
> were rewarded with its confidence.[13]

If the Revolution was indeed precipitated by the actions of
its social and political elite, then lawyers not unexpectedly
took high rank in that privileged order. "Lawyer or merchant
are the fairest titles our towns afford," wrote the Frenchman
Crèvecoeur as he explained to his countrymen just what an
American was like.[14] Of all the professional groups in the
colonies—and they made up only 1–2 percent of the population—lawyers constituted the vast proportion, some 70 percent. And they were the wealthiest of all the professionals,
earning as a group ten times as much as doctors and minis-

---

[12] *Comprehensive Dissertation Index, 1861–1972,* 37 vols. (Ann Arbor,
1973), XXVIII, 430–431. The number of dissertations listed in these vol
umes is about 417,000. The figure of 13,579 in history is given in Warren
F. Kuehl, *Dissertations in History* (Lexington, 1972), p. x. The total includes U.S. and Canadian dissertations completed between 1873 and 1970.

[13] David Ramsay, *History of the American Revolution,* 2 vols. (London,
1793; reprinted, New York, 1968), I, 134.

[14] J. Hector St. John de Crèvecoeur, *Letters from an American Farmer*
(1782; Dutton Everyman ed., New York, 1957), p. 36.

ters and as much as the very wealthiest merchants and planters.[15] A recent study of some 231 high office holders in all the
colonies finds that while planters and merchants included some
who possessed average wealth only, all the lawyers in this
group were wealthy or well-to-do.[16] Commenting on the economic status of lawyers in Virginia shortly after the Revolution, the French traveler, La Rochefoucault-Liancourt, observed: "The profession of a lawyer is here, as in every other
part of America, one of the most profitable."[17]

250   How, then, are we to explain the relative inattention paid by
historians to the vital role played by this signally important
intellectual group in the coming of the Revolution? Apart
from the sheer magnitude of the task—scores of important
figures and hundreds of lesser ones must be dealt with—perhaps historiography and self-imagery suggest an explanation.
The earliest historians of the Revolution represented the event
as the rising of a united people, "under no general influence,
but that of their personal feelings and opinions," led by no
special powerful individuals, and motivated by democratic
sentiments produced by "nature and society" with which
they "grew up, from their earliest infancy."[18] George Bancroft,
who fixed this view in our historiographical literature for more
than a half-century, reiterated that the Revolution stemmed
from "the excitement of a whole people." Each event in the
unfolding process was ascribed to the efforts of a united citizenry. It was universal watchfulness that prevented Britain
from eroding American rights and liberties by the Stamp Act;
and the "whole continent" applauded the sacking of Hutchinson's house in Boston. Obviously, there was no need to stress
the leadership role of any group in a movement which did not
stem from the novelty of any single tax but was deeply rooted,
divinely ordained, and one "which no human policy or force
could hold back"—"as certain as the decrees of eternity."[19]

[15] James Kirby Martin, *Men in Rebellion* (New Brunswick, N. J., 1973),
pp. 66, 68–69; Jackson T. Main, *The Social Structure of Revolutionary
America* (Princeton, 1965), p. 101.
[16] Martin, *Men in Rebellion*, p. 85.
[17] Quoted in Main, *Social Structure*, p. 102.
[18] Jeremy Belknap, *History of New Hampshire* (1812), III, 172, quoted
in Arthur H. Schaffer, "The Shaping of a National Tradition: Historical
Writing in America, 1783–1820" (unpublished Ph.D. dissertation, UCLA,
1966), p. 69; Samuel Williams, *Natural and Civil History of Vermont* (Walpole, N. H., 1794), p. 376; Ramsay, *American Revolution*, I, 31.

This nationalist school of historians would have found it awkward to suggest that the American people had to be led into revolution by any elite segment rather than arising in righteous unity to achieve a heaven-sent mission.

The Progressive historians, who dominated American historiography at the beginning of the twentieth century, emphasized internal conflicts within the colonies and economic and social issues within the empire. For one of these, Louis Hacker, the contest was not at all over "high-sounding political and constitutional concepts: over the power of taxation and, in the final analysis, over natural rights." It was, rather, issues such as manufacturing, trade, currency, and western lands which lay at the heart of the struggle.[20] And to another historian of this persuasion, Arthur M. Schlesinger,

251

> The popular view of the Revolution as a great forensic controversy over abstract rights will not bear close scrutiny. . . . At best, an exposition of the political theories of the anti-parliamentary party is an account of their retreat from one strategic position to another . . . . it may as well be admitted that the colonists would have lost their case if the decision had turned upon an impartial consideration of the legal principles involved.[21]

To historians for whom principle was subordinate to material self-interest, and legal rhetoric a mere camouflage for more basic matters of economic and financial import, the role of lawyers was necessarily minimal. For the Progressives, the Revolution was made in the streets, not in the council chambers; and artisans, merchants, and planters were the protagonists, if not the heroes. Far from stressing the role of law in American history, the Progressives emphasized that "lawlessness has been and is one of the most distinctive American traits." In the dual movement which the Revolution represented to Carl Becker, legal resistance was employed in the contest with England; but in the more important struggle over who should rule at home, spontaneous explosions of popular feeling and outbursts of mass violence were more determina-

---

[19] George Bancroft, *History of the United States from the Discovery of the American Continent*, 10 vols. (Boston, 1870–1879), V, 291, 313, 321; VII, 21.

[20] Louis M. Hacker, "The First American Revolution," *Columbia University Quarterly*, XXVII (1935), 290.

[21] Arthur M. Schlesinger, *New Viewpoints in American History* (New York, 1922), p. 179.

tive of events than those petitions and resolves which bespoke constitutional and legal principles.[22]

Curiously, members of the legal profession did not fare much better with the neo-Conservative school of American historiography which flowered in the post-World War II era. For a principal spokesman of this school, Daniel Boorstin, what distinguished the American Revolution from others was its failure to give birth to a new political theory. Assuming that American history represented a continuity based upon those persistent values that were "givens" from the past, Boorstin stressed the failure of the Revolution to disrupt this continuity by producing any new dogma. At best, the event was for Americans merely an opportunity to affirm what was traditionally British in their heritage. If lawyers argued the case at all, it was not as theorists but merely as more articulate spokesmen of sentiments which all Americans understood—their English birthright. In a curious paradox, Boorstin concedes that what was at issue in 1776 was not a large political principle but merely a technical legal question, the constitution of the empire. The Declaration of Independence thus did not have to expound any new "high-flown political philosophy"; Americans already possessed it. Yet while one would have expected Boorstin to thereupon emphasize the role of the bar in expostulating the American legal position, he does not, escaping the dilemma by suggesting that since all Americans were versed in law, they required no specialists to speak for them. It was the "universal voice of our country" (quoting Jefferson) which responded to the British challenge. English principles did not have to be justified anew: they were already well known; no new American principles had to be explained: they were still to be discovered. In an era of law without lawyers, of institutions and principles so "given" that they need not be reduced to theoretical definition, there was obviously no call for lawyers to make the American case.[23]

252

---

[22] James T. Adams, "Our Lawless Heritage," *Atlantic Monthly*, CXLV (1928), 732; Carl Becker, *History of Political Parties in the Province of New York* (Madison, Wis., 1909), pp. 21–22, 26, 28, 79–80; Arthur M. Schlesinger, "Political Mobs and the American Revolution, 1765–1776," *Proceedings* of the American Philosophical Society, XCIX (1955), 244–250.

[23] For Boorstin's views, see his *Genius of American Politics* (Chicago, 1953), chap. 3, and *The Americans: The Colonial Experience* (New York, 1958), pp. 191–205. For other neo-Conservative historians, who see the Revolution essentially as a war of national liberation, the transition from

One of the most recent schools of historiography, represented by Bernard Bailyn, stresses the centrality of the new world view which Americans developed by 1776 of their relationship with Great Britain. The sources of this general mood or "map of social reality," which Bailyn designated as ideology, were widespread; and they included the tradition of English common law. But, as Bailyn defined it, common law was less a collection of legal principles and experiences than "a form of history" which, presumably, was understood, appreciated, and cited by broader elements in the population than merely the practitioners of the law. Besides, common law as a source of American ideology ranked well below Enlightenment ideas and attitudes, the Classics, New England Puritan thought, and the political theories of the English "Commonwealthmen" in shaping American perceptions of themselves and their relationship with Britain. In any case, what moved Americans to action in 1776, according to Bailyn, was a cluster of fears, emotions, and convictions of almost evangelical fervor arising from their settled belief that the colonists' whole way of life was being endangered by British tyranny. Surely, the "abstruse points of constitutional law that so engaged the mind" of lawyers like John Adams did not propel Americans into revolution; implicitly, neither did the lawyers.[24]

253

For the most recent school of American historians, the angry young men of the profession and its "New Left," lawyers no less than merchants, planters, and clergymen represent skewed mirrors of the past. Our preoccupation with their thoughts and deeds has caused us to view history from the top down. These radical members of the profession would prefer an account from the other perspective, and although they have not yet drawn its outlines fully, it is clear that the history of the powerless and the inarticulate will not be exposited in their pages through the mouths of the lawyer class.[25]

---

colonial to national status required no special philosophical or legalistic justification. See, for example, Thomas C. Barrow, "The American Revolution as a Colonial War for Independence," *William and Mary Quarterly,* XXV (1968), 452–464.

[24] For Bailyn's view, see his *Ideological Origins of the American Revolution* (Cambridge, Mass., 1967), chap. 2, and "The Central Themes of the American Revolution," in Kurtz and Hutson, eds., *Essays on the American Revolution,* pp. 3–31.

[25] For the New Left view of the Revolution, see Jesse Lemisch, "Jack Tar in the Streets: Merchant Seamen in the Politics of Revolutionary America," *William and Mary Quarterly,* XXV (1968), 371–407; and his "The American

Explanatory as our historiographical survey is for the neglect of the lawyers, it is insufficient; but it is buttressed by a historical phenomenon. The revolutionary generation may have been led by lawyers, but it was also suspicious of them. It was as much mistrustful of law as it was willing to employ the law in defense of its constitutional rights. The love-hate syndrome extended into the years of the early republic, when Jeffersonians attacked the common law for its intricacies and its authoritarianism, yet were unwilling to abandon it. The American constitutional system, it was clear, was based on principles of law, equity, and justice, but these principles ought to be so plain and simple that any man could understand them. The spirit of the law was the foundation of republican virtue; its letter must not be appropriated by shrewd lawyers as an instrument of anti-republican self-interest.[26] The ambivalence of early America was neatly expressed by James Fenimore Cooper's Natty Bumppo: "The law—'tis bad to have it, but I sometimes think it is worse to be entirely without it."[27]

The dualism was evident in colonial America. New York's merchant prince John Watts was an intimate of the colony's lawyers and employed them in his own business; yet he denounced the law as a "System of confounding other People and picking their Pockets." William Livingston studied the law and became a leading member of the profession, but he objected to many of its principles as against "Reason and common sense" and many of its practitioners as "unletter'd Blockheads."[28] The general attitude was early expressed by a Welshman after a fifteen-year residence in Pennsylvania: "Of Lawyers and Physicians I shall say nothing, because this Country is very Peaceable and Healthy; long may it so continue and never have occasion for the Tongue of the one, or the Pen of

254

Revolution Seen from the Bottom Up," in Barton J. Bernstein, ed., *Towards a New Past: Dissenting Essays in American History* (New York, 1968), pp. 3–45.

[26] On early America's ambivalence about the law, see Gordon S. Wood, *The Creation of the American Republic* (Chapel Hill, 1969), pp. 303–305; Linda Kerber, *Federalists in Dissent* (Ithaca, 1970), chap. 5; and Richard E. Ellis, *The Jeffersonian Crisis: Courts and Politics in the Young Republic* (New York, 1971), chap. 8.

[27] James Fenimore Cooper, *The Prairie* (1827), quoted in Perry Miller, *The Life of the Mind in America* (New York, 1965), p. 99.

[28] Watts to Sir William Baker Knight, Jan. 22, 1762, *Letter Book of John Watts* (N.Y. Historical Society *Collections*, 1928 [New York, 1928]), p. 13; *New-York Weekly Post-Boy*, Aug. 19, 1745; [William Livingston], *The Art of Pleading* (New York, 1751), p. 7.

the other, both equally destructive of Mens Estates and
Lives. . . ."[29] Governor Bellomont echoed the same complaint
at almost the same time in New York, informing the British
authorities at home that the province's lawyers bore such "a
scandalous character" that it would grieve an Englishman to
see his noble laws so "miserably managed and prophaned" in
the colony.[30] Despite the increasing professionalization of the
law by the eve of the Revolution, the rising social and economic status of the bar, and its improved qualifications for
practice, the lawyer class remained publicly suspect. Elections,   *255*
such as those in 1768 and 1769 in New York, could turn
upon the success of one faction in persuading the public that
its opponents were led by lawyers and by proposing for public
debate the question "Whether a Lawyer could possibly be an
honest Man."[31]

It is this double vision with regard to the law that explains
why colonial Americans could permit the lawyers to be their
spokesmen in the debate with the mother country without
abandoning their intrinsic distrust of the profession, why they
could continue to regard courts as sources of both protection
and of persecution.[32] It also explains (or at least clarifies) why
New York, which was the scene of some of the most turbulent
lawlessness during the years 1765–1776, was at the same time
under the leadership of lawyers.

In view of this confusion of public attitudes, the magnitude
of the task, and the problem of inadequate sources of information, it would seem foolhardy and fatuous to define precisely what the role of the lawyers was. But a tentative hypothesis in the form of a paradigm is at hand. It is not even
original but can be drawn almost intact from the paradigm
which Arthur M. Schlesinger offered over fifty years ago to
explain the evolution of merchant leadership during the revolu-

[29] Gabriel Thomas, *An Historical and Geographical Account of Pennsylvania and of West-New-Jersey* (London, 1698), in A. C. Myers, ed., *Narratives of Early Pennsylvania, West New Jersey, and Delaware, 1630–1707*
(New York, 1912), p. 328.
[30] Bellomont to the Lords of Trade, Dec. 15, 1698, in E. B. O'Callaghan,
ed., *Documents Relative to the Colonial History of the State of New York,*
15 vols. (Albany, 1856–1887), IV, 441–442. See also "Representation of the
Lords of Trade on the Administration of Justice in New-York," Dec. 14,
1699, in *ibid.*, pp. 598–599.
[31] *New-York Gazette*, Feb. 15, 1768.
[32] This is one of the paradoxes which Michael Kammen describes so in-
cisively in his *People of Paradox* (New York, 1972). See pp. 240–241 for
his comments on the law and the courts.

tionary era. In his study, Schlesinger postulated that the merchants went through several fairly distinct phases of opposition to British measures after 1763. Basically conservative in temperament and socio-economic disposition, the merchants responded cautiously to the economic challenge of the Revenue Act of 1764, urging legislative protests and organizing local non-consumption societies. The Stamp Act was broader in impact, affecting other than the commercial classes. It consequently elevated the controversy, provided a broader ground for opposition, and unfortunately enlisted the lower classes into the protest movement. While a "little mobbing" was useful to give point to the constitutional argument, violence was a two-edged sword, as dangerous to men of property as to the officers of the Crown. The merchants no less than the southern planters "lent the weight of their influence against popular demonstrations." Repeal of the Stamp Act obviated a confrontation between merchant leadership and the "rougher" elements who had intruded into the ranks of the anti-parliamentary forces. The Townshend Acts revived both merchant countermeasures and the division within the American leadership. The commercial classes, repelled by their experience in 1765–1766, were more than ever resolved "to conduct their campaign for redress along legal and peaceful lines." The extended duration of this second contest with England made such a moderate course even more difficult than before, violence soon erupting in the form of smuggling, tarring and feathering of customs officials, and the destruction of royal naval vessels. By the end of the campaign against the Townshend Acts, the merchants were fully alienated from the more radical lower classes. In Cadwallader Colden's words, as men of property, they were "so sensible of their danger, from Riots and tumults" that they would not "readily be induced to enter into combinations, which may promote disorder for the future, but will endeavour to promote due subordination to legal authority."[33]

When the Tea Act and Boston's "tea party" revived the imperial crisis, the merchants were placed on the horns of a dilemma. The rising tide of radicalism threatened to change the character of the anti-parliamentary opposition and to place its leadership in new hands. Some merchants withdrew entirely

[33] Colden to the Earl of Hillsborough, July 7, 1770, *N. Y. Col. Docs.*, VIII, 217.

from the now extra-legal movement, reflected in the actions
of the First Continental Congress. These men ultimately became tories. Others among the moderates, equally disturbed
by the changed complexion of the colonial protest movement,
chose perforce to remain within its ranks in order to curb its
temper and to control its course. While independence sheared
off still additional moderates and made them active loyalists,
those merchants who remained patriots exerted sufficient influence to insure the ultimate victory of conservative principles
in the Federal Constitution of 1787.[34]

New York's lawyers fit Schlesinger's paradigm almost per-   *257*
fectly, but if anything, their role in each phase of its development is even more sharply etched and their imprint more deliberately impressed. And, more, the lawyers in New York began playing out their role even before the imperial crisis became full-blown. If the central question confronting colonists
and Englishmen during the fateful decade after 1765 was the
proper constitutional relationship between provinces and
mother country, then lawyers in New York had defined the
lines of disagreement years before. In response to the British
contention that the plantations overseas were mere corporations of the Crown, ruled through royal instructions by the
King's viceroys, the governors, three of New York's lawyers
argued as early as 1754 that the colony possessed by virtue
of long usage a "Political Frame and Constitution" that no
royal instructions could "Destroy nor Restrain inlarge nor
Abridge."[35] If the political ideology which nurtured the Revolution was the fear of encroaching prerogative power at the
expense of popular liberties, then these same lawyers had given
New Yorkers fair warning, as early as 1753, that an institution such as a college founded by royal charter stood on
precarious grounds. If it was "the King's Prerogative, to grant
a Charter," it was also his prerogative "to grant it upon certain Terms" and also to abrogate it for non-compliance. A
college established by act of Assembly, in contrast, provided
surety of its permanence and also of its representative character, since the Assembly which created it would itself be truly

---

[34] Schlesinger's theme is expounded throughout his *Colonial Merchants
and the American Revolution*, but it is briefly summed up in pp. 591–606.
[35] "Wm. Bryant agt. John Obriant, In Error," [1754], William Smith Papers, New York Public Library; William Smith, Jr., *History of the Late
Province of New-York*, 2 vols. (New York, 1829), II, 204–205.

representative of the entire political community.[36]

If, as the Declaration of Independence put it, the Crown had sought to establish a tyranny over the colonies by making judges dependent upon the Crown for the tenure of their offices, then, again, New York's lawyers had made that point emphatically by their strenuous contest with Lieutenant Governor Colden over that very issue between 1760 and 1762. The Crown was victorious, but for two years lawyers reiterated to New Yorkers the danger to popular rights of a judiciary sitting at royal pleasure. More, New Yorkers had been assured that for English judges to serve on more secure terms than their American counterparts was to deprive Englishmen overseas of the "Liberties and Privileges" possessed by their countrymen at home, an invidious distinction. And, if the Declaration of Independence reminded Americans of the threat to their ancient right of trial by jury through the establishment of juryless Admiralty Courts in the colonies, New York's lawyers had already sounded that alarm in 1764, when Colden challenged the inviolability of the decision of a jury in a civil suit. With near unanimity, New York's bar insisted, in public and private, that Colden's action threatened "to deprive the Subject of his most valuable Rights" and to subvert the constitution of the province.[37]

258

Like the merchants, New York's lawyers responded to Britain's new imperial policy out of self-interest as well as principle; but unlike the former, principle was for the members of the bar neither adventitious nor supererogatory; it was both the language and the substance of their profession. Coke was "the lamp by which young [American] Aladdins of the law secured their juristic treasures," and Coke had been the champion of English opposition to the extension of royal prerogative and the source of the notion that there was a fundamental law controlling even the acts of Parliament.[38] New York's lawyers were undoubtedly social conservatives, linked by ties of blood,

[36] William Livingston and others, *The Independent Reflector*, ed. Milton M. Klein (Cambridge, Mass., 1963), pp. 195, 197 (April 12, 1753).

[37] On these two issues, see Klein, "Prelude to Revolution . . .," *William and Mary Quarterly*, XVII (1960), 439–462.

[38] On Coke, see Charles F. Mullett, "Coke and the American Revolution," *Economica*, XII (1932), 457–471. Coke had declared that "when an act of Parliament is against common right and reason . . . the common law will control it, and adjudge such act to be void." Americans may well have misinterpreted Coke's intention in his pronouncement in this case. See Bailyn, *Ideological Origins*, p. 177 n.

marriage, and economic interest to the ruling commercial and landed families; but, in the words of Richard B. Morris, they nevertheless "acted with plausible consistency in erecting a code of political liberalism upon the legal foundations of social reaction to which they were devoutly attached."[39] Three of the colony's young lawyers had gone beyond Coke, and in the pages of a popular journal of the mid-eighteenth century expounded in peculiarly American idiom the political philosophy of the English Commonwealthmen that ultimately became appropriated by the Americans for their own.[40]

In action, New York's lawyers behaved much like Schlesinger's merchants between 1764 and 1776. They protested the Revenue Act and the Stamp Act on constitutional grounds, penning the New York Assembly's petitions on the subject to King, Lords, and Commons. These legislative resolves, adopted on October 18, 1764, have been described by one modern historian as "among the great state papers of the pre-Revolutionary period."[41] They took an advanced position on the illegality of both the revenue measures and the contemplated stamp duties. Rejecting any distinction between external and internal taxes, the Assembly insisted that "all Impositions, whether they be internal Taxes, or Duties paid, for what we consume, equally diminish the Estates upon which they are charged." The new acts deprived New Yorkers not only of this birthright but also of the benefits of the common law, by placing enforcement in the hands of admiralty courts which "proceed not according [to] the old wholesom[e] laws of the land." Disclaiming any aspiration to independence, the Assembly nevertheless challenged all attempts to deprive the colonists of rights long enjoyed and "established in the first Dawn of our Constitution." And in an even more advanced statement of the American case, the petition to the House of Commons argued

---

[39] Richard B. Morris, "Legalism versus Revolutionary Doctrine in New England," *New England Quarterly*, IV (1931), 214.

[40] Bernard Bailyn, *The Origins of American Politics* (New York, 1968), pp. 114, 128. A recent student of colonial history observes that "the more I read the Livingston articles in *The Independent Reflector* . . ., the more certain I become that Livingston most clearly articulated a mature version of the political ideology that Bailyn describes." Joseph J. Ellis, *The New England Mind in Transition: Samuel Johnson of Connecticut* (New Haven and London, 1973), p. 284.

[41] The estimate is that of Bernhard Knollenberg in his *Origin of the American Revolution* (New York, 1960), p. 205.

that the right to exemption from any but self-imposed taxes
was a "natural Right of Mankind."[42]

In addition to their reactive measures in the halls of the
legislature, the lawyers, like Schlesinger's merchants, were not
unwilling to have opposition voiced in the streets as well; and
a number of them were active members of the Sons of Liberty, both in New York City and in Albany. But as violence
erupted and disobedience rather than non-compliance was
urged upon them, the lawyers drew back, fearful—in the words
of William Smith, Jr.—that "partial tumults" would escalate
into "a general Civil War [that] will light up and rage all
along the Continent" and lead to a "most Melancholy State of
Anarchy under the Government of a Mob."[43] British officers
were certain that the lawyers were the source from which the
Stamp Act troubles flowed; the members of the bar were "at
the bottom" of the "disloyal Insur[r]ection . . . the Hornets
and Firebrands" of the violence.[44] What these observers did
not record was the alacrity with which these same lawyers
sought to quell the disorders and quiet public tempers and
their refusal to accede to radical pressure that the courts be
opened and legal business conducted without stamps. Lawyers
instead took vacations; commercial litigation ceased; only
criminal cases which did not require use of the hated stamps
were tried between November 1765 and April 1766. The
lawyers might pen fiery resolves and encourage the development of home industries through the establishment of a "Society for the Promotion of Arts, Agriculture and Oeconomy";
but they would not defy the law by doing business without

260

[42] *Journal of the Votes and Proceedings of the General Assembly of the
Colony of New-York,* [1691–1765], 2 vols. (New York, 1764–1766), II,
769–779. The petition to the King was penned by John Morin Scott, that
to the Lords by William Livingston, and the one to the Commons by William Smith, Jr. See William H. W. Sabine, ed., *Historical Memoirs . . . of
William Smith,* 2 vols. (New York, 1956, 1958), I, 24.

[43] William Smith, Jr., to General Robert Monckton, Nov. 8, 1765, Chal-
mers Papers, N. Y., IV, 19–20, New York Public Library. On lawyers and
judges in the Sons of Liberty, see Beverly McAnear, "The Albany Stamp
Act Riots," *William and Mary Quarterly,* IV (1947), 486–498; Roger
Champagne, "Liberty Boys and Mechanics in New York City, 1764–1774,"
Labor History, VIII (1967), 115–135; and Herbert Morais, "The Sons of
Liberty in New York," in Richard B. Morris, ed., *The Era of the American
Revolution* (New York, 1939), pp. 272–273.

[44] Gage to Henry S. Conway, Dec. 21, 1765, in Clarence E. Carter, ed.,
*The Correspondence of General Thomas Gage with the Secretaries of State
. . . 1763–1775,* 2 vols. (New Haven, 1931–1933), I, 79; G. D. Scull, ed.,
The Montresor Journals (N. Y. Historical Society *Collections,* 1881 [New
York, 1882]), p. 339.

stamps. As with the merchants, their separation from the radicals had begun.[45]

Lawyer William Smith, Jr., penned the Assembly's address of thanks to the Crown for the repeal of the Stamp Act. It emphasized both the "due subordination of the Colonies, to the Mother Country" and "an equal distribution of Rights" between the inhabitants of both. The sentiments were so unexceptionable that even the Council and the governor could endorse them. The moderation of the Assembly was revealed, too, in its action to erect an equestrian statue of George III and an "eloquent" one of Pitt in appreciation of their friendship for the American colonies.[46] The lawyers expressed their

261

[45] Herbert A. Johnson, "John Jay, Colonial Lawyer" (unpublished Ph.D. dissertation, Columbia University, 1965), pp. 29, 41–43, 53–58, 61.

[46] *Journal of the Votes and Proceedings of the General Assembly . . .,* *June 11, 1766, to July 3, 1766* (New York, 1766), pp. 10, 11, 16; "Address to the King from the Governor, Council and Assembly of New-York," June 24, 1766, CO 5/ 1098, Public Record Office, London; *Smith Memoirs*, I, 32.

Stamp Act protest in New York. From Lossing, Seventeen Hundred and Seventy-Six.

"Is it, then, your opinion, gentlemen, that the tea should be landed . . .? There was one prolonged and vociferous shout . . . 'No! No! No!'" From Lamb and Harrison, History of the City of New York.

own conservatism by assuming leading roles in the prosecution of tenant rioters on the Hudson Valley estates who took violent action during the spring of 1766 to improve the terms of their leases. The bar's posture as advocates of law and order in this instant led one of the accused to sneer, at his trial, that if opposition to government constituted the crime for which he was being prosecuted, then none of the lawyers who sat on the court was himself guiltless.[47]

The Townshend Acts revived the estrangement between the lawyer-moderates and the more radical elements of the American opposition. Lawyer Robert R. Livingston's hopes that "our disputes will end, and the greatest harmony will subsist between us and our mother country" were shattered.[48] Again, the members of the bar sought to secure redress through lawful means, two of them penning "proper and constitutional Resolves" to the Crown and Parliament on the Assembly's behalf, late in 1768. The legislative addresses asserted "the Rights of his Majesty's Subjects within this Colony, which they conceive

[47] Irving Mark, *Agrarian Conflicts in Colonial New York* (New York, 1940), chap. 5; *Montresor Journals*, p. 384.

[48] Livingston to John Sargent, May 2, 1766, Robert R. Livingston Papers, Bancroft Transcripts, NYPL.

have been greatly abridged and infringed."[49] The abridgment to which the Assembly referred was not merely the new revenue measures but also the infamous suspension of the New York Assembly for failing to comply with the letter of the Quartering Act. When the legislature circumvented the act by a voluntary grant for troop support, the radicals accused it of kowtowing to Parliament and in the elections of 1768 and 1769 blasted the lawyers as "a pack of hipocritical, Cheating, Lying, canting, illdesigning Scoundrels."[50]

Nevertheless, the lawyers persisted in keeping the opposition to Britain within constitutional bounds, penning a second set of appeals, on the Assembly's behalf, to the Crown and the House of Lords in the spring of 1769. As in the earlier resolves, they disclaimed any notions of independence but stood firm on the right of New Yorkers "by uninterrupted Usage" to "a civil Constitution" and to an equality with Englishmen that "no Distance from the Mother Country" could diminish. Accepting general parliamentary authority, the Assembly rejected the idea of virtual representation as impractical and claimed exemption from all taxes not levied by the colonies' own legislatures. In blunter language than before, and reflective of the pressure of the more radical elements in the New York population, the address to the House of Lords noted gloomily that the colony's "confidence in the Tenderness of Great-Britain, seems to have suffered a very sensible Abatement." "We are Englishmen," the petitions declared, "and, as such, presume ourselves entitled to the Rights and Liberties, which have rendered the Subjects of *England* the Envy of all Nations."[51]

263

Britain's retreat in 1770 brought a three-year period of relief to New York's troubled legal profession. United in their insistence on colonial rights, they were already beginning to be divided in their view as to how best to assert those rights. Of the old triumvirate of lawyers who had led the constitutional opposition thus far, John Morin Scott became increas-

[49] *Journal of the Votes and Proceedings of the General Assembly . . .*, Oct. 27, 1768, to January 2, 1769 (New York, 1769), p. 55; *Smith Memoirs*, I, 49

[50] John Wetherhead to Sir William Johnson, Jan. 9, 1769, Division of Archives and History, University of the State of New York, *Sir William Johnson Papers*, 14 vols. (Albany, 1921–1965), VI, 575.

[51] *Journals of the Votes and Proceedings of the General Assembly . . .*, April 4, 1769, to May 20, 1769 (New York, 1769), pp. 12–16. William Livingston wrote the address to the King, William Smith, Jr., the one to the House of Lords.

ingly radical, William Smith, Jr., assumed a seat on the Governor's Council and turned increasingly conservative, and William Livingston, standing midway between them, abandoned the province for a country home in New Jersey. But the moderates were strengthened by the rise of a newer and younger group of attorneys, safely conservative, such as John Jay and James Duane. Political divisions were subordinated, however, as the members of the bar debated technical questions of law in their professional society, The Moot, where "any discourse about the Party Politics of this Province" was strictly forbidden. The differences could not be entirely ignored, and in a Debating Society, less restricted in its deliberations, lawyers Robert R. Livingston and Egbert Benson wrestled with the question of whether colonial liberties and the "just Ballance" of the constitution were more endangered by the "additional Weight of Influence . . . gained by the People" than by the increasingly oppressive conduct of the Crown.[52]

The tea episode of 1773 and its consequences confronted the New York bar with more than an academic exercise; and the lawyers, like the merchants, faced their penultimate dilemma. Future loyalists like William Smith, Jr., strove for accommodation with the Crown but took no part in the extra-legal apparatus of committees and mass meetings created to pursue the contest. Other future loyalists like Peter Van Schaack were willing to serve in these extra-legal bodies during the initial phases of their activity but then bowed out, not persuaded that British measures were "undue and oppressive" enough to constitute the "system of slavery" of which more militant patriots were already convinced.[53] Equally conservative lawyers like Robert R. Livingston, James Duane, and John Jay chose to remain within the revolutionary movement, despite their distaste for its excesses. Like William Smith, they dreaded "the Violence of the lower Sort"; but prudence dictated, in the words of Robert R. Livingston, "the propriety of swimming with a stream, which it is impossible to stem." Livingston's dictum explains the grounds on which many of the patriot lawyers made their ultimate decision for independence: "I long ago advised that they should yield to the torrent if they

264

---

[52] Moot Club Papers, 1770–1775; Minutes of the Debating Society, [1768]; both in New York Historical Society.
[53] Henry C. Van Schaack, *Life of Peter Van Schaack* (New York, 1842), 54–58.

hoped to direct its course." James Duane thought similarly. The prospect of a permanent rupture with the mother country was a "most dangerous Extremity," but if the sword had to be drawn by the Americans, licentiousness must be prevented by placing command of the troops "in the hands of Men of property and Rank who, by that means, will preserve the same Authority over the Minds of the people which they enjoyed in the Hour of Tranquillity."[54] Duane's modern biographer notes that this New York patrician became a rebel "through necessity," that of keeping an independent state from surrendering to the dangers of mob rule, and "to save her from the excesses of democracy." The point was not missed by the mob leaders of 1776: rich and designing men were assuming active leadership of the movement for independence so that it would "not . . . go too fast and run into danger." William Gordon, the contemporary historian of the Revolution, confirmed the basis of the conservatives' seemingly paradoxical decision to join the revolutionary tide: "The people were ripe for it [i.e., independence]. Prudence dictated a compliance with their expectations and wishes. A disappointment might have disgusted, and produced disorder."[55]

265

Hence conservative lawyers like Duane, Livingston, and Jay attended the First Continental Congress as delegates from New York. Here they joined the conciliationists, fought for the Galloway Plan of union, and pursued every effort to end the "unnatural convulsions" by lawful means. As late as January 1776, they were hoping for reconciliation; and when in that month a self-styled Scottish nobleman, Lord Drummond, came to Philadelphia with a compromise peace plan, allegedly from Lord North himself, it was to Duane, Jay, and Livingston that he hurried, having been assured that the New Yorkers were most likely to be sympathetic to any plan for accommodation.[56] And it was New York's lawyer-led delegation which delayed the province's approval of the decision for independence

[54] *Smith Memoirs,* I, 186; Robert R. Livingston to William Duer, June 12, 1777, quoted in George Dangerfield, *Chancellor Robert R. Livingston of New York* (New York, 1960), 94; James Duane to Robert Livingston, June 7, 1775, Livingston-Redmond Papers, Franklin D. Roosevelt Library, Hyde Park, N. Y.
[55] William Gordon, *History of the Rise, Progress, and Establishment of the Independence of the United States of America,* 3 vols. (London, 1788), II, 297; Edward P. Alexander, *A Revolutionary Conservative: James Duane of New York* (New York, 1938), 121; Peter Force, ed., *American Archives,* 9 vols. (Washington, D. C., 1837–1853), 4 Series, VI, 996.

so long that an irritated John Adams complained: "What is the reason that New York must continue to embarrass the Continent?"[57]

With independence effected, New York's conservative lawyers strove to insure that the new state constitution would retain power in the hands of those same men of rank and property who had held them in the earlier "Hour of Tranquillity." The constitution of 1777 was essentially the work of the lawyers, Jay, Duane, Livingston, and Gouverneur Morris, with Jay playing the central role. Despite some democratic features, the constitution as adopted represented, on the whole, "a victory for the minority of stability and privilege."[58] New York's was one of the more conservative of the new state constitutions, yet it did not guarantee that permanency of control for the "better sort" that James Duane had hoped for. And herein lies the irony in the role played by the lawyers in this enigmatic drama. Devoted to conservatism but arguing their case against Britain on the highest grounds of legality and constitutionalism, they were driven by the logic of their exposition and the language of their rhetoric to become republicans despite themselves. The differences in temperament, social position, economic status, and political principles that made patriots of some lawyers and loyalists of others are barely discernible. The profession appears to have split almost evenly on the issue of independence. Of 36 lawyers practicing in the New York Supreme Court between 1762 and 1765, the position of 25 can be determined: 12 of these remained loyal, and 13 became patriots. A similar division marked the members of The Moot. Of 20 whose names are recorded in the club's minutes as members between 1770 and 1774, 9 can be identified as loyalists and 11 as patriots.[59]

266

---

[56] On this proposal, see Klein, "Failure of a Mission: The Drummond Peace Proposal of 1775," *Huntington Library Quarterly*, XXXV (1972), 343–380.

[57] John Adams to Samuel H. Parsons, June 22, 1776, in *The Works of John Adams*, ed. C. F. Adams, 10 vols. (Boston, 1850–1856), IX, 407.

[58] Richard B. Morris, *John Jay, the Nation, and the Courts* (Boston, 1967), pp. 10–14; Frank Monaghan, *John Jay* (New York and Indianapolis, 1935), p. 97.

[59] The first computation is that of Johnson, "John Jay," Appendix A; the second is my own. For the bar generally, there are no adequate statistics as to the division between patriots and loyalists. Sabine, in 1864, estimated that a majority of the lawyers were patriots, but the "giants" of the law in all the colonies were loyalists. Wallace Brown, studying the loyalist

What made republicans of some was neither change of economic and social position nor of principle; their "radical" posture after 1776 was rather the consequence of their earlier decision to swim with the tide in order to control its course. What the moderate men of the bar could not foresee was that their flaming rhetoric and high-sounding constitutionalism could be as useful in advancing democratic principles as in preserving conservative doctrines. The press, which moderate lawyers employed to plead for restraint and tempered action, made politics everyone's concern, especially in a province with a long history of political interest and dynamism such as New York; and whatever the intent, the language of moderation became the rhetoric of democracy.⁶⁰ The "new politics" that emerged in New York by 1776 was the lawyers' creation, but it could not remain their creature. Natural rights theory might be good old-fashioned English whiggism, but its limits far transcended Locke and limited monarchy when someone like Alexander Hamilton, perhaps innocently, converted it into words of timeless import:

267

> The sacred rights of mankind are not to be rummaged for, among old parchments, or musty records. They are written, as with a sun beam, in the whole *volume* of human nature, by the hand of the divinity itself; and can never be erased or obscured by mortal power.⁶¹

---

claimants in England, concluded in 1965 that Sabine was probably right. Friedman, in his recent study, states casually that "many lawyers, if not most, were of the loyalist persuasion." In Massachusetts, Morris found that the bar split fairly evenly. Flick, in his volume on New York loyalism, lumped lawyers with other professionals and concluded that a "very large proportion" of all of them were loyalists. However, he offers only seven names of New York City lawyers to illustrate his generalization and lists James Duane as a merchant rather than a lawyer. The fullest study of the early bar, that of Chroust, estimates that only one-fourth of the colonial legal profession left the country or retired from their practice because of their loyalty to the Crown. See Lorenzo Sabine, *Biographical Sketches of the Loyalists of the American Revolution*, 2 vols. (1864; reprinted, Port Washington, N. Y., 1966), I, 59–60; Wallace Brown, *The King's Friends* (Providence, R. I., 1966), p. 265; Morris, "Legalism versus Revolutionary Doctrine," *New England Quarterly*, IV (1931), 206–207; Alexander C. Flick, *Loyalism in New York during the American Revolution* (1901; reprinted, New York, 1969), pp. 31–32; Lawrence M. Friedman, *A History of American Law* (New York, 1973), p. 88; Anton-Hermann Chroust, *The Rise of the Legal Profession in America*, 2 vols. (Norman, Okla., 1965), II, 11.

⁶⁰ On this development, see Gary B. Nash, "The Transformation of Urban Politics, 1700–1765," *Journal of American History*, LX (1973), 605–632.

⁶¹ *The Farmer Refuted* (1775), Harold C. Syrett, Jacob E. Cooke, and others, eds., *The Papers of Alexander Hamilton*, 19 vols. to date (New York, 1961–   ), I, 121–122.

Nor could John Jay anticipate the implications of his reminder to the people of New York late in 1776 that "You and all men were created free, and . . . it is therefore . . . the duty of every man, to oppose and repell all those, by whatever name or title distinguished, who prostitute the powers of Government to destroy the happiness and freedom of the people over whom they may be appointed to rule."[62] Nor could William Livingston appreciate the infinitely prescient significance of his 1765 pronouncement that "Without liberty no man can be a subject. He is a slave."[63]

268

The republic which Americans finally fashioned in 1787 was not the one the lawyers anticipated in 1776, but it bore the stamp of their conservative legalism clothed in democratic dress, just as the moderate rebellion they visualized after 1765 became a revolution of transcending character by 1776. If their role in these events has not been better understood, it is perhaps because the lawyer class, as de Tocqueville observed in the 1830s,

adapts itself with great flexibility to the exigencies of the time and accommodates itself without resistance to all the movements of the social body. But this party extends over the whole community and penetrates into all the classes which compose it; it acts upon the country imperceptibly, but finally fashions it to suit its own purposes.[64]

The lawyers who made the Revolution in New York accommodated themselves adroitly to its changing configurations, and in the process they fashioned it to suit their own purposes. But, ironically, and unperceived by the lawyers who were enacting the drama, they were also being acted upon by the force of events. They not only transformed the Revolution, they transformed themselves; and they became thereby bulwarks of constitutional republicanism as they had once been supporters of constitutional monarchy.

[62] Henry P. Johnston, ed., *The Correspondence and Public Papers of John Jay*, 4 vols. (New York and London, 1890–1893), I, 103 (Dec. 23, 1776).

[63] *New-York Gazette*, March 14, 1765.

[64] Alexis de Tocqueville, *Democracy in America*, ed. Phillips Bradley, 2 vols. (New York, 1954), I, 290.

Political Mobilization and the American Revolution: The Resistance Movement in Philadelphia, 1765 to 1776

R. A. Ryerson*

RECENT studies of the causes of the American Revolution have tended to emphasize its ideological origins to the comparative neglect both of the political processes by which principles, beliefs, and anxieties were translated into revolutionary action and of the considerable conflicts among Americans that were provoked or intensified by British imperial measures.[1] These conflicts were undoubtedly muted by ideological consensus in those areas where, as in New England and Virginia, the colonists, led by relatively united, native, established political elites, appear to have risen up virtually unanimously against the Empire and achieved independence with little internal social stress. But where America's rebellion deeply challenged the local established order and sharply divided the community, as was the case in most of the colonies, the key to understanding the success of the Revolution seems less likely to be found through an examination of ideology than through a close analysis of political process, specifically the process by which disaffected colonists were mobilized for resistance and revolutionary endeavor.

For the province of Pennsylvania, and particularly for the city of Philadelphia, where many if not most of the established political leaders linked their fortunes to the Empire and opposed or lagged far in the

* Mr. Ryerson is a member of the Department of History, The University of Texas, Austin. This article is based upon his unpublished doctoral dissertation, "Leadership in Crisis, The Radical Committees of Philadelphia and the Coming of the Revolution in Pennsylvania, 1765-1776: A Study in the Revolutionary Process" (The Johns Hopkins University, 1972). He wishes to thank Jack P. Greene and Robert Crunden for their helpful criticism.

[1] Three recent, partial exceptions are Merrill Jensen, *The Founding of a Nation: A History of the American Revolution 1763-1776* (New York, 1968); Richard D. Brown, *Revolutionary Politics in Massachusetts: The Boston Committee of Correspondence and the Towns, 1772-1774* (Cambridge, Mass., 1970); and Pauline Maier, *From Resistance to Revolution: Colonial Radicals and the Development of American Opposition to Britain, 1765-1776* (New York, 1972).

rear of popular sentiment, four phases of the process of mobilization were crucially important: (1) The development of a commitment to resistance by a few dedicated leaders. (2) The creation of a new set of political institutions capable both of pressuring existing governmental organs to demand that Great Britain treat Pennsylvania in the manner that the province desired and, when the established order proved intractable, of acting as alternative executors of political authority until the polity could be redesigned on a permanent basis. (3) The shaping and maintenance of a virtually unanimous popular commitment to any plan that could secure Pennsylvania's autonomy, either within or outside the British Empire. (4) The rapid recruitment of new leaders, both to perform new political tasks and to represent a greater proportion of the potentially active population than had found a voice in the pre-Revolutionary polity.

The present inquiry will focus primarily upon this last activity—leadership recruitment—the very core of Revolutionary political mobilization in Philadelphia. The immediate objectives are to delineate the patterns of that recruitment, to identify the factors shaping those patterns, and to assess the impact of this activity upon Revolutionary politics in Pennsylvania. The larger goal is to demonstrate the central role of political mobilization in achieving the Revolution in one colony. Our questions and our methods for answering them, if fruitful, may serve as a foundation for a more precise understanding of the Revolution in every colony where the success of the resistance movement remained in serious doubt almost until the Declaration of Independence. On the broadest scale, to place mobilization at the center of America's Revolution is to relate that event intimately to the continuing and now global process of political modernization. In America, the most striking element of political modernization has always been the "extension of political consciousness to new social groups and the mobilization of these groups into politics."[2]

In the late 1760s and early 1770s, while Pennsylvanians grew increasingly distressed over the steady deterioration of relations with Britain,

---

[2] Samuel P. Huntington, *Political Order in Changing Societies* (New Haven, Conn., 1968), 266. For Huntington's general treatment of the American Revolution as a mobilizing and modernizing process see vii, 32-39, 93-139, 264-274. For another succinct definition of political mobilization see J. P. Nettl, *Political Mobilization: A Sociological Analysis of Methods and Concepts* (London, 1967), 32-33. The processes of mobilization are also of central importance in the recent, highly analytical work of such students of the general phenomena of revolutionary change as Chalmers Johnson and Ted Gurr.

their provincial government ignored the larger imperial questions of the day. Governor John Penn, cautious and divided in his loyalties, offered neither guidance nor opposition.[3] Pennsylvania's assemblymen, still predominantly Quaker in faith or background, had long engaged the proprietor in political battles and, perhaps for that very reason, understood little or nothing of the frustrations and dangers of royal government. As the imperial crisis deepened they closed their eyes to parliamentary statutes and royal decrees that threatened their autonomy and went calmly on governing their no longer quiet province.[4] By the early 1770s Pennsylvanians were rapidly losing confidence in their public officials. In June 1774 they began to turn to new men to lead them in resisting Great Britain.

271

The new radical leadership that emerged in Philadelphia and then throughout Pennsylvania arose out of a decade of mixed triumphs and frustrations.[5] Established Quaker merchants and proprietary faction leaders alike, working through the city's first resistance committees, did

[3] James H. Hutson, *Pennsylvania Politics 1746-1770: The Movement for Royal Government and Its Consequences* (Princeton, N. J., 1972); *Minutes of the Provincial Council of Pennsylvania (Colonial Records of Pennsylvania* [Harrisburg, Pa., 1852-1853]), IX, X, hereafter cited as *Minutes of Provincial Council; Votes and Proceedings of the House of Representatives of the Province of Pennsylvania*, in Samuel Hazard *et al.*, eds., *Pennsylvania Archives*, 8th Ser. (Philadelphia, 1931-1935), VII, VIII, hereafter cited as *Votes and Proceedings*; Ryerson, "Leadership in Crisis," 32-34, 46, 76-78, 79.

[4] Hutson, *Pennsylvania Politics*, esp. Chaps. 3-4; Benjamin H. Newcomb, *Franklin and Galloway: A Political Partnership* (New Haven, Conn., 1972); Richard Bauman, *For the Reputation of Truth: Politics, Religion, and Conflict among the Pennsylvania Quakers, 1750-1800* (Baltimore, 1971), 27, 103-180; Hermann Wellenreuther, *Glaube und Politik in Pennsylvania 1681-1776: Die Wandlungen der Obrigkeitsdoktrin und des* Peace Testimony *der Quäker* (Cologne, 1972), esp. Chaps. 5-6, 10-12, and appendixes I-III, 432-437; David Hawke, *In the Midst of a Revolution* (Philadelphia, 1961), 151-153; Theodore Thayer, "The Quaker Party in Pennsylvania, 1755-1765," *Pennsylvania Magazine of History and Biography*, LXXI (1947), 21n; Wayne L. Bockelman and Owen S. Ireland, "The Internal Revolution in Pennsylvania: An Ethnic-Religious Interpretation," *Pennsylvania History*, XLI (1974), 124-159, esp. 127-134; and my counting of Quakers in the Assembly in the summer of 1774, taken from "Leadership in Crisis," 39-41, 56, 651-653. Of 40 members, 11 were Friends in good standing by my count, while 9 had a strong Quaker background and may still have worshipped with the Friends.

[5] I here employ the term "radical" strictly in relation to resistance strategy and tactics. Persons or groups herein labeled radical on any given date were those who were willing to go farthest in opposing British policy at that particular time. Thus an individual might be a "radical" in 1774 but only a "moderate" in 1776, if his attitudes and ideas had undergone no change in a period when public opinion was changing rapidly around him. I have tried to use the terms "moderate" and "conservative" in the same fashion.

strongly oppose the Stamp Act in 1765.[6] The next several years, however, were lean ones for the resistance movement. Its few Assembly spokesmen lost their seats in 1766, and the city's leading Quaker, Anglican, and Presbyterian merchants, whom Charles Thomson and John Dickinson welded into a committee to direct an anti-Townshend Act boycott only with great difficulty in 1769, fell to arguing among themselves and soon abandoned nonimportation.[7] It finally became evident to many Philadelphians that neither the city's merchants as a body, nor any established elite, nor any branch of the provincial government would go far to defend them.

272

Impelled by this widespread conviction, concerned Philadelphians organized around the city's first faction dedicated to resisting Britain's imperial policy. The new committee of twenty heading this faction, recruited in September 1770 from among citizens noted for both their economic prominence and their ideological zeal, did not enjoy wide enough support, especially with the merchants, to last long as a body.[8] As a leadership core, however, it not only survived the "quiet period" (1770-1773) but mobilized the city's mechanics behind it.[9] When the Tea Act of 1773 suddenly aroused the colonists, a radical leadership was at hand. The decision of the provincial government and of the older and wealthier merchants to accept the act allowed the radicals, again organized into a resistance committee, to incite the community to humiliate the local tea agents and send back the tea ship. Indeed, the dynamic orator Charles Thomson, "the Samuel Adams of Philadelphia," so thoroughly infused several thousand of his townsmen with anti-British zeal that they voted

[6] Arthur Meier Schlesinger, *The Colonial Merchants and the American Revolution, 1763-1776* (New York, 1917); Edmund S. and Helen M. Morgan, *The Stamp Act Crisis: Prologue to Revolution* (Chapel Hill, N. C., 1953); Benjamin H. Newcomb, "Effects of the Stamp Act on Colonial Pennsylvania Politics," *William and Mary Quarterly*, 3d Ser., XXIII (1966), 257-272; Hutson, *Pennsylvania Politics,* Chap. 4; James H. Hutson, "An Investigation of the Inarticulate: Philadelphia's White Oaks," *WMQ*, 3d Ser., XXVIII (1971), 3-25; Ryerson, "Leadership in Crisis," 87-92. For portrait data on the two committees of 1765 see Table I.

[7] Schlesinger, *Colonial Merchants*, 105, 114, 115-120, 125-129, 191-194, 211, 215, 217-223, 226-233; Hutson, *Pennsylvania Politics*, Chap. 4; Hutson, "Philadelphia's White Oaks," *WMQ*, 3d Ser., XXVIII (1971), 22-23; Newcomb, *Franklin and Galloway*, Chaps. 4-8; *Votes and Proceedings*, VII, 6168-6169, 6181-6184, 6187-6192, 6193, 6244-6245, 6269-6282; Bauman, *For the Reputation of Truth*, 130-134; Ryerson, "Leadership in Crisis," 93-110.

[8] The names of these committeemen, 11 from the 1769 board who were loyal to the boycott and 9 fresh recruits, appear in the *Pennsylvania Chronicle* (Philadelphia), Oct. 1, 1770.

[9] Hutson, *Pennsylvania Politics*, Chap. 4; Hutson, "Philadelphia's White Oaks," *WMQ*, 3d Ser., XXVIII (1971); Newcomb, *Franklin and Galloway*, 212-213.

a full endorsement of the destruction of the tea at Boston.[10]

Thomson's triumph drew a sharp reaction from Philadelphia's more moderate Quaker and Anglican merchants, who moved quickly to regain control of city politics. Although with the arrival of news of the Boston Port Act in May 1774, the larger pattern of imperial affairs began to favor the resistance faction, Philadelphia's radicals had to accept an alliance with the moderate merchants in forming a committee to represent their city in response to Boston's call for aid and support. This committee urged Governor Penn to summon the Assembly into emergency session and endorsed the idea of a continental congress.[11]

Yet almost immediately the radicals sensed a favorable shift in public opinion. As counties, cities, and towns to the north and south flocked to the banner of resistance, Thomson, who was Philadelphia's most innovative radical strategist, initiated a campaign to involve every religious congregation in the city in a vigorous protest against British policy.[12] The success of this appeal and Penn's refusal to call the Assembly gave the resistance faction its majority. In mid-June, by recruiting younger men of more modest fortune who followed many different trades and represented Presbyterians, Baptists, and Lutherans, as well as the dominant wealthy Quakers and Anglicans, radical resistance leaders doubled the city committee. This new board, directed by the town to insure Pennsylvania's participation in the Continental Congress, even if opposed by the

273

[10] Schlesinger, Colonial Merchants, 240, 262, 268-281, 290-291; Benjamin Woods Labaree, The Boston Tea Party (New York, 1964), 97-103, 156-160; Pennsylvania Gazette (Philadelphia), Oct. 20, 1773; Thomas Wharton, Sr., to Thomas Walpole, May 2, 1774, Thomas Wharton, Sr., Letter-Book, Historical Society of Pennsylvania, Philadelphia; Ryerson, "Leadership in Crisis," 111-127. John Adams first recorded this epithet for Thomson Aug. 30, 1774. L. H. Butterfield, ed., Diary and Autobiography of John Adams, Vol. II: Diary, 1771-1781 (Cambridge, Mass., 1961), 115.

[11] The best accounts of Pennsylvania politics in the spring and summer of 1774 appear in Charles H. Lincoln, The Revolutionary Movement in Pennsylvania, 1760-1776 (Philadelphia, 1901), 159-184; Schlesinger, Colonial Merchants, 341-356; and Labaree, Boston Tea Party, 230-232, 243-248. The account given here summarizes Ryerson, "Leadership in Crisis," 131-231. The basic sources are the Pa. Gaz., Pennsylvania Journal (Philadelphia), and Pennsylvania Packet (Philadelphia); the accounts of the radical leaders Joseph Reed and Charles Thomson, "The Papers of Charles Thomson," New-York Historical Society, Collections, XI (1878), 215-229, 269-286; and the rich manuscript holdings in the Pa. Hist. Soc., esp. the Gratz, R. R. Logan, Society, and Thomas Wharton, Sr., collections, and the Col. William Bradford, Henry Drinker, James & Drinker, and Charles Thomson papers. Cf. the 19 committeemen chosen on May 20, 1774 (Table II), with the 1769, 1770, and 1773 committeemen (Table I).

[12] Pa. Packet, May 30, 1774; Pa. Jour., June 1, 1774; Rivington's New-York Gazetteer (New York City), June 2, 16, 1774; letters of May 29-June 9, 1774, Henry Drinker and James & Drinker Papers.

governor or the Assembly, quickly abandoned the cautious policy of the committee chosen in May.[13]

At once both Penn and the conservative Assembly agreed to the Congress in order to try to control the Pennsylvania delegation and check the resistance movement. But the legislature's appointment of moderate and conservative congressmen and its contemptuous rejection of the sweeping instructions framed in July by a convention of resistance committee delegates from throughout Pennsylvania proved ineffective.[14] The resistance movement now had the confidence of the province. In the fall Joseph Galloway's hand-picked congressional delegation, sensing the popular mood, rejected its archconservative leader, abandoned the Quaker faction's accommodationist policy, and on October 20, 1774, endorsed the Continental Association, a declaration of open commercial warfare upon Great Britain.[15]

The decision of Congress to entrust the enforcement of the Association boycott to newly elected committees throughout the colonies put Philadelphia's resistance movement on a semi-official and quasi-governmental basis. This congressional mandate solved the question of the committees' institutional status, but their functions and goals continued to change, developing in three distinct stages.

274

---

[13] *Minutes of Provincial Council,* X, 170-180; "Papers of Thomson," N.-Y. Hist. Soc., *Colls.,* XI (1878), 278; *At a Meeting at the Philosophical Society's Hall on Friday, June 10th* . . . [Philadelphia, 1774]; Charles Thomson, Memorandum Book, 1754-1774, 159-162, Gratz Coll.; "list of Committee" [John Dickinson?], Dickinson material, R. R. Logan Coll.; "Papers relating to the shipment of tea" [misdated and mistitled], Pa. Hist. Soc.; official accounts of committee transactions, *Pa. Gaz.,* June 8, 15, 22, 1774; Wharton to Samuel Wharton, July 5, 1774, Wharton Letter-Book.

[14] *Minutes of Provincial Council,* X, 180; "Papers of Thomson," N.-Y. Hist. Soc., *Colls.,* XI (1878), 278-280; John Penn to the earl of Dartmouth, July 30, 1774, in Peter Force, ed., *American Archives,* 4th Ser. (Washington, D. C., 1837-1846), I, 514; reports of committee and convention activity in the city and province, *Pa. Gaz.,* June 22, 29, July 6, 1774; *Pa. Packet,* June 18, July 4, 18, 1774; *Pa. Jour.,* July 20, 27, 1774; provincial convention's proceedings, *Pa. Arch.,* 2d Ser. (Harrisburg, Pa., 1874-1893), III, 545-622; Wharton to Walpole, Aug. 2, 1774, Wharton Letter-Book; "Notes and Papers on the Commencement of the American Revolution" [1869 transcription], Dr. William Smith Papers, Pa. Hist. Soc.; Joseph Reed to Charles Pettit, July 16, 1774, Reed Papers, N.-Y. Hist. Soc., New York City; letter from the Pennsylvania Assembly to the Massachusetts Assembly, June 28, 1774, printed in *Pa. Gaz.,* July 13, 1774; "A Freeman" [Joseph Galloway?], "To the Representatives of the Province of Pennsylvania," *Rivington's N.-Y. Gaz.,* July 28, 1774; *Votes and Proceedings,* VIII, 7097-7101. For two recent views of the politics of this period see Hutson, *Pennsylvania Politics,* 236-240, and Newcomb, *Franklin and Galloway,* 243-259.

[15] Worthington Chauncey Ford *et al.,* eds., *Journals of the Continental Congress,* I (Washington, D. C., 1904), 42-51, 75-81, 102n; *Votes and Proceedings,* VIII, 7148, 7163.

In November 1774 Philadelphia's radical merchants broke with their moderate colleagues and joined the city's mechanics to elect a new, enlarged city committee dominated by young merchants, shopkeepers, and craftsmen of modest fortune.[16] The triumphant radical-mechanic faction then sought to accelerate resistance by arming the still pacific province.[17] This attempt failed utterly, and the committee had to exert its full strength to enforce the Association and to bar from the city press all criticism of the resistance strategy of Congress.[18]

Lexington and Concord ended open opposition to the resistance movement in Philadelphia. Even young Quakers rushed to arms, and the Assembly set to organizing and supplying the province's new militia forces. In May the city committeemen won election to over half of the command posts in Philadelphia's militia. Thereafter, militia leadership and committee leadership were nearly identical.[19] In August the city, in electing a new and again expanded committee, chose leaders even less wealthy and more radical than their predecessors.[20] These zealots soon joined the even more ardent spokesmen of the militia privates in pressuring the Assembly to require that every adult male either bear arms or pay heavy additional taxes in lieu of military service.[21] By November

275

[16] *Pa. Gaz.*, Nov. 2, 9, 16, 23, 1774; *Pa. Packet*, Nov. 7, 1774; *Pennsylvania Ledger* (Philadelphia), Mar. 16, 1776; two election tickets, 960.F. 52, 53, Philadelphia Library Company, Philadelphia.

[17] *Pa. Gaz.*, Dec. 28, 1774, Feb. 1, 1775; Force, ed., *American Archives*, 4th Ser., I, 1066, 1180, 1211; William B. Reed, *Life and Correspondence of Joseph Reed*, I (Philadelphia, 1847), 90, 94; Reed to [Pettit], Jan. 14, 1775, Reed Papers; Reed to Dennis DeBerdt, Feb. 13, 1775, Joseph Reed Letter-Book, 1772-1774 [*sic*], 129, N.-Y. Hist. Soc.; William Duane, ed., *Passages from the Remembrancer of Christopher Marshall* (Philadelphia, 1839), 15.

[18] On the regulation of commerce see Schlesinger, *Colonial Merchants*, 498-500; James & Drinker to Pigou & Booth, Jan. 18, 1775, James & Drinker Letter-Book (Foreign), James & Drinker Papers; Henry Drinker to Benjamin Booth, Feb. 21, 1775, Drinker to Samuel Cornell, Apr. 22, 1775, Henry Drinker Letter-Book (Domestic), Drinker Papers; *Pa. Jour.*, Jan. 4, 1775; *Rivington's N.-Y. Gaz.*, Mar. 30, 1775; *Pa. Gaz.*, Jan. 4, 11, 18, 25, Feb. 1, 8, 1775; and Force, ed., *American Archives*, 4th Ser., II, 238-242. On the committee's suppression of dissent see *Rivington's N.-Y. Gaz.*, Dec. 1, 8, 1774, Mar. 30, 1775; *Pa. Ledger*, Feb. 11, 1775; *Pa. Gaz.*, Feb. 23, 1775; *Pa. Jour.*, Feb. 15, May 17, 1775; Duane, ed., *Passages from Marshall*, 24; Force, ed., *American Archives*, 4th Ser., I, 1231-1232, 1233, 1243; and Ryerson, "Leadership in Crisis," 293-317.

[19] *Votes and Proceedings*, VIII, 7243-7249; Peters Papers, VIII [Richard Peters, Jr., militia papers], 44, 71, Pa. Hist. Soc. (Cf. the committee list, *Pa. Gaz.*, Nov. 16, 1774.)

[20] *Pa. Gaz.*, Aug. 9, 16, 23, 30, 1775; *Pennsylvania Evening Post* (Philadelphia), Aug. 10, 1775; three election tickets, 962.F. 70, 72, 73, Philadelphia Lib. Co.

[21] Peters Papers, VIII, 43, 54-65; *Pa. Packet*, Aug. 21, 1775; *Pa. Evening Post*, Sept. 14, 19, 28, 1775; *Pa. Gaz.*, Oct. 11, 18, Nov. 1, 15, 1775; Duane, ed., *Passages*

1775 Pennsylvania's pacifism was at an end.

Having failed either to persuade the Assembly or to compel it to act by threatening to convoke another provincial convention, Philadelphia's radical committee movement finally broke with it utterly and called for termination of its authority. But it was the Assembly, not the city committee, which brought on this confrontation. So desperately did the legislators oppose independence between November 1775 and April 1776 that the radicals, only recently accustomed to their uneasy alliance with their lawmakers, turned bitterly mistrustful of them.²² In May the current city committee, elected in February and completely controlled by the most radical young merchants and lawyers and the most zealous mechanics, reached two conclusions: first, that their liberties would never be secure short of independence, and, second, that Pennsylvania would never become independent under its present government.²³

Thus it was to escape permanently from what they felt to be British oppression that Philadelphia's radical leaders summoned committee delegates from throughout the province. In June these spokesmen repudiated the Assembly and arranged for the Constitutional Convention of 1776

276

---

from Marshall, 49-50, 53-54, 55-56; Christopher Marshall, Sr., to "S. H.," Sept. 30, Oct. 31, 1775, Christopher Marshall, Sr., Letter-Book, 146, 151, Pa. Hist. Soc.; Drinker to Booth, Oct. 3, 1775, Drinker Letter-Book (Domestic), 160, Drinker Papers; *Pa. Evening Post,* Oct. 3, 1775; *Votes and Proceedings,* VIII, 7301-7302, 7306, 7311-7313, 7323-7324, 7326-7330, 7334-7343, 7351-7352, 7356-7363, 7365-7366, 7369-7384.

²² See *Votes and Proceedings,* VIII, 3750, 7353, 7455, 7513; *Pa. Jour.,* Nov. 22, 1755; *Pa. Ledger,* Nov. 25, 1775; *Pa. Jour.,* Nov. 29, Dec. 6, 1775, for the Assembly's opposition to independence. For early arguments favoring independence that appeared in the Philadelphia press see *Pa. Packet,* Nov. 14, 1774, Aug. 21, 1775; *Pa. Jour.,* Oct. 18, Dec. 27, 1775; Thomas Paine, *Common Sense* (Philadelphia, 1776); *Pa. Jour.,* Jan. 24, 1776; *Pa. Evening Post,* Feb. 3, 1776; Thomas Paine, "Epistle to Quakers," appended to the 3d ed. of *Common Sense* (Philadelphia, Feb. 12, 1776); *Pa. Jour.,* Feb. 14, 1776; *Pa. Evening Post,* Feb. 17, 1776. The only rebuttal to these arguments, before late February, was the Quakers' *Ancient Testimony and Principles of the People called Quakers renewed . . .* [Philadelphia, Jan. 20, 1776]. On the committee's alienation from the Assembly see Duane, ed., *Passages from Marshall,* 69; Reed to Pettit, Mar. 3, 1776, Reed Papers; *Pa. Packet,* Mar. 11, 1776; "The Apologist," *Pa. Evening Post,* Feb. 29; "The Censor," *ibid.,* Mar. 5, 1776; and *Votes and Proceedings,* VIII, 7412, 7436. The independence debate continued in the "Cato" letters [Dr. William Smith], *Pa. Gaz.,* Mar. 13-Apr. 24, 1776; *Pa. Jour.,* Mar. 6, 13, 1776; the "Cassandra" letters [James Cannon], *Pa. Packet,* Mar. 25, Apr. 27, 1776; and the four "Forester" letters [Thomas Paine], *Pa. Jour.,* Apr. 3-May 8, 1776.

²³ *Pa. Gaz.,* Feb. 14, 21, 1776; Duane, ed., *Passages from Marshall,* 65, 71-75, 79-84; "The Forester," no. 4, *Pa. Jour.,* May 8, 1776; *The Alarm: or, An Address to the People of Pennsylvania . . .* [Philadelphia, 1776]; "Protest" of Philadelphia's mass meeting, May 20, 1776, and Philadelphia City Committee to the county committees, May 21, 1776, in Force, ed., *American Archives,* 4th Ser., VI, 519-521; William Bradford, Jr., A Memorandum Book and Register for May and June 1776, 23 (May 20), Bradford Papers.

which, by reforming both the Assembly and the franchise, finally revolutionized Pennsylvania's polity.[24] Through the committee movement the Revolution had at last triumphed in Pennsylvania.

How did the radicals achieve this victory? A quantitative analysis of their strategy of community mobilization through leadership recruitment, an assessment of the probable motivations behind that strategy, and a brief discussion of the central role of this recruitment in the coming of the Revolution in Pennsylvania may suggest some answers to this question.

In examining a group of about three hundred Philadelphians involved in resistance politics—many very prominent, yet easily as many very obscure—I have attempted to answer seven major questions. To what extent did the same men serve on one committee after another? How old were the committeemen at the time of their service? What was their economic status? How did they make their living? From what countries or colonies did they, or their immediate ancestors, come? To what religious faiths did they belong? Finally, do the answers to these questions show a change during the period under consideration, and if so, does that change indicate any purposeful shift in the pattern of leadership recruitment?

Persistency and Continuity. In the decade before independence certain names appear repeatedly on Philadelphia committee lists. How many of these committee veterans were there, and what does their presence indicate about the committee movement? The short-term persistency of committee service—the number of men on a given committee who sat on the succeeding committee—and the long-term continuity of that service—the number of men on a given board who had previous committee experience—together form a clear pattern of committee membership between 1765 and 1776. First, both the persistency and the continuity of committee service rose, although quite unevenly, despite the rapidly increasing size of city committees.[25] Neither the bitter struggles between conservatives,

277

---

[24] For the proceedings of the Provincial Conference see *Pa. Arch.*, 2d Ser., III, 635-665, and *Pa. Gaz.*, June 26, 1776. See also Marshall to "J. B.," June 30, 1776, Marshall Letter-Book, 191-192, and Duane, ed., *Passages from Marshall*, 87-88.

[25] The forward-looking persistency index is included here because of increasing committee size. Had only the backward-looking index of continuity been employed, a doubling of committee size would determine a relatively low percentage of carryover, even if *all* members of the first committee served on the second. Thus the fact that 17 of the 19 committeemen of May 1774 continued to sit on the June committee gives a persistency rate of 89%, but a continuity rate of only 39.5%.

moderates, and radicals nor the mobilization of new leaders for ever larger boards prevented the resistance leadership in Philadelphia from becoming increasingly more experienced. Second, there were two sharp breaks in this growing continuity. Only 30 percent of the 1770 committee sat on the tea committee of 1773, and only 29 percent of the 1773 committeemen had ever served before. Again, only 42 percent of the June 1774 committeemen were elected to the November 1774 board, while only 35 percent of the latter body were committee veterans (Tables I and II). These breaks suggest that the tea committee and the November 1774 committee were somehow different from all other boards formed before 1775-1776, when a strong continuity was gradually reestablished. Quite apart from the slender literary evidence on committees, certain facts about the committeemen themselves confirm this view.[26]

Age. It is harder to determine the age of Philadelphia's resistance leaders than any other simple fact about them. Yet three relationships

278

[26] The portrait data on age, nationality and nativity, and religious affiliation come from the *Dictionary of American Biography; PMHB* (particularly the pre-1920 issues); John W. Jordan *et al.*, eds., *Colonial and Revolutionary Families of Pennsylvania*, 17 vols. (New York, 1911-1965); William Wade Hinshaw, ed., *Encyclopedia of American Quaker Genealogy*, II (Ann Arbor, Mich., 1938); denominational data on Anglicans and Lutherans in *Pa. Arch.*, 2d Ser., VIII, IX; *A Record of the Inscriptions on the Tablets and GraveStones in the Burial-Grounds of Christ Church, Philadelphia* (Philadelphia, 1864); William White Bronson, *The Inscriptions in St. Peter's Church Yard, Philadelphia* (Camden, N. J., 1879); Norris Stanley Barratt, *Outline of the History of Old St. Paul's Church, Philadelphia, Pennsylvania* (Philadelphia, 1917); and William Montgomery, "Pew Renters of Christ Church, St. Peter's, and St. James's from 1776 to 1815, Compiled from Existing Records" (1948), American Philosophical Society, Philadelphia; manuscript Quaker meeting records on microfilm, Friends' Historical Library, Swarthmore College, Swarthmore, Pa.; and manuscript records of Presbyterian congregations, Presbyterian Historical Society, Philadelphia.

For data on wealth and occupation I have relied principally on "A Transcript of the Assessment of the Seventeenth 18d. Provincial Tax for the City and County of Philadelphia, taken in April, 1774," Pennsylvania Historical and Museum Commission, Harrisburg, Pa., and on a contemporaneous official summary of that transcript, Department of Archives, Philadelphia City Hall, Philadelphia. Figures from this assessment have been supplemented by the 1775 18d. provincial tax assessment and the 1775 Philadelphia constables' assessment, Dept. of Arch., Philadelphia City Hall, and with a printed version of the 1774 summary, *Pa. Arch.*, 3d Ser. (Harrisburg, Pa., 1894-1899), XIV, XV.

Tax assessment figures are often misleading and sometimes completely inaccurate indexes of the wealth of particular individuals. The assumption made in the economic analysis of the committeemen presented in this article, however, is that such errors tend to average out so that alterations in the assessments of whole groups of men (the committees) bear some relationship to the collective wealth of these groups, especially when, as is the case with the committees, successive alterations form a clear trend.

among those whose ages are known are unmistakably clear. First, the committeemen were younger than members of the established government. In 1774 Pennsylvania's ten governor's councilors averaged 56 years of age, and twenty-two assemblymen whose ages are definitely known averaged 45.5 years. Yet on no city committee, at any time between 1765 and 1776, was the average age as great as 42, and on at least three committees the average fell below 40 (Tables I and II). Second, the membership of those committees that were the more radical in behavior was, in nearly every case, younger than that of the more cautious boards. This is especially noticeable in the 1770, 1773, and November 1774 committees, the last two of which also had the greatest turnover in membership of all the resistance bodies. Finally, although the known ages of the committeemen chosen in 1765 and of those elected in 1775 and 1776 average about the same, the trend through the decade shows a clear, if markedly irregular, age decline. Moreover, the surprisingly high age averages tabulated for the committeemen of 1775 and 1776 are almost certainly the result of inadequate data. The two committees elected in these two years contained by far the greatest proportion of men whose ages are not known. If, as seems plausible, their obscurity (which is reflected in a general dearth of information about them) indicates that their careers were in their early stages, it is probable that the average age of Philadelphia committeemen declined right up to independence. Significantly, the May 1774 resurgence of conservatism in resistance politics interrupted this decline, as many committee veterans of 1765 and 1769 joined the new city committee.

Wealth. The changing economic status of the committeemen, while paralleling the pattern of age change both in fluctuation and in general decline, presents a far clearer and more dramatic picture. Officials of the government were much wealthier than the committeemen. The ten councilors were assessed an average of £309 by the provincial tax officials in 1774, at a time when only one city taxpayer in ten owned over £40 in assessed property. Sixteen assemblymen living in the city averaged £211.5. Yet only two Revolutionary committees representing Philadelphia averaged more than £128, and the three boards elected after the meeting of the First Continental Congress all fell well under £100 in assessed wealth per member (Tables I and II).

Radicalism was generally paired in committee politics with modest fortune, as was conservatism with substantial wealth. The tea committee of 1773, which approved the destruction of the tea in Boston, was the

279

poorest board chosen before the convening of the First Continental Congress. The committee of May 20, 1774, the most conservative chosen in that year, was the wealthiest board since 1765 and far exceeded any of its four successors in economic standing. Similarly, the moderates' ticket in the November 1774 election averaged £105, but the radical slate only £83. After removing twenty-one notables who appear on both cards, one discovers thirty-nine moderates with an average assessment of £101, while thirty-nine radicals were rated at an average of only £59. Finally, the tendency of the committees to become less wealthy as they became larger and more radical was very pronounced, describing one downward slope in average assessments from 1765 to 1773, and a second, after a strong resurgence by the city's moderates and conservatives, from May 1774 to February 1776 (Figure 1).[27]

Occupation. The ever more modest wealth of Philadelphia's committeemen was partly a function of their increasing youthfulness and of the city's growing disenchantment with those wealthy importers who traditionally enjoyed close connections with the established Quaker and proprietary factions. Fully as crucial, however, and far more demonstrable in quantitative terms, is the correlation between decreasing average wealth and a rapid increase, beginning in November 1774, in the acceptability of mechanics—artisans, petty manufacturers, and assorted shopkeepers—as political spokesmen (Table II and Figures 1 and 2).[28] This last development undoubtedly owed something to the election of very large committees as the Revolution reached a crisis. By 1775 the committees had more than enough seats for every wealthy merchant. This same factor of size also favored the recruitment of poorer men as leaders, and it may even have effected changes in the committees' age profiles.

Yet Philadelphia's mechanics did not enter radical politics automatically as the city's committees became larger. Between 1770 and 1774 Thomson and other radical merchants sought out and secured the sup-

[27] The reader should not assume that the writer has here slipped into the easy error of identifying the several committees as conservative or radical on the basis of age or wealth. Each board's degree of radicalism, relative to earlier and later committees, to current community standards, and to important policy questions, is quite clear from the contemporary literary evidence cited above.

[28] All persons labeled "merchants" in the 1774 and 1775 assessors' returns who were not elsewhere called retailers or craftsmen have been classified as merchants, regardless of the amount of their assessment. All artisans and manufacturers assessed £50 or more are also classified as merchants, because such persons were generally wholesalers and nascent industrialists. Professionals include doctors, lawyers, and ministers. "Others" include one farmer, several "gentlemen" without any known occupation, and the elder statesman Benjamin Franklin.

port of these men. Thereafter, from June 1774 until the Declaration of Independence, the mechanics organized themselves as a political force, formed alliances with radical young merchants and professionals, composed election tickets upon which they themselves appeared in increasing numbers, and swept first conservative and then moderate merchants from committee office.[29]

The introduction of Philadelphia's mechanics into participatory politics had an immediate and profound impact upon the city's commitment to the Revolution. In 1765 and in 1769 middle-aged, wealthy, generally moderate merchants dominated both establishment politics and committee-led resistance activities. Between 1770 and 1773 resistance politics became more radical as younger and somewhat less wealthy merchants took control of the movement. A strong resurgence of more conservative Philadelphians in early 1774 again brought older and wealthier merchants into power. But Thomson's coalition of radical young merchants and newly mobilized artisans, carefully fostered by every radical strategist, finally broke the wealthy merchants' domination of the city's political life. In June 1774 three-fourths of the committeemen were merchants, while only one-tenth were mechanics. After November the merchants held two-thirds of the places and the mechanics over one-fourth. After August 1775 the artisans occupied one-third of the seats. And in February 1776 the merchants were able to secure less than one-half of the places on the city committee (Table II and Figure 2).[30] Their forty-seven members only slightly outnumbered the forty mechanic spokesmen, and many of these "merchants" were poor young men of trade who, in economic status at least, differed little from their artisan colleagues.

Ethnic Origins and Places of Birth. Just as those who were of only modest fortune and those who worked with their hands were finally having their day in Philadelphia politics, the city's Germans, together with other Philadelphians of several nationalities born outside Pennsylvania, discovered that the Revolution opened up dramatic new political opportunities. Between 1765 and May 1774 fifty-six English, Scots, Welsh, or Scotch-Irishmen, and three thoroughly assimilated Frenchmen served on city committees. Yet not one German was chosen for committee service

281

[29] Schlesinger, *Colonial Merchants*, 215, 217-218, 219-220, 227, 232, 254-255, 271, 273n, 277, 279-281, 290-291, 345-347, 351; Charles S. Olton, "Philadelphia's Mechanics in the First Decade of Revolution 1765-1775," *Journal of American History*, LIX (1972-1973), 311-326; sources cited in nn. 9, 16, and 20 above.

[30] For another count of the occupations of the committeemen of 1774, which discovers even more mechanics than I do, see Robert F. Oaks, "Philadelphia Merchants and the First Continental Congress," *Pa. Hist.*, XL (1973), 149-166, esp. 157-158.

in this period. Thus when Philadelphians placed five Germans on the city committee elected in June 1774, they brought that nationality, which comprised at least one-sixth and perhaps as much as one-fourth of the population of the city, into participatory politics for the first time. Thereafter, some 10 to 15 percent of the seats on the committees were always held by German-Americans, and in 1776, when the province became an independent commonwealth, Germans began entering the legislature in appreciable numbers for the first time in Pennsylvania's history.[31]

Perhaps more significant is the number of persons born outside the province who became prominent radical leaders. Joseph Reed had come from New Jersey, Thomas McKean from Delaware, John Dickinson from Maryland via Delaware, and Dr. Thomas Young from Albany, New York, by way of Boston, Newport, Rhode Island, and New York City. The principal foreign-born leaders included Robert Morris and Thomas Paine from England, and Thomson from Northern Ireland. Several more obscure committeemen were immigrants from Ulster and Germany. To some extent the political prominence of immigrants was natural, for a very large proportion of Pennsylvania's population in the 1770s was not Pennsylvania-born. But Scotch-Irish and German immigrants became far more prominent in the Revolution than they had ever been in either the economic or the political life of pre-Revolutionary Pennsylvania. This is yet another indication of how thoroughly Pennsylvanians rejected their established, largely native-born leaders as they approached the Revolutionary crisis.

Religion. A strong commitment to the Revolutionary movement in Philadelphia would appear to have been closely connected with youth, modest income, and even a manual occupation or immigrant status. Were most Revolutionaries also members of just one or two religious faiths? The literary evidence strongly suggests this, indicating that the leading

282

---

[31] See *Pa. Gaz.*, Nov. 16, 1774, Aug. 23, 1775, Feb. 21, 1776, for lists of committeemen. *Votes and Proceedings*, VIII, 7023-7024, and *Journals of the House of Representatives of the Commonwealth of Pennsylvania* . . . (Philadelphia, 1782), give the number of Germans in the Assembly. Sam Bass Warner, Jr., estimates that about 1/6 of the city was German in the 1770s. *The Private City: Philadelphia in Three Periods of Its Growth* (Philadelphia, 1968), 14-15. However, the burial and baptismal figures given in "historical Notes and Memoranda respecting Philadelphia, etc.," Box 2, Item 161, 25, Proud Collection, Pa. Hist. Soc., and in *An Account of the Births and Burials in the United Churches of Christ-Church and St. Peter's . . . From December 25, 1774, to December 25, 1775* [Philadelphia, 1775], and *An Account of the Baptisms and Burials in all the Churches and Meetings in Philadelphia. From Dec. 25, 1774 to Dec. 25, 1775* [Philadelphia, 1775], suggest that between 1/5 and 1/4 of the city was German in the 1770s.

Revolutionaries were Presbyterians, that Quakers became neutrals or even tories, and that Anglicans split, with the younger communicants tending toward radicalism. In general terms, our quantitative findings present much the same picture, yet the portrait data also reveal that the matter is not nearly so simple.

Religious divisions, in Philadelphia and throughout Pennsylvania, had long been intense, despite the traditional public display of harmony and good will among the province's many faiths. By the mid-eighteenth century these divisions were intimately connected with factional politics in both city and province. They were a determinative factor in Pennsylvania politics in the 1750s and early 1760s, and recent scholarship suggests that they may have been even more fundamental to political contention in the late 1770s and the 1780s.[32]

In the coming of the Revolution, however, religion played a very different role. Several of the greatest radical organizers and propagandists in Philadelphia were indeed Presbyterians: Reed and McKean, who served as chairmen of several city committees; Paine's close friend, Dr. Benjamin Rush; James Cannon, author of the radical Pennsylvania Constitution of 1776; and Thomson. And it is also true that after 1775 Quakers could not engage in Revolutionary politics without risking disownment by the Society of Friends. Yet Thomas Mifflin was both a Quaker and a hero of the resistance until his service with the Continental Army led to disownment. Several other Philadelphians, raised as Quakers and many of them still Friends in good standing until 1775-1776—for example, Owen and Clement Biddle, Christopher Marshall, Sr., Timothy Matlack, Samuel Meredith, Samuel Morris, Jr., Thomas Wharton, Jr., and Dickinson— were important resistance leaders. The role of Philadelphia's Anglicans was fully as important. Without the zealous dedication to the cause of resistance on the part of John Nixon, George Clymer, Robert Morris, John Cadwalader, and scores of less prominent activists, the Revolution might well have failed in Philadelphia.

A quantitative assessment of the coincidence between religious affiliation and committee activity confirms this view (Tables I and II and Figure 3). To be sure, the most heavily Quaker committees tended to be the

283

[32] The best recent treatments of the religious-political linkage in the 1760s are Hutson, *Pennsylvania Politics*, 200-243; Newcomb, *Franklin and Galloway*, Chaps. 8-9; and Bockelman and Ireland, "Internal Revolution," *Pa. Hist.*, XLI (1974), 127-144. For a fresh and stimulating look at this relationship after the Declaration see Owen S. Ireland, "The Ethnic-Religious Dimension of Pennsylvania Politics, 1778-1779," *WMQ*, 3d Ser., XXX (1973), 423-448.

most moderate.[33] Conversely, in 1776 when Friends in good standing could no longer serve on Revolutionary committees, the political activity of all Quakers, whether in full membership or disowned, reached its nadir. Yet the most radical committees, if the least Quaker, were not the most Presbyterian, as the conventional wisdom on Revolutionary politics would lead one to expect. In fact, Anglicans were usually the most numerous group on the more radical boards. These committees were also more evenly balanced in religious composition than the more moderate boards that preceded them.

Throughout the Revolution the connections between religious affiliation and political activity were evident in relation to the imperial question, just as they had been in provincial matters. To Scotch-Irish Presbyterians, anti-London sentiment came easily, while the prospect of violent resistance would deter the Quakers, who were at once a pacifist sect and a minority experiencing a continuing relative economic and political decline in Pennsylvania. What is important here is the extent to which the committee movement overcame this natural pattern of political perception and behavior.

The most meaningful and potentially explosive divisions within Philadelphia may well have been those between the leading religious faiths, rather than between economic, occupational, or ethnic groups. To heal those divisions, the city's resistance leaders determined, early on, to secure religiously balanced, inclusive committees.[34] The result of their policy was not just show. The city's Anglicans, for example, were mobilized: they rallied, wrote, and fought for colonial autonomy. And conservative Quakers, who might easily have become a major obstacle to the Revolution, were quickly reduced to political impotence as over one hundred young, energetic, and often wealthy Friends abandoned the meetinghouse for the committee room or the drill field.[35] What is most striking in all this is

[33] Note esp. the number of Friends on the committees of 1765, 1769, and May 1774.

[34] See above pp. 569-570 and nn. 12 and 13 on Thomson's balanced denominational recruiting in May and June 1774. It should be mentioned here, however, that the balance and particularly the inclusiveness achieved in 1774-1776 were really impressive only in relation to the earlier committees. On the last three committees, the dominant Anglicans, Presbyterians, and Quakers together held at least 76% of the seats. According to the vital statistics cited in n. 31, however, these three groups composed only 39% of the city's population. Among these three faiths representation generally did follow population distribution; thus the greatest number of delegates were Anglican. Germans and British-descended members of minor sects, however, remained underrepresented right up to the Declaration.

[35] Records of the Philadelphia Monthly Meeting (center city), and of the Northern and Southern District Monthly Meetings (the suburbs), microfilm, Friends' Hist. Lib.

the cooperation between radicals of different religious faiths.

Change and Development. The foregoing discussion of the age, wealth, occupation, nationality, and religion of Philadelphia's committeemen manifests two distinct patterns of change in the eight years between the Townshend Act boycott and independence. First, those committees that were larger and that had a greater proportion of men new to committee activity (1773 and November 1774), those whose members were younger and poorer and included many artisans and shopkeepers (November 1774, 1775, and 1776), and those in which Quakers did not outnumber Anglicans or Presbyterians (1770, 1773, November 1774, and especially 1776) adopted a more radical stance than the older, wealthier, more veteran, more mercantile, and more Quaker boards (1765, 1769, and May 1774). Second, no matter how radical the committees became, they continued to draw their members from all major economic, occupational, ethnic, and religious groups within the city, and to keep the most powerful of these groups roughly in balance.

Several factors lay behind these two leadership patterns. First, the tendency for Philadelphia's younger and poorer men to become more radical than older and wealthier residents most probably relates to the former group's relatively small investment in the present compared with their much grander hopes for the future. Wealthy merchants over forty found it harder to take this attitude toward the Revolution. For middle-aged Quakers who were past their political and even their economic zenith, passive neutrality and even bitter reaction were natural responses to the imperial crisis, inadequate though they might be. All of this is speculation, however, and lies within the shadowy realm of the motivation of individuals long deceased. More central to our inquiry are the social and collective motives and methods whereby the young, the poor, and the mechanics, the Anglicans, the Presbyterians, and the Germans came forward as many of the old elite faded, or were forced, into the background.

In part, these new men may have consciously seized on the imperial crisis as their opportunity to play a more important role in politics than even the veteran radicals who sought their support expected or desired. Between 1770 and 1774 the mechanics, in particular, readied themselves to take a leading part in public life.[36] Yet even in 1776, well-to-do and well-

---

[36] One may trace the gradual organization of the mechanics as a conscious, distinct political force in "A Brother Chip," *Pa. Gaz.*, Sept. 27, 1770; broadside by 10 candidates, *Fellow Citizens and Countrymen* (Philadelphia, Oct. 1, 1772); "At a

educated Philadelphians played the leading roles in city politics. In large measure, the changing composition of Philadelphia's political leadership was the product of a conscious, well-planned program, dimly visible as early as 1769-1770 and fully operational from June 1774 to independence. Philadelphia's committees were balanced and inclusive because those who composed the election tickets and led the boards had willed it so.[37] Philadelphia's radical leaders did not abandon elitist politics in the Revolution, but redefined them. It remains to consider why they did so, and to offer a few reflections on the results of their policy.

286

In 1765 Philadelphia's merchants appointed a small extra-constitutional board to administer a voluntary boycott of English imports. Just ten years later the full city electorate placed one hundred men on a committee that enforced a comprehensive embargo, aided the city militia in securing arms and ammunition, petitioned the Assembly for a new militia law and an expanded legislature, tried persons accused of obstructing the resistance and condemned those convicted to public ostracism, engaged in controlling propaganda in the city press, and served as the chief liaison group between Philadelphia and the Continental Congress. By 1775 Philadelphia's committees governed the city, not in law but in fact. This new government faced unprecedented duties of the most serious and taxing nature.

The primary reason for the expansion of political recruitment was the need for governmental, even bureaucratic, manpower. Every city district, eventually every block, had its committee delegates who scrutinized their neighbors for fidelity to the embargo and dedication in opposing British authority.[38] Merchants and mariners, manufacturers and craftsmen, shop-

---

Meeting of Respectable Inhabitants," June 17, 1774, and letter from the mechanics to Dickinson, June 27, 1774, Dickinson material, R. R. Logan Coll.; letter from a mechanic assembly to the city committee, July 8, 1774, 20-22, Du Simitière Coll., Pa. Hist. Soc.; notices of the election of the city committee of 66, *Pa. Gaz.*, Nov. 2, 9, 16, 23, 1774; *Pa. Packet*, Nov. 7, 1774; and in the 3 election tickets for the Aug. 1775 committee, 962.F. 70, 72, 73, Philadelphia Lib. Co. The best modern treatments of this process are Schlesinger, *Colonial Merchants*, 215, 217-218, 219-220, 227, 232, 254-255, 271, 273n, 277, 279-281, 290-291, 345-347, 351; Hutson, "Philadelphia's White Oaks," *WMQ*, 3d Ser., XXVIII (1971), 3-25; Hutson, *Pennsylvania Politics*, Chap. 4; Newcomb, *Franklin and Galloway*, 212-213; and Olton, "Philadelphia's Mechanics," *JAH*, LIX (1972-1973), 311-326.

[37] The winning ticket of Feb. 1776 and probably also that of Aug. 1775 (labeled "the mechanicks' ticket" by a contemporary) were composed by leading active members of the respective existing city committees, and tended to be more balanced and inclusive in their ethnic, economic, and denominational dimensions than the opposing moderate slates. The winning ticket of Nov. 1774 appears to have been composed by leading radicals of the existing committee, chosen in June 1774, plus spokesmen of the city's mechanics. See the election tickets cited in nn. 16 and 20; *Pa. Gaz.*, Nov. 2, 9, 1774; and Duane, ed., *Passages from Marshall*, 65.

[38] The committeemen elected in Nov. 1774, Aug. 1775, and Feb. 1776 were

keepers, printers, and lawyers all turned their talents and knowledge to governing the community and keeping it zealous and faithful in the cause of resistance, both in word and in deed.

To achieve their tasks Philadelphia's Revolutionary leaders sought many men who possessed both general and specific talents and who enjoyed the best possible connections with Philadelphia's many sub-cultures. Strategists of the resistance movement quickly appreciated not only the need for manpower, but also the impression of power and legitimacy that numbers would lend to their cause. Thus Thomson observed: "The Committee . . . which was elected [in 1775] . . . was, for the purpose of giving them more weight and influence, increased to the number of one hundred."[39] And as Philadelphians of all occupations took their committee seats, the merchants began watching the wharves and warehouses, the mariners set to inspecting ships, the manufacturers and artisans turned to procuring armaments and war supplies, the shopkeepers began observing their fellow retailers, and the lawyers started talking and writing to, and negotiating with, everyone about everything.

Numbers, then, provided the basic muscle of Revolutionary politics, impressed and persuaded the public, and afforded a broad range of expertise. They gave the Revolution another dimension as well. A committee of one hundred men could represent a city of twenty-five thousand in a way that no board of twenty could.[40] The use of larger bodies permitted the constant communication—the passing up from freemen to public officials of attitudes, needs, and desires, and the passing down to the freemen of orders, resolves, and explanations—that Philadelphia needed in the stress of revolutionary times.

Moreover, this intimate and intense form of representation did not involve twenty-five thousand undifferentiated constituents. Pennsylvania was run by English and Welsh Quaker and Anglican merchants and farmers, plus a few Scots and Scotch-Irish Presbyterians. The majority of artisans, Germans, and Scotch-Irish were at best on the periphery of the political community. Their talents and drive, fully harnessed in the economy, were lost to the polity. This was perhaps unimportant before 1765, when the city and province were seldom subjected to great political or military pressure from outside forces. In the Revolution, however, to disregard so much manpower—so desperately needed in combating an

287

---

evenly divided up and assigned to six geographical districts covering the city and the suburbs for the purpose of observing all importing, exporting, and wholesale and retail trade. *Pa. Gaz.*, Dec. 7, 1774, Aug. 30, 1775, Feb. 26, 1776.

[39] "Papers of Thomson," N.-Y. Hist. Soc., *Colls.*, XI (1878), 283.

[40] For this estimate of the city's population see Warner, *Private City*, 12.

external foe and defeating its internal sympathizers—was unthinkable for the city's radical organizers. The last function of increasing popular participation in committee politics, then, was to draw a greater proportion of the community into resistance activity. The Revolution tore Pennsylvania politics wide open. Hundreds of theretofore obscure Anglicans, Presbyterians, Germans, Baptists, craftsmen, and shopkeepers grasped this occasion to take part in the public life of their community.

In the 1770s Pennsylvanians began to enter the age of mass politics. While both the concept and the practice of elitist leadership were very much alive in Revolutionary Pennsylvania, they were evolving rapidly under the impact of an enlarged public role for the ordinary freeman. Between 1774 and the Jeffersonian era, Pennsylvania politics would exhibit an ever-changing blend of older elitist and newer mass-oriented elements. This was new in eighteenth-century politics. It has been suggested that the world's first modern political parties appeared in Pennsylvania in the late 1770s and the 1780s.[41] And it was the Philadelphia committee movement that initiated this transition.

The mass mobilization that accompanied the recruitment of a new and broader elite led to the rapid achievement of the radicals' basic goal. In 1774 and 1775 Pennsylvania's governmental institutions yielded to the popular demand for broad resistance to British authority. In 1776 the established order, after belatedly attempting to draw the line at independence, quickly collapsed under the onslaught of Pennsylvania's Revolutionary recruits. Without the creation of this new leadership by the committee movement, it is most doubtful that independence could have come to Pennsylvania except through the violent coercion of Continental regiments and a civil war. In the 1760s and early 1770s Pennsylvania lacked nearly every ingredient for revolution found variously in the New England colonies and in Virginia: a strong dissenting tradition, widely felt economic grievances, or a legislature intimately acquainted with royal government.[42] Only the painstaking enlistment of a strong leadership core, the construction of new political institutions, and the rapid mobilization of the majority of the community could overcome these deficiencies. In Pennsylvania British authority succumbed to the activity of a few hundred men who were drawn into public life by perhaps twenty veteran politicians within just two years. To these men and to their committees Pennsylvania owed its Revolution.

288

---

[41] William Nisbet Chambers, *Political Parties in a New Nation: The American Experience, 1776-1809* (New York, 1963), 19-20.

[42] Philadelphia's Quakers were, of course, dissenters. Due to their pacifism, however, their dissent did not present as sharp a challenge to the established order of the British Empire as did that of the Calvinist denominations.

TABLE I
COMPARATIVE PROFILE OF PHILADELPHIA'S RESISTANCE COMMITTEES, 1765 to 1773

Committee	Merchants' Committee Oct. 1765	Merchants' Committee Mar. 1769	Merchants' Committee Sept. 1770	Tea Committee Dec. 1773
No. of Members	11	20	20	24
Persistency[a]	27%	55%	30%	38%
Long-term Continuity[b]	--	30%	60%	29%
Age[c]				
20-29	-	2	5	3
30-39	5	8	7	9
40-49	2	6	6	5
50-59	2	1	1	2
Unknown	2	1	1	5
Average[d]	41.0	40.8	36.8	38.8
Occupation				
Merchant	9	20	17	17
Mechanic	2	-	1	1
Professional	-	-	2	2
Unknown	-	-	-	4
Wealth (£)				
0-49	2	2	4	9
50-99	1	3	3	5
100-199	2	12	9	4
200+	4	1	3	3
Unknown	2	2	1	3
Average	191	128	126	89
Religion				
Quaker	6	8	5	4
Anglican	1	6	7	8
Presbyterian	2	6	6	5
Other	-	-	1	3
Unknown	3	-	-	4

289

Notes:
 [a] The percentage of the members of each committee who served on the succeeding committee.
 [b] The percentage of the members of each committee who had served on any earlier committee, including the seven-man delegation (not discussed in this article) that called on John Hughes to resign his commission as Stamp Agent in 1765.
 [c] In the year of each committee's formation.
 [d] Based on exact known ages only: 7 of 11 in 1765, 14 of 20 in 1769, 15 of 20 in 1770, and 16 of 24 in 1773. The decennial breakdowns, in contrast, include both ages known exactly and those known approximately or estimated from tax data.
Sources:
 Lists of the committeemen (partial for 1769) appear in Morgan and Morgan, *Stamp Act Crisis*, 315-317; Schlesinger, *Colonial Merchants*, 79; *Pa. Gaz.*, June 10, Sept. 20, 27, 1770; *Pennsylvania Chronicle* (Philadelphia), Oct. 1, 1770; *Pa. Gaz.*, Oct. 20, 1773; and Philadelphia tea committee to Boston, Dec. 25, 1773, Reed Papers.

TABLE II
COMPARATIVE PROFILE OF PHILADELPHIA'S
FIVE MAJOR RADICAL COMMITTEES, MAY 1774-FEBRUARY 1776

Date of Election	May 1774	June 1774	Nov. 1774	Aug. 1775	Feb. 1776
No. of Members	19	43	66	100	100
Persistency	89%	42%	67%	69%	--
Long-term Continuity	68%	58%	35%	49%	73%
Age					
20-29	-	-	3	3	4
30-39	7	16	29	30	29
40-49	11	17	14	19	18
50-59	-	5	5	7	7
60+	1	1	2	4	4
Unknown	-	3	13	37	38
Average[a]	41.8	41.9	39.4	41.5	41.1
Occupation					
Merchant	15	33	44	54	47
Mechanic	1	4	18	35	40
Professional	3	3	3	4	5
Other	-	3	-	4	4
Unknown	-	-	1	3	4
Wealth (£)					
0-49	6	16	35	57	62
50-99	3	10	12	17	14
100-199	7	12	12	14	10
200+	3	5	6	9	7
Unknown	-	-	1	3	8
Average	155	112	82	73	64
Religion[b]					
Quaker	8	14	18	29	22
Anglican	5	8	20	26	30
Presbyterian	5	11	18	18	21
Baptist	1	3	1	2	3
Lutheran	-	2	3	2	2
Other	-	1	2	-	1
Unknown	-	4	4	23	21

Notes:
[a] Based on exact known ages only: 16 of 19 in May 1774, 35 of 43 in June 1774, 41 of 66 in Nov. 1774, 51 of 100 in Aug. 1775, and 48 of 100 in Feb. 1776. The decennial breakdowns, as in Table I, include both ages known exactly and those known approximately or estimated.
[b] Including Friends disowned or inactive before 1774: 3 of 8 on the May 1774 board, 3 of 14 in June 1774, 5 of 14 in Nov. 1774, 8 of 29 in Aug. 1775, and 7 of 22 in Feb. 1776.
Sources:
The committee lists appear in *Pa. Gaz.*, May 25, June 22, Nov. 23, 1774, Aug. 23, 1775, Feb. 21, 1776.

290

FIGURE I
Average Assessed Wealth of the Philadelphia Committees, 1765 to 1776

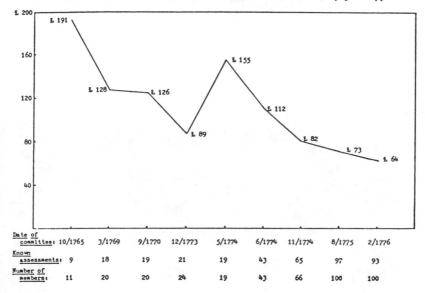

FIGURE 2
Percentages of Merchants, Mechanics, and Professionals on the
Philadelphia Committees, 1765 to 1776

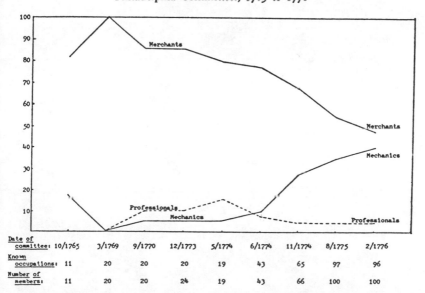

FIGURE 3
Percentages of Committeemen Known to Have Been Quakers, Anglicans, or
Presbyterians, 1765 to 1776

292

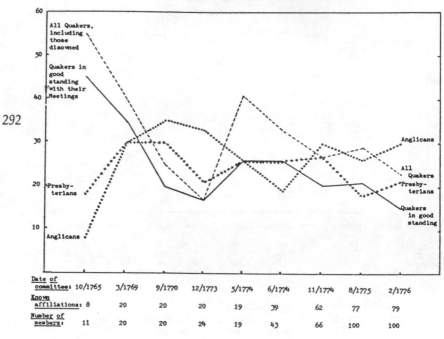

Dramatizing the Ideology of Revolution:
Popular Mobilization in Virginia, 1774 to 1776

Rhys Isaac

Thursday the 21st ult. [December, 1775] in Lancaster county, a Negro fellow was tried and found guilty of sheepstealing; he was sentenced to be burnt in the hand, but instead of saying *God save the King* (as is usual upon such occasion) he roared out, with the greatest seeming sincerity, "God d—n the K—g, and the Governor too."[1]

W E are brought abruptly into the presence of the Revolution by this cryptic report of a trial in northern Virginia during the last months of King George's reign in America. No other record of this court of oyer and terminer under the king's commission survives, and we shall never know the answers to most of the questions that rise in our minds as we read the newspaper report. We do not even know the name and fortunes of the not-so-humble slave momentarily caught in the limelight. Following ancient English custom, extended to include enslaved Africans and their descendants, he was allowed "benefit of clergy" so that, in place of hanging as a convicted felon, he might this once be burnt in the hand in open court, lashed, and released. We do not know whether the cry was drawn forth primarily by relief at the mercy shown by the court, or pain at the impress of the hot iron, or whether a different exclamation on the part of the slave was distorted by nervous slaveowners into the form reported. A month previously, the governor, Lord Dunmore, had raised the royal standard and promised freedom to the slaves and servants of rebels who would rally to it. Masters were understandably anxious to believe that their slaves were faithful to them, sharing their hatred of the governor.[2]

The enigmatic quality of this episode, however, may make it more, not

Mr. Isaac is a member of the Department of History, La Trobe University, Australia. He would like to acknowledge the invaluable assistance of Mr. John W. Dudley and his colleagues at the Virginia State Library. Much of the research for this study was carried out under the auspices of the American Council of Learned Societies, while the work was done mainly in the Research Department of the Colonial Williamsburg Foundation, through the kindness of Dr. Edward M. Riley and his staff. The following persons gave invaluable help in the writing and revising: Inga Clendinnen, Donna Merwick, and Margaret Peart.

[1] *Virginia Gazette* (Dixon and Hunter), Jan. 6, 1776.
[2] Richard Starke, *The Office and Authority of a Justice of the Peace* (Williamsburg, Va., 1774), 86-91.

less, suitable as a point of departure for an essay devoted to exploring aspects
of the "Spirit of '76" about which the advancement of our understanding.
after two hundred years, is most urgent. Preserved for us, like a fly in amber,
this little fragment of forensic drama is most suggestive concerning important
general issues, for it brings us into touch with the experience of revolutionary
overturn, not at the level of the ideologues who constructed the frameworks
of meaning and legitimacy for the emergent new order, but at the level of
country folk—squires, farmers, and bondsmen—whose symbolic universe
was thrown into turmoil by the transformations in process. Momentarily at
least, coherence for them could best be maintained by emphatic inversion,
"God *damn* the King!"

294

    Furthermore, the episode confronts us directly with the county court-
house and its ceremonial. It was at the courthouse that men gathered to hear
the news and arrive at an interpretation of the progress of events; it was to
the courthouse that they came first of all in answer to the beat of the drum;
and so it was at the courthouse—or at the meetinghouse or the townhouse—
that the armies were formed to terminate George III's dominion in the
colonies. Our interpretation of the Revolution will be radically deficient until
we refine our understanding of the interactions and communications that
centered on the courthouse or its equivalent in other social-geographic
regions.

    The special significance of the courthouse, and of other comparable
places of congregation in early America, is closely related to the phenomenon
which is characterized by the phrase "face-to-face society." We have intuited
the existence of a distinctive social dynamic in premodern communities. Is it
not time to systematize our awareness of the peculiarities of that past world?
It is with the functioning of language and communication—the bonding of
society—that we may most profitably begin such an inquiry.

    Consideration of the impact of different media of communication upon
the psychology of individuals reared in diverse cultural systems has come into
being only since electronic devices have liberated observers from the un-
stated, and therefore unquestioned, assumption that writing is the true form
of language and that written statements and diagrams are an ultimate
reality.[3] Words (and other signs) are the elements of which our perceptions
of the world are composed. It is now recognized that persons who are
socialized into a reading-and-writing culture, and who are endowed with a

    [3] Marshall McLuhan, *The Gutenberg Galaxy: The Making of Typographic
Men* (London, 1962). The subject is treated more systematically and in chronological
framework in Walter J. Ong, *The Presence of the Word: Some Prolegomena for
Cultural and Religious History* (New Haven, Conn., 1967). I am grateful to Norman
Fiering for this reference and for many stimulating discussions.

printed-book orientation with respect to information of all kinds, have a sense of words as essentially written (and not sound) signals. When writing becomes the paradigmatic form of knowledge, there is, for those whose perceptions are molded by this medium, a decisive tipping of the balance in the interplay of the senses toward sight.[4] Furthermore, since writing has a permanence in isolation from other media, it can be divorced from compelling social context in a way in which sound cannot be without the aid of recording devices. The shift from an ear-centered to an eye-centered mode of learning about, and hence knowing, the world is at most some three thousand years old—and that for a tiny proportion of humanity. The emergence of entire populations or social systems, so conditioned, is a phenomenon scarcely more than a century old. The patterns of society are inevitably very different on either side of this sensory-experiential watershed, which probably constitutes the most important component in the elusive distinction between modern and premodern. The structures of oral society are necessarily closely dependent on face-to-face interaction for their establishment and reinforcement in a way that is not so for modern societies where impersonal media are primary and continuing sources of knowledge about the social world. These media make possible a level of withdrawal from close immediate dependence on others—individualism, it might be called—which is inconceivable in premodern society.[5]

The distinction between societies with a large residual oral component and our own predominantly literate world is not confined to the way words themselves are experienced. Verbalization functions differently in traditional oral culture and is a less dominant mode, since gesture and dramaturgical forms are habitually called upon to carry a far greater burden of the message. Erving Goffman has superbly revealed the possibilities of dramaturgical analysis as a means of illuminating the structures and processes of our own society. There can be no doubt, however, that in the world of early America, the positional and body-language component of the communication process was much greater and more significant than pre-television generations of historians were able to conceive. Speech in such traditional milieux is imbedded in social structure, and verbalization is thereby circumscribed. In face-to-face societies, where words are not experienced only as sounds but as sounds accompanied by gestures and facial expressions, communication is essentially a "verbo-motor" phenomenon. The sensitivities of persons reared in such a culture intensify both the possibility and the inevitability of dramatic forms of statement: the purely verbal must necessarily seem incomplete, unachieved.[6] Thus the written word in such cultural contexts

295

---

[4] Ong, *Presence of the Word*, 6-8, 66-69, 72-73, 220-222.
[5] *Ibid.*, 40, 54, 72, 231-233.
[6] Erving Goffman, *The Presentation of Self in Everyday Life* (Garden

strives to transcend these keenly felt limitations. We shall find the passionate language of the polemics and apologetics of the American Revolution replete with body-language implications and imagery: "the hand of power raised," "rapacity opens wide her mouth." Such residual oral-culture traits in the printed output of the patriots are important to note, especially at a time when it is not uncommon for the whig publicists and leaders to be viewed as paranoid. Oral culture, created and sustained in the intensities of face-to-face encounters, has an inherent tendency to interpret the social world in terms of the direct interactions of friends and enemies. Gordon Wood has suggested that the whigs' conspiracy interpretation of politics, because secular, should be regarded as a notable step into modern thought patterns. The modernity of the secularism, however, is more than offset by the personalized perspective—a diagnostic feature of oral, as opposed to typographic, culture.[7]

The cry has gone out in recent years for the history of the "inarticulate," and this is well because it draws our attention to the many, so long ignored, whose needs and capacities have always governed the performances of the actors who monopolize the limelight of "history."[8] It is sobering, however, to reflect that we have been arrogant enough to call inarticulate those many whose language we have not understood. It is true that the humble and the illiterate are silent in the presence of conventional historical methods, since they leave few, if any, personal written statements revealing the meaning of their lives. How "typical" are those who do? For most people most of the time, and for the overwhelming majority of persons raised in premodern, verbo-motor cultures all of the time, the most profound expressions of the meanings they find in life are surely made in highly charged forms of patterned action. In Virginia, for example, there is every reason to believe that dancing, to which people of all ranks were passionately addicted, was a primary medium for some of the most powerful declarations of self. These

City, N.Y., 1959), is an invaluable handbook for historians concerned with the analysis of social situations. For an outline on positional or restricted code communication see Mary Douglas, *Natural Symbols: Explorations in Cosmology* (London, 1970), 20-32. For verbo-motor culture see Ong, *Presence of the Word*, 30, 148, 174-175.

[7] Virginia House of Burgesses resolution of May 24, 1774, in *Va. Gaz.* (Rind), May 26, 1774; "W.H.O.," *ibid.*, June 30, 1774; Gordon S. Wood, *The Creation of the American Republic, 1776-1787* (Chapel Hill, N.C., 1969), 40-41. On the polemic character of oral culture—its tendency to see the world in terms of a personalized dichotomy of good and evil (hence of conspiracies)—see Ong, *Presence of the Word*, 255-262.

[8] Jesse Lemisch, "Listening to the 'Inarticulate': William Widger's Dream and the Loyalties of American Revolutionary Seamen in British Prisons," *Journal of Social History*, III (1969-1970), 1-29; James Hutson, "An Investigation of the Inarticulate: Philadelphia's White Oaks," *William and Mary Quarterly*, 3d Ser., XXVIII (1971), 3-25.

declarations were the more powerful because resonant all the way up and down society. The notorious overrepresentation of New England in early American historiography may be attributed in part to the natural preference of typographic-age scholars for a society that expressed itself copiously in print over a cultural region like Virginia where statements of the meaning of life were most naturally and fully presented in vivid dance forms.

The dominance of verbalization, especially of the printed word, in shaping both perception and expression in our literate culture has not only reduced the importance of body-language communication (tending, until the advent of electronic media, to restrict it to the private domain), but has also weakened our capacity to generate and respond to intense communal excitement. The shared ecstasies of religious awakenings were the most spectacular manifestations of the persistence of that capacity in the eighteenth-century world.[9] In modern society, before the electronic age, this form of response remained powerful only in marginal social milieux with a high residual oral component.

The objection naturally arises that, important as this component of communication may have been, it is by its nature swept away in the stream of time and lost to the historian. The objection has less force than might be supposed. The enterprise of recovering the dramatic statements of plain folk from the past is comparatively new, but already it is clear that, although the record is fragmentary, it is serviceable for the purposes of reconstruction. The very importance of body-language communication to those lost worlds increased the likelihood that revealing descriptions of significant postures and gesticulation would be included in written accounts of action.[10]

We are not yet able to locate precisely any of the North American provinces on the scale which extends from wholly oral, through largely or residually oral, to primarily literate, but we begin to have sophisticated estimates of levels of literacy which we may seek to refine and to interpret in relation to other indications of cultural patterns. In a pioneer systematic comparative study Kenneth Lockridge has concluded that white male literacy, outside New England, held fairly steady at or below two-thirds (the same level that prevailed in England) for the whole of the eighteenth century. This measure is of minimal literacy as tested by the ability to sign

297

---

[9] Much of the best evidence of residual oral characteristics in 18th-century Virginia is to be found in the field of religion (outside the scope of this essay). See Rhys Isaac, "Preachers and Patriots: Popular Culture and the Revolution in Virginia," in Alfred F. Young, ed., *The American Revolution: Explorations in the History of American Radicalism* (DeKalb, Ill., 1976), 125-156.

[10] For an example see E. P. Thompson, "The Moral Economy of the English Crowd in the Eighteenth Century," *Past and Present*, L (1971), 76-136, in which a superb discussion of socially resonant values and expectations is derived primarily from a dramaturgical analysis of grain riots.

one's name—a low level of performance in relation to the internalization of the alphabet. Among females the proportion of signers was much lower. The literacy of slaves cannot be measured, but we may be sure that it was negligible. In Virginia society it seems that no more than 25 percent of adults could sign their name. Only a tiny proportion of the population in such a society would have their information-orientation toward writing rather than speech. Even the fully literate elite would be socialized and attuned to the predominantly oral-aural medium of the society in which they lived.[11] This is not to deny the fact that Virginia possessed a numerous gentry, most of whom were keenly literate, at least in the field of law as it was understood in the province, and sometimes highly cultured in the cosmopolitan mode of their time.[12] In a society like that of late eighteenth-century Virginia, where a large portion of the people lived enveloped in the oral medium of folk culture, the roles, status, and power of the fully literate minority constitute a theme of special importance, for they may hold the key to the transmission of revolutionary ideas and the mobilization of revolutionary sentiments.

The purpose of this essay is both to commemorate the popular upsurge that culminated in July 1776 and to explore means of advancing our understanding of the oral-dramaturgical processes through which emotions were communicated, intensified by sharing, and channelled into social action. Great advances have been made in American Revolution studies during the last decade with the elucidation of the political worldview that united the literate genteel leaders in the colonies. We have, however, made only slow progress in the task of investigating the manner in which the literary-ideological formulations of the elite were communicated to the humbler ranks, to whom the pamphlets were rarely addressed, nor have we gone far in analyzing the ways in which ideological commitment was translated into a mass social movement.[13] These tasks must prove very complex, for while the

[11] Kenneth A. Lockridge, *Literacy in Colonial New England: An Enquiry into the Social Context of Literacy in the Early Modern West* (New York, 1974), 77-81. In New England alone did literacy rates rise markedly in the 18th century, until near universal male literacy (as measured) was reached by 1800. In the present discussion our concern is not with minimal ability to sign one's name or read painfully through the pages of a book, but with habitual print orientation in relation to words and information.

[12] See Charles Sydnor, *American Revolutionaries in the Making: Political Practices in Washington's Virginia* (New York, 1965 [orig. publ. Chapel Hill, N.C., 1952]), 17-18.

[13] Cf. Bernard Bailyn, *The Ideological Origins of the American Revolution* (Cambridge, Mass., 1967), and Wood, *Creation of the Republic*. Pauline Maier, *From Resistance to Revolution: Colonial Radicals and the Development of American Opposition to Britain, 1765-1776* (New York, 1972), traces, in a perspective that tends to merge the colonies, the stages of disillusionment and activation of literate, ideologized leaders, principally in the urban centers. The markedly genteel orienta-

success of the ideological interpretation of the Revolution depends largely on the persuasive demonstration that there existed an elite political culture whose features were remarkably uniform throughout the colonies, a corresponding uniformity at the level of popular culture almost certainly did not exist. When we turn from the synchronizing ideological system by which the "thirteen clocks" were made, miraculously it seemed, to strike as one, to investigate the operation of that system upon the social-political mechanisms of the individual provincial clocks, we shall need to divest ourselves of the notion of a single "American" society and to concentrate instead upon the particularities of the regional sub-cultures and on the manner of their response to the mounting crisis.

299

The distinctness of the regional social-cultural systems of British North America is intentionally stressed as a counter-hypothesis to the implications of uniformity often introduced by social historians who organize their analyses in terms of "class." Marx's insights, together with our own experience of modern urbanized society, conspire to freight this word with connotations of broad national—indeed, international—strata of society, sharing not only a common relationship to the means of production but a common mentality. The limitations of scale inherent in oral, face-to-face cultural systems militated against such uniformities. Furthermore, the different dynamics of such societies imposed a distinctive pattern on the forms of status differentiation. If we are going to apply the term "class," we must divest it of unexamined connotations of widely shared values and expectations. We must recognize the limitations to its usefulness, as a category outside economic history, for analyzing sub-cultural systems and for interpreting the "experienced" meanings of life and events available to those who lived within such systems. Eighteenth-century perception was more commonly expressed in terms of "ranks" of men—a word more apt to convey the sense of a community pecking-order, composed of known persons, which was the prevailing experience in premodern agrarian society.[14] Com-

---

tion of pamphlet and newspaper writing in this period has been stressed in Gordon S. Wood, "The Democratization of Mind in the American Revolution," *Leadership in the American Revolution*, Library of Congress Symposia (Washington, D.C., 1974), 63-88.

[14] The deadlocked debate concerning the social composition of the Philadelphia "White Oaks" might yield more insight into the functioning of a social institution if the "White Oaks" were conceptualized as a ranked, vertical structure rather than as a "class" association within a single horizontal social stratum (a model we derive from the dominant institutional forms of *our* day). Hutson, "Investigation of the Inarticulate," *WMQ*, 3d Ser., XXVIII (1971), 3-25; Jesse Lemisch and John K. Alexander, "The White Oaks, Jack Tar, and the Concept of the 'Inarticulate'," *ibid.*, XXIX (1972), 109-134. For an elaborated historian's model of a vertically organized 18th-century society, highly relevant to students of early British North

parative studies will ultimately have an important place in the advancement of our overall understanding, but we must first seek to develop insights into the folk cultures of the North American Atlantic seaboard by the approach which the anthropologist Clifford Geertz has luminously expounded under the heading "Thick Description." We shall need to apply our minds to interpreting individual systems, understood *from within*.[15] By way of exploring modes of procedure in that enterprise, this essay will attempt an analysis of aspects of Virginia courthouse culture and the patterns of communication and mobilization centering there, as the defense of the rights of British America turned into a war for independence.

300

The courthouse in its physical setting is readily pictured—usually an isolated little brick structure with a simple, round-arched, loggia-style porch on the front. It generally stood at a crossroads in the midst of woods and fields, since most counties had no towns, and central location was the prime concern. The courthouse itself would never be quite solitary, for it engendered a small cluster of its own. Thus when William Byrd passed by the newly established Caroline County courthouse, located some distance from the rivers that were the arteries of the county's commerce, he noted that "Colonel Armistead and Colonel Will Beverley have each of 'em erected an ordinary well supplied with wine and other polite liquors for the worshipful bench. Besides these, there is a rum ordinary for persons of a more vulgar taste. Such liberal supplies of strong drink often make Justice nod and drop the scales out of her hands."[16] Such institutions as ordinaries were an important part of the word-of-mouth communication system.

In seeking to understand the social significance of the courthouse in its traditional context we must force our historical imagination out of our own diffuse, map-based sense of geographical extension and back into the particularized social space of premodern communities. This was a close world of familiar places, known, as people were known, by personal and family associations. Indeed, the linkage of places to persons was formally celebrated and reinforced every three years by the memorization ritual of boundary processioning. Within this personalized landscape the courthouse was a focal point of the most intense social significance.

Only in their comings together did premodern, face-to-face communities have real existence. It was in its monthly concourse at the courthouse that Virginia community was most fully embodied and represented, in ranked

America, see Harold Perkin, *The Origins of Modern English Society* (London, 1969), 17-62. I am indebted to Gordon S. Wood for this reference.
[15] Clifford Geertz, *The Interpretation of Cultures* (New York, 1973), 3-30.
[16] Louis B. Wright, ed., *The Prose Works of William Byrd of Westover: Narratives of a Colonial Virginian* (Cambridge, Mass., 1966), 374.

order, to itself. A brief newspaper report of a moment of drama serves to reveal the customary forms of society. We may see a courthouse green literally illuminated for an instant one Thursday in July 1768: "Last Sussex court day at night, a flash of lightning struck near the end of the courthouse of that county, killed two horses (the property of one Ehren Horn . . .) and three hogs. . . . There were upwards of an hundred people in and about the ordinary, within thirty yards of where the mischief was done. The poor man that owned the horses was indemnified upon the spot, by the generous contribution of the Gentlemen who attended that court."[17] Court day had drawn so large a multitude that more than one hundred remained at the ordinary after dark. The horse trader, Ehren Horn, was no doubt one of a number of dealers and peddlers who had come to offer their goods for sale—a custom that turned court days into regular country fairs. The gentlemen in attendance displayed that liberality proper to their rank by making up the unfortunate's losses. Earlier in the day some of these same gentlemen would have conducted the court, lending their personal authority to what was nearly the sum and substance of government at that time—the adjudication of disputes, the recording of transactions, and the distribution of small favors. We must picture the gentlemen justices, bewigged and clad in their fine coats and waistcoats, seated on the raised "bench"—His Majesty's Commissioners, presiding over the communal dispensation of "justice."

Reviewing the records of court proceedings, the twentieth-century observer is struck by the incessant oath-taking. Periodically, the county's commission of the peace was renewed, and the court would then solemnly and publicly constitute itself by an elaborate, carefully recorded round, in which a junior justice administered the oaths to the senior justice present, who then duly swore in all the rest. No justice or militia officer could act until he had qualified himself by taking the oaths in open court. Even the execution of such quasi-executive orders as the assessment of estates carried the requirement that the persons appointed (often the justices themselves) be "first sworn before some justice of the peace." We have to resist the temptation to dimisss all this as a tiresome preliminary to the real business. Procedures of this kind were central to the functioning of courts in pre-modern society. Bernard Bailyn has shown how the analogy between the colonial constitutions and the British original "was compelling; ran deeper than thought; shaped the very process of thought."[18] In the same way Virginians could only conceive of law and authority in their society as an extension of English custom. This was a world of government not overarched (as we now take for granted) by a written constitution; rather, it was one in which the forms of power and authority were encapsulated in the oaths and ceremonies by which they were legitimated. Only a few had direct acquaintance with the authoritative writings in which the customary English constitution was expounded. For most men the nature and sources of authority were learned primarily through participation in courthouse ceremonial forms.

In this light, aspects of the courthouse rituals become clearer. Written instruments and records (commissions, writs, indentures, and so forth) were of course a central part of the proceedings, but they could not be valid as social facts or serve as a basis for action until they had been incorporated into the oral-aural information system by being read aloud, by the emphatic forms of oath-taking, and by a dramatic "subscribing" in the presence of the community. Variations of this dramaturgical linking of forms of writing to the communal fund of knowledge-by-witnessing fill a large part of the records. A single example will illustrate the form: "A Deed of Feeofment from Henry Hinton to William Steptoe, for and Concerning ten acres of Land, commonly known by the name of Steptoes Ordinary was acknowledged in Open Court by Both parties and Ordered to be Recorded." A considerable part of the logic of the continual calling and swearing of juries lay in this process. Freemen arraigned for felony were sent to the General Court in Williamsburg for trial, and society paid not only for the witnesses to attend but for a jury of twelve "venire men" to come from the vicinage of the crime to judge the facts. Quite explicitly, then, the community's fund of knowledge and received wisdom was incorporated in formal proceedings. In the county courts juries were frequently impanelled and sworn to determine causes and assess damages. In boundary suits they went into the fields with a surveyor to adjudicate the running of the line and to witness to its settlement, thus incorporating the fact into the communal store of information. The custom of processioning, supervised by the parish vestry on orders from the court, has already been mentioned. Neighborhood worthies would lead a body of inhabitants around all the boundaries in a designated area, in a ritual that confirmed the community's knowledge of essentials. There are no accounts from Virginia of beating the bounds at the important marks, but such a practice would have been thoroughly consistent with the processes here considered—a little drama to assist memorization. Conducted "in open court" to the accompaniment of cries of "God save the King!," the burning in the hand of felons who had been allowed benefit of clergy was similarly a staged event, serving not only to affirm authority structures but to impress upon memory an important fact.[19] Such customary dramatic means for the reinforcement of values and forms of authority, combined with the range of

---

[19] Lancaster County Order Book No. 14, 1768-1770, May 18, 1769 (microfilm), Virginia State Library, Richmond; Hugh F. Rankin, *Criminal Trial Proceedings in the General Court of Colonial Virginia* (Williamsburg, Va., 1965), 90-91; Starke, *Office and Authority*, 86-91.

activities that took place at the court-day fair, shaped social identity and communal experience.[20] That was why the concourse of people at such centers as the courthouse was so important; and it is against this background that we must view the remarkable phenomenon of Virginia's almost dissent-free mobilization for rebellion and revolution.

The Revolution began in Virginia with two solemn rituals enacted by the county representatives gathered at Williamsburg—the "courthouse" of the province. On May 24, 1774, the House of Burgesses resolved to keep the first day of June (the date for the enforcement of the act of Parliament closing the port of Boston) as a day of fasting and prayer for "divine Interposition that the Minds of his Majesty and his Parliament . . . may be inspired from above with Wisdom, Moderation, and Justice." Faced with such calculated drama-tization of identification with Boston and opposition to Parliament, Governor Dunmore felt obliged to dissolve the assembly. Eighty-nine of the burgesses met the next day in an assembly room near the capitol, to subscribe solemnly to an "Association" for common action in the crisis.[21] This public signing revived a form of behavior that was to become an important ceremonial means of mobilizing the populace behind the patriot cause. On June 1 the burgesses, led by their Speaker and preceded by the mace, walked in procession to the parish church on the governor's palace green, there to hold their fast-day service. By that time some of their number had already gone home; these added the weight of their dignity to the little replications of the Williamsburg enactment that took place in many of the parishes throughout the province. George Mason could not return to Fairfax County, but to his family he sent instructions that reveal the striving of the gentry for dramaturgical effects. They were "to pay strict attention" to the fast, and his three eldest sons, with his two eldest daughters, were to "attend church in mourning."[22]

There followed a brief but tense period of suspense. Nearly ten years had passed since the Stamp Act crisis had occasioned an astonishing demonstra-tion of Virginia's potential for patriot mobilization. During the intervening period the commitment of the leading gentry, as demonstrated in formally drafted resolves and remonstrances, had not been matched by the overall

303

---

[20] See Sydnor, *American Revolutionaries in the Making*, 74-85, for an account of court days in Virginia. Brief analyses of the significance of some of the forms of action at places where Virginians came together have been presented in Rhys Isaac, "Evangelical Revolt: The Nature of the Baptist Challenge to the Traditional Order in Virginia, 1765-1775," *WMQ*, 3d Ser. XXXI (1974), 348-353, and Isaac, "Preach-ers and Patriots," in Young, ed., *American Revolution*, 125-156.

[21] *Va. Gaz.* (Dixon and Hunter), May 26, 1774.

[22] George Mason to Martin Cockburn, May 26, 1774, in Robert A. Rutland, ed., *The Papers of George Mason, 1725-1792*, I (Chapel Hill, N.C., 1970), 191.

performance of either the gentry at large or the common folk. The non-importation movement of 1769 had quickly weakened, and after attempts to revive it had failed, it was simply allowed to die.[23] The crisis of 1774 arose over events in the remote city of Boston and over acts of Parliament directed at Massachusetts; it was far from certain that Virginians generally would respond with vigor. Philip Fithian, a New Jersey tutor residing in West-moreland County, noted in his journal for May 31: "The lower Class of People here are in tumult on account of Reports from Boston, many of them expect to be press'd and compelled to go and fight the Britains!"[24]

It was imperative for the patriot gentry to communicate to the populace not only their dark and fearful view of what awaited Virginians should they remain supine but also their vision of the good life in the pursuit of which they would lead the struggle. At stake were "fortunes . . . liberties . . . and every thing that is held most dear among men," the heritage of "a brave, virtuous and free people." "Virtue," at the heart of patriot aspirations. was not just a moral quality or disposition; it was a program for the preservation and regeneration of society. The threatened British constitution was "the Gift of God . . . to relieve Virtue from every Restraint to its benificent Operation, and to restrain Vice. It elevates the Soul, by giving Consequence to every Individual, and enabling him to support that Consequence."[25] By the operation of virtue the necessary ranking of society could be rendered compatible with the dignity and worth of free men. It was to this vision that the patriot leadership thrilled. The means by which they were able to communicate that thrill, so as to make it the basis for popular action, are the principal subject matter in this case study of Virginian mobilization.

The newspaper in which the burgesses' responses to the closing of the port of Boston were announced is revealing of the communication dynamics of the period. A small-print notice in Dixon and Hunter's *Virginia Gazette*, following news from London, Boston, New York, and Philadelphia, pre-sented only a simple outline of the steps taken by the burgesses and the governor. We might be inclined to suppose from the absence of typographic dramatization that contemporaries did not attach great importance to these actions. There is abundant evidence, however, of an immediate and wide-

[23] William Nelson to Lord Hillsborough, Dec. 1, 1770, in William Van Schree-ven and Robert L. Scribner, eds., *Revolutionary Virginia, I: Forming Thunder-clouds and the First Convention, 1763-1774: A Documentary Record* (Richmond, Va., 1973), 85.
[24] Hunter Dickinson Farish, ed., *Journal and Letters of Philip Vickers Fithian, 1773-1774: A Plantation Tutor of the Old Dominion* (Williamsburg, Va., 1945), 148.
[25] "W.H.O.," in *Va. Gaz.* (Rind), June 30, 1774; "D.C.," *ibid.* (Purdie and Dixon), Dec. 22, 1774; *ibid.* (Purdie), Nov. 10, 1775.

spread sense of their momentousness.[26] It is, indeed, in the very rapid spread of shock throughout Virginia that the explanation for the seeming non-chalance of the newspaper lies, for the press served, especially in connection with local news, rather to authenticate reports passing by word of mouth than to carry news in its fullness. The newspapers of that time, with their fine print, their long reports from the courts of Europe, and their polemical exchanges in learned literary style, replete with Latin quotations, were not directed to the general populace. Persons of this rank were expected to receive the more important messages contained in the fine print through reading aloud and through conversation at courthouses, ordinaries, and other places of assembly as news became part of the common stock of knowledge, opinion, and feeling.

There are a few records of explanatory and exhortatory verbal forms addressed directly by the patriot gentry to ordinary men. On June 6, 1776, Landon Carter felt impelled to go to the Richmond County courthouse:

[T]here I endeavoured by my Conversation to Convince the People that the case of the Bostonians was the case of all America. . . . I farther hinted to our own Peo[ple] that as the People of Great Britain had seemed to be quite Patient under this Arbitrary Proceeding of their Parliament, it behoved us to have as little Commerce with them as Possible; and farther to refuse to do them the service to determine their suits for their debts since they had consented to a Manifest Violation of our whole Constitution. There seemed to be an assent to all I said and I do hope that at some meeting that our two representatives will be active soon in getting together[.] We shall all be Pretty unanimous in Associating against any Commerce or use of . . . Manufactures of Great Britain or of any Place that shall be passive in this grand affair of Liberty.[27]

Eleven days later it was reported to Carter that the common people felt that since they did not drink tea they were not involved in the current disputes.[28]

A single text of a courthouse oration survives from the initial period of uncertainty. It was probably delivered in the summer of 1774 and was later sent to the printer with the explanation that it was "an address delivered to the inhabitants of a certain county in this colony, . . . adapted to the understandings, and intended for the information of, the middling and lower classes of people." It was directed explicitly to those who lived primarily

305

---

[26] Farish, ed., *Journal of Fithian*, 251-252, 255; Jack P. Greene, ed., *The Diary of Landon Carter of Sabine Hall, 1752-1778*, II (Charlottesville, Va., 1965), 817-818.

[27] Greene, ed., *Diary of Carter*, II, 821-822.

[28] Dr. Walter Jones to Landon Carter, June 17, 1774, in Paul P. Hoffman, ed., *The Carter Family Papers, 1659-1797* (microfilm publication, Charlottesville, Va., 1967).

within the oral medium, as may be seen from the observation that "your circumstances in life are such that you have little to do with *letters*." The basic strategy was to open with an expatiation on the happy state of affairs before 1763 and on the willing and loyal compliance of Americans with the restraints placed upon them, and then to recite the list of British attempts at exploitation and encroachment, concluding with a series of rhetorical questions to which the orator supplied the response: "But methinks I see the blood of *true Britons* swelling your veins, and hear you cry, with one voice, *We will be free*." The heroic strain was muted, however, by the difficulties with which the speaker felt he had to deal. Social distance and social tensions were a significant part of the initial lag in the translation of the patriot gentry's sense of crisis into forms of communal action. "You are told, that the present dispute ... is concerning the duty on *tea*. ... Perhaps some of you may now tell me that it is a dispute with which you have nothing to do, as you do not make use of that commodity, and ... that the *high-minded gentlemen* are ... bringing you into difficulties to support their extravagance and ambition." But the courthouse orator firmly directed attention away from insignificant causes: "Is it possible that you can be so blind to ... the oppression daily coming upon you from Britain? Can you suppose the *gentlemen* of all *America* would be so mad as to risk their lives and fortunes merely to save a trifling duty ... ? Are not the *gentlemen* made of the same materials as the lowest and poorest amongst you? ... Have you found, in the course of your observations, that the *gentlemen* (as they are styled) are so very frugal and saving of their money as to bring themselves into the smallest difficulties for so small an advantage?" The speaker exhorted all ranks to unite "to preserve freedom to our posterity. Fortunes we shall not leave them, but we shall be despicable indeed if we tamely suffer them to become *slaves*." The oration concluded with a tirade against the coercive acts, and an admonition: "On the virtue and courage of the people of these colonies does it depend whether we shall be happy or miserable."[29]

It is hard to judge speech from a written text, and the few reports we have cannot constitute a sample, but it does not appear that oratory was an important medium for the mobilization of ordinary Virginians. The language of secular political culture, in terms of which the literate gentry conceived the struggle, could not readily serve as a source of verbal expressions resonating with the worldview of a populace whose higher cultural

306

---

[29] *Va. Gaz.* (Purdie), July 14, 1775. This speech is not dissimilar in approach to a paper, signed "W.H.O.," circulated at Westmoreland courthouse on June 22, 1774, and printed in *Va. Gaz.* (Rind), June 30, 1774. See also David Wardrobe's description of an address by Richard Parker, "mounted on an eminence," at Richmond County courthouse, in Richard B. Hartwell, ed., *The Committees of Safety of Westmoreland and Fincastle Counties* (Richmond, Va., 1965), 35.

orientations were to the Bible rather than the classics. The adulation bestowed on the one leader—Patrick Henry—who could obliterate this distinction indicates an exception so spectacular as to prove the rule.[30] In general, it was through participation in patterned forms of communal action that the rallying process can be seen to have proceeded most effectively.

Since the coercive acts were the occasion for the crisis, dramatization of the plight of the Bostonians and of Virginia's identification with them played an important part in the activation of the patriot movement. Gentlemen like Landon Carter labored to fire such sentiments in the hearts of the freeholders, and ceremonies of concern soon began to be developed, fixing attention on the victims of oppression. Subscription lists were opened, involving the dramaturgical display of a solemn public promise by gentlemen who, in the courthouse setting, offered an example to the community by "subscribing," in writing, to make a generous donation to the cause. The celebration of this patriotic zeal was a powerful means of intensifying commitment.

307

The social process involved is clearly revealed in a notice from Fredericksburg that "very liberal contributions have been made, in this place, for the relief of the poor in *Boston*. Mr. *Mann Page*, Junior, one of our Representatives, has taken uncommon pains to promote the subscriptions . . ." An example of the community mobilization thus striven for is seen in the announcement late in July that "the county of Surry, from the highest to the lowest, are actuated with the warmest affection towards the suffering town of Boston . . . [and] that immediately after the meeting of freeholders and others . . . upwards of 150 barrels of Indian corn and wheat were subscribed . . . for the benefit of those firm and intrepid sons of liberty, the Bostonians." The printer went on to state that "it would be needless to recognize the particular generosity of each county . . . as . . . all Virginians are unanimous in their endeavours."[31]

Above all, when the county community was gathered at the courthouse, the quest was for unanimity. This was especially evident in what a hostile observer called "the grand meetings for signing the association." In Princess Anne County, to take a well-documented example, the process evidently began in July 1774 with "a meeting of a respectable body of Freeholders . . . at the Courthouse, for the purpose of choosing Deputies . . . and of entering into resolutions expressive of the sentiments of the County in support of their just rights and privileges." One Mr. John Saunders alone "obstinately

---

[30] The relationship between Henry's oratorical power and the conflicting classical and evangelical styles is analyzed in Isaac, "Preachers and Patriots," in Young, ed., *American Revolution*, 125-156.

[31] Peter Force, comp., *American Archives* . . . , 4th Ser. (Washington, D.C., 1837-1853), I, 787; *Va. Gaz.* (Rind), July 28, 1774.

refused to sign the resolves though particularly solicited by some of the principal gentlemen then present." Subsequent events were to reveal the agony occasioned the county leaders by this open breach of solidarity. For this reason, perhaps, the official minutes passed over it in silence, noting that "the above resolutions being unanimously agreed to, and signed . . . they then repaired to a place prepared for the occasion" where they drank a series of toasts expressive of unifying, patriotic sentiments. Three weeks later, at the courthouse again, "the Provincial Association . . . was read and offered the people that they might express their approbation by signing it." Once more Mr. Saunders dissented publicly. Eventually the county committee published an account of his recalcitrance and declared him an enemy to the American cause. (Such committees clearly embodied the traditional county community, for they contained a high proportion of the men who had formerly presided at the courthouse as justices. It was not unusual for the committees to meet on court days.)[32]

The reports of these county meetings at the courthouse reveal once again the dramaturgical possibilities available through the display of formal documents in a society where the written word was not yet commonplace. At the first meeting a set of resolutions was ceremoniously adopted. These were then embodied in a draft, prepared in a gentleman's library and cast in the latinate language of the literary-legal culture of that age—largely opaque to common folk, who, if they had any instruction in reading, had it in the very different language of the Bible. At the second meeting, three weeks later, the printed text of the Provincial Association, composed by some of the colony's most cosmopolitan gentlemen, was formally read aloud. This procedure was strongly calculated to dramatize the dominance of the culture of the gentry. Later, when the copies of such papers were handed about, literary and body-language media were spliced together, as public signing in a communal context gave to writing the character of dramatic gesture.[33]

The account given by the Association committee of Princess Anne County of their tireless but unsuccessful efforts to persuade Mr. Saunders to adhere to the nonimportation agreement reveals the depth of the patriot yearning for communal unanimity and the special importance attached to the public dissent of a gentleman. His ultimate publication as an enemy to American liberty was a boundary-marking ceremony. Ostracism formally restored consensus by putting the dissenter outside the community. For a movement that conceived of itself initially as a defensive mobilization to preserve the threatened status quo, such rituals of detestation were of primary

[32] Force, comp., *America Archives*, 4th Ser., II, 76-77; Van Schreeven and Scribner, eds., *Revolutionary Virginia*, I, 153-155.
[33] On the general use of the Bible as a reading primer see Thomas Jefferson, *Notes on the State of Virginia*, ed. William Peden (Chapel Hill, N.C., 1955), 147.

importance in defining the danger and amplifying the community's alarm at it.

The execution of symbolic figures in effigy had constituted, from the time of the Stamp Act, an important part of patriotic rituals in urban centers of other colonies. In Virginia such ceremonies were seldom staged, and on the occasions when they were attempted they seem to have had little impact. There was at least one episode, made famous by the participation of the young James Madison, when a bundle of confiscated tory pamphlets was ordered by the Orange County committee to be publicly burned, "which sentence was speedily executed in the presence of the Independent Company, and other respectable inhabitants . . . all of whom joined in expressing a noble indignation against such execrable publications, and their ardent wishes for an opportunity of inflicting on the authors . . . and their abettors, the punishment due to their insufferable arrogance, and attrocious crimes." This was, however, an isolated instance; in Virginia such communal displays of execration almost always took the form of the socially and economically ruinous ostracism of enemies discovered within the community.[34]

309

It was more reassuring, and therefore more confirmatory of the values of communal harmony, when the denunciation of deviants was the preliminary, not to exclusion from the benefits of society, but to a public act of contrition on the part of the offender. The offenders might be moved by the general fervor for the cause to purge their guilt by confession. Thus "Silas Kirby, James Ingram [and others] voluntarily appeared before [the Southampton County] committee, and acknowledged they had been guilty of violating the . . . association, by gaming . . . that it was an error they were unthinkingly led into, and are convinced of its evil tendency." The committee magnanimously declared that, although these men had been guilty, "yet, in consideration of their candid behaviour," they hoped that "the public will join . . . in considering the aforesaid persons as not inimical to American liberty."[35]

Elaborate acts of contrition might be demanded, as in the case of Andrew Leckie, who had "attended at the courthouse for colonel EDMUND PENDLETON'S address to the people of Caroline County." After "the resolutions of the association were read in a company of people convened for the purpose of acceding to the association, and of raising contributions for the town of Boston," Leckie "was so unguarded and imprudent as to address

---

[34] *Va. Gaz.* (Dixon and Hunter), Apr. 15, 1775. Irving Brant in *James Madison*, I: *The Virginia Revolutionist* (New York, 1941), 163, suggests that Madison was the author of the account published in the newspaper. There was a hanging and burning of Lord North's effigy at Richmond County courthouse, and a report of a tarring and feathering in Southampton County. *Va. Gaz.* (Pinkney), Aug. 24, 1775. In Nov. 1774 a pole with a bucket of tar and a bag of feathers was said to have been set up in Williamsburg. "Letters from Virginia," *Magazine of History* (Jan. 1906), 156.

[35] *Va. Gaz.* (Dixon and Hunter), May 6, 1775.

[himself] . . . to a negro boy who was present in this indecent manner: 'Piss, Jack, turn about, my boy, and sign.' " For this indelicacy he was made to read before the committee and "a great concourse of people" on Caroline court day a full detailed confession and a hearty avowal of friendship to the principles and measures of the patriots, concluding with an open supplication "to regain the favour and good opinion of the public; an assurance of which would be the greatest consolation . . . under the insupportable weight of public censure and public hatred."[36]

310   The rituals of detestation and the striving to bring deviants into conformity were, in some sense, negative celebrations of harmonious community. Yet as popular enthusiasm became engaged, the movement also elaborated a set of rituals whose tendency was to affirm, in the face of doubt, the "virtue" of challenged Virginia society. The most direct of these rituals of affirmation were the enactments of frugality and industry. These were of particular importance because they served as palliatives to nagging doubts concerning the moral soundness of Virginia—anxieties over indebtedness (supposed to arise from luxurious extravagance) and over slavery (supposed to be the source of a debilitating indolence that exacerbated the same extravagance).[37] Public declarations of frugality through the wearing of homespun also provided the patriot gentry with a means of setting an example to their inferiors while at the same time narrowing visible social distance as signalled by richness of apparel. George Washington had reflected in a letter to George Mason on the occasion of the proposed anti-Townshend duty association of 1769 that it would be possible to check purchases "if Gentlemen in their several Counties would be at some pains to explain matters to the people, and stimulate them to a cordial agreement." The more he considered the scheme, the more ardently he wished success to it "because . . . there are private as well as public advantages to result from it." By being "curtail'd in . . . living and enjoyments . . . the penurious Man . . . saves the money, and . . . saves his credit . . . The extravagant and expensive man has the same good plea to retrench his Expenses. He is thereby furnished with a pretext to live within bounds . . . And in respect of the poor and needy man, he is only left in the same situation he was found; better I might say, because as he judges from comparison, his condition is amended in Proportion as it

[36] *Ibid.* (Rind), Nov. 11, 1774.
[37] Evidence concerning Virginia anxieties at signs of moral decline is collected in Gordon S. Wood, "Rhetoric and Reality in the American Revolution," *WMQ*, 3d Ser., XXIII (1966), 27-30. The relationship between republican moralism and the austere codes being introduced among the common people as part of the evangelical movement is discussed in Isaac, "Preachers and Patriots," in Young, ed., *American Revolution*, 125-156.

approaches nearer to those above him." Encapsulated in this statement, and in its enactment in the wearing of homespun, lay an epitome of the whig-republican ideal for society. Distinctions of rank based on material fortunes were to be ennobled and legitimated by distinctions based on moral excellence.[38]

But true virtue in that face-to-face social order could not be "private" or individualistic. Ultimately it must contribute to, and draw from, a communal harmony (itself an oral-aural metaphor) which could most readily be restored and sustained by readiness to sacrifice oneself to the general good. The ideal of harmony in community was conceived in terms of a profoundly felt analogy between it and the healthy functioning of the human body, and so in terms of a complementarity, rather than an equality, of the parts. As the sound body was ruled by the head, its rational part, so society was expected to be ruled by the learned and liberal part, the gentry. As with the healthy body, however, all the members must be responsive to each other's true needs. It was to the affirmation of virtuous harmony or bodily health of this kind that the most subtle and the most important rituals were necessarily directed in a crisis the favorable resolution of which was believed to depend upon the moral soundness of Virginia society. The rallying to the support of Boston, the Association, the purging of unsound members, and the displays of frugality all contributed to this necessary demonstration, but the vital display could best come through the dramatization of the aspect of government most dear to the patriots, namely elections.[39]

In order to understand the dramaturgical possibilities of elections we have to divest ourselves of nearly all our current assumptions. Trials of strength between contending interests and even popular choice between rival programs were precisely the lines upon which it was believed elections should *not* be conducted. Polling was a testing, face-to-face procedure in old Virginia, with the candidates confronting the voters over the table as the latter publicly declared their preferences. The true purpose, in accordance with the organic conception of society, was to enhance the authority of virtue, or right reason combined with manly courage. The idealizations according to which the election process was to be judged had been set forth with superb clarity in a paper signed NO PARTY MAN, addressed to the freeholders of Accomac County in 1771. This broadside outlined the model which the patriots would seek to represent dramatically at the county courthouses. The

311

[38] *Va. Gaz.* (Rind), Dec. 14, 1769; *ibid.* (Purdie and Dixon), Dec. 29, 1774; *ibid.* (Dixon and Hunter), Jan. 28, 1775; George Washington to George Mason, Apr. 5, 1769, in Rutland, ed., *Papers of Mason,* I, 97-98.
[39] See Wood, *Creation of the Republic,* 29, and J. G. A. Pocock, "Virtue and Commerce in the Eighteenth Century," *Journal of Interdisciplinary History,* III (1972-1973), 125-134.

voters should give their suffrages to gentlemen of "penetrating Judgement," able "to scan every Proposal, to view it in every Light . . . and, piercing into Futurity, behold even how remote Posterity may be thereby effected." The ideal representative should be "able to strip every Measure of that Disguise under cover of which it may be artfully obtruded on his Mind, and penetrate through all the sinister Designs and Machinations of the Enemies of Freedom, the Slaves of Interest. . . . It is absolutely necessary that he be a Man of Probity . . . One who regards *Measures* not *Men*" and who will follow his country's interest regardless of the effect of his course upon either his friends or his foes. To this end he must have "that Fortitude, or strength of Mind, which enable a Man, in a good Cause to bear up against all Opposition, and meet the Frowns of Power unmoved."[40]

The qualities demanded of the voters who were to select such a representative were scarcely less precious. To begin with, they were to be imbued with a strong sense of their exalted roles: "It is your greatest Glory . . . that you give Being to your Legislature, that from you they receive their political Existence. This renders an American Planter [i.e., farmer] superiour to the first Minister of an Arbitrary Monarch, whose glittering Robes serve but to veil from vulgar Eyes the Chains of Slavery. Guard it then, as the most precious Pledge committed to you by the Deity. Let every Gentleman's true Merit determine his Place in the Scale of your Interest." Altogether it is an inspiring vision, conjuring up a sturdy yeomanry who with dauntless honesty would elevate, by their virtuous trust, the wisest and sternest of the "Gentlemen" to give laws and "to meet the Frowns of Power unmoved."[41]

Actual representations of this scenario, dramatically affirming the virtue that inspired the patriot cause, were enacted in a series of unanimous elections at the commencement of the final crisis in 1774. A single example will convey how the vision was translated into action. Rind's *Virginia Gazette* of July 14, 1774, reported: "On Wednesday . . . came on the election of burgesses to represent the county of Prince George in the ensuing general assembly, when the people, sensible that their late representatives had discharged their duty to their country, in opposing those baneful, ministerial measures, which have been lately taken to enslave this continent, and highly applauding those sentiments of union among the colonies which occasioned the dissolution of the last assembly, unanimously agreed to re-elect RICHARD BLAND and PETER POYTHRESS, esquires, who were returned without a poll being taken." This simple courthouse enactment—the acclamation of the representatives and the explanation of the reasons for according this honor—was highly effective in dramatizing to freeholders the awful menace of British power and the noble solidarity of Americans, as

[40] *Va. Gaz.* (Dixon and Hunter), Apr. 11, 1771.
[41] *Ibid.*

well as in engendering in them a glow of virtue at their participation in this brave defiance on a world stage.[42]

There was another possibility. The affirmation of the highest political virtues might be combined with the affirmation of frugality, by the simple inversion of the time-honored custom of the candidates' treating the voters. On July 8, 1774, "a considerable number of the inhabitants of [Williamsburg] . . . met at the courthouse" to present an address to their representative, proposing that as they were "greatly scandalized at the practice which has too much prevailed . . . of entertaining the electors (a practice which even its antiquity cannot sanctify) and being desirous of setting a worthy example . . . for abolishing every appearance of venality (that only poison which can infect our happy constitution) and to give the fullest proof that it is to your singular merit alone you are indebted for the unbought suffrages of a free people . . . we earnestly request that you will not think of incurring any expence . . . , but that you will do us the honour to partake of an entertainment, which we shall direct to be provided for the occasion."[43] Five days later the freeholders met their representative, "attended by many respectable inhabitants, at the courthouse . . . to elect him again . . . , when he was immediately unanimously chosen." After the election the voters "conducted him to the Raleigh, where almost every inhabitant had met, a general invitation having been given by the generous electors, whose conduct . . . will be long remembered as a laudable . . . precedent, and highly worthy of every county . . . to adopt. Notwithstanding the festivity, and the pleasing, social intercourse, which here prevailed, harmony, decency, and decorum, were strictly maintained."[44] The gentry still showed their liberality by treating and patronizing the freeholders, but their role could now be freed of "every appearance of venality," while the prevailing "harmony, decency, and decorum" were signs of virtue diffused through all the ranks of the free community.

The dramaturgical possibilities available in the celebration of local notables were even more fully realized in the fêting of the heroes of Virginia and America at large. In these ceremonies they and their cause could be celebrated in such a way that their own virtue and that of the people who identified with them were simultaneously affirmed. The sense of immediate engagement in drama on a world scale (already noted in the acclamation of

---

[42] For other reported instances of unanimous elections see *ibid*, May 20, 1775; *ibid*. (Purdie), May 26 and June 1, 1775; *ibid*. (Pinkney), Mar. 9, 1775; and Force, comp., *American Archives*, 4th Ser., I, 1203.

[43] *Va. Gaz*. (Rind), July 7, 1774.

[44] *Ibid*., July 14, 1774. The practice of reversing the charges of treating went back at least to 1769. See *ibid*., June 1, 1769, and *ibid*. (Purdie and Dixon), Sept. 14, 1769. For other reported examples in 1774 see *ibid*. (Rind), July 21, 28, 1774.

the Prince George representatives) could thereby be most readily intensified. The patriot leaders, of course, owed a great deal of their charisma to their own sense that they were engaged in a momentous struggle in which the destiny of mankind would be determined.[45] Peyton Randolph, Williamsburg's representative, Speaker of the House of Burgesses, and president of the Continental Congress, had this quality of transcending local and provincial forms of authority. He combined this with the manners and outlook of a "liberal" Virginia gentleman in the traditional style—a clubman at ease with persons of all ranks. We may see these elements united in the report of a ceremony that took place on May 28 and 29, 1775:

314

> *Last Monday, about 10 o'clock, the* WILLIAMSBURG TROOP OF HORSE *left this city, well accoutred, in order to meet our good and worthy speaker on his return from the continental congress. Notwithstanding the inclemency of the weather, these hardy friends and supporters of American liberty pursued their journey with the utmost eagerness, whilst the most unfeigned joy diffused itself in every countenance.*
>
> *For order, good discipline, and regularity, this company was greatly applauded. Ruffen's ferry was the place where they met the object of their wishes, whom, after giving three hearty cheers, they conducted until they arrived within two miles of the city, when they were joined by the* COMPANY OF FOOT, *who also gave three cheers, and shewed every other mark of decency and respect. The pleasing deportment of the speaker, on account of this peculiar honour done him, animated, in the highest degree, every person that attended; and on Tuesday, about 5 o'clock in the afternoon, the whole body arrived . . . surrounding the* FATHER *of his* COUNTRY, *whom they attended to his house, amidst repeated acclamations, and then respectfully retired.*[46]

In the feeling expressed through the postures adopted (or believed by contemporaries to have been adopted) toward Peyton Randolph, we catch a vivid glimpse of the way in which the patriot movement momentarily evoked (or was intended by its leaders to evoke) the spirit of the traditional, deferential social order. But, as we see also in this account, men in arms were on the march. The struggle was unleashing forces that would not find their fullest expression in marks of "decency and respect."

The preceding accounts reveal how, in a set of *tableaux vivants*, communicating more than words could do, there was engendered a collective

---

[45] Thus Patrick Henry in accepting the governorship of Virginia on June 29, 1776, was moved to reflect "that, from the events of this war, the lasting happiness, or misery, of a great proportion of the human species will finally result." *Ibid.* (Dixon and Hunter), July 6, 1776. This feeling was expressed in the correspondence of nearly all the leaders. See Bailyn, *Ideological Origins*, 138-143.

[46] *Va. Gaz.* (Pinkney), June 1, 1775.

consciousness of belonging to a virtuous community, unanimously roused in support of its dearest rights. The Anglo-American ideal of civic virtue was not, however, confined to frugality and political incorruptibility, for it enshrined martial valor at its heart. Military rituals and occasions for the self-presentation of the warrior that was expected to exist in every free man had ultimately the greatest potential for stirring this aggressive, contentious people. During the initial phase of uncertainty in the summer of 1774, when the Association was being promoted as a peaceful measure, involving only "some inconveniencies," warlike notes were not much sounded. By December 1774, however, the governor reported to the home authorities that every county was now "arming a Company of Men, whom they call an independent Company." We may get a sense of this new development from the record of a gathering at the Fairfax County courthouse on September 21, 1774. The proceedings reflect the valiant endeavor to produce a moral regeneration of the old order by an ostentatious assumption of public burdens on the part of the gentry. The minutes show that the gentlemen and freeholders who had attended were "hoping to excite others by . . . Example." They formed themselves into "the Fairfax independant Company of Voluntiers," who would meet at times appointed for "learning and practising the military Exercise and Discipline; dress'd in a regular Uniform of Blue, turn'd up with Buff; with plain yellow metal Buttons, Buff Waist Coat and Breeches and white Stockings," and furnished with a complete set of arms and equipment. Further, they would keep by them considerable stock of powder, lead, and flints. On the principle of *noblesse oblige,* the gentlemen, who alone could afford this dress and equipment, were setting an example of valiant patriotism and at the same time incorporating the principles of popular government into their organization by electing their officers.[47]

315

By February 1775 a plan "for Embodying the People" was being circulated in Fairfax County, and a new conception of uniform heralded the intrusion of more popular styles. The drive was now for a volunteer militia, "intended to consist of all the ablebodied Freemen from eighteen to fifty Years of Age." The enlistment of poorer men rendered the prescription of uniform impossible, but the proposal did call for those who could "procure Riphel Guns . . . to form a Company of Marksmen . . . distinguishing [their] Dress . . . by painted Hunting Shirts and Indian Boots."[48]

The shifting of the balance in favor of more popular assertion, as well as the excitement engendered by the rise of martial formations, became manifest during the next phase of Virginian patriot mobilization, after the governor seized the colony's store of gunpowder from the magazine in

[47] "W.H.O.," *ibid.* (Rind), June 30, 1774; Rutland, ed., *Papers of Mason,* I, 211.

[48] Rutland, ed., *Papers of Mason,* I, 215-216.

Williamsburg on April 21, 1774. It was the morning of Monday, April 24, when news of his lordship's coup reached Fredericksburg. "This being a day of meeting of the Independent Company," the assembled volunteers angrily considered the state of affairs and "came to a unanimous resolution, that a submission to so arbitrary an exertion of Government, may not only prejudice the common cause, by introducing a suspicion of a defection of this Colony from the noble pursuit, but will encourage the tools of despotism to commit further acts of violence." They informed the commanders of the companies in nearby counties that "this Company could but determine that a number of publick spirited gentlemen should embrace this opportunity of showing their zeal in the grand cause, by marching to *Williamsburgh*." They declared that "to this end, they have determined to hold themselves in readiness to march as Light-Horse, on *Saturday* morning; and in the mean time to submit the matter to . . . the neighbouring counties."[49]

316

The letters, conveying so clearly a body-language sense of valiant warlike posture, evoked immediate responses. The Prince William company was "called together . . . , and had the vote put whether they would march to *Williamsburgh* . . . which was carried unanimously." Companies began to gather at Fredericksburg for a massive display of patriotism in martial array. The excitement, and the new tone that was becoming dominant, can be sensed in the words of a young gentleman volunteer, Michael Brown Wallace, of Falmouth, who described for the benefit of his brother how the governor's action "occasioned upwards of 1,000 men to assemble together at Fredericksburge among which was 600 good Rifle men." He was sure that "if we had continued there one or two days longer we should have had upwards of 10,000 men [as] all the frontier Countys of Virginia were in motion . . . [and that] Fredericksburge never was honour'd with so many brave hearty men since it was a Town[,] evry Man Rich and poor with their hunting shirts Belts and Tomahawke fixed of[f] in the best manner." However, Wallace also reported that "thir was a Council of war held three days saturday sunday and monday[.] [T]he third day in the evening we were all draw'd up in ranks and discharg'd—some promise of the governor's delivery of the Powder."[50]

Patrick Henry, at the head of a body of men assembled at Hanover courthouse, was not so easily dismissed. He marched toward Williamsburg

[49] Hugh Mercer [*et al.*] to Capt. Grayson, Apr. 24, 1775, in Force, comp., *American Archives*, 4th Ser., II, 387. A detailed chronological account of events can be found in Ivor Noël Hume, *1775: Another Part of the Field* (New York, 1966).

[50] Capt. Grayson to George Washington, Apr. 26, 1775, in Force, comp., *American Archives*, 4th Ser., II, 395; Michael Brown Wallace to Gustavus Brown Wallace, May 14, 1775, Wallace Family Papers, 1750-1781, Alderman Library, University of Virginia, Charlottesville. I am indebted to Emory Evans for this reference.

until some £330 was exacted from His Majesty's receiver-general by way of reprisal for the confiscated powder. Henry was uneasy for an instant at the possible consequences of his action, but addresses from courthouses throughout the province revealed that the patriot movement was ready to go decisively into military action. He and his volunteers were congratulated upon showing "resentment" like true Virginians. When Henry rode off soon after to the second Continental Congress, he was fêted on his journey by a succession of armed escorts. Ostensibly these were to protect him from arrest or insult; they were in fact a defiant celebration of patriotism in martial array.[51]

The new tone of the patriot movement—more popular and more martial—was sharply and dramatically signalled by the appearance of the men in hunting shirts. These "brave hearty men" had honored Fredericksburg with their presence in early May 1775. By June a Norfolk tory was writing home that Dunmore would only return to Williamsburg "provided the shirtmen are sent away" and explaining that "these Shirt men, or Virginia uniform, are dressed with an Oznab[urg] Shirt over their Cloaths, a belt round them with a Tommyhawk or Scalping knife." The term initially had been applied by their enemies—"the damn'd shirtmen"—and then adopted as a badge of pride.[52] The revolution in cultural orientation that was taking place is most readily seen in the contrast of the shirtmen's attire with the "Uniform of Blue, turn'd up with Buff . . . yellów . . . Buttons, Buff Waist Coat and Breeches and white Stockings," appointed for the gentlemen of the Fairfax Independent Company. For all their intense provincial patriotism, the Virginia gentry had always boasted a strong Church-and-King loyalty and, looking to the English metropolis for cultural values, had tended to despise the "buckskin" of the backwoods. Now suddenly the riflemen from the west were the "heroes in huntingshirts," to whom even the most cosmopolitan gentlemen looked for protection. James Madison wrote on July 19, 1775, to a friend in Pennsylvania that "the strength of this Colony will lie chiefly in the rifle-men of the Upland Counties, of whom we shall have great number." This sentiment occurs in a great many places and had evidently become almost universal. The intensity of the reorientation westward and the adoption of the new woodsman identity by the gentry can be seen in a published recommendation to the burgesses, before the assembly called for June 1, 1775, that they attend in shirtmen's attire, "which best suits the times, as the

317

---

[51] Force, comp., *American Archives*, 4th Ser., II, 516; Patrick Henry to Francis Lightfoot Lee, May 8, 1775, in Paul P. Hoffman, ed., The Lee Family Papers, 1742-1795 (microfilm publication, Charlottesville, Va., 1966); *Va. Gaz.* (Purdie), May 19, 1775.

[52] James Parker to Charles Steuart, June 12, 1775, "Letters from Va.," *Mag. Hist.* (Jan. 1906), 159.

cheapest, and the most martial." The advice was taken, and "numbers of the Burgesses" did attend in the uniform of "Coarse linnen or Canvass over their Cloaths and a Tomahawk by their Sides."[53]

The committee for Cumberland County, meeting in May 1775, considered the news of the battles of Lexington and Concord and resolved "that the Military Powers of this County be immediately collected and ... that Wednesday the 10th ... be appointed for a general Muster ... and that all free Men be summoned ... to appear at the Court House on that day" equipped with their arms.[54] Preparation for war was now the principal source of excitement for the patriot movement. The classical Graeco-Roman attitudes so characteristic of the early phases were being overlaid by more robust and popular styles. A blend of the two may be seen in the correspondence of Col. Adam Stephens who had written in August 1774 that in the Virginia Convention he "should expect to see the spirit of the Amphyctions shine, as ... in their purest Times before Debauch'd with the Persian Gold." Later Stephens wrote that, having heard "that Lord North has declar'd that he has a Rod in piss for the Colony of Virginia," he wished he could see his lordship in America, for "in Spite of all the armies of Commissioners, Customs house officers and soldiers, I would make the meanest American I know piss upon him."[55]

With this last we are in touch with the scatological ribaldry of the military camp. Although this form of communication appears little in the written records, it represented an important aspect of that male warrior fraternity which was more decorously manifested in the stirring resolves of

318

[53] William Byrd to Ralph Wormeley, Oct. 4, 1775, photocopy in Virginia Historical Society, Richmond; James Madison to William Bradford, June 19, 1775, in William T. Hutchinson and William M. E. Rachal, eds., *The Papers of James Madison*, I (Chicago, 1962), 159. The general diffusion of this reliance is strongly suggested by entries in a Spottsylvania County servant's diary. Edward Miles Riley, ed., *The Journal of John Harrower: An Indentured Servant in the Colony of Virginia, 1773-1776* (New York, 1963), 111. See also *Va. Gaz.* (Purdie), Oct. 20 and Nov. 17, 1775; "An American," *ibid.*, May 19, 1775; Lord Dunmore to earl of Dartmouth, June 25, 1775, C.O. 5/1353, 160-172, Public Record Office, London (typescript at the Colonial Williamsburg Foundation). On Mar. 25, 1775, the Virginia Convention, following trends already at work, had instructed the upland counties to concentrate on mobilizing riflemen in hunting shirts. Force, comp., *American Archives*, 4th Ser., II, 169.

[54] H. R. McIlwaine, ed., "Proceedings of the Committee of Safety of Cumberland and Isle of Wright Counties, 1775-1776," *Fifteenth Annual Report of the Library Board of the Virgina State Library, 1917-1918 ...*, V (Richmond, Va., 1919), 11.

[55] Adam Stephens to Richard Henry Lee, Aug. 24, 1774, and Feb. 1, 1775, Letters to Richard Henry Lee, American Philosophical Society, Philadelphia (microfilm [M-63-2], Colonial Williamsburg Foundation).

the spring and summer of 1775.[56] In this ethos the country squirearchy, many of whose members were schooled in boxing and quarter-racing, could hold their own; but social distance was inevitably reduced, special advantages derived from cosmopolitan education were diminished, and distinctions of rank were rendered less sharp. By the same confusions in society at large the momentary sense of a precious harmony was drowned and deference was abased, so that by the spring elections of 1776 the celebrated unanimity with which the freeholders of many counties had affirmed community virtue was replaced by "many . . . warm contests" in which even "Colonel Mason [was only] with great difficulty returned for Fairfax."[57]

The shift in dramaturgical forms from tableaux of civic virtue and constitutional loyalty to courthouse musters of men in hunting shirts inevitably contributed to the increasing alienation of Virginians from the mother country. No accounts exist of popular ceremonies at the courthouses directed to the dramatic "killing" or dethroning of the king. There was the vehement inve.sion with which this essay began; and something more of the persistence of old forms—and of the readiness to see them changed—is caught in a report of April 1776 from Gloucester County: "We hear . . . that as the sheriff was opening the court . . . he was going to conclude with *God save the King*, when, just as he was abo:t pronouncing the words a *five's ball*, struck by a soldier of the 7th regiment, entered the window, and knocked him in the mouth, which prevented him from being guilty of so much impiety."[58] Perhaps the impropriety of regicide enactments, before an alternative locus of sovereignty was declared, inhibited more deliberate performances—or the reporting of them.

In Williamsburg there was an official celebration of the formal decision of the Virginia Convention for independence on May 15, 1776. In accordance with ancient Virginia custom, "some gentlemen made a handsome collection for treating the soldiery." After a parade and salutes to the "American independent states," to Congress, and to General Washington, refreshments were taken "and the evening concluded with illuminations . . . and other demonstrations of joy." The report stated that everyone seemed "pleased that the domination of Great Britain was now at an end, so wickedly . . . exercised for these twelve or thirteen years past." It had already noted that independence was "universally regarded as the only door which will lead to

319

---

[56] For examples of verbal expressions of a posture of armed defiance see Force, comp., *American Archives*, 4th Ser., II, 539, 547, 578, 710-711, 872, 938; *Va. Gaz.* (Pinkney), May 25, 1775; and *ibid.* (Dixon and Hunter), June 17, 1775.

[57] Robert Brent to Richard Henry Lee, Apr. 28, 1776, in Kate Mason Rowland, *The Life of George Mason, 1725-1792*, I (New York, 1892), 222.

[58] *Va. Gaz.* (Purdie), Apr. 19, 1776.

safety and prosperity."[59] The matter-of-fact, even complacent tone suggests that anguish at denying loyalties, once so strongly affirmed, was already over.

At a Court held for Lancaster County on the 18th Day of July, 1776, In Pursuance of the Ordinances of the general Convention of this Colony of Virginia, being the first Court . . . after the Establishment of the new Form of Government . . . and the Declaration of Congress for the Independency of the American States.

James Ball Gent, first Justice having taken the Oath prescribed by the Convention, administered the same to John Chinn . . .[60]

320

We seem to be witnessing a cyclical repetition as old forms reassert themselves. The patriots' revolution came and went; the continuities in the life that ebbed and flowed about the courthouse were very great. The question about how much was changed by the Revolution, at the level of community life, still presents itself as one of the most often asked and least satisfactorily answered in the field of early American history. Approaching the question, we need to be less exclusively preoccupied with "social structures" conceived in terms of wealth and status. It will also be necessary to extend the new and fruitful interest in ideology and the symbolic order to include the media and dynamics of communication.

We have been taught to think of the Revolution primarily in terms of its apparently timeless statements of principle, but those statements can only be understood historically in relation to the passions of the movement of which they were the fruit. The courthouse (or its equivalent elsewhere) was the central exchange point of that movement. It was the forum for the translation of the patriot gentry's essentially literary vision into a powerful communal enthusiasm, and for the counter-assertion of popular aspirations and identifications, as in the emergence of the "shirtmen" and the new cultural orientation they represented.

The courthouse had been the place where, through formulaic oaths and ceremonies, the source and nature of authority under a customary constitution had been continually intoned, to be learned and internalized. For the system of authority conceived and sustained in this way the Revolution substituted frameworks of government, delineated in written documents, immediately cast in type, multiplied in many copies, and soon to become milestones in the literate world of cosmopolitan culture. There were three newspapers in pre-Revolutionary Virginia, emanating from a single center. In the 1780s twelve new ones, from eight centers, appeared. For the 1790s

[59] *Ibid.*, May 17, 1776.
[60] Lancaster County Court Order Book, No. 14, July 18, 1776, Va. State Lib.

thirty-one newspapers have been listed from twelve centers.[61] At the oath-taking ceremony in Lancaster County on July 18, 1776, the courthouse community was on the threshold of a world, dominated by print—modern-ized—as it had not been before.

[61] Clarence S. Brigham, *History and Bibliography of American Newspapers, 1690-1820*, II (Worcester, Mass., 1947), 1105-1138. For the impact of the American constitution making on the cosmopolitan political culture of the day see Robert R. Palmer, *The Age of the Democratic Revolution: A Political History of Europe and America, 1760-1800*, I: *The Challenge* (Princeton, N.J., 1959), 213-217, 518-521.

Choosing Sides:
A Quantitative Study of the Personality Determinants of Loyalist and Revolutionary Political Affiliation in New York

N. E. H. HULL
PETER C. HOFFER
STEVEN L. ALLEN

INDIVIDUAL choice is the essence of aggregate political affiliation. In the crisis of 1776, loyalism and revolution grew from particular colonists' adoption of opposing partisan stances. In the course of a political and military upheaval lasting an entire generation, almost every Anglo-American faced this decision. For many of these individuals, known only by cryptic references in muster lists or confiscation rolls, the question of choice remains unanswered. Whatever gross surmise there may be about this faceless multitude—many perhaps victims of geographical accident or invading armies—as individuals, they chose to stay or flee, sign oaths of allegiance or resist the oath givers. One can couch this fact in psychological terms: "human action is *never* directly caused by situations; it is invariably mediated by psychological variables." A relative handful of loyalists and revolutionaries did leave behind them sufficient evidence for the historian to probe the psychological dimensions of individual choice. This essay is a report on the application of modern psychological scaling techniques and quantitative methods to study political affiliation among loyalists and revolutionaries in New York.[1]

The colony of New York presents the problem of revolutionary political choice at its most complex. Recent investigators have agreed that New York loyalists and revolutionaries "cannot readily be placed into predetermined categories." Aristocratic planters, merchants,

N. E. H. Hull is a graduate student at Columbia University.
Peter C. Hoffer is assistant professor of history in the University of Georgia, Athens.
Steven L. Allen is a graduate student at New York University.

[1] Fred. I. Greenstein, *Personality and Politics: Problems of Evidence, Inference, and Conceptualization* (New York, 1975), xviii.

yeoman farmers, and professional men can be found in both camps. In centers of intense political activity, such as Kings County, partisans regularly switched sides, and for the colony as a whole, it was "impossible to determine with exactitude the division of the people into Whig and Tory." In this situation it clearly makes sense to seek the psychological components of individual political choice.[2]

In recent years, students of the American Revolution have increasingly concerned themselves with the psychological dimensions of political action. Thus far, psychohistorians have primarily relied upon childhood-centered "dynamic" or "ego" psychology to explain the behavior and thought of leading figures of both parties. Though these investigations reveal the potential of psychological inquiry, they are by their nature self-limiting. While dynamic psychology must have specific documentation on the subject's early years to be effective, material for childhood studies is not available for more than a very few eighteenth-century individuals. As one spokesman in the field has written, "no childhood, no psychohistory." What is more, even the most able dynamic psychohistories vary greatly in texture and emphasis according to the particular authors' intuition. Finally, analysis of political group affiliation requires a higher level of consistency and comparability than a simple collation of individual psychobiographies can attain.[3]

323

[2] Jacob Judd, "Frederick Philipse III of Westchester County: A Reluctant Loyalist," Robert A. East and Jacob Judd, eds., *The Loyalist Americans: A Focus on Greater New York* (Tarrytown, N.Y., 1975), 25–28; Bernard Mason, *The Road to Independence: The Revolutionary Movement in New York, 1773–1777* (Lexington, Ky., 1966), 64.

[3] Lloyd DeMause to the authors, May 1975. Other investigators of the revolutionary era employing dynamic psychology are Edwin G. Burrows and Michael Wallace, "The American Revolution: The Ideology and Psychology of National Liberation," *Perspectives in American History*, VI (1972), 167–225; Winthrop D. Jordan, "Familial Politics: Thomas Paine and the Killing of the King, 1776," *Journal of American History*, LX (Sept. 1973), 294–308; and John J. Waters, "James Otis, Jr.: An Ambivalent Revolutionary," *History of Childhood Quarterly*, I (Summer 1973), 142–50. A very informal use of ego psychology has appeared in a number of recent revolutionary period biographies, including Bernard Bailyn, *The Ordeal of Thomas Hutchinson* (Cambridge, 1974); and Carol Berkin, *Jonathan Sewall: Odyssey of An American Loyalist* (New York, 1974).

The loyalists used in this study were Samuel Auchmuty, William Axtell, Goldsbrow Banyar, Gerard G. Beekman, Evert Byanck, Cadwallader Colden, Myles Cooper, John H. Cruger, James DeLancey, Oliver DeLancey, Phila DeLancey, Andrew Elliot, Edmund Fanning, Benjamin Floyd, Hugh Gaine, Samuel Gale, Daniel Horsmanden, Charles Inglis, Guy Johnson, John Johnson, Thomas Jones, John Tabor Kempe, Isaac Low, John McKenna, David Mathews, Frederick Philipse III, John Peters, James Rivington, Beverley Robinson, Philip Skene, Samuel Seabury, William Smith, Jr., Henry Van Schaack, Peter Van Schaack, John Vardill, Abraham Wagg, John Watts, and Isaac Wilkins.

The revolutionaries were James Beekman, Egbert Benson, George Clinton, Henry Cruger, James Duane, William Duer, Stephen Gano, Leonard Gansevoort, Henry Glen, Alexander Hamilton, Nicholas Herkimer, John Sloss Hobart, John Holt, John Jay, John Jones, Samuel Kirkland, John Lamb, Hayman Levy, Francis Lewis, Philip Livingston, Peter Van Brugh Livingston, Robert Livingston, Jr., Robert R. Livingston, Walter Livingston, William Livingston,

This essay presents a different approach. Its chief contention is that measurable differences in adult personality characteristics differentiate loyalists from revolutionaries as well as the best established socioeconomic and political analyses. To test this contention, a "PEF" scale, of standard historical explanations of the political, economic, and family causes of loyalist and revolutionary affiliation, was composed, along with an "LR" scale of those personality traits linked to public activity and conviction. From the colony were winnowed a group of thirty-eight loyalists and forty-two revolutionaries—all the individuals about whom sufficient biographical data and manuscript materials for the two scales are available. Only eighty of over 1,200 potential subjects fit the criteria. The loyalists and revolutionaries were selected in the same fashion; no systematic effort was made to include or dismiss a subject other than availability of sufficient biographical and manuscript sources to complete at least one-half of the items of the PEF and LR scales for that individual. The size of the final population, small by comparison with the total number of loyalists and revolutionaries in the colony, does not handicap the ability to assess the discriminatory power of PEF and LR hypotheses. These eighty individuals do not represent a sample. The goal is to determine whether psychological factors differentiate loyalists from revolutionaries as well as political, economic, and social forces, and not to discover what proportion of either group in the colony as a whole fit any particular socioeconomic or psychological category.

324

Samuel Loudon, Alexander McDougall, Gouverneur Morris, Lewis Morris, Jr., Richard Morris, Samuel Provoost, Philip Schuyler, John Morin Scott, Isaac Sears, Melancton Smith, Abraham Ten Broeck, Philip Van Cortlandt, Pierre Van Cortlandt, Marinus Willett, Henry Wisner, Peter W. Yates, and Robert Yates.

Lists of loyalists were taken from Alexander C. Flick, ed., *The American Revolution in New York: Its Political, Social and Economic Significance* (Albany, 1926); William Kelby, *Orderly Book of the Three Battalions of Loyalists Commanded by Brigadier-General Oliver De Lancey, 1776-1778; to which is appended a list of New York loyalists in the city of New York During the war of the Revolution* (New York, 1917), 115-31; and Lorenzo Sabine, *Biographical Sketches of Loyalists of the American Revolution, with an Historical Essay* (2 vols., Boston, 1864), in addition to materials included in the *Journals of The Provincial Congress, Provincial Convention, Committee of Safety and Council of Safety of the State of New-York* (2 vols., Albany, 1842); and "Minutes of the Commitee and of the First Commission for Detecting and Defeating Conspiracies in the State of New York, December 11, 1776-September 23, 1778, with Collateral Documents. To which Is Added Minutes of the Council of Appointment, State of New York, April 2, 1778-May 3, 1779," *Collections of the New York Historical Society for the Year 1924*, LVII (1924). The names of revolutionaries came from *Journals of the Provincial Congress; Journals of the Continental Congress, 1774-1789* (34 vols., Washington, 1904-1937), I, II; Roger J. Champagne, *Alexander McDougall and the American Revolution in New York* (Schenectady, N.Y., 1975); George Dangerfield, *Chancellor Robert R. Livingston of New York 1746-1813* (New York, 1960); and Don R. Gerlach, *Philip Schuyler and the American Revolution in New York 1733-1777* (Lincoln, Neb., 1964). Invaluable throughout the research was Milton M. Klein, *New York in the American Revolution. A Bibliography* (Albany, 1974).

Included in the PEF scale is biographical information that permits testing of established political, social, and economic hypotheses on political choice. The "PE" items include sex, age of the subject in 1776, education, place of birth, place of residence, officeholding record, religious affiliation, occupation, wealth, travel experience, ethnic background, and military experience. Also on this scale are "F" items on family composition, to test a number of social-psychological hypotheses on the cause of political choice. These items are family generation in the colony, number of siblings, sibling position of the subject, age at father's death, age at marriage, and whether the place of residence is the same as the place of birth.

325

The following seven hypotheses composed from the PE items will be familiar to students of revolutionary historiography. First, loyalists were older than revolutionaries. Second, loyalists were members of the Protestant Episcopal Church and the revolutionaries were dissenters. Third, relatively speaking, the loyalists were the "haves" and the revolutionaries the "have-nots" in the colony. Fourth, loyalists tended to hold better jobs and live closer to the shore than the revolutionaries, for the loyalists were more dependent for livelihood and influence upon the center of the empire, across the Atlantic. Fifth, loyalists tended to be multiple officeholders, royal officeholders, and executive officeholders, while the revolutionaries held fewer offices, and these tended to be local and legislative. Sixth, the revolution in this colony was a struggle between two great families, the loyal DeLanceys and the revolutionary Livingstons. Seventh, British ethnic background, better education, wider travel experience, and service in the royal military forces were likely to lead to loyalist attachments. The degree to which any or all of these fit a profile of either political persuasion was then ascertained.[4]

The F items on the PEF scale were adopted from the work of historian Philip Greven and psychologist Alfred Adler. Greven postulated a causal relationship between the social independence of the fourth and fifth generation and those generations' participation in the rebellion. The children of earlier generations were more dependent upon their parents, and tended to live nearer home, marry later, and seek less personal autonomy than the fourth and fifth generations. The latter left

[4] These hypotheses were suggested by Stanley Elkins and Eric McKitrick, "The Founding Fathers, Young Men of the Revolution," *Political Science Quarterly*, LXXVI (June 1961), 181–216. Flick, *New York*; James Kirby Martin, *Men in Rebellion: Higher Governmental Leaders and the Coming of the American Revolution* (New Brunswick, N.J., 1973); and Carl Lotus Becker, *The History of Political Parties in the Province of New York, 1760–1776* (Madison, Wisc., 1960).

the family sooner and were consequently more accustomed to independence. For these individuals, ''Thomas Paine's call for independence in 1776 from the mother-country and from the father-king might have been just what Paine claimed it to be—common sense.'' Following Greven, it was hypothesized that if the subject is fourth generation or later, marries before the father's death, and does not reside at his place of birth, the subject should be a revolutionary.[5]

The second group of F items expresses in historical terms a facet of Adler's ''individual psychology.'' Adler argued that the ''family constellation'' had a major impact on the behavioral goals of its members. Older children, after losing the attention of parents to younger siblings, sought to regain adult approval. Middle children lost some but not all of the parents' attention and so wished approval but not with the same intensity as the eldest child. The youngest child, spurred and tutored by older siblings, while still bathed in the love of parents, could feel secure enough to devote his or her attention to personal goals. Recent experiments indicate that oldest children indeed require more approval from peer group and parental figures, while children lower in sibling order are more personalized, introspective, and independent in their goals. It was hypothesized that older children were more likely to be loyalists and younger children in the family more likely to be revolutionaries.[6]

While the primary aim of this essay is not to prove or disprove any of the PEF hypotheses so much as to comapre their discriminating power with that of the LR scale hypotheses, the quantitative results on the PEF scale were interesting in their own right. In some cases they represent the first numerical test of these theories, and the results are highly informative.

The LR scale is a nine-item personality inventory, designed to investigate adult personality characteristics of loyalists and revolutionaries. Fortunately for historians who wish to evaluate adult personality, experimental social psychologists have developed many scales to test adult cognitive and affective characteristics. Although the protocols of sophisticated modern personality inventories are too specific for surviving manuscript sources, they have been used here to create a simplified test of traits. With the LR scale, personality origins of political

[5] Philip J. Greven, Jr., *Four Generations: Population, Land, and Family in Colonial Andover, Massachusetts* (Ithaca, 1970), 279–81.

[6] Heinz L. Ansbacher and Rowena R. Ansbacher, eds., *The Individual Psychology of Alfred Adler: A Systematic Presentation in Selections From His Writings* (New York, 1956), 379; Salvatore R. Maddi, *Personality Theories. A Comparative Analysis* (Homewood, Ill., 1972), 476–78.

326

choice may be measured. It is assumed that personality is a mental structure that governs the individual's response to external stimuli, including political crisis. It is further assumed that "the political, economic, and social convictions of an individual often form a broad and coherent pattern, as if bound together by a 'mentality' or 'spirit,' and that this pattern is an expression of deeply [felt] trends in his personality."[7]

To isolate and evaluate major personality traits in historical figures, one must, as Robert Calhoon has written, find the subjects' "statements of self-consciousness and self-awareness." For many years, political scientists have employed individual attitude scales as indicators of aggregate political motivation. In this essay, the same thing is done using historical manuscripts, public orations, and privately recorded conversations as the raw data. Although the authors, who served as scorers of this material, avoided including a person on the scale without an adequate sample of his writing, they did accept the principle that scoring could be applied to any surviving document.[8]

327

[7] Roger Brown, *Social Psychology* (New York, 1965), 422; T. W. Adorno, Else Frenkel-Brunswick, Daniel J. Levinson, and R. Nevitt Sanford, *The Authoritarian Personality* (New York, 1950), 1.

[8] Robert M. Calhoon, "The Loyalist Perception," *Acadiensis*, II (Spring 1973), 3.

Relevant manuscript collections were consulted at the Albany Institute of History and Art, Columbia University, the New York Historical Society, the New York Public Library, and the New York State Library (Albany).

Published sources include: "Aspinwall Papers, Part II," *Collections of the Massachusetts Historical Society*, X (1871); Edmund C. Burnett, ed., *Letters of the Members of the Continental Congress* (8 vols., Washington, 1921–1936), I, II; Philip L. White, ed., *Beekman Mercantile Papers, 1746–1799* (3 vols., New York, 1956), I, II; "Cadwallader Colden Papers," *Collections of the New York Historical Society*, IX–X (1876–1877); [Peter Force, ed.] *American Archives: Fourth Series. Containing a Documentary History of the English Colonies in North America, from the King's Message to Parliament, of March 7, 1774, to the Declaration of Independence by the United States* (6 vols., Washington, 1837–1846); Hugh Hastings, ed., *The Public Papers of George Clinton, First Governor of New York, 1777–1795—1801–1804* (10 vols, New York, 1899–1914); Daniel Horsmanden, *The New York Conspiracy*, Thomas J. Davis, ed. (Boston, 1971); Paul Leicester Ford., ed., *The Journal of Hugh Gaine, Printer* (2 vols., New York, 1902); Henry P. Johnston, ed., *The Correspondence and Public Papers of John Jay* (4 vols., New York, 1890–1893), I, II; [Philip Livingston] *The Other Side of the Question: or, A Defense of the Liberties of North-America. In Answer to a Late Friendly Address To All Reasonable Americans, on the Subject of Our Political Confusions. By a Citizen* (New York, 1774); "Letters to General Lewis Morris," *Collections of the New York Historical Society for the Year 1875* (1876), 433–512; Richard B. Morris, ed., *John Jay, the Making of a Revolutionary: Unpublished Papers 1745–1780* (New York, 1975); E. B. O'Callaghan, ed., *The Documentary History of the State of New York* (4 vols., Albany, 1848–1851); William H. W. Sabine, ed., *Historical Memoirs of William Smith, Historian of the Province of New York, Member of the Governor's Council and Last Chief Judge of that Province Under the Crown Chief Justice of Quebec* (3 vols., New York 1956–1959); Kenneth Scott, comp., *Rivington's New York Newspaper: Excerpts from a Loyalist Press, 1773–1783* (New York, 1973); [Samuel Seabury] *Free Thoughts on The Proceedings of the Continental Congress, Held at Philadelphia Sept. 5, 1774* (White Plains, N.Y., 1930); Harold C. Syrett, ed., *The Papers of Alexander Hamilton* (26 vols., New York, 1961–1976); L. F. S. Upton, ed., *The Diary and Selected Papers of Chief Justice William Smith, 1784–1793* (2 vols., Toronto,

1963–1965); Philip Van Cortlandt, "Autobiography of Philip Van Cortlandt, Brigadier-General in the Continental Army," *Magazine of American History*, II (1878), 279–98; "Letter Book of John Watts, Merchant and Councillor of New York January 1, 1762–December 22, 1765," *Collections of the New York Historical Society for the Year 1928*, LXI (1928).

The published essays of the subjects were scored, including Egbert Benson, "Memoir Read Before the Historical Society of the State of New York December 31, 1816," *New York Historical Society Collections*, Second Series, II (1849), 77–148; E. C. Chorley, ed., "Letters of the Rev. Dr. Jeremiah Leaming to the Rev. Samuel Peters," *Historical Magazine of the Protestant Episcopal Church*, 2 (Sept. 1932), 116–42; Cadwallader Colden, *The History of the Five Indian Nations of Canada, which are dependent on the Province of New-York in America and Are the Barrier between the English and French in that Part of the World* (London, 1747); [Myles Cooper] *Patriots of North America: A Sketch with Explanatory Notes* (New York, 1775); Myles Cooper, *Poems on Several Occasions* (London, 1761); James DeLancey, *A Letter to . . . Mr. Pitt* (London, 1788); Stephen Gano, *Narrative of My Life* (Providence, 1826); Charles Inglis, *The True Interest of Americans Impartially Stated* (Philadelphia, 1776); Thomas Jones, *The History of New York During the Revolution and of the Leading Events in the Other Colonies at that Period*, Edward Floyd de Lancey, ed. (2 vols., New York, 1879); William Livingston and Others, *The Independent Reflector, or Weekly Essays on Sundry Important Subjects More particularly adapted to the Province of New-York*, Milton M. Klein, ed., (Cambridge, 1963); William Smith, Jr., *The History of the Province of New-York*, Michael Kammen, ed. (2 vols., Cambridge, 1972).

Various secondary sources, memoirs, and lives reprinted portions of primary sources and gave valuable assistance on biographical data. They include: Eben E. Beardsley, *The Life and Correspondence of the Right Reverend Samuel Seabury, D.D., First Bishop of Connecticut, and of the Episcopal Church in the United States of America* (Boston, 1881); E. C. Chorley, "Samuel Provoost, First Bishop of New York," *Historical Magazine of the Protestant Episcopal Church*, 2 (June 1933), 1–25; 2 (Sept. 1933), 1–16; L. Effingham De Forest, *The Van Cortlandt Family* (New York, 1930); Dorothy Rita Dillon, *The New York Triumvirate: A Study of the Legal and Political Careers of William Livingston, John Morin Scott, William Smith, Jr.* (New York, 1949); Elizabeth Ellet, *Women of the American Revolution* (2 vols., Philadelphia, 1900); Edward Hagaman Hall, *Philipse Manor Hall at Yonkers, N.Y.; the Site, the building and its occupants* (New York, 1912); J. T. Headley, *The Chaplains and Clergy of the Revolution* (New York, 1864); Mary Gay Humphreys, *Catherine Schuyler* (New York, 1897); Isaac Q. Leake, *Memoir of the Life and Times of John Lamb, an Officer of the Revolution* (Albany, 1857); Alfred Lawrence Lorenz, *Hugh Gaine: A Colonial Printer-Editor's Odyssey to Loyalism* (Carbondale, Ill., 1972); Benson J. Lossing, *The Life and Times of Philip Schuyler* (2 vols., New York, 1872); John W. Lydekker, *The Life and Letters of Charles Inglis, His Ministry in America and Consecration as First Colonial Bishop* (London, 1936); Richard K. McMaster, "Parish in Arms: A Study of Father John McKenna and the Mohawk Valley Loyalists, 1773–1778," *U.S. Catholic Historical Society Historical Records and Studies*, XLV (1957); Max M. Mintz, *Gouverneur Morris and the American Revolution* (Norman, 1970); John Pell, "Philip Skene of Skenesborough," *Quarterly Journal of the New York State Historical Association*, IX (Jan. 1928), 27–44; David de Sola Pool, *Portraits Etched in Stone: Early Jewish Settlers, 1682–1831* (New York, 1952); Victor H. Paltsits, "John Holt—Printer and Postmaster," *Bulletin of the New York Public Library*, 24 (1920); Emma Runk, *Ten Broeck Genealogy* (New York, 1897); Cecil Roth, "A Jewish Voice for Peace in the War of American Independence. The Life and Writings of Abraham Wagg, 1719–1803," *Publications of the American Jewish Historical Society*, 31 (1928), 33–75; Theodore Sedgwick, Jr., *A Memoir of the Life of William Livingston, Member of Congress in 1774, 1775, and 1776; Delegate to the Federal Convention in 1787, and Governor of the State of New-Jersey from 1776 to 1790, with Extracts from His Correspondence, and Notices of Various Members of His Family* (New York, 1833); John Nicholas Norton, *The Life of Bishop Provoost* (New York, 1859); Jared Sparks, *The Life of Gouverneur Morris, with Selections From His Correspondence and Miscellaneous Papers* (3 vols., Boston, 1832), I; E. Wilder Spaulding, *His Excellency George Clinton, Critic of the Constitution* (New York, 1938); Howard Thomas, *Marinus Willett, Soldier-patriot, 1740–1830* (New York, 1954); L. F. S. Upton, *The Loyal Whig: William Smith of New York & Quebec* (Toronto, 1969); R. W. G. Vail, "A Patriotic Pair of Peripatetic Printers, Upstate Imprints of John Holt and Samuel Loudon," *Essays in Honor of Lawrence C. Wroth* (Portland, Me., 1954), 391–427; Henry Cruger Van Schaack, *Memoirs of the Life of Henry Van Schaack Embracing Selections From His Correspondence During The American Revolution* (Chicago,

To create a suitable personality scale, the ideas of various social psychologists and personality theorists were combined. This eclecticism can be justified. In the first place, the experimental psychologists and theoreticians had themselves drawn measures and theses from disparate sources. In the second place, many of these psychologists have expressed a personal interest in the historical application of their work, and some of them have tried to apply their ideas to historical events. Finally, as a leading political scientist in this field wrote, borrowing from psychologists himself, "It is unsatisfactory for the analyst whose primary interest is in how the actor's personal chracteristics guide the full range of his behavior simply to rely on a set of propositions. . . ." Of course, no theoretical formulation can be any better than its results, as David C. McClelland has remarked.[9]

329

The final version of the LR scale composed for this study is as follows: (1) need for order; (2) intolerance of dissonance; (3) intolerance of ambiguity; (4) submission to authority; (5) power orientation; (6) hierarchical thinking and authoritarian aggression; (7) traditionalism; (8) conformity; and (9) stereotyped thinking. The items measure attitudes toward order, authority, and social values—components of personality

1892); Henry C. Van Schaack, *The Life of Peter Van Schaack, LL.D., Embracing Selections From His Correspondence and Other Writings, During the American Revolution, and His Exile in England* (New York, 1842); Mary Voyse, *John Sloss Hobart—forgotten patriot* (New York, 1959); A. J. Wall, "Samuel Loudon (1727–1813)," *New York Historical Society Quarterly*, 6 (Oct. 1922), 75–92; and Philip L. White, *The Beekmans of New York in Politics and Commerce, 1647–1877* (New York, 1956). Standard works including Allen Johnson, ed., *Dictionary of American Biography* (20 vols., New York, 1928–1936); Franklin B. Dexter, *Biographical Sketches of the Graduates of Yale College* (6 vols., New York, 1885–1912); and Clifford K. Shipton, *Sibley's Harvard Graduates: Biographical Sketches of Those Who Attended Harvard College* (14 vols., Cambridge, 1933–1975) were also used.

[9] Greenstein, *Personality and Politics*, xx; David C. McClelland, *The Achieving Society* (New York, 1961), 79; Adorno, Frenkel-Brunswick, Levinson, and Sanford, *Authoritarian Personality*; and Leon Festinger, *A Theory of Cognitive Dissonance* (Evanston, Ill., 1957), 249–51, have all expressed their interest in history. Full technical exploration of the origins and interconnectedness of the items created for the LR scale would be out of place here.

The methodological decision to use modern psychological concepts to study eighteenth-century figures, in full cognizance of the "culture-bound" limitations of all psychological theory, was made for a number of reasons. In the first place, a great similarity exists between the private concerns of the eighteenth-century subjects and men and women today. In a more technical vein, to view or translate proven modern psychological methods into impressionistic eighteenth-century cultural terms would so weaken the validity of the psychological measures as to render them meaningless. Even if strict and consistent "linkages" were proposed between eighteenth-century cultural, political, and social norms and the subjects' lives, and then these linkages used to revise the terminology of modern personality tests, a criticism would still remain: "Which collectivity should the psychohistorian select as the social context in which the individual personality develops?" See Alfred J. Rieber, "Comment on 'The Psychoanalysis of Groups,'" *Group for the Use of Psychology in History Newsletter*, IV (March 1976), 28. The use of potentially anachronistic technical terminology in the LR scales cannot weaken the discriminatory power of the LR scale items—simply because loyalists and revolutionaries were scored using the *same* terms and concepts.

which can be ascertained from informed reading of historical manuscripts.

The first item seeks to discover the need for order, neatness, control of possessions and situations, and the desire for regularity in life experiences. Closely allied to the need for order is a need for definition in expectation, deliberateness, and sobriety. Threats to personal and social stability are magnified by those who have a positive need for order. Pierre Van Cortlandt, for example, expressed this need for order in a report he drafted to the state committee of safety late in 1776: "At a time when the utmost resources of this State were laid open to their [the soldiers'] wants, . . . and after frequent losses of provisions and barracks, to supply two numerous armies, . . . with every article which they required, . . . wherever our troops have marched or been stationed, they have done infinite damage to the possessions and farms, and pilfered the property of the people." In Cadwallader Colden's plea for "as much quietness as could be expected in the present situation" and his demand for suppression of "riots and tumults" during the Stamp Act crisis, there is the same need for order. A negative scorer, like Henry Wisner, required far less order. It did not seem to disturb him that settlers following his directions got lost or that he was not available to sign the Declaration of Independence which he approved the day before.[10]

The next item, intolerance of dissonance, probes the subject's perceptual style. Cognitive dissonance is the product of conflicting cognitive elements within a person's mind, for example, conflicting ideas about what is happening and what ought to be happening. Dissonance is uncomfortable and every individual works to reduce it. For some, dissonance is more unbearable than for others, and this study is based on the belief that "variation in 'toleration for dissonance' would seem to be measurable." An individual's methods of reducing dissonance, such as denial of reality, shifts in group attachment, and selective perception, indicate that individual's ability to handle dissonance. In William Duer's admonition to his untrustworthy apprentice, "be assured I will leave no stone unturned either to confirm what I have strong reason to suspect, or to remove those suspicions," he tried to reduce an intolerable dissonance by seeking new information. Duer showed a low threshold for dissonance on questions which would not have disturbed others,

[10] Henry A. Murray, *Explorations in Personality: A Clinical and Experimental Study of Fifty Men of College Age* (New York, 1938), 80–81, 241–42; *Journals of the Provincial Congress of New York*, II, 211; "Colden Papers," X, 66–67; Henry Wisner to William Alexander, April 25, 1767, Alexander Manuscripts. The above and all subsequent quotes are examples to illustrate the definitions of LR items and by no means the sole criterion by which an individual was scored on a particular item.

hence scored positively on the item. One rarely sees William Smith, Jr., so beset by dissonance. Instead, as he noted in his journal of June 5, 1775, "In times of so much heat, a wise man will set a double guard upon his steps to avoid precipitation." So, too, Beverley Robinson coolly told the state committee for the detection of conspiracies, "Sir, I cant take the oath [of allegiance], but should be exceedingly glad to stay in the country. . . . It is very uncertain who will rule yet for the matter is not determined." Robinson, like Smith, a negative scorer, could have waited out the war, dealing with both sides, without being unduly disturbed by dissonance.[11]

The next four items are loosely derived from the concept of "authoritarianism." Intolerance for ambiguity, item three, is the tendency to see events and issues in black and white terms, to make mechanical judgments, and to be rigid in their application. Charles Inglis' delight that "A perfect harmony has hitherto subsisted between me and my people. Many reigning vices are checked, some quite suppressed" shows an intolerance for ambiguity repeated much later in his castigation of Paine's *Common Sense* as "one of the most virulent, artful, and pernicious pamphlets I have ever met with, and perhaps the wit of man could not devise one better calculated to do mischief." Inglis' fear of Paine may not have been unfounded—many revolutionaries feared Paine's radicalism—but Inglis' reaction to the pamphlet was quick and uncompromising: "At the risk, not only of my liberty, but of my live [sic], I drew up an answer, and had it printed here." Others opposed Paine, but nevertheless proved willing to hear both sides of the issue and consider compromise. Among these was Henry Van Schaack, who wrote to his brother Peter, "I told them [the members of the New York delegation to the Continental Congress] that every good man ought to do his endeavors to think of a reconciliation, instead of widening the breach; that perhaps when the House met, some conciliating plan might be suggested and approved . . . ." It should be noted that items two and three are theoretically related.[12]

331

[11] Festinger, *Cognitive Dissonance*, 266–68; Jack W. Brehm and Arthur R. Cohen, *Explorations in Cognitive Dissonance* (New York, 1962), 177; William Duer to Robert Snell, 1773, Duer Papers; Smith to Lewis Morris, June 5, 1775, William W. H. Sabine, ed., *The Historical Memoirs of William Smith, Jr.* (3 vols., New York, 1956), I, 228; Beverley Robinson to Conspiracy Committee, Feb. 22, 1777, *Minutes of the Committee to Detect Conspiracies*, 148–49.

[12] Else Frenkel-Brunswick, "Further Explorations," Richard Christie and Marie Jahoda, eds., *Studies in the Scope and Method of "The Authoritarian Personality"* (Glencoe, Ill., 1954), 257; Lydekker, *Life and Letters of Inglis*, 17; Charles Inglis, "State of the Anglo-American Church in 1776," O'Callaghan, ed., *Documentary History of the State of New York*, III, 1059; *Memoirs of the Life of Henry Van Schaack*, 33.

Item four explores submission to authority. The key concepts here are a need to be dominated, to have visible and rigid rules for dependency, and an affinity for authoritarian leadership. Father figures, a benevolent father-king, for example, are given greater importance by positive scorers on item four than by negative scorers. It is clear where Myles Cooper, president of Kings College, stood on the scale. Comparing rebels to schoolboys in 1775, he rhymed:

So oft the giddy Eton Boys,
Disturb, Oh, Thames, thy peaceful Joys
. . .
Calling their Comrades, Knaves and Fools,
Who tamely crouch, to College Rules
. . .
But they cabal, harrangue, resolve,
Rebel, associate, run away;
Exult in Anarchy's short Day.
. . .
The gen'ral Tenor of its runs,
That Fathers shan't controul their Sons.

James Beekman saw the crisis differently: "But it is impossible that freeborn Englishmen, as we are, . . . should now submit to Parliamentary Taxations, without giving up our Title to Freedom, and become Vassals and Slaves." Beekman's attitude was what Else Frenkel-Brunswick has called "principled independence," the opposite of authoritarian submission.[13]

Power orientation, item five, traces the subject's emphasis upon power relationships in his perceptions of the outside world. Be the situation political, economic, or social, the positive scorer on item five will always be skeptical of idealistic or affective relationships, and instead see interest and advantage as the true motives of others. Positive scorers also tend to divide the world into their own group, family, party, or sect—and "out groups" whose motives and methods are invariably suspect. Robert Livingston, Jr., the third lord of the vast family estates on the Hudson, saw interpersonal conflicts as power struggles for influence, land, and wealth. He warned his son-in-law, James Duane, against continuing to represent the rival DeLancey family in legal matters, for a "violent spirit still reigned in their hearts." Duane was to join with "men of more sense and honor"—the Livingstons. At the same time, Livingston was writing to Philip Schuyler, "There is a great

[13] Authoritarian submission, power-orientation, and aggression, as well as hierarchical thinking, are discussed in Adorno, *Authoritarian Personality*, 223–28, 236–38, 414; Cooper, *Patriots of North America*, 13; "Beekman Correspondence," I, 758.

deal in good management of the votes. Our people are in high spirits, and if there is not fair play shown there will be bloodshed, as we have by far the best part of the bruisers on our side."[14]

Item six, hierarchical thinking and authoritarian aggression, combines two closely related concepts—the subjects' high esteem for those who have power and the subjects' desire to use power themselves. For positive scorers, status is equivalent to worth, and individuals are ranked according to the power they possess. Positive scorers believe strength and decisiveness good, and weakness bad. John Peters, a transplanted Connecticut Puritan, evidenced the first of these attributes in his appeal to the crown for recompense: "Some persons, who have commissions, altho very small ones, treated me and other gentlemen very ill by saying that non-commissioned officers should command us . . . I am a colonel in the militia in Glouster County, and have my commission with me . . . I am also one of the judges of the court of common pleas in that county . . . I am descended from a gentleman who settled in New England and not of the meanest family but one of the best." Alexander Hamilton illustrated the second portion of item six: ". . . my Ambition is prevalent," he wrote while a youth, "that I contemn [sic] the grov'ling and condition of a Clerk or the like, to which my Fortune &c. condemns me and would willingly risk my life tho' not my Character to exalt my Station." Five years later, in 1,774, he expressed the same drives by warning England that military action would be met by bloody, implacable, and obstinate colonial resistance. Where others among the patriot party recoiled from strife, Hamilton embraced it. Samuel Provoost, the assistant rector of Trinity Church, scored negatively on item six, for he believed "my situation perfectly agreeable if it were not for the bigotry and enthusiasm that generally prevail here among people of all denominations. . . . As I found this to be the case, I made it a point to preach the plain doctrine of religion and morality." Throughout the crisis, Provoost avoided power and shunned status, claiming instead to be guided by conscience.[15]

The last three items concern the social ideas, "schematizations" of values, held by loyalists and revolutionaries. Schematizations are cognitive frameworks, lattices of social values and expectations in every individual's mind. Variation in these values by individual loyalists and revolutionaries was a product of their varying personalities. Value

[14] Robert Livingston, Jr., to Duane, Feb. 17, 1772, Duane Manuscripts; Lossing, *Schuyler*, I, 236.

[15] John Peters to unknown correspondent, Oct. 27, 1780, New York State Library; Syrett, *Papers of Hamilton*, I, 4, 54; Chorley, "Samuel Provoost," I, 4.

schematizations are particularly useful tools for the historian, for they are often the substance of self-descriptive and normative essays. Item seven is concerned with the subjects' views of established institutions, customary ways of thought, and traditions. When Justice Thomas Jones of Long Island, for example, warned the rebels, especially William Livingston, against "pulling down the Church and ruining the constitution," he scored positively on item seven. Of all the items on the scale, this one comes closest to the category of ideology. Positive scores are conservative and negative scorers welcome change and reform.[16]

Conformity, item eight, evaluates the subject's desire for peer group acceptance and social harmony. The positive scorer tries to fit his behavior and opinion to the current norms of the group in which the subject finds himself and demands the same conformity from neighbors. While late eighteenth-century New York had its share of conformists, there were notable exceptions. William Livingston was one. In his October 11, 1753, *Independent Reflector*, he opined "that the word *Orthodoxy*, is a hard equivocal priestly Term, that caused the Effusion of more Blood than all the Roman Emperors put together." Support came from young Schuyler. "I esteem the Church and its liturgy," he wrote in 1753, "but I believe [William Livingston] is right in opposing the ridiculous pretensions of the clergy, who would make it as infallible as the popish church claims to be. I wish liberty of conscience in all things."[17]

The last item in the scale tests the subject's stereotyping of people and events. If the subject labels rather than seeking individual differences, and lumps other individuals together into narrowly defined, demeaning categories, a positive score was assigned on item nine. Merchant Gerard Beekman's descriptions of other groups—"New England men are bad pay," the Irish are "scowbankers," the French are untrustworthy, and Beekman himself "almost Turned Jew" in his business activities—give him a positive score on this item. William Smith, Jr., scored negatively, in part for his willingness to criticize his beloved father for using "an affecting representation of the agonies of the cross" in a speech denying political rights to the Jews of the city of New York. William Smith, Sr.'s, "religious and political creed were [sic] both inflamed by the heat . . . of the times . . . . Perhaps," his son suggested, "he was not himself at that time."[18]

[16] David C. McClelland, *Personality* (New York, 1951), 239–88; Jones, *History of New York*, I, 6.

[17] Livingston, *Independent Reflector*, 391; Lossing, *Schuyler*, 78.

[18] White, *Beekmans of New York*, 223–24; Smith, *History of the Province of New-York*, II, 34–35.

The entire LR scale may be seen as a measure of individual tolerance for disorder, dissent, independence, equality, change, and non-conformity. A positive score, + 1, was given for a subject on an item if the subject showed a positive attitude , a − 1 if a negative attitude appeared, and no score if the evidence was missing or ambiguous. Although, as is evident from the examples above, not every revolutionary obtained a negative score nor every loyalist a positive score on each item, the two groups did tend to score differently. The hypothesis was that revolutionaries were likely to be negative scorers on every item and overall, and loyalists the reverse. Because the results depended so much upon the scoring of the manuscript documents, every effort was made to insure that the scoring would be both sensitive and objective. To guarantee that no systematic bias crept into the scoring, two of the authors scored "blind," that is, without knowing the identity or political affiliation of the subject. Conferences were held after the scoring was completed to discuss disputed results. If the authors could not then agree, the item was not entered for that individual. After a practice session on a small sample of the group, the authors found they tended to agree on their scores.[19]

Throughout the scoring, the authors were aware of the problem of possible post-decisional personality change. It was assumed that personality differences were the causes of individual decision making in the crisis, yet a small portion of the documentary material came from the period after the Declaration of Independence. Were the traits measured in these cases created by events rather than the reverse? Two recent technical essays were reassuring on this matter. First, Raymond Cattell and his associates have established the fact that personality traits such as "radicalism" and "self-sufficiency"—closely related to the first, fourth, fifth, sixth, seventh, and eighth items—change very little, if at all, between sixteen and sixty. Of course, a stress situation as severe as the revolutionary crisis might have affected personality—but to what extent? The latest cognitive dissonance experiments suggest that important decisions, far from changing established opinions and attitudes, tend, after a period of regret, to "fix" the pre-decisional state of mind. The question remains open whether such attitudinal hardening is also true of underlying personality traits, but the extant cognitive dissonance literature confirms a belief that while the magnitude of attitudes may be changed by a decision, their direction, and hence the direction of the

[19] David C. McClelland, Russell A. Clark, Thornton B. Roby, and John W. Atkinson, "The Effect of the Need for Achievement on Thematic Apperception," John W. Atkinson, ed., *Motives in Fantasy, Action, and Society* (Princeton, 1958), 80.

personality characteristics beneath them, is not generally changed after a
difficult choice.[20]

The primary method used to determine the validity of both PE and LR
hypotheses was to determine the percentage of errors made in classifying
individuals as loyalist or revolutionary using those hypotheses. It is
important to note that every hypothesis was two-sided. For example, it
was hypothesized that subjects who held executive offices were likely to
be loyalists, and it was found that nineteen executive officers were in fact
loyalists and twelve were revolutionaries. This gives twelve classification
errors out of thirty-one cases. For the converse of the hypothesis—that
non-executive officeholders would tend to be revolutionaries—twenty
revolutionaries and seven loyalists were obtained, a total of seven

336

TABLE 1

Political and Economic (PE) Hypotheses

Hypotheses	Percent error	rb percent	λb percent
Highly Discriminatory			
Royal officeholding	25	24	46
Legislative officeholding	25	23	46
Church affiliation	29	15	35
Place of Birth	33	11	30
Executive officeholding	33	10	27
Marginally Discriminatory			
Age at 1776	40	4	12
Generation family in colonies	31*	4	12
Wealth	40	3	17
Non-Discriminatory			
European travel	36	2	5
Occupation	42	1	6
Residence	46	0	3
Education	48	0	0
Military service	49	0	0
Travel in American colonies	52	•	•
Officeholding	53	—ᵇ	—
Ethnic derivation	59	—	—
Multiple officeholding	60	—	—

* Variance caused by difference in number of subjects classified.
ᵇ Values of rb and λb not meaningful for hypotheses with greater than 50 percent errors.

[20] Raymond B. Cattell, *Personality and Motivation: Structure and Measurement* (Yonkers-on-
Hudson, N.Y., 1957), quoted in Allan R. Buss and Wayne Poley, *Individual Differences, Traits
and Factors* (New York, 1976), 142; Robert A. Wicklund and Jack W. Brehm, *Perspectives on
Cognitive Dissonance* (New York, 1976). See also Leon Festinger, *Conflict, Decision, and
Dissonance* (Stanford, 1964), 42–44, 61.

classification errors out of twenty-seven cases. Thus there was a total of nineteen errors for fifty-eight cases. This level of error, 32 percent is low enough to indicate a substantial relationship between executive officeholding and loyalism.[21]

The various PE hypotheses were tested in the above manner for discriminatory power, with results presented in Table 1. Next to each hypothesis is shown the percentage of classification errors and two statistical measures of the strength of discrimination: τb and λb. The hypotheses are listed in descending order of discriminatory power as measured by τb, which gives more accurate rankings of items than λb.

In addition to computing the discriminatory power of each hypothesis singly, all the non-discriminatory hypotheses were adjusted for interaction with other PE hypotheses to see if the former might then provide some discriminatory power. Even with adjustments, the non-discriminatory hypotheses showed no substantial discriminatory power.[22]

337

The combination of PE hypotheses that would most strongly discriminate between loyalists and revolutionaries was sought next. This ''short PE scale'' would later be compared with the most discriminatory combination of LR hypothesis to test the principal contention. Royal officeholding and age at 1776 were excluded. The former was omitted because by the time of the arrival of Governor William Tryon, in 1771, royal offices were only given to those men who had already shown their aversion to dissent. Age at 1776 was dismissed because young loyalists did not have the same opportunity to gain political prominence or economic status, and so leave manuscripts behind them, as the young revolutionaries. Had the loyalists won the war, the reverse would have been true.

To find the best combination of PE hypotheses, each subject was assigned a score on all remaining hypotheses. A positive score, $+1$, was given a subject if he fulfilled the loyalist condition of a hypothesis, and a negative score, -1, if he fulfilled the converse revolutionary condition, regardless of his actual political affiliation. A form of discriminant analysis was then used to find the best combination of hypotheses by

[21] For a full discussion of these measures, see Herbert M. Blalock, Jr., *Social Statistics* (New York, 1972), 300–03.
[22] This was done by means of a partial F-test; see N. R. Draper and H. Smith, *Applied Regression Analysis* (New York, 1966), 71.

TABLE 2

Distribution of Scores on Combined Political-Economic Hypotheses
(Short PE Scale)

Score on short PE scale		Actually loyalist	Actually revolutionary
	5	1	0
	4	5	0
"High"	3	3	0
	2	5	0
	1	6	3
"Middle"	0	4	5
	−1	10	8
	−2	1	5
"Low"	−3	2	16
	−4	0	2
	−5	1	3

338

TABLE 3

Combined Political-Economic Hypotheses (Short PE Scale)

Classifications	Actually loyalist	Actually revolutionary
Loyalist (high combined score)	20	3
Unclassified (middle combined score)	14	13
Revolutionary (low combined score)	4	26

Classification errors, 7; total classified, 53; classification error, 13%.
Equivalent classification errors, 15.9; number of subjects, 80; equivalent classification error, 20%.

TABLE 4

Personality Characteristics (LR) Hypotheses

Hypotheses	Percent error	rb percent	λb percent
Highly Discriminatory			
Tradition	20	39	59
Sumbission	24	25	51
Conformity	30	14	38
Power orientation	37	11	16
Hierarchical thinking/authoritarian aggression	36	9	24
Marginally Discriminatory			
Order	43	4	8
Stereotyping	41	3	10
Non-Discriminatory			
Dissonance	46	1	8
Ambiguity	53	—	

adding together each subject's scores on all the hypotheses in various groups.[23]

As Table 2 above indicates, adding scores on a number of hypotheses produces a range of scores. When the scores were added, some subjects had high positive scores, some had low scores, and a middle group emerged with + and − scores that tended to cancel one another out. An individual with a preponderance of + scores was classified as a loyalist, and one with a preponderance of − scores, was classified as a revolutionary. In cases where the scores tended to balance each other, the subject was not classified. While the ideal would have been to classify all the subjects as either loyalist or revolutionary according to the short PE scale, the authors did not wish to do this at the expense of having a large proportion of classification errors. To determine how large this middle group should be, the number of classification errors that could be committed in order to avoid leaving subjects unclassified had to be decided. It was determined that the middle group would consist of those subjects with the same score who could not be classified as either loyalist or revolutionary without committing greater than 33 percent classification errors. The discriminatory power of the short PE scale was evaluated according to "equivalent classification error" and 33 percent of the number of subjects left unclassified.[24]

The combination of PE hypotheses which made the fewest equivalent classification errors was the combination of all four remaining highly discriminatory hypotheses and one of the marginally discriminating hypotheses—wealth. This distribution of scores is displayed in Table 2. Table 3 shows the results of the classification using this short scale. The combined PE hypotheses have only 13 percent errors on the subjects classified and 20 percent equivalent errors on all subjects,

[23] Adding together scores on different items to form a single score that provides better discrimination than any of the individual items is called discriminant analysis. In discriminant analysis, one usually multiplies the scores on each item by a weight before adding the scores on the items together. The method used in this essay is equivalent to discriminant analysis with all weights confined to being either 0 or 1. Discriminant analysis with weights was attempted, first using weights assigned by maximizing the ratio of between-groups variance to pooled within-groups variance, and second using weights assigned by dummy regression, where regressands were dichotomous variables. These procedures are discussed in Robert A. Eisenbeis and Robert B. Avery, *Discriminant Analysis and Classification Procedures: Theory and Applications* (Lexington, Mass., 1972). The scores produced by the two procedures did not have substantially greater discriminatory power than the scores produced without using multiplicative factors. The latter method was used to present the results. For a more detailed comparison of the two kinds of discriminant analysis, see footnote 25 below.

[24] The exact value of the multiplicand in the equivalent classification error measure is not important. Scores on the combined hypotheses would not have been changed if 32 percent or 34 percent replaced 33 percent. The selection of 33 percent was based on a visual interpretation of Tables 2, 5, and 8.

compared with 25 percent errors on the best of the individual PE hypotheses.

Using the same classification techniques as on the PE hypotheses, LR scale items could be separated according to their discriminatory power. The results appear in Table 4.

Next, the combination of LR hypotheses that would produce the strongest discrimination between loyalists and revolutionaries was sought. Until further study of the scoring of traditionalism, including replication on another data set, this item was temporarily excluded. So uniform was the loyalist scoring on this item that it was feared that it reflected the psychological phenomenon of rationalization, rather than the schematization of values being tested. The remaining LR hypotheses were then tested and combined in the same method used for the PE hypotheses. A short JR scale combining all of the four highly discriminatory hypotheses with ''order,'' one of the marginally discriminatory hypotheses, produced the fewest equivalent classification errors. The distribution of scores appears in Table 5.

340

TABLE 5

Distribution of Scores on Combined Personality Characteristics Hypotheses
(Short LR Scale)

Score on short LR scale		Actually loyalist	Actually revolutionary
"High"	5	14	1
	4	5	2
"Middle"	3	4	4
	2	1	3
	1	9	9
	0	2	2
"Low"	−1	2	8
	−2	0	1
	−3	1	10
	−4	0	0
	−5	0	2

TABLE 6

Combined Personality Characteristics Hypotheses (Short LR Scale)

Classifications	Actually loyalist	Actually revolutionary
Loyalist (high combined score)	19	3
Unclassified (middle combined score)	16	18
Revolutionary (low combined score)	3	21

Classification errors, 6; total classified, 46; classification error, 13%.

Equivalent classification errors, 17.2; number of subjects, 80; equivalent classification error, 22%.

Table 6 shows the results of classification of the subjects using the short LR scale. A comparison of Table 6 with Table 3 reveals that the combined LR hypotheses commit exactly the same amount of error—13 percent—as the combined PE hypotheses on the subjects classified by each of the short scales, and the former commits only a slightly higher percentage of equivalent classification errors on all subjects than the latter—22 percent versus 20 percent. There is thus no way to choose between the combined LR hypotheses and the combined PE hypotheses for discriminatory power.[25]

It is revealing to compare the classification of subjects according to the short PE scale with the classification of subjects under the short LR scale. This is done in Table 7.

TABLE 7

Political and Economic, and Personality Characteristics Combined Hypotheses
(Short PE and LR Scales) Compared

Combined Short PE Scale Score	Combined Short LR Scale Score		
	High	Middle	Low
High	12	10	1
Middle	7	13	7
Low	3	11	16

One should note that all twelve subjects who received high scores according to both the PE and LR short scales were in fact loyalists, and that all sixteen subjects who received low scores in both short scales were in fact revolutionaries. For the twenty-eight subjects for whom situational and psychological factors agree, no classification error was made. One should also note that only four subjects out of eighty got a

[25] Other statistical measures of association confirm that the short PE scale has only slightly better discriminatory power than the short LR scale. Goodman and Kruskal's rb is 36 percent for the short PE and 31 percent for the short LR. λb is 47 percent for the short PE and 42 percent for the short LR. Kendall's correlation coefficient rb (correlating the rank orderings of the individual subjects' scores with whether they were loyalists or revolutionaries) was 51 percent for the short PE and 48 percent for the short LR. The comparison of the two short scales is presented in terms of equivalent classification errors rather than any of the above statistical measures because these measures place too heavy a penalty upon the number of unclassified individuals. See Blalock, Social Statistics, 300–03, 418–20.

Had discriminant analysis with weights been used, as described in footnote 23, to compare the two short scales, the conclusions would have been the same. The best PE discriminant score obtained with this method made three errors out of a total of forty-six individuals classified and left thirty-four subjects unclassified, for a total of 14.2 equivalent classification errors, and an equivalent classification error of 18 percent. The best LR discriminant score so obtained made seven errors out of fifty-four individuals classified and twenty-six subjects unclassified, for a total of 15.6 equivalent classification errors and an equivalent classification error of 20 percent.

low score according to one short scale and a high score according to the
other. These two results suggest that there is some tendency for the PE
and LR scores on a subject to agree. This agreement is far from perfect,
however, as can be seen by noting that subjects with middle scores
according to the LR short scale are evenly distributed among the PE
high, middle, and low scorers. This argument is confirmed by computation of the correlation between the two scores of each subject using
the Spearman rank order correlation coefficient. A 47 percent
correlation between the two scores is high, but far from the 100 percent
which would indicate perfect correlation.

342

TABLE 8

Distribution of Scores on Summed Short Political and Economic (PE) and
Personality Characteristics (LR) Scales

Summed PE and LR Scores		Actually loyalist	Actually revolutionary
"High"	9	3	0
	8	4	0
	7	3	0
	6	4	0
	5	1	0
	4	3	1
	3	5	2
"Middle"	2	3	5
	1	4	4
	0	3	1
	−1	2	3
"Low"	−2	1	4
	−3	1	5
	−4	1	7
	−5	0	1
	−6	0	6
	−7	0	0
	−8	0	2
	−9	0	1

TABLE 9

Results of Summed Short Political and Economic (PE) and Short Personality
Characteristics (LR) Scales

Classifications	Actually loyalist	Actually revolutionary
Loyalist (high combined scores)	23	3
Unclassified (middle combined scores)	12	13
Revolutionary (low combined scores)	3	26

Classification errors, 6; total classified, 55; classification error, 11%.
Equivalent classification errors, 14.3; number of subjects, 80; equivalent classification error, 18%.

Given the degree of correlation between the two scores, a combination of the two short scales to show a slight but not substantial decrease in the number of classification errors from those committed by each scale separately would be expected. The scores are combined in Table 8. Table 9, which shows the results of classification using the sum of the scores of the short PE and short LR scales, indicates that the assumption is true.

Other tests were performed with the F items, to determine if there were other ways of explaining political affiliation in the colony. The Greven thesis was not found to be discriminatory. Of those subjects who fit the revolutionary prescription, two in fact were revolutionaries, and two were loyalists. The converse of the Greven hypothesis, which described conditions leading to loyalism, fared better, fitting four loyalists and one revolutionary. Sibling order did fit the Adlerian hypothesis, but the results were only marginally discriminatory. Of the eldest children, ten were loyalists and seven were revolutionaries. This gives a total of fifteen classification errors out of forty-four subjects classified, an error of 34 percent. The Livingston-DeLancey thesis did hold almost perfectly for those who were born or married into these two great families. But when all of these subjects were removed from the group, very similar results were obtained from the short PE and LR scales as were obtained with these subjects included. The hypothesis thus merely explains the actions of members of the two families, not the political choices of those outside the families.

While this study is but a first step toward a sophisticated use of personality scaling in historical explanation and the synthesis of personality research and more conventional socioeconomic analysis, some clear conclusions have been reached. It has been possible, using a suitable personality scale, to discriminate between loyalist and revolutionary political affiliation better than one can with any single, current, conventional political or socioeconomic hypothesis, and as well as with a combination of the most discriminatory of such hypotheses. Political choice in the crisis could be determined as well from a scoring of personality characteristics as from any combination of situational factors. While the LR scale and PEF scale produce similar rankings of individuals for both political persuasions, they do not completely explain each others' results. The authors conclude that personality and situation are woven together in the life and choices of each individual; "both classes of determinants are jointly indispensible." For those cases in

343

which neither scale was a very effective discriminator, further individual examination is necessary.[26]

Even the tentative, fragmentary results obtained in this study point the way to future research. Modification, including factor analysis, of the LR scale will increase its reliability and validity. Vertical cross-validation of the scale, in another revolutionary colony, is under way. In addition to a reexamination of the concepts and results used in the New York study, vertical cross-validation will permit a comparison of colonial intergroup psychodynamics. Discriminant analysis of LR scale results measures the "separation" between loyalist and revolutionary personalities. The extent of this "separation" hints at the collective sensitivities and commitments of the two political factions. The degree of separation of loyalists and revolutionaries on the LR may thus be an approximate indicator of the capacity of the two groups, as groups, to be able to compromise their differences and avoid confrontation, or conversely, the likelihood and probable speed of violent conflict between them. Comparison of "separation" of loyalists and revolutionaries in various colonies of the LR scale may help to explain why political breakdown and violence occurred in some colonies long before it occurred in others. Finally, horizontal cross-validation of the LR scale in other periods of American history can be contemplated. The more manuscript materials available for empirical groups—political parties, religious sects, cultural groups—the more confident will be scoring of those groups on the LR scale. The present study has attempted to open these questions; its authors invite broad application and modification of their tentative answers.

344

[26] M. Brewster Smith, "A Map For the Analysis of Personality and Politics," *Journal of Social Issues*, XXIV (July 1968), 18–19.

The London Mercantile Lobby and the Coming of the American Revolution

Alison G. Olson

Over the first half of the eighteenth century three different types of London interests—churches, ethnic groups, and mercantile communities—developed connections with corresponding interest groups in the American colonies. Although on occasion they might consider their own interests to be at odds with those of their American counterparts, as a general rule the British interest groups came to serve as channels through which their American colleagues and correspondents could convey local demands directly to the British government and as lobbies through which Americans could bring pressure on the government for or against local and imperial policies that affected them.

In the London lobbies Americans of a variety of persuasions had "friends" capable of influencing the government: English interest groups recommended candidates for appointive local offices, arranged the personal solicitation necessary for approval of private acts benefiting friends in America, and lobbied to get official sanction for fund-raising campaigns on behalf of American interests. At the same time the lobbies provided the government with information about local conditions in America, information, for example, which helped the government decide when to back down in enforcing a law that might be unworkable with a section of the colonial population or when to disallow a provincial law prejudicial to a local minority. London-American interest groups, therefore, more often than not contributed to the development of a responsive, tolerant, and tolerated imperial administration; most of them provided an effective lubricant for imperial machinery.

Then, within a decade and a half after 1760, many of them, for a variety of reasons, ceased to work effectively at all within the imperial structure. When the lobbies declined, the Americans lost one of their main sources of influence on the imperial administration, and the British became increasingly unable to develop policies that were realistic and acceptable to the colonists.

Foremost in the decline were the lobbies of the London merchants. Of all the types of interest groups active early in the eighteenth century, the London

Alison G. Olson is professor of history at the University of Maryland, College Park.

merchant lobbies were among the most effective; yet of all the interest groups active in the decade just before the Revolution none were more notorious among the Americans for the ineffectiveness of their support. Americans who earlier had seen "their interest . . . closely interwoven with ours" now perceived them as turning "cool."[1] They had, as American correspondents interpreted the situation, lost sympathy for American resistance to Parliament as they came to see the Americans as aiming at rebellion and as they found increasing outlets for trade in other parts of the world.

The purpose of this essay is not to deny that such coolness existed, but to suggest another, possibly more important, reason for the merchants' ineffectiveness: on the eve of the Revolution the merchants were experimenting with new forms of lobbying, indeed, even with new ideas about the way in which interest groups should function. In the first half of the eighteenth century the merchants of London and the outports had developed informal but effective organizations for working mainly with the executive part of the government on measures affecting individual colonies or colonial regions. At the same time, they and the politicians they sought to influence had developed some common assumptions about the nature and limits of legitimate interest group activity and the proper relationship between government and interests.[2] In the 1760s, however, when Parliament began considering a series of important measures affecting all or most of the American mainland colonies, a group of highly placed London mercantile leaders became concerned that the traditional lobbying was too fragmented and on a scale too small to be effective with Parliament for any sustained period, and they attempted to bind the smaller units into a larger organization capable of bringing pressure on the government on behalf of all the London merchants trading to America. The very attempt to lobby on an expanded scale was controversial. In addition, shortly after the changes were initiated the followers of John Wilkes began experimenting with new types of lobbying activity, and the merchants divided further over the merits of using the Wilkesite movement as a model. Thus the merchant efforts were weakened as much by doubt about the changing role of interest groups in English politics as by any coolness on the American issues themselves.

One of the most notable features of the earlier mercantile activity was its fragmentation.[3] For one thing, while the merchants of London and the various

---

[1] Robert Beverley to J. Backhouse, July 25, 1769, Beverley letter book (Library of Congress, Washington); Michael G. Kammen, *A Rope of Sand: The Colonial Agents, British Politics, and the American Revolution* (Ithaca, 1968), 196–98.

[2] For discussion of eighteenth-century attitudes toward lobbying, see Graham Wootton, *Pressure Groups in Britain, 1720–1970: An Essay in Interpretation with Original Documents* (Hamden, Conn., 1975), 11, 19–20, 33, 39, 47; Samuel H. Beer, "The Representation of Interests in British Government: Historical Background," *American Political Science Review*, 51 (Sept. 1957), 613–50; Samuel E. Finer, *Anonymous Empire: A Study of the Lobby in Great Britain* (London, 1958), 2–4; Patricia Hollis, ed., *Pressure from Without in Early Victorian England* (New York, 1974), vii–ix.

[3] The communities of mainland American merchants, unlike the various West Indian committees, left no records, nor did most of their members, but records of the Board of Trade, the Privy

outports often worked together, they were organized quite separately. Within London there was further fragmentation into at least five different groups, the Chesapeake, New York, New England, Carolina, and Pennsylvania lobbies, differentiated by the North American mainland region with which they traded.[4] The interests organized rather loosely around informal centers—the ''Exchange'' walks, coffeehouses, and mercantile clubs. At these places most merchants gathered primarily for commercial purposes—to buy insurance, pick up mail, and exchange information. The centers of activity, in other words, were preexisting institutions whose functions were only incidentally political. Their main functions were social and commercial, but once the merchants gathered, it was possible to politicize them. At any one time a core group of three or four merchants would take the lead in mobilizing the others for political activity, circulating petitions, polling merchants on current

347

Council, and Parliament do give us an idea of the kinds of American issues in which the merchants were interested and the way in which the merchants worked. We have a total of fifty-one petitions from London-American merchants to the Board of Trade, 1702-1775; thirty-five petitions to Parliament listed in Leo F. Stock's *Proceedings and Debates of the British Parliaments Respecting North America;* eleven petitions in the House of Lords Record Office; and unsigned copies of other individual petitions scattered in various periodicals and manuscript collections. See petitions in vols. 116, 400-1332, series 5, Colonial Office Papers (Public Record Office, London); Leo Francis Stock, *Proceedings and Debates of the British Parliaments Respecting North America* (5 vols., Washington, 1924-1941), III-V; House of Lords Mss. (House of Lords Record Office, London); ''Memorial of the Merchants and Others Trading to, and Interested in New England,'' *Gentleman's Magazine,* 19 (March 1749), 116; *Daily Advertiser* (London), Oct. 5, 1775; *London Chronicle,* Oct. 3-5, 1775, p. 334, Oct. 14-17, 1775, p. 372; item 38340, folios 102-03, Additional Manuscripts, Hardwicke Papers (British Library, London); item 30/8/73, folio 160, Chatham Papers (Public Record Office); Papers of William Petty, Earl of Shelburne (William L. Clements Library, University of Michigan, Ann Arbor). Altogether more than one hundred mercantile petitions on American affairs survive for the three-quarters of a century that precede the American Revolution. Signatures on the petitions can be checked against *A Guide to the Mechanic Arts, Manufactures and Trades Established in London and Westminster* (London, 1731-1775). We also have records of the appearances of leading merchants before Parliament, the Board of Trade, and the Privy Council, and the correspondence of leading ministers. A rich set of letter books of the merchants' American correspondents also exists: see, for example, Beverley letter book; William and Thomas Nelson letter book (Virginia Historical Society, Richmond); William Reynolds letter book (Library of Congress); Henry Bromfield letter book, Bromfield Papers (Massachusetts Historical Society, Boston).

[4] The Chesapeake lobby began with the emergence of a Virginia organization as early as the 1670s and a distinct but overlapping Maryland lobby thirty years later. The New York lobby developed in the 1690s; the New England lobby was visible in the 1680s; and the Carolina lobby developed about 1715. Until rather late in the period the politically active Quaker merchants of Pennsylvania worked primarily through London Yearly Meeting of Friends. See petitions to the Board of Trade, [May 14], June 13, [Sept. 6], 1662, Jan. 8, 1662/63, in *Calendar of State Papers: Colonial America and the West Indies, 1661-8* ed. W. Noel Sainsbury (London, 1964), nos. 301, 311, 365, 406; Memorials of Merchants to Board of Trade, Feb. 9, March 10, 1698/99, folios 9-11, 15, vol. 1042, series 5, Colonial Office Papers; Merchants trading to New York to Board of Trade, Feb. 18, 1698-99, *ibid.;* Lords of Trade journals, Feb. 4, 1675, April 6, April 13, 1676, transcripts (Historical Society of Pennsylvania, Philadelphia); petitions, July 18, Sept. 16, 1715, vol. C.O. 5/1264, folio 301, vol. C.O. 5/1265, folio 9, Colonial Office Papers; A. T. Gary, ''The Political and Economic Relations of English and American Quakers (1750-1785)'' (D. Phil. diss., Oxford University, 1935), 29-36, 45-46; London Meeting for Sufferings, minutes, April 20, Aug. 10, 1753, May 24, 1754, March 21, 1755, May 14, 1756 (Friends Historical Library, London).

issues, notifying them of hearings, and arranging for them to appear as a group before Parliament or the Board of Trade.[5]

For the first half of the century, colony-by-colony coffeehouse organizations were quite adequate for the lobbying they needed to do because issues that came up involved the merchants of one or at most two colonies. On daily business the merchants worked mostly with the Board of Trade or the Privy Council, both of which dealt with individual colonial problems. The board and the council exercised four main functions that were of particular interest to the merchants—the preparation of instructions for colonial governors, review of legislation passed by the colonial legislatures, the transportation and settlement of non-English immigrants in the various colonies, and the nomination of colonial councillors. Each of these functions was handled necessarily on a colony-by-colony basis.[6] Far less often, and less comfortably, the merchants lobbied with Parliament, but even at the parliamentary level most issues affected the merchants of one colony or one colonial region. Even issues that at first sight appeared to be of general mercantile interest turn out on closer examination to have concerned only the members of one particular group. Robert Walpole's excise scheme of 1733, for example, was apparently not opposed across the board by merchants trading to all colonies but only by those trading to Maryland and Virginia.[7] American merchant signers of two petitions critical of Walpole's unpreparedness against the Spanish in 1739 and 1742 were largely Carolina merchants; the neighboring Chesapeake merchants refused to support them.[8]

Besides their fragmentation, another notable feature of earlier mercantile lobbies was their assumption of a basically cooperative relationship with the government in handling American problems. They included both representatives of the moneyed interest like John Hanbury, who actively supported the established government, and the middling merchants of London who consistently formed the backbone of Walpole's electoral opposition in the City. As a group they formed something of a cushion between the moneyed men and lesser tradesmen. Yet they very rarely lobbied in opposition to the known opinion of ministers on particular American issues. Part of the reason for this

[5] Participation in political activities seems to have fluctuated greatly from coffeehouse to coffeehouse and decade to decade, varying according to the size of "the trade," the quality of leadership, and the number and importance of current issues. In the first quarter of the eighteenth century, a total of 398 merchants were interested enough in American questions to sign at least one petition or appear at least once before Parliament or the Board of Trade; in the second quarter, the total number was 304. On important questions petitions could carry as many as fifty to seventy signatures. See Alison Gilbert Olson, "Parliament, the London Lobbies, and Provincial Interests in England and America," *Historical Reflections*, 6 (Winter 1979), 367–86.

[6] See Alison Gilbert Olson, "The Board of Trade and London-American Interest Groups in the Eighteenth Century," *Journal of Imperial and Commonwealth Studies*, 8 (Jan. 1980), 33–50.

[7] Paul Langford, *The Excise Crisis: Society and Politics in the Age of Walpole* (Oxford, 1975), 58; John Mickle Hemphill II, "Virginia and the English Commercial System, 1689–1733: Studies in the Development and Fluctuations of a Colonial Economy under Imperial Control" (Ph.D. diss., Princeton University, 1964), 153–228.

[8] The petitions, Feb. 23, 1738/39 and Feb. 1742, were to the House of Lords. They are in bad condition and many of the names are now indecipherable. House of Lords Mss. (Library of Congress).

was that they had little chance of success unless they were pressing for war or unless they dared bring out the London mob. A larger part was that on most American issues they felt no need to oppose the government. They regarded their main role as being that of advisers to the Board of Trade, which was usually sympathetic to the merchants' interest. A significant part of the board's job, in fact, was to neutralize the middling merchants, to keep their discontents within bounds so they would not raise "clamours" against the government.[9]

Moreover, in working with the board, the Privy Council, and Parliament, the merchants soon learned that their greatest strength came not from political pressure but from their access to certain kinds of information the government needed, and their lobbying efforts focused on the careful dissemination of this information. Merchants wrote pamphlets directed at M.P.'s, prepared testimony for Parliament or the Board of Trade, called personally on leading statesmen, and sent ministers copies of excerpts from correspondence or conversations with persons newly arrived from America. If ministers wanted to know insurance rates on American shipping, crop conditions in America, the predicted effect of paper money emissions, even the latest information on the local popularity of colonial governors, they turned to firsthand information from the merchants themselves. When merchants wanted a lighthouse built, they could make a strong case for it because of their extensive knowledge of the colonial coast; if they wanted a currency act repealed, they could make a strong case because of their knowledge of the colonial economic conditions. In developing good working relations with the government, merchants made the most of their access to information about the colonies.[10]

Finally, it was assumed that the merchants lobbied the government only on questions that directly affected their own interests. Those interests, moreover, were commercial, and they were specific. The merchants as a group did not concern themselves with "politics"—the constitution and functioning of the British government were matters beyond their expertise—and they did not take up 'general issues of humanity.'[11] It followed that they did not take up colonial matters as questions of principle, nor did they espouse colonial causes. Their job was simply to inform the government what their interests were because they were in the best position to know them.

Fragmentation among preexisting organizations whose functions were not primarily political, dispersal of power, a preference for working with the Board of Trade rather than Parliament, an emphasis on their ability to provide crucial information, a concern with conveying their "interest" to government, and the assumption of a comfortable advisory relationship with the government— all were characteristic of mid-eighteenth-century mercantile lobbies. After

---

[9] Olson, "Parliament, the London Lobbies, and Provincial Interests," 367–86; Olson, "The Board of Trade and London-American Interest Groups," 33–50.

[10] Olson, "Parliament, the London Lobbies, and Provincial Interests," 367–86; Olson, "The Board of Trade and London-American Interest Groups," 33–50.

[11] Bernard L. Manning, The Protestant Dissenting Deputies (Cambridge, Eng., 1952), 472. This refers to a much later (Feb. 24, 1826) statement, but the deputies' philosophy did not change in nearly a century.

1760, however, these characteristics became increasingly difficult to sustain successfully. As a result of the postwar financial difficulties, the need to defend an expanded empire, and the problems associated with the credit crisis of 1763, the focus of colonial authority shifted from the Board of Trade to Parliament, and in rapid succession Parliament took up a series of measures affecting all or several colonies at once. Altogether in the years 1763–1767 there were nine issues on which London merchants petitioned Parliament or their leaders negotiated with the ministers. In exactly the same period the Board of Trade ceased to consult the merchants on matters where they had traditionally done so, even on the review of colonial legislation. Not one merchant appeared before the Board of Trade to testify after 1764, nor was a single merchant petition submitted to them—a striking and abrupt change from the close cooperation between merchants and the board in the decade before. In the face of these changes the merchants trading to various mainland colonies had to develop new methods of cooperation in order to exert sustained pressure on the legislature; the further the new methods took the merchant group from the customary characteristics of eighteenth-century lobbies, the closer they brought them to an entirely new concept of lobbying as represented in the Wilkesite lobby, and the more the whole mercantile lobby divided over the changes.

In the forefront of the new efforts there emerged as early as 1765 a group of fifteen or twenty leading men representing all the coffeehouse interests and notable both for their breadth of interest and for the continuity of their efforts. As a general rule, two or three represented the merchants trading to each mainland colonial area, and the same men continued to represent their fellow merchants throughout the prerevolutionary years.[12] In the major crises of the decade, from the Stamp Act to the preparation of petitions against the stagnation of trade in March 1775, merchants' committees were chosen to coordinate efforts at mass meetings of the rank and file, and the same men were consistently on the committees. From time to time their position was confirmed by new elections, but they never appear to have had any competition and there was rarely any turnover of members. In addition to heading the mass meetings, the committee members also met frequently among themselves: between 1765 and 1775 there is clear evidence of at least sixteen such meetings, though this number is undoubtedly too small.

The core of the mercantile leadership was a group of seventeen men (or in the case of the DeBerdts, Bakers, and Athaweses, father-son combinations) distinguished by trade to more than one colony, the large size of their American debts, and their highly placed political influence as individuals. All were active on the committee to repeal the Stamp Act; all but two were still active on the 1775 committee to petition Parliament about the general stagnation of trade, and those two, James Russell and Dennys DeBerdt, Jr., both signed the more extreme October 1775 petition urging the government to take steps to restore

[12] This can be seen by comparing the committee of 1766 with the committee of 1775. See "Letters of John Hancock," *Proceedings of the Massachusetts Historical Society*, 55 (Feb. 1922), 217–23; *American Archives*, ed. Peter Force (6 vols., Washington, 1837–1846), I, 1086.

peace with America. The core included well-known men like Edward
Athawes, dean of the Virginia tobacco merchants and a man regarded by
ministers and the Board of Trade alike as their chief spokesman since the
1750s; John Norton, more conservative and less influential than Edward
Athawes; the well-known Quakers David Barclay and Daniel Mildred; the
Marquis of Rockingham's friends Sir William Baker and his lawyer-son
William Baker, Jr., who succeeded him. It also included less well known men
like the Carolina merchants Edward Bridgen and John Nutt, New England merchants Alex Champion and Thomas Lane, Maryland merchants James Russell
and William Molleson, the Virginia merchant Duncan Campbell, along with
William Neate and Frederick Pigou who traded to New York and Pennsylvania.
In the 1760s the long-run core group was supplemented by a few others, men
like Barlow Trecothick, Capel Hanbury, Charles Crokatt, and James Crokatt
who were very active at the time of the Stamp Act crisis but were dead or
retired by the time of the mercantile agitation on the Intolerable Acts. In the
crisis immediately before the Revolution, a small group of merchants new to
politics joined them—some Englishmen like Thomas Wooldridge and John
Blackburn who remained active in mercantile politics through the 1780s and
some Americans like Thomas Bromfield, William Lee, and Joshua Johnson
who briefly attempted to push the mercantile leadership into cooperation with
the Wilkesites in 1775, then vanished to France when the Revolution began.[13]

Just where the idea of a merchant committee transcending coffeehouse
politics came from is not at all clear. The initial idea for a mercantile organization may have come from the colonial agents who themselves had met
together on several occasions before 1760. It may also have come by way of
Dennys DeBerdt, Sr., from the Protestant Dissenting Deputies, whose
organization closely resembled that of the merchants. The example of the
Committee of West Indian Merchants may also have been significant, although we do not know exactly how that group was organized in the 1760s.
More generally, we do know that during the mid-century wars the city merchants had established a committee including four representatives each from
among merchants trading to North America, South America, the East Country, and the "Italian Streights" to "consider the numerous captures of ships

351

[13] The average core-group member claiming debts after the Revolution claimed them in 2.6 colonies; the average inactive merchant also claiming prewar debts claimed them in 1.6 colonies. See
"Report on American debt claims," Feb. 5, 1791, P.R.O. 30/80/343, folios 168–70 (Public Record
Office). Of fourteen core group members whose trade can be fully identified, only four traded to
only one colony as compared with eight from a similar number of politically inactive merchants.
This suggests not only that the core group was more likely to be interested in broader problems
than the noncore, but also that they were more likely to know merchants in more than one coffeehouse club and might find intercolonial cooperation easier. Seven, at least, of the seventeen long-
term members are known to have had easy access to the leading ministers at one time or another,
while Barlow Trecothick, Charles Crokatt, James Crokatt, Capel Hanbury, and John Blackburn,
whose careers did not cover all the prewar decade, were also influential with various ministers.
Yet another distinguishing feature of the core group was the size of their claims for prewar debts,
their average claim being a staggering £100,964 as opposed to an average of £15,574 claimed by
politically inactive merchants. Whether the core group had larger businesses or simply extended
more generous credit there is no doubt they had an enormous financial incentive for keeping the
American distresses from coming to a head. Katherine A. Kellock, "London Merchants and the
Pre-1776 American Debts," *Guildhall Studies*, 1 (Oct. 1974), 109–49.

and the prevention of the same for the future."[14] A more important influence may well have been the Quaker merchants who began for the first time in the 1760s to participate in the general lobbying activities of non-Quaker merchants and brought with them a knowledge of the very sophisticated organization of the London Meeting for Sufferings, which was itself a general meeting subdivided into committees of merchants trading to each of the American colonies.[15]

In addition, part of the initiative for mercantile organization almost certainly came from the leading English politicians, both in and out of government, who attempted to politicize the merchants for their own purposes. One of their objectives was simply to gain information on American problems, and to this effect the Rockingham, Chatham, and North ministries either met with the committee on American issues or circularized them on particular problems. Beyond this, some of the younger members of the Rockingham party (and to a lesser extent, apparently, some of the Earl of Chatham's followers) attempted to organize their own mercantile support in the City. They were better able to do this because the Duke of Newcastle's departure from government in 1763 put an end to a forty-five-year-old informal alliance between the old Whig government and the London moneyed interest, making it possible for politicians to attract a few moneyed men into opposition ranks.[16] Of the committee members whose political leanings can be identified, the largest group by far associated with Rockingham. The defection of some of the moneyed interest from the government in turn made it easier for wealthy merchants to take the lead with lesser merchants who had hitherto resented the political favors they received.[17]

[14] *The West India Monthly Packet of Intelligence: An Account of News Foreign and Domestic. Extracted from the Best Authorities,* Jan. 25–Feb. 22, 1745–46.

[15] Before the 1760s Quakers had held back from cooperating with non-Quaker merchants. The most powerful had lobbied with ministers and the Board of Trade on their own; lesser ones had channeled their influence through the London Meeting for Sufferings, but their names were conspicuously absent from mercantile petitions. In the 1760s Quakers like William Neate, David Barclay, Daniel Mildred, and, before his early death, Hanbury had begun cooperating with the larger merchant community. Quaker influence is also suggested by John Fothergill's statement that three or four Quaker merchants got the merchants mobilized on the Stamp Act opposition, though Fothergill was clearly writing for Quaker consumption. John Fothergill to James Pemberton, April 8, 1766, in *Chain of Friendship: Selected Letters of Dr. John Fothergill of London, 1735–1780,* ed. Betsy C. Corner and Christopher Booth. (Cambridge, Mass., 1971), 257–61.

[16] Thomas Lane and Frederick Pigou were the only core-group members actually in the moneyed interest, but others were clearly on its fringes, and William Molleson, Duncan Campbell, and John Norton identified with it enough to sign on anti-Wilkesite petition in 1769. George F. E. Rudé, "The Anti-Wilkite Merchants of 1769," *Guildhall Miscellany,* 2 (Sept. 1965), 283–304.

[17] See L. Stuart Sutherland, "Edmund Burke and the First Rockingham Ministry," *English Historical Review,* 46 (1932), 46–72; and L. Stuart Sutherland, "The City of London in Eighteenth Century Politics," in *Essays Presented to Sir Lewis Namier,* ed. A. J. P. Taylor and Richard Pares (London, 1956), 68–69. Another possible reason for the development of a merchants' organization was the need to negotiate periodically with sailors. William Baker, Jr., mentioned in 1768 that "Trecothick told us the sailors in general were far from being quiet and gave an account of the meetings they had appointed with the merchants to come to terms, etc." Since William Baker, Jr., referred to a particular crisis, long after the merchant committee was first established, his account cannot explain the committee's origin; it does, however, suggest that the committee had other functions besides lobbying on American issues. William Baker, Jr., to William Baker, Sr., n.d. [probably 1768], folio 32, Baker Mss. (Hertfordshire County Record Office, Hertford, Eng.).

Just when the group began meeting is no clearer than the sources of its inspiration. Clearly it did not spring up overnight with its first visible performance concerning the Stamp Act. Probably it dated back to the fall or winter of 1763. In June of that year nine of the core group signed an address of congratulations to the king on the successful conclusion of the Seven Years' War, but the signers did not include any Quakers except the Athaweses nor did they include merchants closely allied with the Duke of Newcastle.[18] The duke had recently been dismissed from office; in his interpretation, the inspiration for the address came not from the merchants but from the court, and the signatures were "obtained by much solicitation, and from an Inclination, in weak and Interested men, to take any pretence grounded or not, to make their court."[19] By the spring of 1764 the Rockingham merchants and the Quakers had joined the other core group members in preparing a petition to Parliament for a revival of bounties on hemp, and Barclay, a prominent Quaker, was being mentioned as chairman of a committee of North American merchants. Thirteen of seventeen core group members signed the hemp petition, which contained a total of ninety-seven signatures of merchants trading to every colony from Massachusetts to Georgia. Indeed, if Newcastle's suggestion that the signing of the congratulatory address of 1763 was court-directed is true, then the hemp petition is really the first indication of a coordination of mercantile efforts by an organization transcending the coffeehouse clubs. In the same year when the Board of Trade violated its traditional policy of consulting separately with merchants trading to different colonial areas and heard testimony from merchants trading to every colonial region in its review of Virginia's Currency Act, the merchants called to testify were all part of the core.[20]

The fact that the merchants' committee was composed of wealthy, highly respectable merchants who had several well-established precedents for organizing themselves as they did suggested that they would pursue a largely traditional approach to lobbying, and so, for the first several years, they did. While the committee itself was an informal association sustained only by reelection at mass meetings, its constituents were members of the individual coffeehouse communities. With the appointment of Rockingham as prime minister in summer 1765 the merchants began a four-year period of cordial relations with successive ministries: Rockingham, Chatham, and the Duke of Grafton all consulted the merchants' committee on questions pertaining to American trade. When the Rockingham ministry revised the Navigation Acts, for example, it worked so closely with the committee that Capel Hanbury had to "request our Friends to excuse our not now entering into the answering . . . letters . . . [because] we are now very closely engag'd in endeavouring to procure beneficial extention regulations of the American Commerce."[21]

[18] *St. James Chronicle*, May 21-24, 1763.
[19] Duke of Newcastle to William Baker, Sr., June 28, 1763, item 32,949, folio 220, Additional Mss., Hardwicke Papers.
[20] Joseph Albert Ernst, *Money and Politics in America. 1755-1775: A Study in the Currency Act of 1764 and the Political Economy of Revolution* (Chapel Hill, 1973), 111-14.
[21] Capel Hanbury and Osgood Hanbury to George Washington, March 27, 1766, Custis Papers (Virginia Historical Society).

In addition, when the merchants did petition Parliament, their early petitions concentrated on providing information about conditions of trade. The Stamp Act petition, for example, stressed the inability of American customers to pay their debts; the message of the petition against the Townshend Duties was "that this commerce so necessary to afford employment and subsistence to the manufacturers of these Kingdoms, to augment the public Revenue, to serve as a nursery for Seamen, and to support and increase our Navigation and Maritime Strength, is at present in an alarming State of Suspension."[22] The information presented, moreover, was directed toward explaining the merchants' interest, rather than justifying the Americans' cause, and American correspondents helped by putting questions in terms of self-interest: "Their interest ought to be closely interwoven with ours & they sh⁴ consider an Injury done to us must ultimately affect them."[23] "Believe me we are so connected in Interest that we sh⁴ have fallen together."[24] Even such a politically active merchant as Samuel Athawes could argue that he "never meddled with politics," meaning that he kept his lobbying activities within the eighteenth-century limits of propriety.[25]

Even though the merchants' committee attempted to follow mainly traditional methods of lobbying, the very fact that they attempted the consolidation of coffeehouse lobbies in a larger group was alarming to some of the merchants. Particularly disturbing were the lobby's size, its intercolonial base, and its impersonality. For one thing, there had been fringe benefits to coffeehouse participation that rallies at the King's Arms could not offer. Coffeehouses had newspapers, the inevitable presence of ship captains, the latest mail, insurance dealers, and the like; they were places where some merchants carried on their entire business and others came to discuss the trade. In the normal course of business the merchant would naturally attend the coffeehouse, where fellow merchants could exert a friendly pressure that King's Arms orators could not.[26]

For another thing, the lobby's size and impersonality meant that participation in it was no longer likely to be recognized by American correspondents as a personal favor exchanged for American business. In fact, the rank-and-file merchants had no economic incentive to sign the petitions which the merchants' committee had prepared because the Americans did not distinguish between signers and nonsigners in doing business. Merchants like William Lee pleaded with them to be more selective: "Does it not occur to you as a measure absolutely requisite to be adopted in America, to agree in supporting those Merchants effectually & only, who have openly & avowedly espoused your cause with infinite danger to themselves while so many have been busy in traducing you & forwarding the late iniquitous measures with all their

[22] Petitions, n.d., item 38,340, folio 102, Additional Mss., Hardwicke Papers.
[23] Beverley to Backhouse, July 25, 1769, Beverley letter book.
[24] William Nelson to John Norton, July 25, 1766, Nelson letter book.
[25] Thomas Nelson to Samuel Athawes, Aug. 7, 1774, Nelson letter book.
[26] Aytoun Ellis, *The Penny Universities: A History of the Coffee Houses* (London, 1956), 108-17.

force?"[27] But it was only on the very eve of the Revolution that Americans began considering selective retaliation against merchants who did not help them.[28] Not until August 1775 did Congress vote "not to give any orders in future to those merchants who have publickly or privately favored those measures which are inimical to the trade and liberties of the American continent."[29] Nonimportation agreements affected all English merchants indiscriminately, and when nonimportation agreements were not in effect Americans made no effort to deal only with sympathetic merchants. Samuel Athawes and Edward Athawes, for example, took countless hours off their own business working on the Americans' behalf. Their competitors Thomas Hunt and Rowland Hunt never signed a single pro-American petition—they were described by William Lee as inveterate enemies to America in 1774 and in fact signed an anti-American petition in 1775—but there is no evidence of any Virginia planter switching business from the Hunts to the Athaweses because of their political sympathies.[30] Indeed, the Hunts retained an affectionate correspondence with leading Virginians down to the Revolution. Similarly, Nutt was on every committee to draft pro-American petitions but there is no evidence that this gained him any business from his rivals in the South Carolina trade, Graham, Johnson, and Company, who did nothing at all.[31]

355

The lack of American selectivity did not proceed from ignorance; if newspapers did not provide lists of signatures, then correspondents did, and colonists in London like William Lee and Josiah Quincy provided lists of American sympathizers.[32] Rather, Americans were acting with perfect economic rationality. Even the largest London businesses were family affairs, two- or three-man partnerships, and there were limits to the numbers of customers they could handle. If some Americans shifted their business to political sympathizers, the Americans who did not would stand to profit because of the extra time their English associates had for handling their business; the unsympathetic British merchants might do so well as to make it financially essential for American correspondents to shift back to them.[33]

[27] William Lee to Richard Henry Lee, Sept. 10, 1774, Lee Papers (University of Virginia Library, Charlottesville).

[28] *Daily Advertiser*, Sept. 30, 1775.

[29] *Ibid.*

[30] *London Gazette*, Oct. 10–14, 1775.

[31] Henry Bromfield wrote his brother in England, "Mr. Sheriff Lee writes his friends here highly in your fav.r, as being the only merch.t trad.g to America that had appeared in opposition to the late Acts of Parliament. I doubt not when matters come to be settled our house will have considerable business," but added, more than formally, "if we can give satisfaction in the management of it." Henry Bromfield to Thomas Bromfield, Oct. 30, 1774, Henry Bromfield letter book.

[32] See the list in "Journal of Josiah Quincy, Jr., during His Voyage and Residence in London, from September 28, 1774, to March 3, 1775," *Proceedings of the Massachusetts Historical Society*, 50 (June 1917), 467.

[33] American letters to the tobacco merchants especially are full of warnings not to let their business get too large. William Reynolds, for example, warned George F. Norton that his father's business was getting so big that it "must necessarily prevent his paying that particular attention a man might do with 5 or 600 hhds." William Reynolds to George F. Norton, June 3, 1774, Reynolds letter book. Robert Beverley advised John Morton Jordan, "I would persuade you not to increase the size of y.r vessels but be satisfied with a snug comfortable Trade of 4 or 500 hhds p.an." Beverley to John Morton Jordan, March 3, [1762?], Beverley letter book.

Thus, despite the attempt of the merchants' committee to preserve traditional methods of lobbying, such essential departures from tradition as they did accept were enough to discourage some merchants in the committee's early years. The lesser merchants found that lobbying activities brought them no extra business in America and did not even produce the fringe benefits they were used to from coffeehouse lobbying in London. After 1769, it became increasingly difficult for merchants to perpetuate any of the traditional methods at all, as the Wilkesite movement thrust into the lobby fundamentally divisive questions about what a lobby should be and how it should function in contemporary politics.

The divisions arose during two crisis periods, 1769–1770 and 1774–1775. In each case the merchants responded slowly to parliamentary legislation affecting the American colonies—the Townshend Duties in the first period, the Coercive Acts in the second—because as was customary they hesitated to criticize the acts directly and were waiting for an American economic response upon which they could base their petitions for repeal. In the period when they were waiting, London radicals in the Wilkesite movement did take up the American issues, attacking the government directly upon political grounds, and when the merchants finally met, they faced the choice of sticking as nearly as possible to traditional methods or of using Wilkesite activity as a model for their own. In the first period, the bulk of the merchants considered Wilkesite methods and, on the whole, seem to have rejected them; in the second, the merchants were far more sharply divided. In the early months of 1775 they continued to reject the Wilkesite model, but by late in the year the Wilkesite pressure had become so strong that the mercantile lobby split apart.

The first crisis began in spring 1769, nearly two years after the Townshend Duties were passed. That year Wilkes's repeated exclusions from Parliament despite his repeated elections as M.P. for Middlesex gave London radicals a new personal leader, and the establishment of the Bill of Rights Society to support Wilkes and pay his debts introduced a new kind of institution in British politics—the public opinion lobby. One of the most significant (but least studied) effects of the Wilkesite movement was that it forced existing lobbies to consider whether they would be better off abandoning traditional methods and developing new ones, using the Wilkesite movement as a model.

The question was particularly pointed in the case of the mercantile lobby because within three months of its establishment the Bill of Rights Society had added American grievances to those of the electors of Middlesex. In May 1769, the Middlesex freeholders' petition, prepared under Wilkesite direction, linked the ministry's mismanagement of American affairs with its violations of subjects' rights in England.[34] But the Wilkesites went even further than merely superimposing American grievances on their own list: at one level they blended American complaints inseparably with their own. They applied the

[34] Robert E. Toohey, *Liberty and Empire: British Radical Solutions to the American Problem, 1774–1776* (Lexington, Ky., 1978), 10; John A. Sainsbury, "The Pro-American Movement in London, 1769–1782: Extra-Parliamentary Opposition to the Government's American Policy" (Ph.D. diss., McGill University, 1975), 60; *Public Advertiser* (London), May 24, 1769, p. 199.

American demand for "no taxation without representation" to the plight of the unenfranchised in England, using it as the rationale for demanding an expansion of the English electorate.[35]

Despite the Wilkesite interest in American affairs the London-American merchants were, as a whole, hesitant to take up either the Wilkesite program or their methods of lobbying, both of which diverged sharply from the merchants' traditional approach. The mercantile lobby, for example, had derived support only from members of the London coffeehouse communities, men directly or indirectly involved in the American trade; the Wilkesite movement, by contrast, appealed to "the public" by means of mass meetings indiscriminately attended, "fortuitous concours[es] of people," as the *Annual Register* described them to distinguish them from "lawful assemblies" like the merchants' meetings.[36] The merchants had cultivated a cooperative, advisory relationship with the government; the Wilkesites assumed a position of open hostility to the ministry, successfully urging the Middlesex freeholders to petition the king against continuing the existing ministry in May 1769.[37] The merchants had defended their own practical interests, providing government with information it might not otherwise have about them; the Wilkesites, by contrast, espoused a cause—"the cause of Constitutional liberty," "Mr. Wilkes' cause," "the public cause"—and they provided constitutional theory, not practical information.[38] Their support, moreover, for the political principle of "no taxation without representation" was clearly offensive to merchants who prided themselves on "never meddling with politics."

Inevitably the Wilkesite innovations raised disturbing questions. Should the merchants expand their base to include, for example, lesser tradesmen unconnected with the American trade? Could they continue lobbying in the face of ministerial hostility? Did they take up American issues as a cause?

It would be misleading to suggest that the merchants divided into pro- and anti-Wilkesite "camps" on these questions; rather, their attitudes formed a continuum, with Wilkesites and their opponents at the extremes. At one end of the continuum the traditionalists argued (with Samuel Johnson) that if lobbying activities expanded beyond the mercantile community and beyond the mercantile interest, the motives for people to sign petitions would be so diverse as to render the petitions meaningless; to act in the face of ministerial hostility, moreover, would turn the merchants' lobby into an antigovernment agency.[39] At the other end of the spectrum, however, were merchants who found in the new methods their only chance of success because they were finding it difficult to oppose the Townshend Duties in traditional ways. When the merchants finally petitioned against the Townshend Duties in spring 1770, the American nonimportation agreements of the previous year were breaking down, and it was clear that the merchants were having a hard time making the

[35] John Brewer, *Party Ideology and Popular Politics at the Accession of George III* (Cambridge, Eng., 1976), 201–16.
[36] *The Annual Register for 1770* (London, 1771), 113.
[37] Toohey, *Liberty and Empire*, 10.
[38] *London Chronicle*, Feb. 28–March 2, 1769, pp. 201–08.
[39] Samuel Johnson, *The False Alarm* (London, 1780), 48.

case that their economic interests were hit by an American boycott. Moreover the Grafton ministry, with whom the merchant committee had enjoyed cordial relations, was replaced in January 1770 by the ministry of North, who was less responsive to mercantile pressure. "The Merchants trading to America," wrote Benjamin Franklin, "not well liking the ministry . . . were backward in petitioning the Parliament."[40]

The merchants at the extremes of the continuum constituted slightly more than 25 percent of the total merchant community. The rest were undecided or hedging, as one would expect, since the American merchants were a cross section of the London mercantile community and included all economic ranks from the small merchants who tended to support Wilkes to the wealthy ones who opposed him. Nevertheless, the divisions could be bitter. On the committee itself Samuel Athawes, Edward Athawes, and William Baker, Jr., opposed Wilkes's expulsion from Parliament; Molleson, Campbell, and Norton supported it; and the others, apparently disliking Wilkes, attempted to avoid antagonizing their American correspondents by public involvement. Among the coffeehouses there were substantial variations from one group to another. In the Virginia lobby, which was the most sharply divided, 24 percent opposed Wilkes while 21 percent supported him. Among the Carolina merchants, by contrast, only 3 percent opposed Wilkes while 8 percent supported him. New York, Maryland, New England, and Pennsylvania merchants had 6 percent, 6 percent, 4 percent, and none of their members opposing Wilkes and 12 percent, 20 percent, 19 percent, and 16 percent, respectively, actively supporting him.[41]

Even among small groups of individual merchants, high feelings on the issue were reflected in occasional fistfights; on one well-reported occasion, for example, a Wilkesite leader was reported to have lost two teeth to a merchant who opposed Wilkes, though the loss (not the fight) was later denied.[42] Among the rank and file merchants, a comparison of signatures on an anti-Wilkes petition of 1769 and a pro-Wilkes petition of 1775 suggests that a somewhat higher proportion supported Wilkes than opposed him personally, but the fact that the conservative committee continued to dominate the merchants, drawing up a traditional petition against the Townshend Duties—signed, apparently, only by members of the mercantile lobby—indicates that a majority of American merchants were uneasy about adopting Wilkesite methods for their lobbying activity.[43]

[40] [Benjamin Franklin], "The Rise and Present State of Our Misunderstanding," in *The Papers of Benjamin Franklin*, ed. Leonard W. Labaree and William B. Willcox (22 vols., New Haven, 1959-   ), XVII, 271.

[41] For merchant action against the Stamp Act, see petition to the House of Lords, March 5, 1766, House of Lords Mss. (Library of Congress). For merchant action against the Intolerable Acts, see petition to House of Commons, n.d., item 38,340, folios 102-03, Additional Mss., Hardwicke Papers. The March 1775 petition of sixty firms is in House of Lords Mss. (House of Lords Record Office). For the petition of Oct. 11, 1775, see *London Evening Post*, Oct. 14-17, 1775. It is analyzed in detail in Sainsbury, "Pro-American Movement," 310-45. Names of the anti-Wilkesite signers are analyzed in Rudé, "Anti-Wilkite Merchants," 283-304.

[42] See *London Chronicle*, March 7-9, 1769, p. 230, March 9-11, 1769, p. 234, March 23-25, 1769, p. 286.

[43] Rudé, "Anti-Wilkite Merchants," 283-304; Sainsbury, "Pro-American Movement," 310-45.

The mercantile lobby remained intact until 1775, its committee dominated by conservatives, its differences over the proper methods and functions of lobbies latent or papered over. In 1775, however, the receipt of the Continental Congress's resolutions anticipating a third nonimportation agreement among American merchants raised again questions about whether the merchants should adopt Wilkesite methods of lobbying against government measures. This time the questions were no longer muted but were debated publicly in mercantile meetings and in Parliament. This debate seems to have polarized the lobby much more decisively than the debates of 1769–1770, some merchants being subsumed in the Wilkesite lobby, some digging in their heels against it, and some dropping out of political activity altogether.

The very timing of the early meetings on January 4 and January 11, 1775, indicates that as the year opened, moderate merchants still dominated the lobby. At the very least, it was significant that the merchants waited until 1775 to petition against parliamentary acts passed the year before. In 1774, in response to the Boston Tea Party, Parliament had passed four acts penalizing the port of Boston and reorganizing the government of Massachusetts. Twice during spring 1774, once in March and once again in May, several "Natives of North America" had petitioned Parliament and then the king against the acts: the first set of petitions called the Coercive Acts "repugnant to every principle of law and justice"; the later set called them "fatal to the Rights, Liberties, and Peace of all Americans" and opposed them upon "the principle of justice."[44] In these endeavors, the merchants never cooperated—partly because the majority still opposed the spirit of petitions espousing a "cause," partly because, until they had evidence of American intentions to stop imports, the merchants could make no case that the mercantile interests were affected. Both reasons suggest that moderates still dominated the lobby.

Even more indicative of conservative domination were the circumstances surrounding the failure of the merchant committee to act quickly in December 1774, when resolutions of the Continental Congress, producing the long anticipated nonimportation agreement against British goods, arrived in London. On December 19 of that year, shortly after the congressional resolutions had arrived, the Wilkesite members of the committee advertised a mass meeting of merchants and other Londoners for December 23, at which they presumably intended to present a petition that was pro-American in principle, thereby catching off guard the more conservative merchants who were at their country homes for Christmas holidays.[45] A conservative wing of merchants, including Blackburn, Barclay, and Champion, rushed to head off the meeting by inserting in the papers, on the day the original meeting was to occur, notice of an

[44] Petition from Natives of North America to House of Lords, March 28, May 11, 1774, typescript, Henry Laurens Papers (University of South Carolina, Columbia). See also petitions to House of Commons, March 25, May 2, 1774, *ibid.*; petitions to the King, March 31, May 19, 1774, *ibid.* I am grateful to George Rogers of the University of South Carolina for copies of these letters which are currently being edited for the *Papers of Henry Laurens.*

[45] *London Evening Post*, Jan. 3–5, 1775.

alternative meeting January 4.[46] The delay gave time for the absent merchants to get back to London in sufficient numbers to dominate the meeting. It also gave the conservatives time to map out strategy with a middle group consisting of Samuel Athawes, John Sargent, Bridgen, Norton, and Russell, arranging for one of their own members—the conservative and respected Lane—to preside over the meeting, obtaining supportive letters from the outports, and preparing a petition in the traditional mold.

When the merchants did meet, January 4, 1775, the main questions, as in 1769, concerned the procedure and functions of the lobby, and the decisions on these issues made it clear that moderates still dominated the lobby.[47] The first issue that came up concerned the appropriate membership of the meeting itself. The Wilkesite leaders preferred an open meeting, a mass rally not restricted to merchants. "The people are interested," wrote Arthur Lee; "it is to them I speak."[48]

The majority of merchant leaders, however, wanted the meeting confined to merchants and "others interested in the commerce of America," by which, as they later specified, they meant tradesmen who did business with American merchants. William Baker, Jr., lawyer-son of one of the leading New York merchants, made a point of apologizing for "not being immediately in the American trade, . . . tho connected."[49] When the petition was prepared, three merchants attended its signing to prevent signers "not being known to be concerned in the American trade or from being deemed too inconsiderable."[50] Molleson assured Lord Dartmouth, the secretary of state, that the petition was "supported by all the principal men."[51] One unidentified "principal man" was represented to Dartmouth as saying that four-fifths of the petitioners signed "to preserve appearances and to keep up a good understanding with our correspondents in America and the West Indies," further suggesting that the petitions were confined to those whose interests were directly affected.[52] (It was noted in Parliament that two petitions were received from Birmingham at the same time the London merchants petitioned: "the first petition from Birmingham was signed by persons not concerned in the trade to North America, and therefore ought not to have the least weight with Parliament, the second petition from Birmingham being signed by persons really interested, merited a serious consideration.")[53]

[46] Arthur Lee to Richard Henry Lee, April 3, 1775, Lee Papers; John Blackburn to [Earl of Dartmouth], Dec. 22, 1774, item 1025, section D (W) 1778/II, Dartmouth Mss. [William L. Salt Library, Staffordshire County Record Office, Stafford, Eng.].

[47] The meetings are described at length in *American Archives*, ed. Force, I, 1086-87, 1107, 1219-21.

[48] *An Appeal to the Justice and Interests of the People of Great Britain, in the Present Disputes with America, by an Old Member of Parliament* (London, 1774), 44.

[49] *London Evening Post*, Jan. 3-5, 1775.

[50] *The Parliamentary History of England from the Earliest Period to the Year 1803*, ed. William Cobbett (36 vols., London, 1803-36), XVIII, 187.

[51] William Molleson to Dartmouth, n.d., item 1037, section D (W) 1778/II, Dartmouth Mss.

[52] Molleson to Dartmouth, Oct. 11, 1775, Feb. 28, 1776, items 1560, 1663, *ibid*.

[53] *Parliamentary History of England*, ed. Cobbett, XVII, 195.

The second issue concerned the grounds on which an interest group might legitimately base its appeal to the government. Here the debate was considerably more complicated than before. The majority of merchants seem to have rejected the radical proposal that American issues be argued "not upon partial, self interested principles but upon the comprehensive plan of liberty and your country"; they rejected even the less radical argument that the mercantile interests "and the general liberties of this country are inseparably connected."[54] But what kind of mercantile "interest" did they substitute for "principles of liberty"?

Despite the anticipated nonimportation agreement in America, it was hard to argue consistently that the merchants' interests lay with the Americans. It was difficult to argue, for example, that it was in the merchants' interest to defend men who had destroyed mercantile property (five of the core group had recommended correspondents or partners as consignees of the tea), and indeed it was clearly not in the merchants' interest to criticize a government that might later be responsible for helping to collect their American debts.[55] Moreover, the merchants were receiving a mixed lot of suggestions from their American correspondents, many of whom were quite uncertain whether it was in their own best interest to support the radical movement in America.[56] More generally, government pamphleteers like William Knox advised the merchants that their "interest" lay in obtaining American subordination to a mercantile empire.[57] By 1775, then, it was possible for the wisest merchant to be confused about exactly what was implied by the mercantile "interest." Between January and March 1775, the merchants petitioned Parliament or the king four times, three times on the Coercive Acts and once on the act restraining New England's trade; each petition followed a debate that produced new clarification and new bitterness.

361

The first debate occurred January 11 over the committee's draft of a petition; it centered on whether to include the Quebec Act among the merchants' complaints. A majority of merchants attending the meeting objected to such an inclusion on grounds that reference to the Quebec Act would be "political," not

---

[54] *London Evening Post*, Dec. 31-Jan. 3, 1775; [Joseph Priestley], *An Address to Protestant Dissenters of All Denominations, on the Approaching Election of Members of Parliament with Respect to the State of Public Liberty in General and of American Affairs in Particular* (London, 1774), 4.

[55] Francis S. Drake, *Tea Leaves: Being a Collection of Letters and Documents Relating to the Shipment of Tea to the American Colonies in 1773* (Detroit, 1970), 208-09, 215, 233.

[56] This is clearest in the papers of James Russell. Some correspondents urged the merchants to "excite themselves in such a manner as to get our affairs on their former footing again." Francis Whittington to James Russell, Oct. 24, 1774, James Russell Papers (Messrs. Coutts and Company, London). But certainly an equal number spoke of the danger of local "incendiaries" and "warme men." William FitzHugh to Russell, Nov. 24, 1774, *ibid.*; Samuel Galloway to Russell, June 8, 1774, *ibid.* Pennsylvania merchants had written of their fear of popular reprisals. See Arthur L. Jensen, *The Maritime Commerce of Colonial Philadelphia* (Madison, 1963). William Molleson's correspondence also suggested mixed views in Maryland. Molleson to Dartmouth, Dec. 17, 1774, item 1023, section D(W) 1778/II, Dartmouth Mss.

[57] William Knox, *The Interest of the Merchants and Manufacturers of Great Britain in the Present Contest with the Colonies, Stated and Considered* (Cork, 1775), 25.

"commercial," but the issue was hotly debated for several hours, and the meeting finally agreed to allow the committee's reference to the Coercive Act "and other acts," thus letting merchants and M.P.'s interpret the act as they preferred. The petition went on to assure Parliament that the signers were motivated "essentially" by their interest in trade to North America.[58] Thus conservative merchants could argue that they "confined [them]selves altogether to commerce and have not touched upon politics" while radicals thought that most of the signers were "not at all serious."[59]

In February the merchants went slightly further, still stressing commercial dangers but attacking the wisdom of limiting American trials by jury—something difficult to connect with commerce.[60] In March, on another petition, this time against the parliamentary bill restraining the trade to New England, the merchants edged even closer to principled objection, calling the measure "unjust," "unconstitutional, repugnant to equity and the rights of subjects."[61] This, however, was as far as the moderate merchants were willing to move away from tradition. Wilkesite merchants made lists dividing merchants between those who were willing to go beyond a mere interest to a general support of the American cause and those who were not; not many merchants made it onto the first list.[62]

The third issue concerned the maintenance of the merchants' traditional role as advisors to the government. At issue was not only the radicals' desire to organize a popular opposition to the ministry (Arthur Lee was certain that such an opposition would bring North's government down) but also the ministers' ambivalent attitude toward mercantile advice.[63] Individually or in small groups, members of the core group attempted to hold their earlier ground, establishing or reinforcing old ties with ministers or leading politicians. A delegation called on North. Quakers on the committee began their own efforts with the ministers to preserve peace. At least two of the committee—Blackburn and Molleson—opened communications with Dartmouth, keeping him informed of the day-to-day and sometimes hour-by-hour deliberations of the committee.[64]

While Dartmouth forwarded mercantile representations to the cabinet, North was considerably less responsive. At one point North told the merchants to "return & sett quietly at their compting Houses."[65] Symptomatic of most

[58] *London Evening Post*, Jan. 3-5, Jan. 10-12, 1775.

[59] Molleson to Dartmouth, n.d., item 1037, section D(W) 1778/II, Dartmouth Mss.; Kammen, *Rope of Sand*, 305.

[60] "The Petition of the merchants traders and others of the City of London concerned in the American Commerce," Feb. 7, 1775, House of Lords Mss. (House of Lords Record Office).

[61] Merchants' petition to House of Lords, March 1775, copy in House of Lords Mss. (Library of Congress).

[62] Jack M. Sosin, *Agents and Merchants: British Colonial Policy and the Origins of the American Revolution* (Lincoln, Nebr., 1965), 196.

[63] *Ibid.*

[64] Molleson to Dartmouth, Dec. 17, 1774, item 1023, section D(W) 1778/II, Dartmouth Mss.; Blackburn to unknown, Dec. 1774, item 1025, *ibid.*; David Barclay to Dartmouth, item 1454, *ibid.*; Sosin, *Agents and Merchants*, 175-76.

[65] Quoted in Sosin, *Agents and Merchants*, 175-76.

ministers' attitudes was their motion to send the merchants' petition to a
dead-end committee and their related opposition to hearing the merchants
before the house. A leading ministerial supporter gave these reasons: "the only
end which can be proposed in hearing the petitioners at the bar is information.
What information could they lay before the House? Were they to allege that
whilest the disputes between Great Britain and America subsisted, their trade
would undergo a temporary stagnation? This was to say nothing that was not
already known." In vain did Edmund Burke reply that "whatever the knowledge of any individual in the House might be, there was a great difference between knowledge and feeling . . . the nature of mankind was such, that general
observations affected their minds in a slight and indistinct manner, when the
detail of particulars, and the actual substance of things, made a most forcible
impression."[66] Burke's characteristic attempt to provide a rational justification for what had become custom was too ingenious for the house to accept;
the Rockingham faction settled back into a more common justification of the
merchants' approach in its official protest against the refusal of the Lords to
receive the petitions of the North American merchants. Yet their claim that
"there is no information concerning the state of our colonies (taken in any
point of view) which the merchants are not far more competant to give than
governors or officers, who often know far less of the temper and disposition of
the people, or may be more disposed to misrepresent it than the merchants,"
made clear that the information-giving role of the mercantile lobby had itself
become a political issue. The supporters of the merchants acting in their traditional role were in a small minority.[67]

363

Thus, three issues—whether membership in the lobby should be open to
men not directly involved in the North American trade, whether the lobby
should espouse a cause rather than explain an interest, and whether the lobby
should continue its efforts in the face of ministerial hostility—sharply divided
the London-American merchants in the first three months of 1775. This was
evident from the length of the debates (some ran to three or four hours) and the
chairman's apparent difficulty in keeping order. It was also evident from the
committee's reversal, on at least one occasion, of a decision made by the
general meeting. It was most evident in the signers of the petitions. When the
January petition was circulated, only 105 men signed out of roughly 450 who
attended the meeting. Nearly a quarter of the signers were members of the
merchants' committee, and the other 83 were men who had previously shown
little interst in politics: not one had signed the petition for repeal of the Stamp
Act. By March the number of signers was down to representatives of 60
firms.[68]

By spring the core group was in disarray, "shuffling," as William Lee
described them. Both William Lee and Quincy sent home lists of American

[66] *Parliamentary History of England*, ed. Cobbett, XVII, 186–88.
[67] *Ibid.*, XVII, 292–94.
[68] See merchants petition to House of Lords against Intolerable Acts, March 15, 1775, House of
Lords Mss. (House of Lords Record Office); *American Archives*, ed. Force, III, 1009–10; Sainsbury,
"Pro-American Movement," 310–45.

friends and enemies among the merchant group and most of the core group appeared on the "enemies" list.[69] When the radicals proposed petitioning the king, Rockingham wrote Burke, "Baker is very doubtful what to do, his opinion is against the measure and yet he don't like that a disunion should arise." Sargent dined with William Baker, Jr., and shared his doubts.[70] Molleson despaired, "Left without resource, without aid from government, what can we do?" "The Merchants trading to North America are in a most disagreeable predicament."[71]

The nadir of the core group's fortunes came in October 1775, when William Lee approached the committee again about petitioning the Crown, this time in response to a new address from the Continental Congress. The committee voted twenty to three not to do so, but this time, with the support of Wilkesite leaders in the City of London, William Lee went ahead and advertised a meeting anyway, and the moderates and conservatives on the committee could not outflank him. Lee's intention was to subsume the merchant movement under the Wilkesite movement, and with the moderates unable to head him off, both core group and lesser merchants were left to decide for themselves whether to go along with him. It was a last chance to protest American policy, but it was such a departure from legitimate lobbying methods that most merchants could not stomach it. The ground of the petition prepared was political, not economic; its purpose was to plead a cause, not to provide information on the needs of a particular group; and its signers were drawn from such a variety of occupations, that they could not be said to represent an "interest."[72] At issue was not only the American question but also the integrity of the mercantile interests. William Baker, Jr., for example, wrote "warmly" and anxiously to Burke on behalf of the Continental Congress, urging him to present the congressional address to Parliament, but Baker was a reluctant figurehead at the City meeting.[73] Barclay pleaded strongly in private with Dartmouth not to let the ministry reject the American address, but he would not sign the City petition.[74] Most of the merchants agreed with Barclay: only 39 of the 105 merchants who signed the January petition signed the October one, and only 7 of the core group signed.

The crisis of 1775 ended the mercantile lobby's usefulness to the Americans, though it did not, as it turned out, end the existence of the lobby itself. In the last years of the American Revolution the lobby reemerged in a role in which it was comfortable, pressing in traditional ways for government assistance in col-

---

[69] See, for example, William Lee to Richard Henry Lee, Feb. 25, 1774, Lee Papers; "Journal of Josiah Quincy," 467.

[70] Lord Rockingham to Edmund Burke, Feb. 9, 1775, *Correspondence of Edmund Burke*, ed. George Guttridge III (Cambridge, Eng., 1961), 113.

[71] Molleson to Dartmouth, Oct. 11, 1775, Feb. 28, 1776, items 1560, 1663, section D(W) 1778/II, Dartmouth Mss.

[72] *Daily Advertiser*, Oct. 5, 1775; *London Chronicle*, Oct. 3-5, 1775, Oct. 14-17, 1775; *American Archives*, ed. Force, III, 1009-10.

[73] Burke to William Baker, Jr., Oct. [or Aug.?] 23, 1775, folio 53, Baker Mss.

[74] Barclay to Dartmouth, Aug. 23, 1775, item 1454, section D(W) 1778/II, Dartmouth Mss.

lecting their American debts. The question of debt was clearly one of practical interest that could not be elevated to a "cause," and it was one on which ministers needed specific information that only the merchants could give. During the Revolution the Wilkesite mercantile leaders had fled to the continent; the mercantile leaders who remained in England disassociated themselves and the lobby from the new radical reform movements of the early 1780s. For fifteen years at least—the records are unclear after that—the lobby continued to press the government on debt and related questions with considerable success.[75]

For a brief period before the Revolution, however, the lobby had been caught off guard, unable to function as it had traditionally done. New circumstances had called into question both the methods and the rationale of the group. The combination of the ministerial instability of George III's early years and the emergence of London-American radicalism caught the merchant lobby in a squeeze. Long used to operating on the borders of the political nation, they faced increased hostility from dominant groups within the political elite and increased insistence in redefining the borders by militant radicals well outside the political nation. The merchants were left uncertain and divided about adapting to the new situation. By 1800 it was becoming clear that interest-group lobbies and public-opinion lobbies could function side by side and separately. In the years when American legislation was at stake this was not yet clear, and the British empire suffered because of it.

365

[75] For the fate of the merchant lobby, see Kellock, "London Merchants," 109–49; John Adams letter books, 1785-1788, Adams Family Papers (Massachusetts Historical Society); Nutt and Molleson to Henry Dundas, Aug. 31, Nov. 30, 1791, Aug. 18, Aug. 30, 1792, Melville Papers (Clements Library); "Brief Statement of the Claims of the British Merchants," n.d., *ibid.*; Charles R. Ritcheson, *Aftermath of Revolution: British Policy toward the United States, 1783-1795* (Dallas, 1969), 41, 57-58, 80, 125, 148, 150, 319; T. M. Devine, *The Tobacco Lords: A Study of the Tobacco Merchants of Glasgow and Their Trading Activities, 1740 to 1790* (Edinburgh, 1975), 153-58; Edward Papenfuse, *In Pursuit of Profit: The Annapolis Merchants in the Era of the American Revolution, 1763-1805* (Baltimore, 1975), 108, 184-85, 207-09, 216, 218, 223; *The Papers of Thomas Jefferson*, ed. Julian P. Boyd (19 vols., Princeton, 1950-1974), IX, 403-05; *Parliamentary History of England*, ed. Cobbett, XXVIII, 177-80, 243-55, 481-83, 662-95, 738.

AFTERWORD

I believe that most editors of such collections as this will agree that the appropriate "afterword" is a sigh of relief. For my own part, I had no idea when I agreed with Garland Publishing to do the series that it would entail as much labor as it did. To be sure, it was enlightening to have the chance to re-read so many superb articles in my own field. The effort has enriched my teaching and redirected my thinking on many issues. The painful part was deciding which articles to reprint and which to omit. To my "board" of advisors, Timothy Breen, Ken Coleman, Natalie Hull, Milton Klein, Allan Kulikoff, Tom Slaughter, and Alden Vaughan, I am indebted immeasurably, though the blame for any oversights is and must remain my own. I must admit that on more than one occasion I had to referee disagreements among my advisors; I hope but cannot therefore guarantee that they will be entirely pleased by the final version of the collection.

Having done the work, I find myself asking about its ultimate value. Surely its intrinsic value cannot be less than the summed worth of the articles. If they have merit, reprinting them shares that merit. Their dispersion in so many journals makes this collection an affordable and fair-minded (in the legal sense) alternative to xeroxing articles for scholarly, teaching, archival, bibliographical, and reference uses. Moreover, the total worth of the collection exceeds the sum of its parts, for gathered in this way, the articles tell us something about the development of scholarly methods, research strategies, interests, and theories in early American history in our century. We can see the social sciences taking firm root. No chronicler can now ignore them, and the best modern narrative history quietly borrows from them. We can trace the discovery and full utilization of new sources, and even new kinds of sources. We can follow the careers of scholars. We can, in sum, recover something of the history of early American historical writing.

Peter Charles Hoffer
University of Georgia

The publisher and editor gratefully acknowledge the permission of the authors and the following journals and organizations to reprint the copyright material in this volume; any further reproduction is prohibited without permission:

The William and Mary Quarterly; *The Journal of American History* & Organization of American Historians for material in the *Journal*; the Regents of the University of California for material in the *Pacific Historical Review*; the New York State Historical Association for material in *New York History*.

CONTENTS OF THE SET